W9-CCZ-824
No. 1101
$15.95

How to Design & Build Your Own Custom TV Games

By David L. Heiserman

TAB BOOKS Inc.

BLUE RIDGE SUMMIT, PA. 17214

FIRST EDITION

FIRST PRINTING—NOVEMBER 1978
SECOND PRINTING—APRIL 1980
THIRD PRINTING—APRIL 1981

Library of Congress Cataloging in Publication Data

Heiserman, David L. 1940-
    How to design and build your own custom TV games.

    Includes index.
    1. Video games—Equipment and supplies—Design and
construction—Amateur's manuals. I. Title.
TK9971.H44   688.7′28   78-11389
ISBN 0-8306-9859-0
ISBN 0-8306-1101-0 pbk.

Preface

America is a nation accustomed to fads. Novel ideas and products catch on rather quickly, sweeping the country with new products and services. More often than not, these fads gradually change form or fade away with time.

TV games had all the earmarks of being one of these fads at first. Once the idea caught on, video game products captured the fancy of all sorts of people—people willing to put out $50, $60 or, in some cases, more than a $100 to play the fascinating little games in their own homes.

But it appears that TV games are here to stay. The games are becoming more sophisticated and diverse, and product sales skyrocket every Christmas. What's more, commercial, coin-operated versions have already transformed the game arcade industry into something totally new and different. It now seems that video games are replacing the pinball machine as America's number-one arcade game.

This is a book about TV games. It shows how they work and, more importantly, how to design and build custom versions. This book is not merely a collection of complete TV game circuits. To be sure, there are a number of complete game circuits presented as design examples; the real emphasis is on designing and building custom TV games. In fact the reader will loose much of the fun of the whole thing by simply copying the circuits shown here.

The whole idea of the book is to release the reader's creative instincts, transforming them into custom games that are a delight to the designer as well as others who have an opportunity to enjoy them.

The game systems as they are presented here might seem rather cumbersome compared to the slick, cassette-programmed game systems on the market today. But how creative can one be with someone else's prescribed programs? Sure it is possible to get a dozen games on one program tape, but it really doesn't take long to want more. The game-design scheme presented in this book is wholly open-ended—there is no real limit to the number and types of games that can come from it. It's all a matter of learning how to design the games and exercising some degree of creativity and imagination.

It is not necessary to have a great deal of know-how concerning digital electronics to begin the work in this book. The first few chapters have been planned with the digital novice in mind. As the work progresses, however, the need for learning more about basic digital electronics becomes more apparent. Unfortunately, a book of this size cannot stand up as both a design manual for video games and a text book on basic digital electronics.

While the information regarding game design is thus adequate for building custom games of any sort, a reader not fully acquainted with basic digital electronics will eventually become lost without the aid of a good digital reference text. This, however, should not discourage a beginner in the digital business. Rather, it should provide some motivation and direction for learning more about digital electronics in general.

What better way to learn digital electronics than by seeing each newly learned fact transformed into moving image on the TV screen?

David L. Heiserman

Contents

Special Notes to the Reader

- FCC regulations prohibit connecting the output of any rf source to an external antenna. The antenna must be completely disconnected from the TV receiver before any of the video circuits described in this book are connected to the set via rf modulators.

- While most of the circuits in this book have been orginated by the author, one or more circuits, techniques, and names of games may be covered by current U.S. patents and trademarks.

Chapter 1

Television and Television Games

Television has been an important part of home life in America for better than 25 years now, but television games, in their most popular forms, have been around for only a few years. It might seem that TV games could have been invented in the very early days of TV technology, but they were not. Why not? Because the right kind of game technology wasn't available at an affordable cost until recently.

This chapter describes the technologies of TV and TV games, showing in a very general way how modern TV games are interfaced with conventional TV receivers. Without at least a basic understanding of the interfacing problems, an experimenter can have little hope for designing custom TV games. One might be able to duplicate some of the specific game circuits shown in this book, but without that overall view of what the system is doing, the whole point of investing money in this book will be lost.

THE TV RASTER

In the simplest terms, the TV raster is that pattern of fine horizontal lines that can be seen on the screen of a TV receiver. The set generates these lines whether it is tuned to a station or not. The raster generating process is built into the TV set itself.

As indicated in Fig. 1-1a, the raster is drawn on the screen, one horizontal line at a time, beginning near the upper left-hand corner and progressing toward the lower right-hand corner. Each horizontal line is drawn on the screen from left to right. As the beam reaches the right-hand edge, it is first blanked off and then sent back to the left-hand edge to begin the next scanning operation.

This horizontal scanning operation continues until the beam reaches the lower right-hand edge, at which time it is blanked off and returned to the top to begin a new framing sequence.

The raster as it appears on the screen is thus a series of straight lines that result from two different kinds of operations: a relatively fast horizontal scan, combined with a relatively slow vertical scan. The horizontal scanning is responsible for moving the beam from left to right, and the vertical scanning is responsible for setting each line a bit below the previous one.

Figure 1-1b shows the sort of sawtooth waveform that is used for both horizontal and vertical scanning. As the sawtooth level rises with time, the beam responds by moving a proportional distance across the screen. Two such waveforms are required, one for the horizontal- and another for the vertical-scanning operations.

The only difference between the horizontal- and vertical-sawtooth waveforms is their frequency. The horizontal sawtooth waveform runs at a frequency on the order of 15,750 Hz, while the vertical version runs at about 60 Hz. It can be reckoned from these figures that there are 262.5 horizontal scan lines for each vertical scan. The American television scheme, however, uses an interlaced scanning technique calling for two complete vertical scans for one frame.

The framing rate is thus 30 Hz, and there are 525 horizontal lines (262.5 on the first field and another 262.5 on the interlaced field) in each complete frame.

None of the TV game schemes in this book use interlaced scanning, so the figures relevant to our purposes are the 15,750 Hz horizontal-scanning rate and the 60-Hz vertical-scanning rate.

The horizontal- and vertical-sawtooth waveforms are generated within the receiver by the horizontal and vertical oscillators. When receiving a TV signal from a broadcast station or TV game system, these oscillators must be synchronized in order to hold the picture together properly. Vertical rolling or horizontal tearing of a video signal are familiar signs of a loss of sync from the incoming video signal.

Figure 1-1c shows a typical video signal as it arrives from a conventional TV station. The horizontal-sync pulses ride in a piggyback fashion on the horizontal-blanking pulses. Since there are far more horizontal-scanning operations than vertical ones, it follows that the composite video signal is dominated by horizontal sync and blanking pulses.

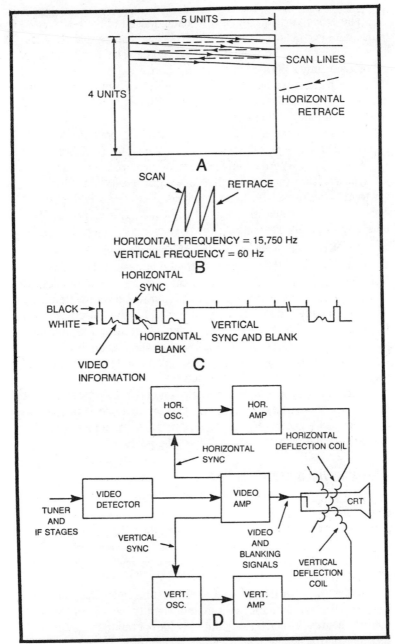

Fig. 1-1. Generating the TV raster. (a) The basic raster as it appears on the screen. (b) The sawtooth waveform characteristic of horizontal and vertical raster scanning. (c) A composite video waveform. (d) TV receiver block diagram showing sections relevant to TV games.

The broad vertical sync and blanking pulse in Fig. 1-1c carries horizontal-sync pulses along its top. This is a feature that is necessary for maintaining horizontal sync during the relatively long vertical retrace time. Without maintaining horizontal sync during this time, the picture would tend to be torn out of sync in the upper left-hand corner of the screen, the place where the beam is located when it is no longer blanked.

The block diagram in Fig. 1-1d shows the portions of a TV receiver that are especially relevant to TV games. Horizontal- and vertical-sync pulses are taken from the video amplifier and are used for synchronizing their respective sawtooth oscillators. Once the sawtooth waveforms have been amplified, they are applied to sets of coils (the yoke) around the neck of the CRT. The magnetic fields thus generated are responsible for positioning the electron beam.

The actual video information and blanking signals are applied to the cathode of the CRT to modulate the brightness of the beam. The blanking pulses have a polarity that cuts off the beam completely. Lower voltages create varying degrees of gray and white. Referring to the composite video waveform in Fig. 1-1c, the "black" voltage levels are near the top, while the "whites" are near the bottom.

The video information, tucked between each horizontal-blanking pulse, thus creates shades of gray, the lower the voltage level, the whiter the spot on the screen.

This is hardly a complete description of the TV system, but it does touch upon those principles relevant to understanding the operation of TV games. Readers interested in more details about TV systems should consult a good TV textbook.

THE BASIC VIDEO GAME SYSTEM

The whole point of the video game system is to create images on the screen that have shapes and motions relevant to a particular game scheme. These images, however, must be created in the context of a conventional TV system, and that means generating horizontal- and vertical-sync/blank pulses as well as game video information.

It turns out that the game system must be under the control of its sync pulses at all times, so it is important to have a reliable and accurate source of such pulses, not only for operating the game, but also for controlling the beam on the screen of a conventional TV receiver.

The whole game system is ultimately synchronized by a crystal oscillator. In this particular case, the oscillator runs at 14 MHz. The

14-MHz pulses from the oscillator operate a 9-bit binary counter that ultimately yields the 15,750-Hz pulses required for horizontal synchronization. During the counting interval, however, the horizontal-count circuit generates a distinctive pattern of binary numbers that actually indicate the horizontal position of the beam on the screen. See Fig. 1-2.

The 15,750-Hz output of the horizontal-counting circuit clocks yet another 9-bit binary counter, the vertical-count circuit. This circuit utlimately produces the necessary 60 Hz vertical-sync pulse, but in the meantime, it also generates a 9-bit binary code that indicates the vertical position of the beam on the screen.

In a manner of speaking, then, the TV game system always knows exactly where the beam is situated on the CRT screen. A pair of 9-bit binary numbers indicate the coordinates in a manner quite similar to the x, y coordinates of a conventional graphing scheme.

Since the game system knows where the beam is located at any given moment, it is possible to generate white or black video levels to create images on the CRT.

Notice in Fig. 1-2 that the sync pulses, blanking pulses, and game video information are combined to create the composite video signal. The only step remaining after that is to place the signal onto an rf carrier that will feed it through the tuner section of a conventional receiver. The rf modulator, incidentally, can be omitted from the system if the composite signal is applied directly to the video amplifier in the TV set. This calls for some surgery on the receiver circuitry, and many experimenters are unable or unwilling to do that sort of job.

As far as this book is concerned, the bulk of the circuits blocked out in Fig. 1-2 is the same for every game. Only the game video generator and external game controls change. Most of the circuitry is thus built into a permanent unit called the Sourcebox unit. This particular part of the system is described in great detail in Chapter 2. The remainder of the book deals with experiments, examples, and design hints for the game video generator and external game controls, units that are plugged into the standard Sourcebox.

HOW TO USE THIS BOOK

This book leads the prospective TV game designer through a series of experiments, examples, and hints that are all intended to make game design possible and fun for just about anyone willing to make the effort. Generally speaking, the material (or "lessons," if you will) are presented in order of importance. It would be difficult,

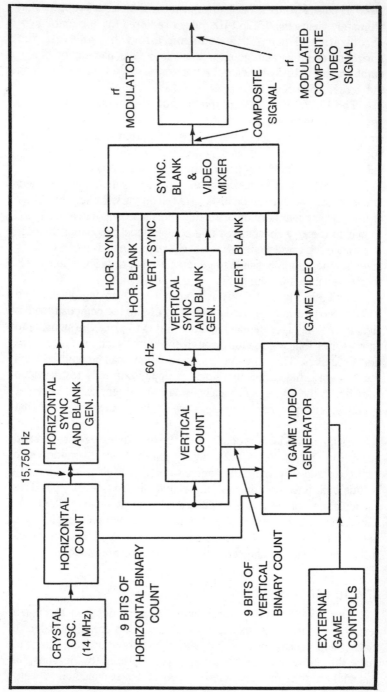

Fig. 1-2. The basic TV game system block diagram.

16

for instance, to begin your study of TV games in the middle of the book, because each chapter assumes an understanding and some experience with the ideas presented in all the previous chapters.

Build up the systems one step at a time, performing the suggested experiments and trying some of your own. Hands-on experience is the key to designing games of your own, and the only way to get that kind of experience is by doing the work suggested here.

LOCATING PARTS

Most of the parts specified in this book are available from stores such as Radio Shack. In many instances, Radio Shack part numbers are specified for the benefit of experimenters who are not fully acquainted with other sources and substitution procedures.

Not all parts are available from Radio Shack, but it is not difficult to locate them from the many mail-order houses advertising surplus in newsstand electronics magazines.

ASSEMBLING THE SYSTEMS

There are few specific notes in this book concerning the final assembly of game circuits. It is left to the experimenter to devise clever assemblies of his or her own, thereby removing the limitations on fun and imagination that characterize commercially available TV game systems.

Of course this approach puts something of an extra burden on the beginner, but what better way to learn than by doing?

Chapter 2

The Sourcebox Unit

The Sourcebox unit described in this chapter contains all the circuitry common to virtually all the TV games described in this book. It is the interface unit that stands between the game itself and the TV receiver. The Sourcebox unit, for instance, generates all the sync and blanking signals that synchronize both the TV raster and the game operations. Unless this system is built and made to operate properly, the experimenter cannot hope to make any real progress in his or her understanding of anything else that follows.

This chapter describes the theory of operation, shows complete circuit detail, and provides some practical hints on construction. The opening section of Chapter 2 gives the experimenter an opportunity to test the system.

The block diagram in Fig. 2-1 shows the basic circuits contained in the Sourcebox unit. The purpose of each block might be self-evident to anyone who has made a thorough study of the material in Chapter 1. The following sections of this chapter, however, describe the purpose and theory of each block in some detail. The construction hints are inserted at appropriate places in the discussion, rather than at the end of the chapter.

SOURCEBOX ORGANIZATION

The Sourcebox unit is organized into 10 basic circuits as described here:

1. *Power supply*—The power supply provides DC voltage levels to all of the circuits in the Sourcebox unit as well as

plug-in game modules and the so-called tinkerboxes (breadboard units intended for self-learning experiments and game design). With the notable exception of the +1.5-V supply voltage for the rf modulator, the power supply gets its power from a standard 120-VAC, 60-Hz source.

2. *7-MHz oscillator*—This is the master clock oscillator for the entire TV game system. For best results, this should be a crystal-controlled, 14-MHz oscillator, followed by a toggling flip-flop that both divides the crystal frequency by two and assures a clean, 7-MHz HCLK waveform.

3. *Horizontal-count source*—The horizontal-count source generates a 9-bit binary counting code that divides the game screen into 455 equal horizontal segments. Each horizontal scan line on the screen is thus divided into 455 discrete sections, each of which is capable of rendering one bit of horizontal video information.

    The nine binary-counting outputs are labeled 1H, 2H, 4H, 8H, and so on through 256H, with 1H being the least-significant (highest-frequency) output and 256H being the most-significant output bit.

    The horizontal-count source also generates an HRST (Horizontal ReSeT) pulse that is used for clocking the vertical-count source and synchronizing the operation of some game circuits. An inverted version of this positive-going HRST pulse, designated $\overline{\text{HRST}}$, is used for generating horizontal-sync pulses.

4. *Horizontal sync and blanking generator*—The inverted HRST pulse from the horizontal-count source is converted to horizontal sync and blanking pulses in this part of the Sourcebox unit. The horizontal-sync pulse (HSYNC) ultimately triggers the TV's horizontal retrace operation. The horizontal-blanking pulse (HBLANK) is likewise used for blanking horizontal retrace on the TV screen and for certain kinds of control operations for the video games.

5. *Vertical-count source*—The vertical-count circuit is almost identical to its horizontal counterpart. It generates a 9-bit binary count that divides the receiver's raster into 262 vertical segments, or lines. In a manner of speaking, this circuit provides information regarding the position of the TV's beam in the vertical sense.

    Like the horizontal-count source, the nine outputs are labeled 1V through 256V, with 1V being the least-

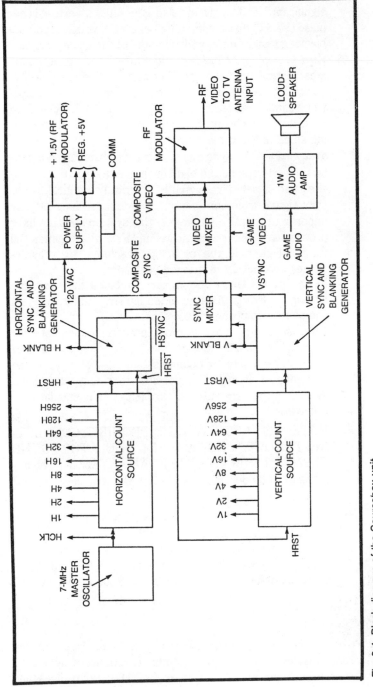

Fig. 2-1. Block diagram of the Sourcebox unit.

21

significant bit. The circuit also generates a vertical-reset pulse (VRST) that is used for clocking the vertical sync and blanking generator as well as some of the game circuits.

6. *Vertical sync and blanking generator*—This circuit generates vertical sync and blanking pulses. The vertical-sync pulse ultimately initiates vertical retrace of the TV's electron beam. The vertical-blanking pulse (VBLANK) is used for blanking the beam through vertical retrace and operating some of the game circuits.

7. *Sync mixer*—The sync mixer circuit combines the horizontal and vertical sync and blanking pulses to create a composite sync signal. This signal is practically identical to the sync signals from commercial TV stations. There is one important exception, however; this system does not have provisions for interlaced scanning. Few video games call for the higher degree of image resolution that characterizes commercial interlaced scanning.

8. *Video mixer*—The video mixer combines the sync and blanking pulses with game video information to provide a complete, composite video signal.

9. *RF modulator*—The rf modulator is responsible for amplitude modulating the composite video signal with an rf frequency tuned to TV channels 2, 3, or 4. This part of the Sourcebox unit makes it possible to connect the game system to the VHF antenna terminals of any standard TV receiver.

   NOTE: FCC REGULATIONS PROHIBIT CONNECTING THE OUTPUT OF ANY RF MODULATOR TO THE TERMINALS OF AN EXTERNAL ANTENNA. The antenna must be disconnected before the modulator is fixed to the TV receiver.

10. *Audio amplifier*—The audio for TV games is not carried via the composite TV signal through the receiver's own audio system. Any audio special effects for a TV game are generated by the game system and merely amplified and reproduced by a small loudspeaker in the Sourcebox unit.

POWER SUPPLY

The power supply, illustrated in Fig. 2-2, services both the Sourcebox unit and external game circuits. This is a conventional IC power supply, taking its main power from the utility lines and

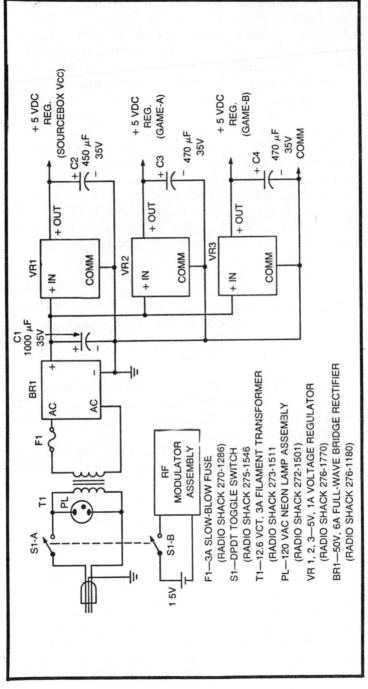

Fig. 2-2. Power supply schematic diagram.

23

converting it to an unregulated +18 VDC. Transformer T1 steps down the 120 VAC from the line cord to about 12.6 VAC at its secondary. The system is fused by F1, and then the lower AC voltage is rectified by a full-wave bridge rectifier assembly, BR1.

The +18-V peaks from the bridge circuit are then filtered to an unregulated 18 VDC by C1 before the voltage is applied to three +5-V, 1-A regulators, VR1 through VR3. The DC output from VR1 supplies its regulated 5-V level to circuits within the Sourcebox unit, including the audio amplifier. This particular +5-V source is also accessible to the outside for operating relatively low-power circuits.

The regulated outputs from VR2 and VR3 are used only for powering external game circuits and design breadboards. Some of the more involved video games described later in this book call for using all three voltage regulators to their maximum 1-A capacity. In fact any experimenter contemplating designs for very elaborate games should count on constructing an outboard 5-V regulated supply capable of providing an additional one or two amps.

The rf modulator assembly, described in more detail later in this chapter, uses a separate 1.5-V AA battery as a power supply. Using a battery for this particular application ensures a clean, ripple-free modulated video waveform. For the sake of convenience, the battery supply for the rf modulator is switched on and off by means of the same toggle switch that applies 120 VAC to the 5-V power supply section.

The line cord is fed through the back of the Sourcebox housing, using a plastic strain relief (Radio Shack 278-1636) to prevent abrasion of the insulation and possible strain on the connections to the switch and power transformer.

Power switch S1 should be mounted at some convenient place on the front panel of the Sourcebox housing, preferably under the neon POWER ON indicator lamp.

Power transformer T1 should be mounted on the bottom, inside surface of the Sourcebox housing. The rectifier assembly, fuse and fuse holder, and all four filter capacitors can be mounted to a small perfboard or custom PC board. This compact power supply board can then be mounted near the power transformer, using insulated standoffs to prevent any short-circuit conditions to the Sourcebox housing.

The 5-V regulator assemblies tend to run a bit hot at times. To reduce the chances of destroying them by overheating, it is a good idea to mount them directly to the inside surface of the metal Sourcebox housing, or to affix a small heat sink to each of them. See the dimensions for one of the three heat sinks in Fig. 2-3. Similar

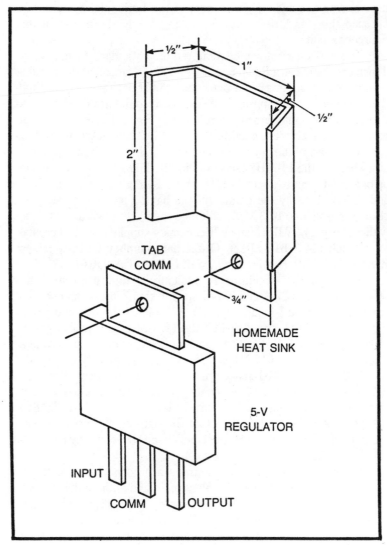

Fig. 2-3. Recommended heat sink for the voltage regulators.

heat sinks are available commercially, but it is rather easy to cut and bend custom versions from standard 1/16-in. aluminum stock.

HORIZONTAL SOURCE BOARD

Figure 2-4 is a complete schematic diagram for the circuit that generates all the horizontal counting, sync, blanking, and reset pulses. This particular circuit board also holds the audio amplifier IC, not because the audio signal is part of the horizontal system, but because there is little space for putting it anywhere else in the Sourcebox unit.

The entire circuit can be mounted on a standard 44-pin, 4- by 4-inch card, such as a Radio Shack 276-153. In fact all of the circuits and systems described in this book can be built onto such a board and then plugged into the appropriate edge-card connector (Radio Shack 276-1551). The numbers in parentheses in Fig. 2-4 indicate card pin numbers arbitrarily assigned to the card-and-connector assembly.

The heart of the horizontal system, and indeed the video game as a whole, is the 14-MHz oscillator circuit. This little circuit is made up of a crystal cut to about 14 MHz and TTL digital inverters IC7-A and IC7-B. Actually the crystal should have a frequency rating as close as possible to 14.3 MHz, although the system will allow values within 2% of 14.3 MHz. James Electronics supplies an ideal crystal for the job (14.31818 MHz). Order part number CY14A, James Electronics, 1021 Howard Ave., San Carlos, CA 94070.

Although the oscillator is basically a digital circuit, the waveforms from IC7-A and IC7-C appear sinusoidal on an oscilloscope. The toggled J-K flip-flop, IC1-A, isolates the oscillator from the rest of the circuitry and divides the 14.3-MHz frequency by two. The output of IC1-A is thus a quasi-sinusoidal waveform having a frequency close to 7.015 MHz. This is the system's HCLK signal.

IC2, IC3, and IC1-B make up the 9-bit horizontal-count source. IC2 and IC3 are ordinary 4-bit binary up counters connected so that they generate an 8-bit binary count. IC1-B is a toggled J-K flip-flop that generates the 9th bit. Note that the outputs of these counters are labeled 1H through 256H, the labels used so frequently throughout this book.

The nine horizontal-count sources are connected directly to output terminals, but there is a selection of five of them that also go to the inputs of IC4, an 8-input NAND gate. This is all part of a circuit that restricts the counting range of the horizontal-count source to 455 HCLK pulses. A 9-bit counter without this resetting circuit would count 511 states.

The resetting circuitry senses a count of 454 at IC4, generating a negative-going pulse at the D input of IC5A. IC5A is an edge-triggered D flip-flop which sets its Q output to the D-input logic level whenever its CLK input shows a positive-going edge. IC5-A is clocked by HCLK in this case; and as long as the horizontal-count source is generating numbers less than 454, the Q output of IC5-A remains at a logic-1 level. The complemented output from $\overline{Q}$ is at logic 0 at the same time.

One HCLK pulse after the count reaches 454, however, IC5-A loads its Q output with a logic-0 level and the $\overline{Q}$ output takes on a logic-1 level. This condition immediately clears all nine bits from the horizontal-count source to zero, thus restarting the 455-step operation all over again.

The signal from the $\overline{Q}$ output of IC5-A is thus a negative-going pulse that lasts for one HCLK pulse interval and occurs at the very beginning of each horizontal-count cycle. A positive-going version of that same pulse, HRST, is directed to IC2, IC3, and the plug assembly leading to the outside world.

The circuit build around the four 2-input NAND gates of IC6 are responsible for generating the horizontal blanking (HBLANK) and inverted horizontal sync ($\overline{HSYC}$) pulses. IC6-B and IC6-C make up what is commonly known as a $\overline{R}$-$\overline{S}$ flip-flop. Whenever the negative-going HRST pulse is directed to the pin-10 input of IC6-C, the output of that same IC is set to a logic-1 level. The device remains in that state while the horizontal-count source is cleared and restarted. The moment the count reaches 80, as determined by the 16H and 64H inputs to IC6-A, this flip-flop circuit is reset so that the pin-8 output of IC6-C returns to logic 0. This point then remains at logic 0 until another $\overline{HRST}$ pulse occurs.

The real significance of the output of IC6-C is that it generates the system's HBLANK pulse, a positive pulse that begins as the horizontal-count circuit is reset to zero and ends 80 HCLK pulses later. Ultimately the beam on the TV screen will be blanked off through this 80-pulse, horizontal blanking interval.

The horizontal sync pulse is generated at IC6-D. This NAND gate is normally gated off by the logic-0 level from IC6-C. Whenever IC6-C is generating an HBLANK signal, however, IC6-D is open to the 32H signal at its pin-12 input. An inverted version of 32H thus appears at the output of IC6-D, but only through the horizontal blanking interval. See the waveforms in Fig. 2-5.

Looking at the HBLANK and HSYNC sequence in detail, the positive HBLANK pulse begins first. Thirty-two clock pulses later, the inverted HSYNC pulse begins, lasting through count 64. HBLANK finally ends at count 80. The overall effect is a combination of horizontal blanking and sync pulses that work very much like their counterparts in a commercial TV broadcast signal.

The only purpose of audio amplifier IC8 is to amplify any special-effects sounds and match the circuit to an 8-ohm loudspeaker. Since audio special effects are not described until Chapter 10, the volume control and loudspeaker need not be connected at this time.

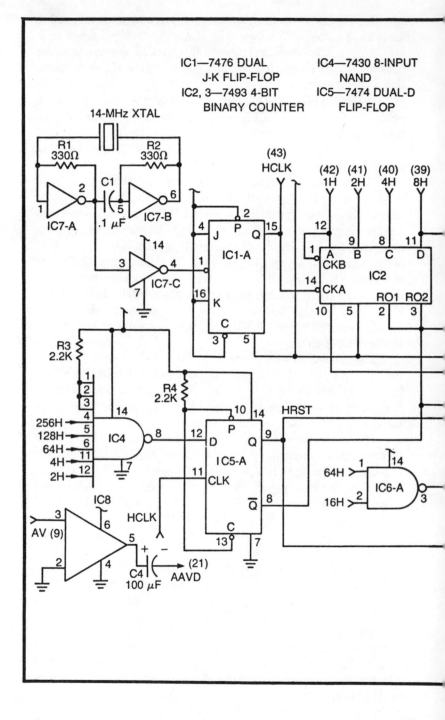

IC1—7476 DUAL J-K FLIP-FLOP
IC2, 3—7493 4-BIT BINARY COUNTER
IC4—7430 8-INPUT NAND
IC5—7474 DUAL-D FLIP-FLOP

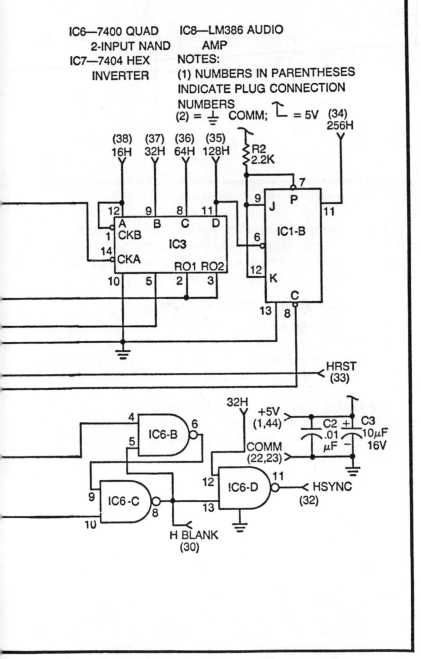

Fig. 2-4. Horizontal source board schematic diagram.

29

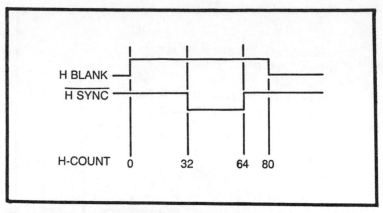

Fig. 2-5. Horizontal blanking and sync waveforms.

The volume control, speaker, and amplifier arrangement are shown in more detail in Fig. 2-6. Control R5 should be mounted on the front panel of the Sourcebox, while the loudspeaker can be positioned at any convenient place inside the box.

VERTICAL SOURCE AND COMPOSITE VIDEO BOARD

The circuit in Fig. 2-7 shows the complete schematic diagram for the vertical-count source and composite video generator. The vertical-count source consists of IC1, IC2, IC3, IC4-A, and IC5. The remainder of the circuit is responsible for composite video operations.

The vertical-count source is a 9-bit binary counter made up of two 4-bit counters and a toggled J-K flip-flop, IC3. The natural counting range for a 9-bit counter is between 0 and 511; but like the horizontal-count generator, this circuit is fixed so that it counts a much more limited range.

Note that the two counters, IC1 and IC2, are cleared by the $\bar{Q}$ output of IC5, while the J-K flip-flop (IC3) is cleared to zero by the Q output of IC5. IC5 is a positive-edge triggered D flip-flop having a Q output that takes on the logic level of its D input whenever the CLK input shows a positive-going edge. The flip-flop in this case is clocked by HRST from the Horizontal Source board—at a frequency very close to 15,750 Hz.

NAND gate IC4-A keeps the D input to IC5 pulled up to logic 1 most of the time, so the repeated HRST pulses at the CLK input keep the Q output of IC5 fixed at logic 1 most of the time. There is a time, however, when the D input to IC5 is set to logic 0: when the 1V, 4V and 256V inputs to IC4-A show logic 1 at the same time. This condition represents count 261 from the vertical-count source, and it is responsible for clearing the counters back to zero.

The vertical-count section thus generates 260 different patterns representing that many vertical lines on the screen.

The vertical-blanking and sync pulses are generated in a fashion almost identical to the corresponding horizontal section. One difference is that this circuit is built around a flip-flop triggered by positive-going, rather than negative-going, pulses.

The VBLANK generating flip-flop is composed of NOR gates IC6-A and IC6-B. The pin-4 output of IC6B is at logic 0 most of the time, rising to logic 1 only when a VRST (vertical reset) pulse occurs at the $\overline{Q}$ output of IC5. This pulse sets the pin-4 output of IC6-B to logic 1 and, as described earlier in this section, clears the vertical-count source to zero.

The VBLANK signal remains at this logic-1 level until the 16 V signal at the input of IC6-B goes to logic 1. This action returns the pin-4 output of IC6-B to zero and, in fact, forces it to remain at 0 until another VRST pulse occurs.

The VBLANK signal thus goes to logic 1 the instant the vertical counters are reset to zero, and it remains in that condition until the counters increment to count 16. VBLANK can then be described as a positive-going pulse that lasts 16 HRST pulses.

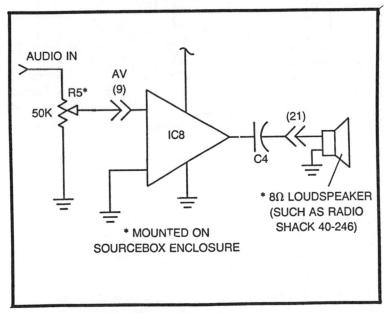

Fig. 2-6. The complete audio amplifier system.

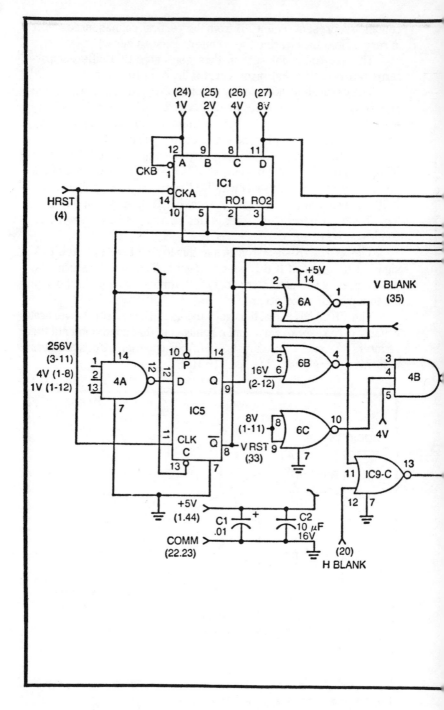

32

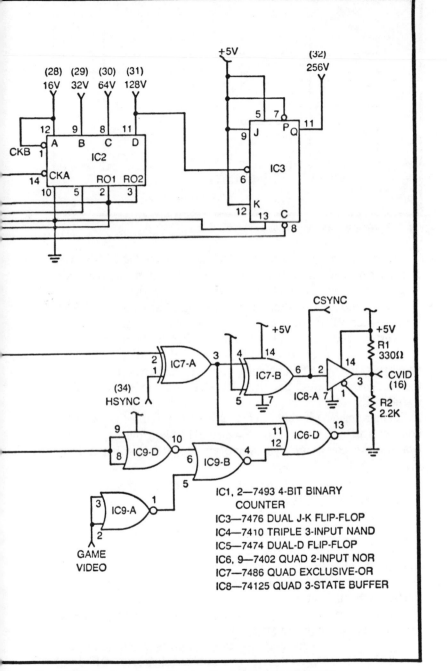

Fig. 2-7. Vertical source and composite video board schematic.

33

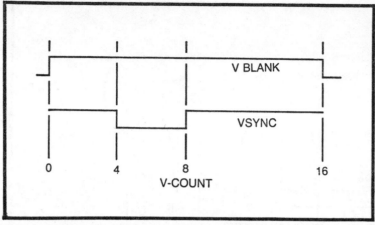

Fig. 2-8. Vertical blanking and sync waveforms.

The vertical-sync pulse, VSYNC, is generated at IC4-B. This particular designation does not appear on the schematic, however, because it is never used alone anywhere else in the system.

IC4-B has an output that remains at logic 1 as long as VBLANK is at 0. When VBLANK rises to logic 1, indicating it is time to blank the vertical retrace on the TV screen, IC4-B allows 4V and an inverted version of 8V to pass. The result at the output of IC4-B is a negative-going pulse that begins a count 4V and ends at 8V. This is the vertical-sync pulse. See the VBLANK and VSYNC pulses illustrated in Fig. 2-8.

The remaining circuitry in Fig. 2-7 is responsible for combining both the horizontal- and vertical-sync and blanking pulses, and then working the composite sync waveform together with the game video.

The horizontal- and vertical-sync pulses are effectively combined in the EXCLUSIVE-OR gate, IC7-A. The output of this gate, shown in Fig. 2-9(a), shows the 15,750-Hz horizontal sync pulses in a positive-going, active-high format until the vertical-sync pulse occurs. At that moment, the horizontal pulses switch to an active-low format, providing the effect of a serrated vertical-sync pulse, an effect that is necessary for maintaining horizontal sync through vertical sync and retrace.

IC7-B serves merely as an inverter for obtaining an inverted version of this composite sync signal.

The horizontal- and vertical-blanking pulses are ORed together in IC9-C and IC9-D, and then these combined signals are ORed with the game video in IC9-B. The output of IC9-B is thus a combination of horizontal- and vertical-blanking pulses and any game video applied from external circuitry to IC9-A.

These two sets of waveforms—the composite sync from IC7-B and video and blanking pulses—are finally amplitude modulated at the 3-state buffer, IC8-A. A precise analysis of this operation is left to experimenters who have some experience with Boolean algebra. The overall effect, however, is shown in Fig. 2-9(b).

The composite video waveform in Fig. 2-9(b) clearly shows three distinct voltage levels. The highest voltage level, about +5V, is the domain of the blacker-than-black sync pulses. At the other extreme is the white-video information, at about 0V. Black-video information and the blanking pulses fall between these two extremes, occuring only when the 3-state buffer is put into its high-impedance state by the output of IC6-D.

The vertical- count and composite-video board in Fig. 2-7 can be assembled on the same kind of 44-pin edge card that the horizontal section is. Both boards should be situated in their respective edge-card connectors in the Sourcebox housing.

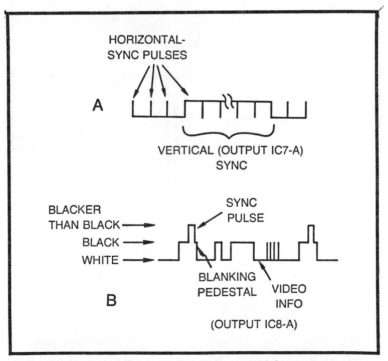

Fig. 2-9. Composite waveforms. (a) Composite sync. (b) Composite video to the modulator.

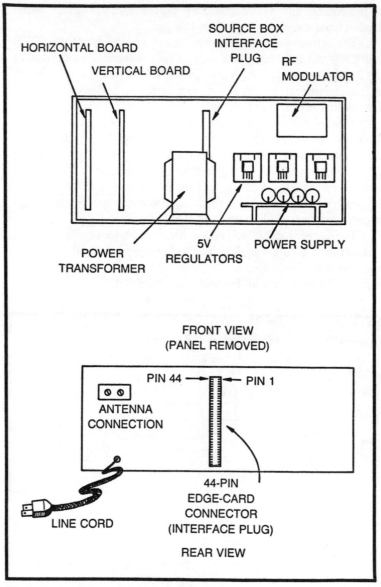

Fig. 2-10. Suggested cabinet layout for the Sourcebox unit.

THE RF MODULATOR

The rf modulator is responsible for modulating the composite video (CVID) from the vertical/video board at a VHF frequency that can be selected on TV channels 2, 3, or 4. In a word, the whole idea is to get all this video, sync, and blanking information into a conventional TV receiver.

It is possible to build VHF modulators from scratch, but considering the fact these little circuits are now commercially available for

PIN	FUNCTION	PIN	FUNCTION
1	+5 V-A	23	COMM
2	+5 V-B	24	1V
3	HBLANK	25	2V
4	HRST	26	4V
5	+5 V (SOURCEBOX)	27	8V
6	nc	28	16V
7	nc	29	32V
8	nc	30	64V
9	audio in	31	128V
10	nc	32	256V
11	nc	33	nc
12	COMP SYNC	34	256H
13	MOD IN	35	128H
14	CVID	36	64H
15	nc	37	32H
16	GAME VID IN	38	16H
17	nc	39	8H
18	nc	40	4H
19	VRST	41	2H
20	VBLANK	42	1H
21	nc	43	HCLK
22	COMM	44	+5 V-A

NOTE:

COMP SYNC = UNMODULATED COMPOSITE SYNC
MOD IN = rf MODULATOR INPUT
CVID = UNMODULATED COMPOSITE VIDEO
GAME VID IN = INPUT FROM ANY EXTERNAL GAME CIRCUIT

MOD IN AND CVID ARE NORMALLY SHORTED TOGETHER

Fig. 2-11. Listing of power supply terminals and signals that must be present at the interface plug.

about $10, the job of building one from scratch is hardly worth the trouble.

Suitable modulators are now being used by microprocessor enthusiasts who want to interface their computer systems with a TV display. So the best source of modulators is the amateur computer shops now springing up all over the country. At the time of this writing, Radio Shack is planning to offer a suitable modulator in the near future. Although it is intended specifically for use with that company's microprocessor system, it would serve our purposes quite well.

Mount the modulator inside the Sourcebox unit, as far as possible from the master clock and crystal (to avoid possible rf interference between the two).

SOME MECHANICAL CONSIDERATIONS

All of the Sourcebox circuitry fits quite nicely into Radio Shack's "compact" 5⅞-by 9- by 4⅞-inch cabinet (Radio Shack 270-281). See Fig. 2-10.

The two major circuit boards can be inserted into 44-pin edge-card connectors mounted vertically on the inside rear surface of the cabinet. The rf modulator is likewise mounted on that surface, using a 2-terminal, feedthrough TV antenna connector (Radio Shack 274-663). The power supply components are mounted inside the cabinet as described earlier in this chapter.

What has not been adequately described thus far is the means for getting access to the horizontal- and vertical-counting signals as well as any other system inputs and outputs that are vital to the operation of game systems. The most convenient way to interface the Sourcebox with the outside world is by means of another 44-pin edge-card connector that feeds through the back of the cabinet.

All of the connections between the Sourcebox and outside world are made through this connector. Its solder connections are inside the cabinet, connected to the appropriate signal sources as suggested in Fig. 2-11. Getting access to these signals from the outside world is thus a simple matter of plugging the appropriate 4- by 4-inch 44-pin PC card into the plug on the back of the cabinet.

No matter how you choose to arrange the circuitry for the Sourcebox unit, bear in mind that you must have convenient access to the supply voltages and signal connections listed in Fig. 2-11.

Chapter 3
Building Static Figures

For the purposes of this book, *static figures* are considered any figures, no matter how simple or complex, that do not move on the screen. Such figures, in the context of TV games, can represent game boundaries, obstacles and nonmoving targets.

A static figure, incidentally, does not have to be a visible one. Invisible figures can add an extra bit of challenge to an otherwise too-simple game; but more importantly, invisible lines and rectangles can serve as "windows" for confining other images to a field that is smaller than the TV screen.

Static figures, whether visible or not, play invaluable roles in TV-games technology; and it turns out that building static figures can be a fascinating and rewarding pastime in itself.

This chapter describes a number of basic techniques for building static lines, bars, and rectangles, while the following chapter takes up the special subject of building complex static figures (circles, figures with diagonal lines, images of people, rocket ships, cars, etc.).

Each technique is illustrated with several specific examples, and the reader will find the procedures used many times and in many different ways throughout the book. It is important to bear in mind, however, that the purpose of this book is to provide some guidelines for creating original TV games and displays. For that reason, alone, it is just as important to understand the essence of each figure-building technique as it is to see how the specific examples work.

None of the figure-building techniques is really any better than the others under all possible circumstances. The most appropriate technique depends on the size, position, general configuration, complexity of the figure, and the role the figure is to play in the display.

The selection of a figure-building technique thus calls for an intelligent decision on the part of the experimenter, so it is important to study this entire chapter and the one that follows before making a firm commitment to the circuit for an original TV-game display.

A prudent student of TV-game technology will breadboard the circuits as they are encountered in these chapters. Of course it takes longer to become acquainted with all the circuits this way, but this doing-while-reading approach makes the learning process much easier, more effective, and a whole lot more fun. Try building the specific examples first, then test your understanding by attempting to create a few static images of your own.

LINES AND BARS DIRECTLY FROM THE COUNT SOURCES

One of the simplest and most straightforward ways to create simple lines and bars on the screen is by combining the wave-forms already available from the Sourcebox unit. All of the horizontal-count outputs quite naturally generate alternate black and white vertical bars or lines on the screen, while the vertical-count outputs create horizontal bars.

Figure 3-1 summarizes five different horizontal- and vertical-count signals as they appear on the TV screen. To view the figures as shown here, simply connect a jumper wire between the designated horizontal- or vertical-count output and the GAME VID IN terminal on the Sourcebox unit. This procedure, incidentally, assumes the CVID and MOD terminals on the Sourcebox unit are jumpered together as described in the previous chapter.

Note that the 256H display shows a vertical black bar that almost reaches the center of the screen. This is a clear indication that the 256H signal is at logic 0 through the first half of each horizontal trace. (A logic-0 video signal always creates a black area on the screen, and a logic-1 signal creates a white area).

The figure for 128H shows twice as many vertical bars as the 256H signal does. The reason is rather easy to understand: the 128H frequency is twice that of the 256H count source. And in a similar manner, each lower-order H output shows about twice as many bars as the one preceding it. Outputs 8H, 4H, 2H, and 1H are not shown here because the lines are too fine and closely spaced to make a meaningful picture in the book. Look at them on your own TV screen, however.

A figure for 256V is not shown here because it does not make a very interesting picture. It is at logic 0 through all but the last four lines of the display. Figure 3-1 does show what you should expect to see from 128V, 64V, 32V, and 16V.

While inspecting these figures for yourself, take careful note of the fact that the bars for 64H and 64V are very close to the same size. The same is true for 32H and 32V, 16H and 16V, etc. From 64H and 64V downward, the lines are about the same size when comparing an H output with its vertical counterpart.

There is, however, an obvious difference between the sizes of the bars for 128H and 128V, and 256H and 256V. Keep these facts in mind for a time when you will be considering your own figure-building procedures.

An experimenter can be justifiably proud of his system when seeing these basic horizontal- and vertical-count bars for the first time. A lot of work and money has gone into building the Sourcebox, and this is the first solid result of all that work. But looking at these bars and lines can become rather boring after a while. So now it is time to begin using these lines and bars as mere building blocks for creating more-useful and interesting figures.

THE LINE/BAR TINKERBOX

Figure 3-2 shows a schematic diagram, physical layout, and parts list for a breadboard system we shall call the Line/Bar Tinkerbox. It is simply a selection of ICs that are most useful for creating certain lines and bars at desired positions on the screen. The main purpose of this Tinkerbox is to let the experimenter find out exactly what IC devices are necessary for building a desired line or bar on the screen. After taking careful note of how it is done with the Tinkerbox, the experimenter can transfer the ideas to a permanent cirucit.

The ICs are plugged into a standard breadboard and bus-strip assembly. (See the parts list in Fig. 3-2 for catalog numbers.) The breadboard assembly is connected to the Sourcebox unit via a multiconductor cable or bundle of wires. These wires are connected to the Sourcebox output connector by means of a standard 22-pin edge-card PC board. Figure 3-3 shows a connection diagram that corresponds with the Sourcebox output terminal configuration described in Chapter 2.

To get a feeling for what the Tinkerbox can do and how to use it, connect the circuit shown in Fig. 3-4a. In this case, 256H is connected to pin 1 of IC3, the 8-input NAND gate. If a test jumper is

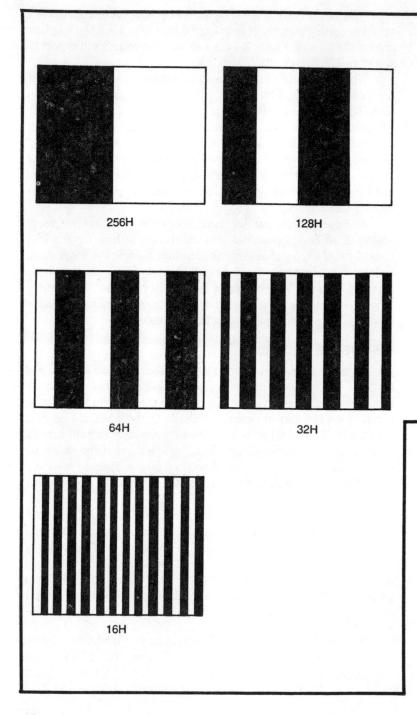

256H

128H

64H

32H

16H

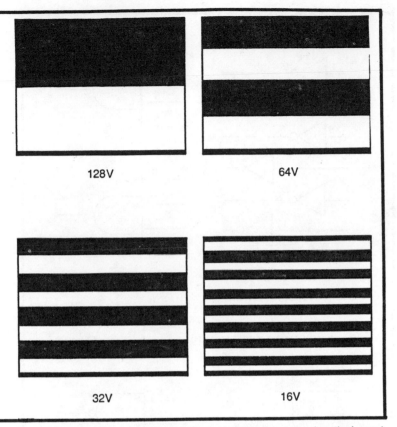

128V   64V

32V   16V

Fig. 3-1. Video images available directly from the horizontal and vertical-count sources.

connected from that input point and the GAME VID IN terminal on the Sourcebox, the screen will show the usual 256H pattern.

But once that same signal passes through the NAND gate, the blacks and whites are reversed. In digital terms, a NAND gate with a single input works like a logic inverter—it reverses the logic-1 and -0 levels.

The signal from the NAND gate is then passed through an inverter circuit where the waveform is reversed once again. This operation brings the signal back to its original phase, thus creating an image on the screen that is in all respects the same as that created by the original 256H waveform.

Any horizontal- or vertical-count waveform can be applied to the input of the circuit in Fig. 3-4a, and emerge in its original form from the output of the inverter circuit, IC1-A.

43

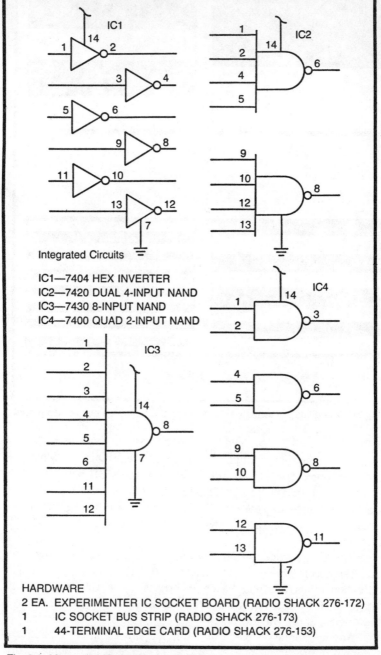

Integrated Circuits

IC1—7404 HEX INVERTER
IC2—7420 DUAL 4-INPUT NAND
IC3—7430 8-INPUT NAND
IC4—7400 QUAD 2-INPUT NAND

HARDWARE

2 EA. EXPERIMENTER IC SOCKET BOARD (RADIO SHACK 276-172)
1   IC SOCKET BUS STRIP (RADIO SHACK 276-173)
1   44-TERMINAL EDGE CARD (RADIO SHACK 276-153)

Fig. 3-2. Most-used ICs for the Line/Bar Tinkerbox assembly. Other useful IC's include a 7486 quad EXCLUSIVE-OR and a 7402 quad 2-input NOR gate.

So what is accomplished by the simple circuit in Fig. 3-4a? Not much in terms of building images for TV games. But the circuit does clearly demonstrate two important facts: a NAND gate inverts logic levels (and hence reverses blacks and whites), and doubly inverting a signal returns it ot its original phase.

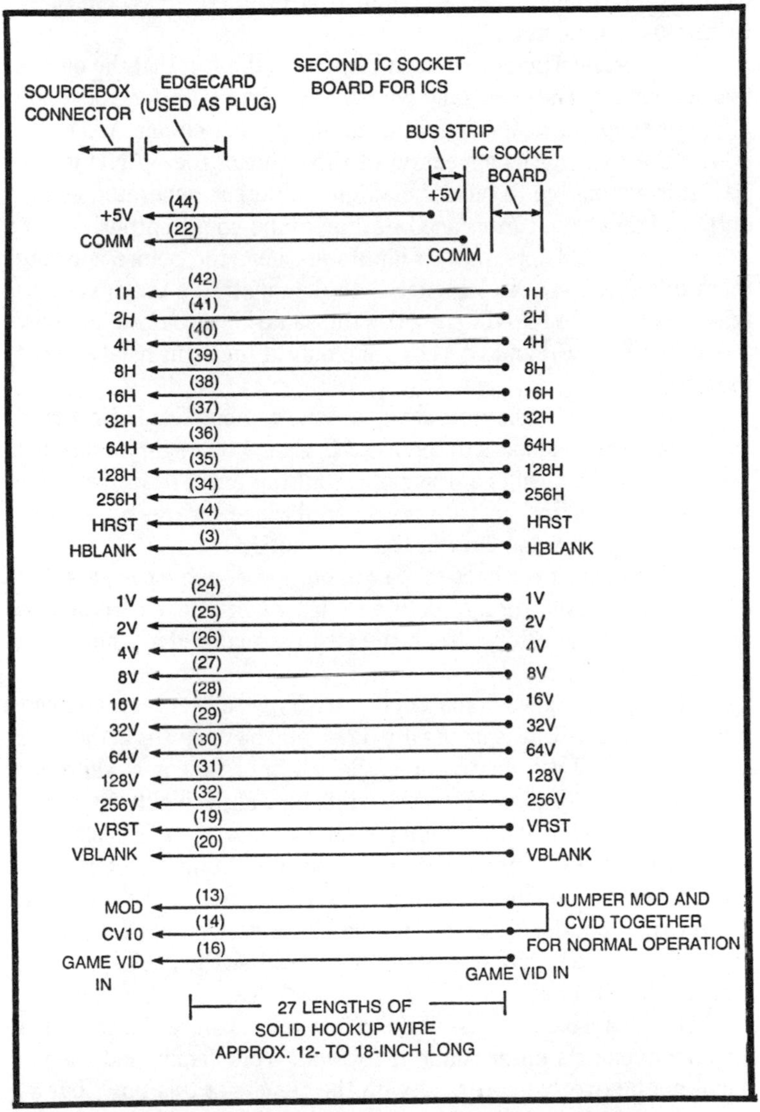

Fig. 3-3. Signal and power supply connections between the Sourcebox unit and Tinkerbox assembly. Note that the Sourcebox MOD and CVID terminals are connected together at the Tinkerbox.

Now wire the circuit in Fig. 3-4b. There are two inputs in this instance. The waveform from 256H is applied to an inverter circuit and then to one input of the 8-input NAND gate. The other input, 128H, goes directly to a second input of the NAND gate. The little screen figures accompanying the diagram in Fig. 3-4b show the patterns appearing on the TV screen as GAME VID IN is connected to various test points.

The essential point to note in Fig. 3-4 is the fact that the output figure shows a white bar only where the white bars for $\overline{256H}$ and 128H overlap. In digital logic terminology, this circuit ANDs together the two signals appearing at the input of the NAND gate.

It is impossible to build the single white bar generated as the output of this circuit from any one horizontal-count output.

What would happen if *both* inputs are inverted before applying them to the NAND gate? Figure 3-4c demonstrates the answer to that question. The NAND gate does the same job as before, but now the whites for $\overline{256H}$ and $\overline{128H}$ overlap only at the right-hand edge of the screen.

Play with this basic idea, using various combinations of inverted and noninverted H inputs to the NAND gate. You might be puzzled with some of the results at this point, but the exact procedures for generating a vertical line at one desired place on the screen are outlined in great detail later in this section.

Incidentally, if you happen to stumble across some patterns that look especially useful or interesting for later work, take careful note of the circuit connections. Keep the results recorded in a notebook for future reference.

Figure 3-5 shows some similar tricks with the vertical-count signals. In Fig. 3-5a, the inputs are 128V and 64V; and as in the case of the horizontal demonstrations, the overall result is a white bar appearing at the location where the white bars at the inputs overlap.

White playing with various combinations of V signals, remember that 256V is not a very useful or interesting waveform. An inverted version of the 256V signal has little noticeable effect on these demonstrations, while a noninverted version applied to the input of the NAND gate blanks out just about all the useful working area of the screen.

The Tinkerbox, as described to this point, can be the source of a whole evening's entertainment for you. Your family and friends might not be overly impressed with the results at this time, but as long as you are having fun with the system and learning things as you progress, that is all that really counts.

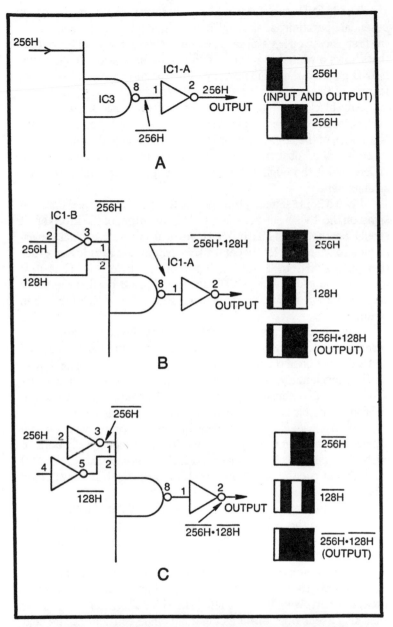

Fig. 3-4. Some vertical lines and bars from the Tinkerbox assembly. (a) A twice-inverted 256H signal yields a 256H pattern on the screen. (b) A NAND gate followed by an inverter combine two different horizontal-count signals such that the resultant is a white area where two white areas of the original signals overlap. (c) Another example of creating a moderately narrow, vertical white bar where two input signals have overlapping white areas.

The NAND gate, followed by an inverter circuit, performs an essential operation as far as building static figures is concerned. In the first place, you have already seen that this circuit yields an output that shows a white bar wherever the white bars at the input of the NAND gate overlap. And now it is time to study a second essential feature of this NAND/invert combination.

Any black or white bar from one of the basic horizontal- or vertical-count sources is always divided equally by a black/white alternation of the next-lower-order signal. Although this might seem to be a rather obscure fact at the moment, it is important you understand it thoroughly. So try an example with your Tinkerbox arrangement.

Feed a 256H signal to the input of the NAND gate and note the signal on the TV screen as generated at the output of the inverter. It should be the now-familiar 256H vertical pattern: a black space turning to white just left of center. Now apply the next lower-order H signal, 128H, to a second input of the inverter. That new waveform should cut the 256H pattern in half. It divides the white portion of 256H into equal-sized black and white—black first, then white.

This demonstrates the fact that any basic horizontal- or vertical-count display has its white section(s) cut in half by a black/white alternation of the next-lower-count input. The black section of 256H is, incidentally, being cut in two also. But since this particular NAND/invert combination yields only overlapping white areas, the division of the black section cannot be seen on the screen.

To check your understanding of this principle, what do you suppose will happen when you add a third input, specifically 64H, to the NAND gate circuit? If 256H and 128H are already there, the 64H input should cut the white area of 128H in half—black first, then white.

The next-lower-order H signal is 32H; and if it is included as a fourth input to the NAND gate, it cuts the bar in half again. This procedure can continue until all eight inputs on the NAND gate are used.

While running this experiment, notice that the white bar on the screen seems to grow narrower as each input is added. Furthermore, it is narrowing from the left-hand side. The right-hand side is remaining fixed. Bear this effect in mind while considering the next set of experiments.

Remove all inputs to the 8-input NAND gate except 256 H. The image on the screen should then be the standard black-to-white 256H signal. Apply the 128H signal again, but run it through an

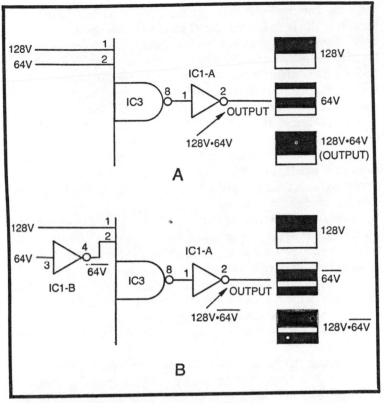

Fig. 3-5. Some horizontal lines and bars from the vertical-count sources. (a) A wide white bar at the bottom of the screen representing the area where white areas of 128V and 64V overlap. (b) Building a broad, horizontal bar just below the center of the screen.

inverter first. The inputs to the NAND gate are now 256H and 128H. How has this inversion of the 128H signal influenced the pattern on the screen?

The white portion of the 256H signal is cut in two by a white/black alternation this time. Recall that connecting a noninverted version of 128H to the NAND gate also cut the white portion of the 256H image in two, but with a black-to-white alternation.

Continue adding *inverted* versions of the H-count signals to the NAND gate until all eight inputs are used. If you are adding these inputs in decreasing order—from $\overline{128H}$ to $\overline{64H}$, to $\overline{32H}$, to $\overline{16H}$, etc.—you will see that the white bar on the screen narrows in from the right-hand side.

As far as the line-building effect on the TV screen is concerned, adding a noninverted version of the next-lower-order H input narrows the bar from the left-hand side, while adding an inverted version of the next-lower-order H input narrows the bar from the right. There is no reason why you cannot use combinations of inverted and noninverted H inputs to place a white bar in virtually any position in the white field of the basic $\overline{256H}$ pattern. And if you want the bar to appear on the left-hand side of the screen, begin with 256H instead of 256H. Furthermore, you can set the width of the white bar by the number of H inputs you use: the larger the number of H-count inputs, the narrower the bar becomes.

Now you are in a position to try some design work of your own. Remove all inputs to the NAND gate and use a grease pencil to mark a point on the TV screen where you want a vertical line to appear. Indicate the desired width too.

Apply the 256H signal to the NAND gate. If your mark is in the white area, that is the proper input signal. If your mark is in the black area, however, you must apply 256H to the NAND gate (by running it through an inverter before applying it to the NAND gate).

Once you have the mark in a white field, add 128H to the NAND gate. Again, if the mark appears in the resulting white field, you are ready to add the next-lower-order signal, but if it is in a black area, 128H must be run through an inverter before applying it to the NAND gate.

Continue this procedure, adding successively lower-order H inputs, inverting them when necessary, until the resulting white bar has the position and width you indicated with the grease pencil on the screen. Allowing a small percentage of placement error, you will be able to place a single vertical line of any desired width anywhere on the screen.

This entire process can be summarized as a recipe for building a vertical line or bar, using the NAND/invert circuit on the Tinkerbox assembly.

Recipe for a Vertical Line or Bar

Begin with a white screen, assuming it is actually a full-screen vertical bar.

1. Is that big bar to be narrowed in from the left or right?
   If from the left, use 256H
   If from the right, use $\overline{256H}$

2. Is the resulting white bar to be further narrowed from the left or right?
   If from the left, use 128H
   If from the right, use $\overline{128H}$

3. Is the resulting white bar to be further narrowed from the left or right?
   If from the left, use 64H
   If from the right, use $\overline{64H}$

Continue including more H inputs, in decreasing order, until the desired line width and position is achieved. Remember that including an inverted H input narrows the bar from the right-hand side, while including a true (noninverted) H input narrows the bar from the left. Always begin with 256H and work one H input at a time toward 1H, but use as few inputs as possible to simplify the final circuit design.

After mastering the preceding technique for placing a vertical bar or line at any desired position on the screen, building horizontal bars will seem quite simple. Use the same combination of an 8-input NAND gate followed by an inverter, but apply vertical-count signals to the input of the NAND gate.

Begin the process with 128V. (256V isn't very useful because its first white-to-black alternation takes place only four lines before vertical blanking begins at the bottom of the screen.) If the desired horizontal line is to appear in the white portion of 128V, you are ready for the next step. But if the line is to be in the black region of 128V, invert that signal before applying it to the NAND gate.

Continue adding inverted or noninverted V-count inputs, in decreasing order, until the resulting white bar has the desired position and width. Note that adding a noninverted V-count input narrows the bar from the top, and adding an inverted version of the same signal narrows the bar from the bottom.

To check your understanding of the horizontal-bar-building procedure, make a grease-pencil mark on the screen where you would like a horizontal bar to appear. Then begin adding inverted or noninverted V-count inputs to the NAND gate, beginning with 128V and working downward through the lower-order V-counts signals.

The process can be summarized in a recipe for building a horizontal line or bar.

Recipe for a Horizontal Line or Bar

Begin with a white screen, assuming it is actually a full-screen horizontal bar.

1. Is that big bar to be narrowed from the bottom or top?
   If from the top, use 128V
   If from the bottom, use $\overline{128V}$
2. Is the resulting white bar to be further narrowed from the top or bottom?

If from the top, use 64V

If from the bottom, use $\overline{64V}$

3. Is the resulting white bar to be further narrowed from the top or bottom?

   If from the top, use 32V

   If from the bottom, use $\overline{64V}$

Continue using more V inputs, in decreasing sequence, until the desired horizontal line width and position is achieved. Bear in mind that including another inverted V input narrows the white bar from the bottom, while including another noninverted V input narrows the bar from the top.

While experimenting with this general procedure for building vertical or horizontal lines, you might have noticed what happens whenever you skip over one of the lower-order signals. Try it. You will find that skipping one input in the normal sequence of high-to-lower-order inputs causes a pair of parallel lines to appear on the screen. Take note of this fact because it might be helpful to you later on.

BUILDING WIDELY SEPARATED PARALLEL LINES AND BARS

Single white vertical or horizontal lines might be useful for certain game designs, but it is more often desirable to create a pair of widely separated parallel lines. A case in point concerns building the border lines for many playing-field type games. Such a border can be built from a combination of widely separated horizontal and vertical lines.

Building a four-sided border figure is getting ahead of the discussion, however. You must first learn how to put a pair of parallel lines of any desired width and spacing you choose on the screen.

This procedure involves three basic steps. First, use the NAND/invert scheme on the Tinkerbox to create one of the two lines. Note the required inputs, then use the same circuit to create the second line. Finally, reduce the two circuits to their simplest possible circuit form and combine them in a Tinkerbox ORing circuit. Use the diagrams in Fig. 3-6 as a reference for studying and experimenting with this procedure in greater detail.

Suppose you want to place two parallel vertical lines on the screen. The two lines can have any desired width and relative position.

Begin by building one of the two lines, using the NAND/invert circuit shown in Fig. 3-6a. Do this by using the Recipe for a Vertical Line or Bar described earlier in this chapter.

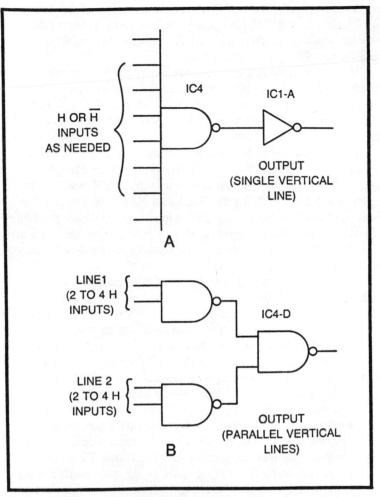

Fig. 3-6. Building white vertical lines and combining them into a single video signal. (a) Circuit for determining the horizontal-count specifications for each line. (b) Combining two simplified versions of the line-generating circuit.

Once you have formed this line, take careful note of the exact H-count inputs you used, and show whether each of them should be inverted or noninverted.

Unless you are trying to build an extremely narrow line, you won't really need more than four combinations of inverted and noninverted inputs to the NAND gate. If it turns out that the line requires only two inputs, transfer the connections to the 8-input NAND gate over to one of the 2-input NAND gates in IC4. (Refer to Fig. 3-2 for the appropriate pin numbers.) If the line calls for three or four inputs, transfer the NAND connections to one of the 4-input NAND gates in IC2. The idea here is to (1) free the 8-input NAND gate for building another line and (2) reduce the circuit to the simplest possible gate configuration.

With the first vertical line designed and reduced to the simplest possible NAND gate circuit form, repeat the entire process for the second vertical line. When you are finished with this part of the project, you should have two separate NAND-gate circuits, one for each of the two vertical lines.

All that remains to be done is to combine the two on the TV screen at the same time. Figure 3-6b shows how this is done. Simply connect the outputs of the two line-generating NAND gates to the inputs of a 2-input NAND gate. That final NAND operation effectively combines the two line signals in a logic ORing fashion, yielding an image on the screen showing both of your designated vertical lines. Note that there are no inverters used past the line-forming NAND gates.

While you are working with this particular parallel-line circuit, connect GAME VID IN to the inputs of the final NAND-gate stage. You will find that the inputs to this gate each carry one of the lines you built—but the image has the blacks and whites reversed. You will see a black vertical line on a white field. The lesson here is that a NAND gate can OR together two signals if they are in an inverted form. This effect takes advantage of something called De Morgan's theorem from basic texts on digital electronics.

After you're convinced you understand how to create parallel vertical lines of any relative width and spacing on the screen, draw an exact diagram of your final circuits for future reference and try the same procedure for building pairs of horizontal lines. First build the lines separately, using the 8-input NAND gate and inverter, then transfer the circuit to smaller NAND-gate devices. Combine the two lines as shown in Fig. 3-6b. Refer to the Recipe for a Horizontal Line or Bar as necessary.

Building Intersecting Horizontal and Vertical Lines

The Line/Bar Tinkerbox assembly can be used for creating intersecting horizontal and vertical lines. Suppose, for example, the experimenter wants to build a tic-tac-toe pattern on the screen. This is essentially a pair of vertical and a pair of horizontal parallel lines combined into one picture. And if the lines are fixed at the extreme edges of the screen, it appears they are creating a border for many different kinds of TV games.

Creating intersecting parallel lines, both horizontal and vertical, is a simple matter of extending the Tinkerbox techniques already described in this chapter. First build the lines one at a time, using the 8-input NAND gate and inverter system. Keep track of the "formula" for each line, then reduce them to simpler NAND-gate inputs.

Next combine the vertical lines as shown in Fig. 3-6, and then combine the two horizontal lines in the same fashion. All that remains to be done at that point is to combine the two sets of parallel lines into one image. Figure 3-7 shows how this can be done.

Figure 3-7a shows the most straightforward technique for combining pairs of horizontal and vertical parallel lines. The idea is to build the horizontal and vertical parallel lines separately as described in the previous section of this chapter. Then combine the two sets of lines by first inverting them and then applying them to separate inputs of a 2-input NAND gate. The output of that final NAND-gate stage yields the composite image.

While this might be the most straightforward technique, it is not the most efficient. It is possible to do the same job using the circuit in Fig. 3-7b.

To understand how the circuit in Fig. 3-7b works, let's assume you have used the recipes for vertical and horizontal lines to get the line-generating specifications—the combinations of inverted and noninverted count inputs for each of the four lines. After reducing these input specifications to the point where you are using the simplest possible input NAND gates for each line, simply connect the outputs of the four NAND gates to a 4-input NAND gate. You will find that the output of that final NAND-gate circuit creates an image identical to the output of the more complicated looking circuit in Fig. 3-7a.

In fact it is possible to use the general circuit in Fig. 3-7b to combine any number of different lines on the screen. Simply build the horizontal and vertical lines separately, reduce the input NAND gate circuits to their simplest form, and then connect the outputs of each of the line-generating NAND gates to an output NAND gate. If the output NAND gate happens to be a 7430 8-input NAND gate, it is possible to combine as many as eight different combinations of horizontal and vertical lines into one image.

The circuits in Fig. 3-8 show the author's circuits for generating the tic-tac-toe pattern and a full-screen border for many different kinds of video games. The circuits are essentially identical, the only difference being the spacing of the pairs of horizontal and vertical parallel lines. Of course it is possible to create the same patterns, but

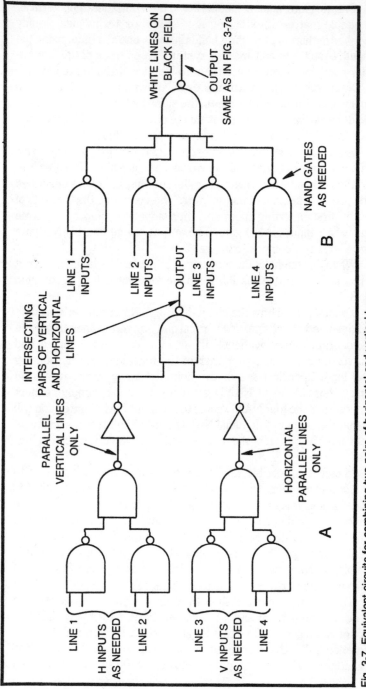

INTERSECTING
PAIRS OF VERTICAL
AND HORIZONTAL
LINES

PARALLEL
VERTICAL LINES
ONLY

LINE 1

H INPUTS
AS NEEDED

LINE 2

LINE 3

V INPUTS
AS NEEDED

LINE 4

HORIZONTAL
PARALLEL LINES
ONLY

OUTPUT

A

WHITE LINES ON
BLACK FIELD

OUTPUT
SAME AS IN FIG. 3-7a

LINE 1
INPUTS

LINE 2
INPUTS

LINE 3
INPUTS

LINE 4
INPUTS

NAND GATES
AS NEEDED

B

Fig. 3-7. Equivalent circuits for combining two pairs of horizontal and vertical bars.

with black lines on a white background, by inverting the composite signal before applying it to the GAME VID IN terminal of the Sourcebox unit.

Figure 3-7b is a key circuit in designing all kinds of video games and effects, so it should be clearly marked for future reference.

Building Narrow Lines More Efficiently

One of the features of the line-building procedure outlined thus far in this chapter is that the width of the line depends on the number of horizontal- or vertical-count inputs used. The narrower the line is supposed to be, the more inputs one must use.

Now this calls for using a lot of inputs to make very narrow lines. It would be nice if there were some way to modify the technique to reduce the number of count inputs required for making narrow lines. Fortunately, there is such a technique, and it quite often reduces the number of inputs to just two or three.

Figure 3-9 shows a Tinkerbox technique for generating narrow lines. Use the 8-input NAND gate to determine the inputs required for setting the position of the line. If you are working with a vertical line, adjust the position of the white bar so that its left-hand edge marks the place where the narrow line is to begin. When working with vertical lines, the narrow line will begin at the top of the position-determining white bar.

After setting the starting point of the narrow line as shown in Fig. 3-9a, remove the output inverter stage, and connect the output of the NAND gate to a combination RC and logic circuit as shown in Fig. 3-9b.

The output from the final inverter stage in Fig. 3-9b is a white line that begins at the same time the original white bar does, but it ends at some time equal to or less than the original bar. The duration (or width) of the line is determined by the time constant of components R and C.

One convenient way to fix the width of the line is by setting R equal to 470 ohms and then varying the value of C until the line has the desired width. For vertical lines, the value of C will be on the order of 0.002 μF. The value of R can be changed a little bit too, but it should always remain between 100 and 470 ohms for the most reliable operation.

In summary, the starting point of the narrow line is determined by the starting point of a white bar, a white bar that is developed by one of the recipes for vertical or horizontal bars. The cutoff time of the line is then determined by the values of R and C in Fig. 3-9b.

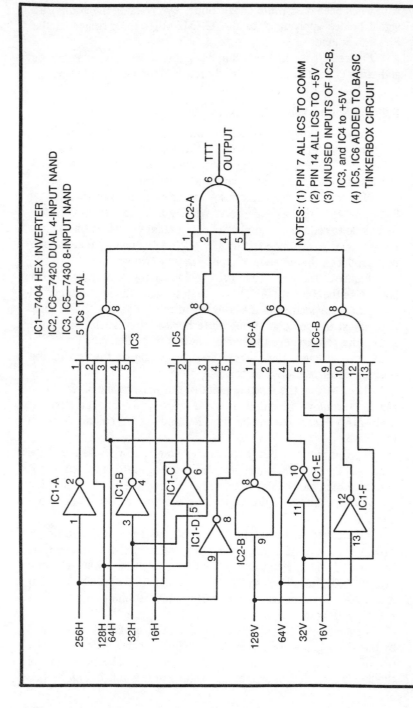

NOTES: (1) PIN 7 ALL ICS TO COMM
(2) PIN 14 ALL ICS TO +5V
(3) UNUSED INPUTS OF IC2-B, IC3, and IC4 to +5V
(4) IC5, IC6 ADDED TO BASIC TINKERBOX CIRCUIT

IC1—7404 HEX INVERTER
IC2, IC6—7420 DUAL 4-INPUT NAND
IC3, IC5—7430 8-INPUT NAND
5 ICs TOTAL

OUTPUT

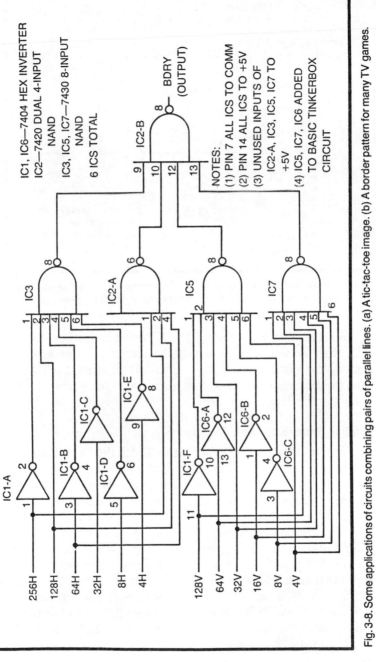

Fig. 3-8. Some applications of circuits combining pairs of parallel lines. (a) A tic-tac-toe image. (b) A border pattern for many TV games.

59

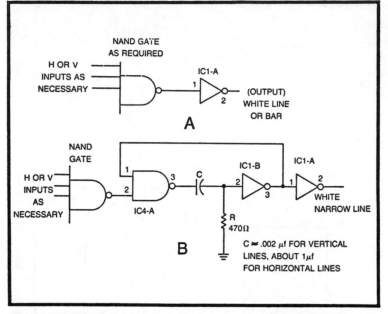

Fig. 3-9. An RC technique for generating very narrow white lines. (a) Setting up the starting point of the line. (b) Modifying the circuit to make the line as narrow as desired.

Any line that is narrowed by this RC technique can be combined with other lines by first removing the output inverter and then applying the signal to one input of a NAND gate, the NAND gate used for combining lines from a number of line-generating circuits. See the example in Fig. 3-10.

Building Broad Bars More Effectively

Anyone who has now experimented with the basic Tinkerbox technique for generating lines and bars might be picking up another shortcoming to the system: it is all but impossible to make a white bar that crosses the dividing line between black 256H and white 256H.

The dividing line between the black and white areas of the basic 256H pattern is a unique point in the overall horizontal-count sequence. At that particular point, every H-count signal switches from logic 1 to logic 0. They all make a transition from white to black. The significance of this fact is that it requires some special logic trickery to make a wide white bar extend continuously through this unique dividing line; and that particular bit of trickery hasn't been fully described yet.

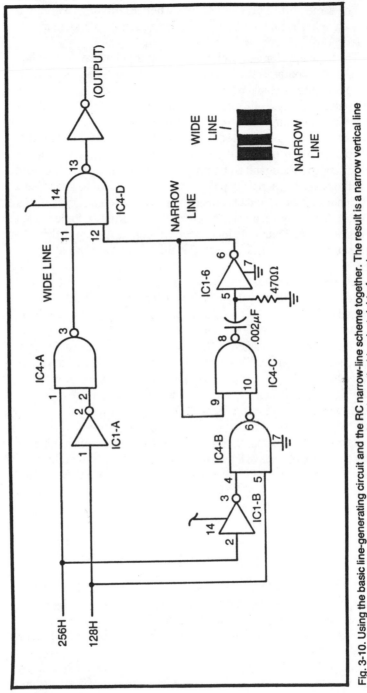

Fig. 3-10. Using the basic line-generating circuit and the RC narrow-line scheme together. The result is a narrow vertical line near the left-hand side of the screen and a moderately wide vertical bar just right of center.

The same sort of problem occurs when attempting to create a broad white horizontal bar that extends through the dividing line of the basic 128V image.

The technique for generating relatively broad white bars, either vertical or horizontal, is the subject of this section. Besides allowing the experimenter to build broad white bars across the center of the screen, this technique often offers a more efficient option to building broad white bars anywhere on the screen.

The basic idea, illustrated in Fig. 3-11, is to build a simple $\overline{R}$-$\overline{S}$ flip-flop from a pair of 2-input NAND gates. To see how this circuit works, suppose the $\overline{R}$ and $\overline{S}$ inputs are normally at logic 1. If indeed this is the case, momentarily pulling the $\overline{S}$ input down to logic 0 sets the Q input to logic 1, and Q remains at logic 1, even after $\overline{S}$ returns to logic 1. The only valid way to return the Q output to logic 0 once again is to pull the $\overline{R}$ input to logic 0 for a moment. And after that, the Q output remains at logic 0 until the $\overline{S}$ input sees another logic-0 pulse.

In summary, the Q output is set to logic 1 whenever the $\overline{S}$ input is pulsed with a logic-0 level, and Q is returned to logic 0 only when $\overline{R}$ is pulsed to logic 0. The $\overline{Q}$ output, as its name implies, is merely an inverted version of the Q output.

What is the significance of this circuit in the context of building broad white lines on the TV screen? It means that a white bar can be initiated at one point on the screen and terminated at any other point to the right of it. It is a matter of coming up with two narrow-line signals, one that switches on the white line and another that switches it off.

Suppose, for example, you have built a Tinkerbox circuit that draws two parallel vertical lines on the screen. The width of the lines isn't really important, just as long as they don't overlap. Now connect the output of the NAND gate generating the line on the left to the $\overline{S}$ input of the flip-flop, and connect the output of the NAND gate generating the second line to the $\overline{R}$ input. You will find that the Q input of the flip-flop circuit generates a broad white, vertical bar that begins when the left-hand line begins and ends where the right-hand line begins.

Any technique you use to generate a pair of parallel lines can be applied here. The resulting white bar will always cover the space between the beginning of the first and last lines. This rule holds as long as (1) the two original parallel lines do not overlap and (2) there are only two parallel lines.

Figure 3-12 shows one of the author's circuits for building a white vertical bar that extends across the center of the screen.

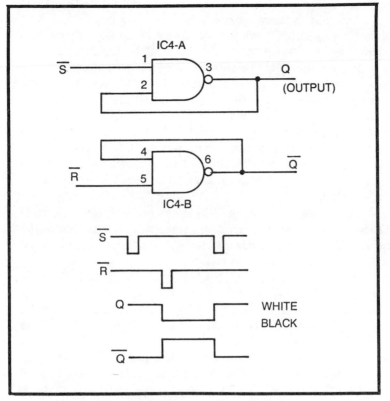

Fig. 3-11. A basic R-S flip-flop circuit and relevant waveforms.

IC2-A defines the starting point of the bar. Viewed on the TV screen, the output of this NAND gate appears as a relatively narrow black bar just left of the center of the screen. IC2-A thus defines the starting point of the white bar being generated in this example.

IC2-B in Fig. 3-12 generates the end-of-bar signal. Looking at the output of this NAND gate on the screen, it appears as a relatively narrow black bar just right of the center of the screen. Combining these two black-bar signals in the $\overline{R}$-$\overline{S}$ flip-flop ICs 4-A and 4-B, yields the final result.

The same $\overline{R}$-$\overline{S}$ technique can be applied to the task of generating broad vertical bars. The only real difference is that the inputs to the first set of NAND gates come from vertical-count sources rather than horizontal-count sources.

Try building some broad white bars, both horizontal and vertical ones, until you are confident you can handle the $\overline{R}$-$\overline{S}$ flip-flop procedure.

A slightly different approach to generating broad white bars calls for a special IC device, a 7474 dual D flip-flop. Figure 3-13 shows the basic layout and truth table for this nice little device.

In the context of drawing wide bars on the screen, the D-type flip-flop works like a short-term memory circuit that remembers whatever logic level (1 or 0) is present at its D input the instant its CLK input makes a transition from 1 to 0. The Q output responds directly to any changes at the D input as long as CLK is at logic 0. As soon as CLK returns to logic 0, however, the circuit "remembers" the D input it saw just before that 1-to-0 transition took place at CLK. D remains fixed at that output level until CLK is pulled up to logic 1 again.

The simple circuit in Fig. 3-14 is just one example of how a D flip-flop can be used for generating a wide, white vertical bar on the screen. The D input in this instance is an inverted version of the 256H signal. The CLK input is 128H.

Whenever 128H is at logic 1 (white) any logic level present at the D input is transferrred immediately to the circuit's Q output. The first time 128H goes white in Fig. 3-14, it so happens 256H is white; thus, the circuit generates a white bar that begins as 128H goes white the first time.

The output then remains white while 128H makes an alternation from white to black. The second time 128H goes white, 256H has switched to olack, so the output of the D flip-flop circuit is switched to logic 0 (black on the screen).

It is left to the experimenter to decide whether the $\overline{R}$-$\overline{S}$ or D-type flip-flop is best under specific conditions. Neither is better under all circumstances.

Building Broad Bars and Multiple Parallel Lines by Foldover

There is yet another technique for building bars and parallel lines on the screen. This technique still uses the basic Tinkerbox approach to getting things started, but it calls for an additional IC to complete the job.

Understand from the outset that this foldover technique is useful only under certain circumstances described later in this section. Usually it is simpler and more effective to use a straight Tinkerbox, RC-modified, or flip-flop-modified technique. The foldover procedure is presented here for two reasons: first, it completes the list of possible ways to generate bars and lines; and second, it introduces a digital principle that will become especially

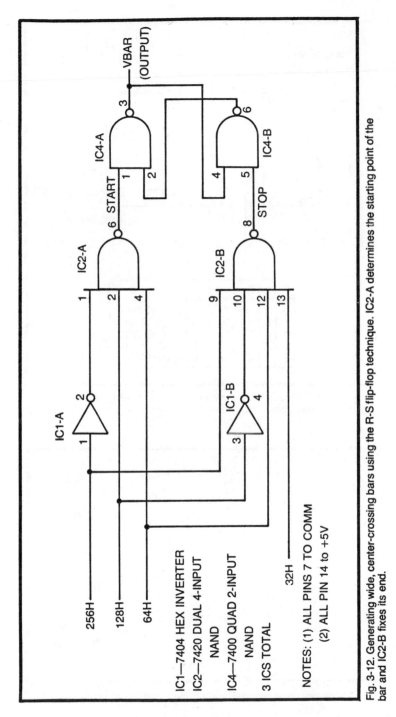

Fig. 3-12. Generating wide, center-crossing bars using the R-S flip-flop technique. IC2-A determines the starting point of the bar and IC2-B fixes its end.

65

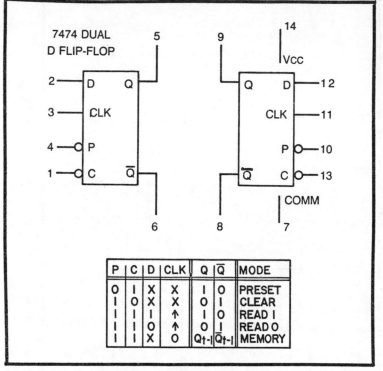

Fig. 3-13. The 7474 dual D flip-flop circuit and truth table. (The Xs designate "don't care" conditions, while the arrows indicate the need for a positive-going level change).

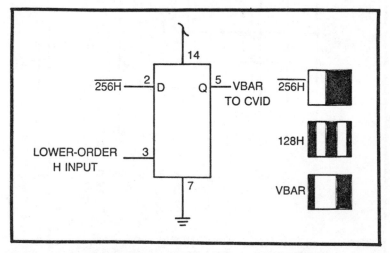

Fig. 3-14. Using the D flip-flop to generate a board, center-crossing vertical bar.

important when attempting to build more-complex figures such as racing cars, people, airplanes, rockets, tanks, and so on.

To see how the foldover procedure works, suppose you have built a vertical white line using $\overline{256H}$, 128H, $\overline{64H}$, and $\overline{32H}$. As shown in Fig. 3-15a, these inputs occupy all four inputs of a 4-input NAND gate on the Tinkerbox assembly. If the output of this gate is run through an inverter before it is applied to GAME VID IN, it generates a moderately narrow white line that is just a bit left of center. See Fig. 3-15b.

Now modify the inputs to the line-generating NAND gate by running them through a set of EXCLUSIVE-OR gates (a 7486 quad 2-input EXCLUSIVE-OR). As long as the control input to the 7486

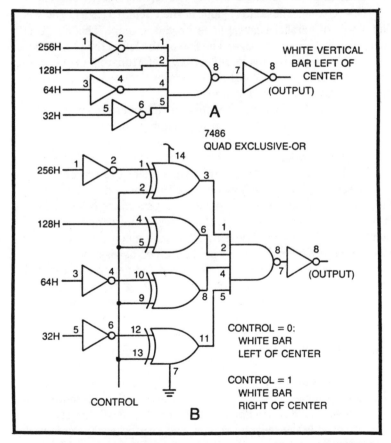

Fig. 3-15. The basic foldover bar-drawing technique. (a) Circuit for establishing the size and position of the left-hand half of the image. (b) Final circuit for doubling or folding over the original image.

67

IC is connected to COMM (at logic 0) the white line appears at the same place on the screen it had before the EXCLUSIVE-OR gates were installed. But connecting that control line to +5V (logic 1), the line shifts to the right of center.

What is happening here is a reversal of the horizontal-count sequence as the NAND gate sees it. Reversing or inverting the outputs from any digital counter circuit makes it appear to count backwards. So when the control input to the EXCLUSIVE-OR gates is a logic 0, the NAND gate sees the H-count inputs arriving in their normal up-coming sequence. Setting the control input to logic 1, however, creates the effect of a counter that is running backwards. In a sense, the NAND gate is fooled into reacting as though the horizontal count is running from right to left across the screen.

Now connect the control input of the circuit to 256H. You will find a pair of parallel vertical lines on the screen. This image is something like a mirror image. The line on the left is the real image, and the one on the right is its reflection. Unfortunately the dividing line is at the point where 256H changes from black to white, and that point is always a bit left of center.

Used with H-count line drawings, the foldover technique yields a double pattern, with the right-hand half being a mirror image of the left-hand side.

The trick works even better with vertical-count signals because the 128V dividing line is closer to the center of the screen.

Create any pattern of horizontal parallel lines on the left side of the screen, then run the inputs to their line-generating NAND gates. Using 256H as the control input, the result is a mirror image on the right side of the screen. Try using 128H as the control and you will find the pattern repeating itself several times across the screen.

This foldover technique can be used for generating a broad white bar if the inputs to the line-generating NAND gate are specified so that they create a white bar that ends at the line where 256H changes from black to white. The mirror image of a white bar ending at that line effectively extends the bar across that point and an equal distance into the right-hand side of the screen. The same sort of thing happens when folding over a horizontal white bar.

Using the foldover technique is purely optional at this point. The flip-flop techniques are equally effective and often more efficient. Compare the two methods as shown in Fig. 3-16. Both circuits generate exactly the same horizontal white bar across the center of the screen. The scheme in Fig. 3-16a uses a $\overline{R}$-$\overline{S}$ flip-flop, while the one in Fig. 3-16b uses the foldover technique.

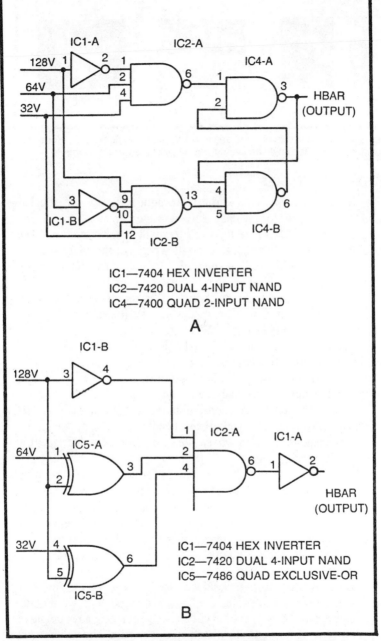

Fig. 3-16. Equivalent circuits for generating a wide, center-crossing white bar. (a) Flip-flop version. (b) Foldover version.

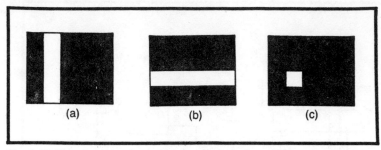

Fig. 3-17. The structure of a rectangle. (a) Vertical component. (b) Horizontal component. (c) Rectangle resulting from ANDing the two components.

BUILDING RECTANGLES

Recall that the basic Tinkerbox technique for building vertical or horizontal bars calls for logically ANDing together white areas. The scheme uses a NAND gate followed by an inverter circuit, and the resulting image is a white bar that exists wherever the white areas of the input signals overlap. Building a rectangular figure on the screen is a matter of first building two white bars, one vertical and the other horizontal. The two signals are then ANDed together such that the resulting image represents the area where their white areas overlap. See the example in Fig. 3-17.

The white vertical bar in Fig. 3-17a is a generated by any one of the bar-generating techniques described in the previous section. The horizontal bar in Fig. 3-17a is generated in a similar fashion, using combinations of vertical-count inputs, of course.

These two signals are then combined in yet another NAND/invert combination on the Tinkerbox breadboard. The image on the screen represents the area where the two white bars overlap. It is always a rectangular figure.

In a very real sense, a rectangle is formed on the screen by specifying its horizontal and vertical coordinates. The vertical coordinate in this case is a vertical white bar, and the horizontal coordinate is a horizontal white bar. It doesn't make any difference how these bar coordinates are generated; if they are ANDed together with a NAND/invert combination, the result is a white rectangle on the screen.

Of course the output could be taken ahead of the inverter portion of this circuit to produce a black rectangle on a white field.

Figure 3-18 shows a model circuit for generating a rectangle of just about any dimensions anywhere on the screen. The vertical and horizontal coordinates are generated by a straightforward NAND-gate procedure, using the Tinkerbox components. The outputs of these line-generating NAND gates are inverted, then applied to a 2-input NAND gate. If the rectangle is to be white on a black field, the signal from the 2-input NAND gate is run through yet another inverter before applying it to GAME VID IN.

One good way to build a rectangle is to sketch its outline on the TV screen with a grease pencil. Then work with the Tinkerbox circuit to build a white vertical bar that runs down through the rectangle drawing, fitting the position and width as closely as possible. That operation specifies the rectangle's vertical component. Write down the H-input specifications and repeat the operation, generating a horizontal bar that fits the rectangle's specified position and height. Again, mark down the V-input specifications.

Reduce the two circuits to their simplest NAND-gate forms and feed their outputs to a 2-input NAND gate and inverter as shown in Fig. 3-18. If you've specified the vertical and horizontal inputs properly, there's your rectangle on the screen.

This rectangle-building procedure can be summarized as follows.

Recipe for Building a Rectangle or Square

1. Build a horizontal white line or bar as described in Recipe for a Horizontal Line or Bar. The position of that bar

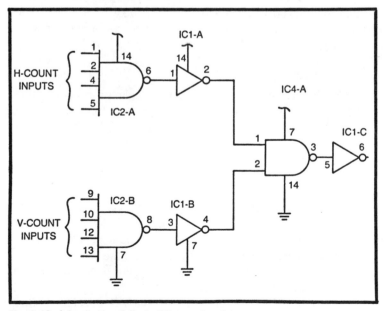

Fig. 3-18. A basic circuit for building rectangles.

determines the horizontal position of the rectangle or square, and its horizontal width determines its final width.

2. Build a vertical white line or bar as described in Recipe for a Vertical Line or Bar. The position of this bar or line determines the vertical position of the rectangle, and its horizontal height fixes the height of the final product.

3. If the 8-input NAND gate is used for building these two lines or bars, transfer them to simpler NAND gates. A line or bar requiring four inputs, for example, can be transferred to one section of the dual 4-input NAND gate.

4. Run the outputs of the two sets of NAND gates through INVERT gates and then to the inputs of a 2-input NAND gate.

5. Invert the output of that 2-input NAND gate and apply the resultant signal to CVID—and presto! There's the square or rectangle. This step, incidentally, is responsible for creating a white square on a black field. The situation can be easily reversed (same square, but black on a white field) by omitting the final inverting operation—take the CVID from the ouput of the 2-input NAND gate described in step 4.

Try building some rectangles of your own, specifying a variety of dimensions and positions on the screen. If you want to make some very small rectangles, you will find the RC line-generating technique is simpler than the basic NAND-gate approach.

Sculpturing Rectangles

There is an alternate procedure for building a rectangle that sometimes saves some time and is perhaps more fun to use. First build the basic rectangle circuit shown in Fig. 3-18, but without specifying the exact horizontal- and vertical-count inputs. The screen should be completely white at this point in the procedure, and it is convenient to assume the circuit is generating a full-screen white rectangle.

Next, apply a 256H or 256H signal to one input of IC2-A. The full-screen rectangle will narrow in from one side or the other, depending on the phase of the 256H signal you use. Then apply a 128V or 128V signal to one input of IC2-B, and the white rectangle will shrink down from the top or bottom, again, depending on the phase of the 128V signal you use.

Then apply an inverted or noninverted 128H signal to another input of IC2-A and watch the rectangle narrow even more. Apply a

64V or $\overline{64V}$ signal to a second input of IC2-B to make the rectangle pull down farther from the top or up from the bottom.

Continue adding more H and V inputs to their respective NAND gates until the resulting rectangle has the relative dimensions and position you desire. I've called this a *sculpturing* technique because it gave the experimenter a feeling of sculpturing or trimming a figure on the screen.

The general procedure for sculpturing a rectangle on the screen can be summarized in a basic "recipe."

Recipe for Sculpturing a Rectangle or Square

Begin with a white screen, assuming it is actually a full-screen, white rectangle.

1. Is that big white rectangle to be narrowed in from the left right?
   If from the left, use $\underline{256H}$
   If from the right, use $\overline{256H}$
2. Is the resulting vertical bar to be reduced down from the top or upward from the bottom?
   If from the top, use $\underline{128V}$
   If from the bottom, use $\overline{128V}$
3. Is the resulting white square to be further narrowed from the left or right?
   If from the left, use $\underline{128H}$
   If from the right, use $\overline{128H}$
4. Now is that white rectangle to be reduced downward from the top or upward from the bottom?
   If from the top, use $\underline{64V}$
   If from the bottom, use $\overline{64V}$
5. The white square can be sculptured further by alternately reducing its horizontal and vertical size and position.

Simplifying the Final Rectangle Circuit

All of the rectangle-building circuits described thus far use at least three inverter circuits, one from each of the line-generating NAND gates and one at the output of the NAND gate that combines the two lines. This circuit is quite appropriate when experimenting with various ways to build a desired rectangle, but there happens to be a simpler way to do the same job. This simpler operation calls for using an IC that is not included on the Tinkerbox parts list, but it ought to be specified in any final circuit that is to be part of a permanent game system.

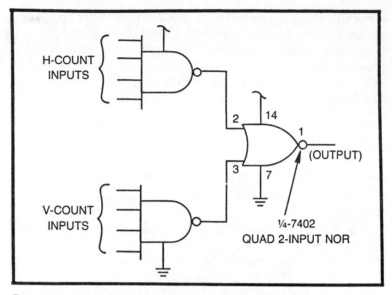

Fig. 3-19. A simplified rectangle-building or sculpturing circuit

Rather than inverting the output of each line-generating circuit, applying the signals to a NAND gate and then inverting the result, simply take the outputs directly from the line-generating NAND gates and apply them to the inputs of a 2-input NOR gate—one section of a 7402 quad 2-input NOR IC package. Compare the basic Tinkerbox rectangle-generating circuit in Fig. 3-18 with the simplified NOR-gate version in Fig. 3-19.

The circuit in Fig. 3-19 takes advantage of one of De Morgan's logic theorems that says two signals can be ANDed together by performing a NOR operation on inverted logic inputs. Well, the signals from the line-generating NAND gates are really inverted versions of the lines they are to generate. (Note that those outputs generate black lines on a white field.) So running them directly to a NOR gate yields an ANDed output; and that's exactly what the rectangle-building operation is based on.

NOR gates are used quite frequently throughout this book where it is necessary to AND together signals that are already in an inverted state. Using that one NOR gate eliminates the need for at least three inverter circuits.

COMBINING ANY NUMBER OF STATIC FIGURES ON THE SCREEN

Single lines, bars, and rectangles—the sort of figures described throughout this chapter—have little value in themselves. Two or more of these basic static figures must be combined on the screen to make up a more useful and interesting game pattern.

Speaking in digital terms, the process of combining two or more static figures on the screen is a matter of ORing together the individual elements. In terms of Tinkerbox technology, this means running the output of each figure-generating circuit to a separate input of a NAND gate. If the output of that NAND gate is then inverted, the resulting signal is a composite image.

The circuit in Fig. 3-20 shows how four different static figures can be combined into a single, composite video waveform. The procedure takes advantage of De Morgan's theorem, where a NAND gate performs an OR operation if the inputs are in an inverted form.

Most of the line, bar, and rectangle generators in this chapter yield inverted signals (black and white) anyway, so the NAND-gate circuit is the most convenient and efficient one for this particular job. Note that the output of the NAND gate is an "upright" or white-on-black signal.

SOME INTERESTING PATTERNS
FROM STATIC-FIGURE COMPONENTS

Figure 3-21 shows a variety of circuits that create some fascinating images on the screen. The basic idea is to combine a certain horizontal-count input with a vertical-count input of the same order, 64H with 64V, for instance.

The circuits built around NAND gates produce a regular pattern of squares on the screen. If the video signal is taken directly from the output of this NAND gate, the result is a set of black squares on a

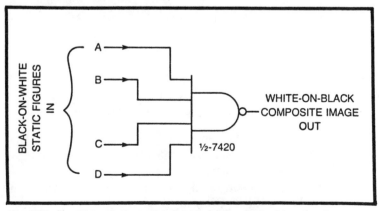

Fig. 3-20. Combining two or more figures into a single video signal

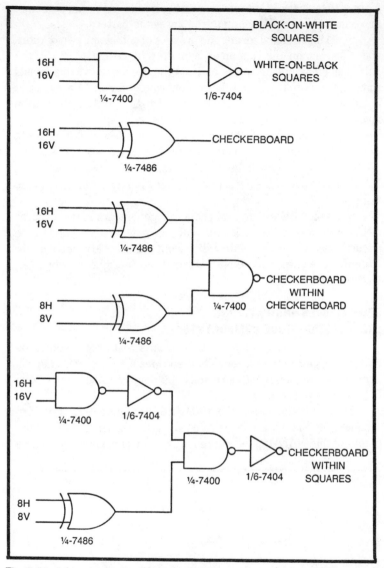

Fig. 3-21. A few circuits for generating some special static-figure effects.

white background. If, on the other hand, the signal from the NAND gate is inverted before applying to GAME VID IN, you will find white squares on a black background.

Combining a pair of horizontal- and vertical-count signals at the inputs of an EXCLUSIVE-OR gate produces a very distinctive checkerboard pattern.

Whether you use the NAND-gate squares or EXCLUSIVE-OR checkerboard, the pattern becomes finer as the input signals decrease in order. A 32H, 32V checkerboard pattern, for instance, is much more coarse than one generated from 8H, 8V inputs.

Checkerboards within checkerboards, checkerboards within squares, squares within checkerboards, and so on make some fascinating images on the screen. Many of them are potentially useful for special effects in TV games you will want to develop later on.

Chapter 4
Building
More-Complex Static Figures

While it is possible to achieve a wide range of static patterns using the principles outlined in the previous chapter, they generally lack the interest that typifies some of the better TV games on the market today. The line and bar patterns are all made from straight lines and right angles; and building something as geometrically simple as a triangle calls for an exceedingly complex Line/Bar Tinkerbox circuit.

This chapter presents one basic approach to building static figures of all kinds, geometric figures as well as an unlimited variety of far-more-interesting figures such as rockets, airplanes, tanks, people, guns, and so on. And to some extent, it is possible to use this technique to build up some of the more complicated line, bar, and rectangle figures described in the previous chapter.

Although this chapter presents only one basic approach, I think you will find it is adequate for just about any figure-building problem you might ever encounter. The range of possible figures that can be built is really limited only by your own understanding of how the scheme works and, of course, your own imagination.

Follow the discussions carefully and in the sequence as presented here. You might get the impression you are studying a textbook from time to time, but if you work out the specific examples and then try a few of your own, you'll have a lot of fun learning how to build complex figures on the TV screen.

This technique, incidentally, can be extended later on to include some animation and figure-motion effects. So the figures you create

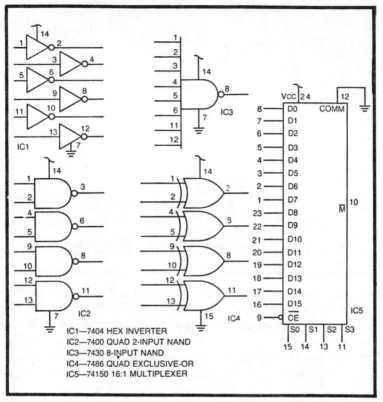

Fig. 4-1. Most-used IC components for the Complex-Figure Tinkerbox.

as part of the discussions in this chapter can be modified at a later time so that they can be moved freely around the screen. Keep a good set of notes concerning the specifications for interesting and potentially useful figures. Such notes will prove invaluable when you decide to work out a TV game of your own.

COMPLEX-FIGURE TINKERBOX

Assemble a Tinkerbox assembly similar to the one described in Chapter 3 for building lines, bars, and rectangles. As indicated in the parts list in Fig. 4-1, you need at least one 7450 16:1 multiplexer and a 7486 quad EXCLUSIVE-OR in addition to the inverters and NAND gates prescribed for the Line/Bar Tinkerbox. There will be a need for as many as four 7450 multiplexers for performing the more advanced experiments in this chapter. But since these large 24-pin ICs take up so much space on the breadboard, it is a good idea to attach them to the board only as they are needed.

For the sake of readers who have no special knowledge of digital electronics, the operation of the 16:1 multiplexer circuit calls for some special consideration. The truth table in Fig. 4-2 represents the operation of a 74150 16:1 multiplexer IC. Note that the device has 16 separate data inputs, labeled D0 through D15. There is a single output, however, $\overline{M}$. Then notice there are four select inputs, S0 through S3, and a chip-enable input, $\overline{CE}$. All of those terminals, plus two more for +5V and COMM, add up to 24 pins.

According to the truth table in Fig. 4-2, the M output of this IC is always at logic 1 whenever the $\overline{CE}$ input is at logic 1. The Xs in the select columns mean those inputs are not relevant as long as $\overline{CE}$=1. The $\overline{CE}$ input, in effect, is capable of disabling the chip altogether—as long as $\overline{CE}$=1, to be specific. Setting the $\overline{CE}$ input to logic 0 thus enables the IC for its normal multiplexing operations.

Suppose the $\overline{CE}$ input is set to logic 0. Whenever that is the case, output M is equal to an inverted version of one of the 16 D inputs. Furthermore, the D input that appears inverted at the M output depends on the status of the select inputs. If the select inputs are all set to logic 0, for instance, an inverted version of input D0

		OUT PUT
	INPUTS	
$\overline{CE}$	S3 S2 S1 S0	$\overline{M}$
1	X X X X	1
0	0 0 0 0	$\overline{D0}$
0	0 0 0 1	$\overline{D1}$
0	0 0 1 0	$\overline{D2}$
0	0 0 1 1	$\overline{D3}$
0	0 1 0 0	$\overline{D4}$
0	0 1 0 1	$\overline{D5}$
0	0 1 1 0	$\overline{D6}$
0	0 1 1 1	$\overline{D7}$
0	1 0 0 0	$\overline{D8}$
0	1 0 0 1	$\overline{D9}$
0	1 0 1 0	$\overline{D10}$
0	1 0 1 1	$\overline{D11}$
0	1 1 0 0	$\overline{D12}$
0	1 1 0 1	$\overline{D13}$
0	1 1 1 0	$\overline{D14}$
0	1 1 1 1	$\overline{D15}$

Fig. 4-2. Operating truth table for the 74150, 16:1 digital multiplexer.

appears at $\overline{M}$. If, on the other hand, the select inputs are set to binary 0001 (S3=0, S2=0, S1=0, S0=1), output M is equal to an inverted version of the D1 input.

The S columns in Fig. 4-2 actually represent a 4-bit binary counting sequence from binary 0000 (decimal 0) through binary 1111 (decimal 15). The D inputs are labeled with numbers running from 0 through 15, and it is no coincidence that setting a particular binary number at the S inputs causes the corresponding D input to appear inverted at $\overline{M}$.

A 16:1 multiplexer thus directs one of 16 different inputs to a single output, depending on the 4-bit number applied to the S inputs. If the select inputs happen to be connected to a 4-bit binary counter, the D outputs would appear at M in sequence—in a scanning-like fashion. And that, dear reader, is a clue to how a multiplexer can be used for generating complex figures on the TV screen.

Just to get the Complex-Figure Tinkerbox going, connect the circuit shown in Fig. 4-3. Note that select inputs S0, S1, S2, and S3 are connected to horizontal-count signals 32H, 64H, 128H, and 256H respectively. These counting signals cause the multiplexer to deliver inverted versions of the D inputs, in sequence from D0 through D15, to the $\overline{M}$ output. Also note that the CE input is connected to COMM in order to permanently enable the multiplexing action. Connect the M output directly to GAME VID IN as shown in Fig. 4-3.

At this point in the experiment, the screen is blank, or should be blank if everything is going well. Then connect the D8 input, pin 23, to COMM. A white bar should appear down the middle of the screen. Its width should correspond to the width of the bars for a 32H signal.

Now remove the COMM jumper from D8 and connect it to other D-input terminals on the multiplexer, inputs D7 (pin 1), D9 (pin 22), and D10 (pin 21). What happens to the bar? It appears at a different place on the screen each time the COMM jumper is moved to a different D-input location. You will notice that the bar does not appear when connecting inputs D8, D7, and D6 to COMM. The bar is being generated by the multiplexer in those three instance, but it so happens the bar is in the horizontal blanking interval. All other inputs fix the location of this vertical white bar in some visible area of the screen.

Using the multiplexer as shown in Fig. 4-3 divides the screen horizontally into 16 equal segments. Each of these segments represents one of the inputs to the multiplexer IC. The D0 input is active during the segment where 256H, 128H, 64H, and 32H are all equal

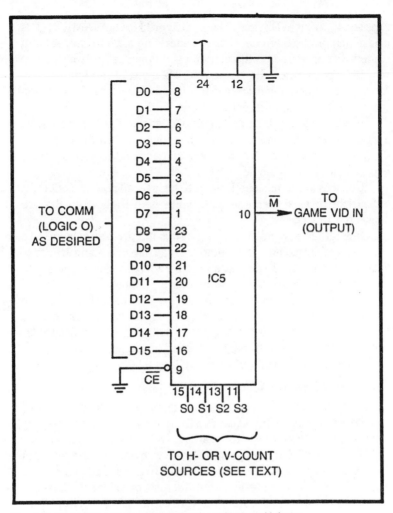

Fig. 4-3. Pinout and nomenclature for the 74150 multiplexer.

to logic 0, the point in the horizontal-count format that initiates the horizontal blanking interval. The blanking interval continues through the time the multiplexer is scanning D0, D1, and D2. But once the count reaches a point where the multiplexer is scanning the D3 input, the horizontal blanking interval is over. Segments representing inputs D3 through D15 thus appear in the useful working area of the screen.

When you connected the D8 input to COMM (logic 0), nothing really happens until the H-count inputs to the multiplexer reached the D8 scanning position. At that moment, an inverted version of the logic level applied to D8 (logic 1) was delivered to the GAME VID IN connection on the Sourcebox, thus generating a white line. A bit of white video appeared on the screen each time the horizontal trace reached a point where it selected the D8 input of the multiplexer. Moving the logic-0 input around to other D-input positions moved the active region to different locations on the horizontal trace.

Incidentally, any D input that is not connected anywhere acts as a logic-1 input. All D inputs that are not connected to COMM (logic 0) thus generate black areas on the screen, and that is why this experiment shows a single white bar on a black field.

Connect more than one D input to logic 0 and note the effect. It is possible to fill the screen with white bars if all 16 inputs are connected to COMM.

It is rather convenient to think of this multiplexer scheme as a type of memory circuit. The memory is capable of holding 16 bits of data, and each of the 16 data locations are addressed in sequence by the signals appearing at the multiplexer's S inputs.

Bear this in mind while substituting vertical-count inputs for the horizontal-count inputs at S0, S1, S2, and S3. Be sure to connect the highest-order V-count input to S3, the next-higher V-count to S2, and so on down the line to S0. Scrambling the sequence at this point might cause more confusion than anything else.

THE ADDRESS MATRIX CONCEPT

Since each of the 16 D inputs on the multiplexer represents 1 of 16 different combinations of 1s and 0s applied to the S inputs, it is possible to organize those 16 locations into a matrix pattern.

The experiments suggested in the previous section of this chapter assumed a matrix 1 unit wide and 16 units long. There was one string of 16 discrete segments across or down the screen, depending on whether the S inputs were connected to horizontal- or vertical-count sources.

What do you suppose happens to the D-input addressing if two of the S inputs, say S0 and S1, are connected to H-count inputs, while the two remaining S inputs, S2 and S3, are connected to V-count inputs? to be more specific, try this: connect S0 to 16H, S1 to 32H, S2 to 16V, and S3 to 32V. Instead of generating a string of 16 segments, you end up with a 4×4 matrix or graph. See Fig. 4-4a.

The H-count pulses determine the horizontal positions on this little matrix, while the V-count pulses determine the vertical coordinates. Position D10, for instance, is enabled whenever the two H-count pulses show the decimal equivalent of 2 and the two V-count signals are at decimal 2.

To get a better feeling for what is happening here, make the connections to the multiplexer as prescribed in Fig. 4-4b. Every one of the D-input positions that are connected to logic 0 (COMM) generates a white area on the screen. (Remember that the multiplexer inverts the data.) So the image on the screen should correspond to the drawing in Fig. 4-4b.

Certainly there are more than one of these "Block-C" figures on the screen. That is a clear indication that the system is generating the little matrix pattern a number of times for each horizontal and vertical scan cycle.

If you are beginning to get a grasp of what is going on here, you should be able to predict what will happen if you connect the D6 input (pin 2) to logic 0. Try it. That operation should fill in the black area designated D6 in Fig. 4-4b, converting the white block-C figure into

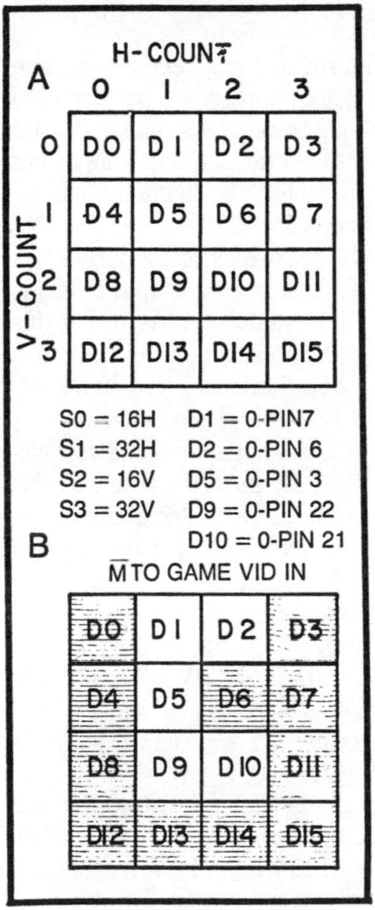

Fig. 4-4. The simplest 4 × 4 figure matrix. (a) The basic matrix format. (b) Specifications for a simple figure generated by the 4 × 4 matrix circuit.

a white rectangle. Remove the grounding wire to D5 and note the effect. You'll get backward block-Cs on the screen if you have left D6 connected to logic 0.

Play around with the logic levels at locations D1, D2, D5, D6, D9, and D10, and note the results. Keep a record of the connections that generate a pattern you think might be useful in the future. Avoid tampering with the matrix blocks surrounding the sides and bottom of the figure—unless you want the white areas of one matrix to butt up against white areas of another one.

Try running the $\overline{M}$ output of the multiplexer through an inverter before applying the signal to the GAME VID IN. You will find that the blacks and whites are then reversed on the screen. Maybe sometime you will have a need for a black block-C on a white field.

Windowing the Matrix Display

Having a number of identical figures on the screen at the same time might create some interesting visual impressions, but it is often confusing and usually undesirable to show more than one particular complex figure on the screen at any given time. Eliminating all but one of the matrix figures is a matter of building a window around the figure in the desired area of the screen.

Figure 4-5 shows the standard 16-cell matrix circuit, including a windowing feature built around IC5. Note that the output of IC5 is connected directly to the CE input of the multiplexer. As long as this terminal is at logic 0, the multiplexer circuit generates its matrix video at $\overline{M}$. The entire multiplexing operation is inhibited, however, when the output of the NAND gate rises to a logic-1 level.

Now notice that the inputs to IC3 are horizontal- and vertical-count sources. An astute reader will recognize the fact that this NAND operation is identical to the rectangle-building circuit described in Chapter 3. And that's precisely what is involved in windowing the matrix display: building a rectangle that encloses one of the matrices and eliminates all the others.

Connect the circuit shown in Fig. 4-5, using window and address inputs as follows: S0=32H, S1=64H, S2=32V, S3=64V; with window inputs $\overline{128H}$, 256H, and 128V. With no connections to the D inputs, you should see a white square in the lower right-hand quadrant of the screen. Now the fun begins.

The square on the screen represents the 4×4 matrix shown in Fig. 4-4a. Since the output of the multiplexer is now inverted before it is applied to GAME VID IN, it follows that logic-1 levels applied to the D inputs creates white matrix cells on the screen. The matrix is

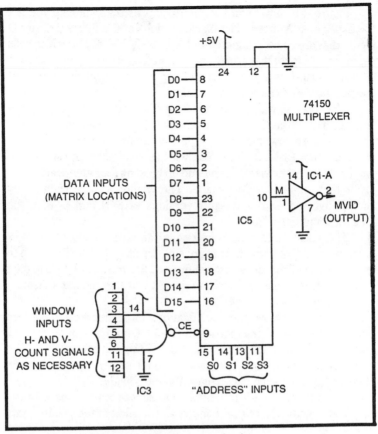

Fig. 4-5. The basic 16-cell matrix generator circuit.

now filled with white cells because any unconnected input of a TTL IC automatically assumes a logic-1 condition.

Connect a single jumper wire to COMM and touch the free end to various D inputs on the multiplexer. You will find that applying a logic-0 level to the D inputs in this fashion causes the corresponding matrix cell on the screen to go black. Connect the jumper to D0 through D15 in succession, and you will see a black square moving through the matrix as you go.

Building Complex Images in the 4x4 Windowed Matrix

Building complex figures using the circuit in Fig. 4-5 is a matter of eliminating white cells by connecting their corresponding D inputs to logic 0. And if you are really putting your heart into the project, you can have a good hour or so of fun playing with this scheme.

Figure 4-6 shows some complex figures that will help you get the experiment started. The black portions of the figure indicate D inputs that are to be connected to logic 0 (COMM). The white cells represent D inputs that aren't connected to any sort of input at all.

As usual, it is a good idea to keep notes concerning the input specifications for the figures you create.

After playing with this circuit for a while, try making the figures smaller. To cut the size of the matrix in half, shift the S inputs to the multiplexer to lower-order H- and V-count sources: S0=16H, S1=32H, S2=16V, S3=32V. You will have to reduce the size of the window, too, otherwise you will end up building four identical figures inside that original window space. The window can be reduced by adding inverted or noninverted versions of 64H and 64V to the window inputs of IC3.

The basic matrix described thus far is made up of 16 cells arranged in a 4×4 pattern. It is possible to alter the configuration to generate 16-cell matrices that are either 2×8 or 8×2. (The first digit indicating the number of horizontal cells and the second indicating the number of vertical cells.)

Figure 4-7 shows the specifications for generating these two different kinds of 16-cell matrices. The 2×8 matrix is generated by connecting S0 to 32H, S1 to 32V, S2 to 64V, and S3 to 128V. The circuit in this case uses only one H-count select input and three V-count inputs, hence it is longer than it is wide.

Changing the width-to-height ratio also alters the shape of the required window. Note the changes as specified in the window data in Fig. 4-7a.

If you ever want to create a complex pattern within an 8×2 matrix as in Fig. 4-7b, simply reorganize the select and window inputs as prescribed in that figure.

In either case you can still eliminate white cells by connecting the designated D input to logic 0, and retain a white cell by making no connection at all to that particular D input.

Carefully compare the shapes, select, and window specifications for the matrix-generating circuits in Figs. 4-4a and 4-7. All 3 have a total of 16 cells. That's quite apparent. But note a more subtle feature. The matrices must have a width-by-height product equal to 16. For example, it is not possible to build a 3×5 matrix using this 16-cell scheme. You do not have to use all the cells (the figure in Fig. 4-4b happens to occupy a 2×3 space), but you must be able to account for all of them in the basic matrix pattern.

Work with this basic 16-cell format, changing select and window specifications, until you are certain you understand how it works. As

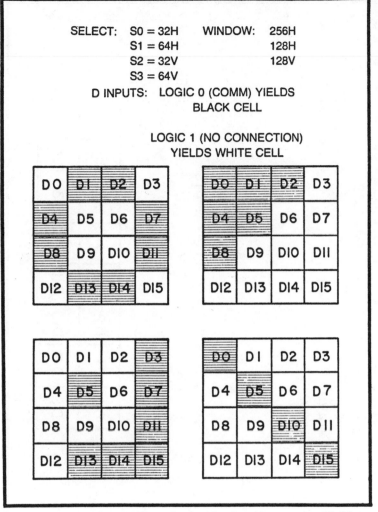

SELECT: S0 = 32H   WINDOW: 256H
         S1 = 64H   128H
         S2 = 32V   128V
         S3 = 64V

D INPUTS: LOGIC 0 (COMM) YIELDS
                BLACK CELL

LOGIC 1 (NO CONNECTION)
YIELDS WHITE CELL

Fig. 4-6. Some experimental figures for the 16-cell matrix generator. All of these figures use a 4 × 4 format.

soon as the experiments seem to be getting a bit dull, move on to the next stage of the project, generating extended matrices.

Extending the Matrix

After experimenting with the basic 4×4 matrix for a while, you will come to the conclusion that it is incapable of generating a very wide selection of interesting figures. The versatility, resolution, and overall quality of TV-game images is directly proportional to the

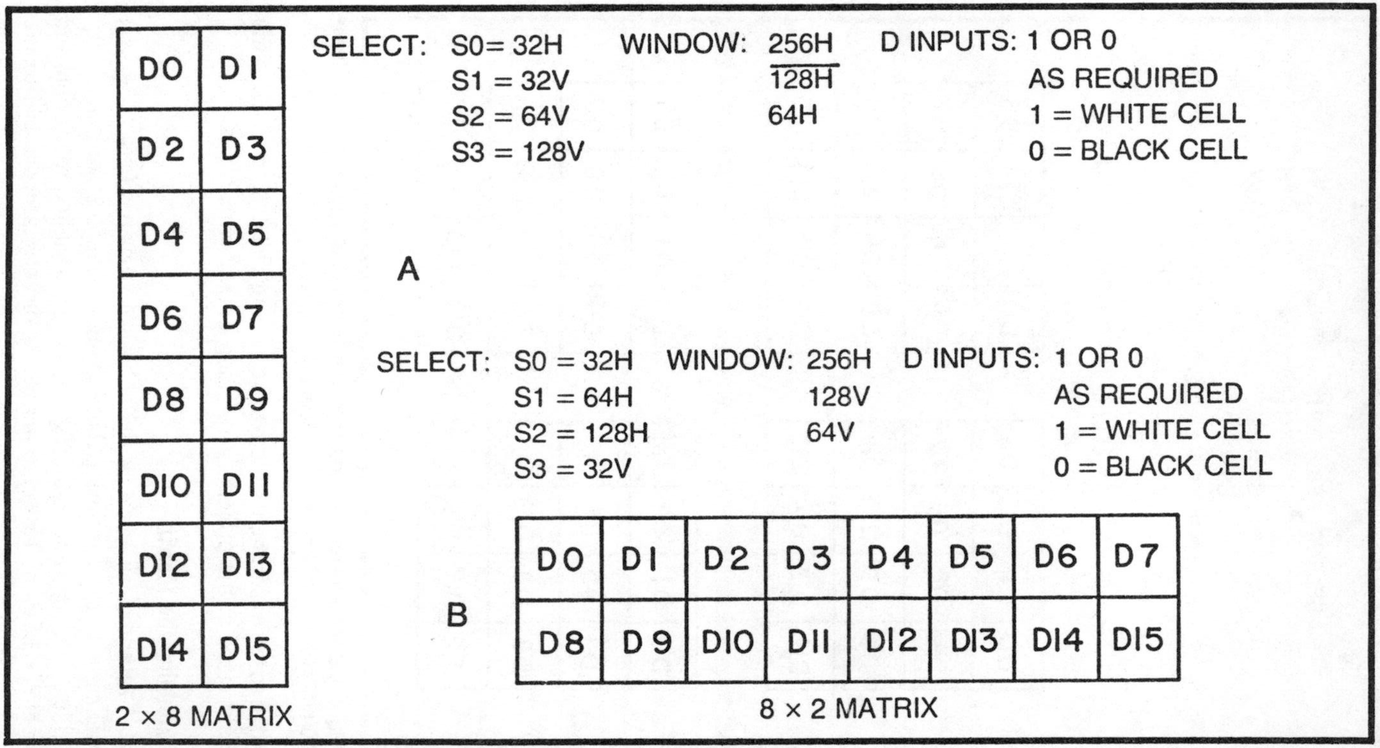

Fig. 4-7. 16-cell matrices organized in patterns other than 4 × 4. (a) 2 × 8. (b) 8 × 2.

SELECT: S0 = 32H   WINDOW: 256H   D INPUTS: 1 OR 0
         S1 = 32V   128H   AS REQUIRED
         S2 = 64V   64H   1 = WHITE CELL
         S3 = 128V   0 = BLACK CELL

A

SELECT: S0 = 32H   WINDOW: 256H   128H   D INPUTS: 1 OR 0
         S1 = 64H   128V   AS REQUIRED
         S2 = 128H   64V   1 = WHITE CELL
         S3 = 32V   0 = BLACK CELL

B

D0	D1	D2	D3	D4	D5	D6	D7
D8	D9	D10	D11	D12	D13	D14	D15

8 × 2 MATRIX

D0	D1
D2	D3
D4	D5
D6	D7
D8	D9
D10	D11
D12	D13
D14	D15

2 × 8 MATRIX

90

number of cells available in the matrix, and unfortunately, the basic 16-cell matrix is a bit too elementary to be of much use.

It turns out, however, that it is possible to apply a simple matrix-extension procedure to double the number of cells in any basic matrix. Using this procedure, for instance, immediately transforms the 4×4 matrix shown in Fig. 4-4a into a 32-cell, 4×8 matrix (See Fig. 4-8).

One of the special features of the matrix-extension technique used in this book is that it does not call for adding any hardware to the basic matrix-generating circuit. The circuit for generating the 32-cell matrix in Fig. 4-8 is exactly the same as that described in connection with the 16-cell circuit in Fig. 4-5.

Thus it is possible to double the essential qualities of a matrix-generating circuit without having to add more hardware. And that is one fine example of applied engineering efficiency.

The only real difference between the specifications for a basic 16-cell matrix and its 32-cell extended version is the D-input format. Whereas a basic matrix calls for inputs of either logic 0 or 1, the extended version calls for logic 1, 0, and inverted/noninverted vertical-count signals. Compare the D-input specification for the 4×8 extended matrix in Fig. 4-8 with those for the basic 4×4 matrix in Fig. 4-6.

Rather than launching a highly technical theory of operation at this point, it is better (in this case anyway) to try the scheme first.

Using the circuit shown in Fig. 4-5, modify its select and window specifications as prescribed in Fig. 4-8. Do not make any connections to the D inputs at this time.

After carrying out this initial setup procedure, you should find a 4×16 white rectangle resting in the lower right-hand quadrant of the screen. This is the extended 4×8 matrix having all D inputs equal to logic 1.

Connect one end of a jumper wire to logic 0 (COMM) and touch the other end to the multiplexer's D0 input. You will find two black squares appearing on the screen. One is in the D0 position of the matrix and the other is in the D0E position. Here is the first important point. A logic-0 level applied to any one of the 16 D inputs on the multiplexer creates 2 black squares. One of these squares appears in the designated D-input position, while the other appears in the corresponding extended-matrix position.

Tap the logic-0 jumper wire to all 16 D inputs in succession and note how it eliminates 2 cells at one time. Of course you can connect all 16 D inputs to logic 0 and end up blacking out all 32 matrix cells—2 at a time.

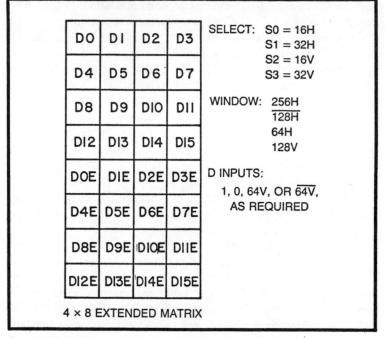

				SELECT:	S0 = 16H

DO	DI	D2	D3
D4	D5	D6	D7
D8	D9	DIO	DII
DI2	DI3	DI4	DI5
DOE	DIE	D2E	D3E
D4E	D5E	D6E	D7E
D8E	D9E	DIOE	DIIE
DI2E	DI3E	DI4E	DI5E

SELECT: S0 = 16H
         S1 = 32H
         S2 = 16V
         S3 = 32V

WINDOW: 256H
         $\overline{128H}$
         64H
         128V

D INPUTS:
         1, 0, 64V, OR $\overline{64V}$,
         AS REQUIRED

4 × 8 EXTENDED MATRIX

Fig. 4-8. A 4 × 8 extended matrix from a basic 16-cell circuit. The Select, Window and D-input specifications are merely examples.

Note that the extended-matrix pattern in Fig. 4-8 shows the usual 16 cells arranged in a 4×4 pattern at the top of the rectangle. The bottom half of the rectangle is composed of another 4×4 matrix with cells designated D0E, D1E, D2E, etc. The "E" suffix indicates an extended matrix cell, and whenever one of the cells in the top half of the matrix is blackened by setting that D input to logic 0, its extended counterpart in the bottom half of the matrix is also blackened.

While this procedure for generating two black squares at the same time is a cute trick, it isn't really very useful (unless the figure you want to create happens to be a symmetrical one). So here is the clincher. Remove any logic-0 connections to the D inputs of the multiplexer and connect one end of the jumper wire to the 64V source. Connect the other end of this jumper to the D0 input of the multiplexer, and presto! There is a single black square in matrix position D0. You are no longer getting the two-square effect you found when connecting the D inputs to logic 0.

Try touching this 64V source to the multiplexer's D inputs, one at a time and in succession. You will be able to blacken any one of the

16 cells in the upper half of the matrix. But notice that it is not possible to darken any of the extended-matrix cells in the lower half of the rectangle.

Next, run the 64V source through an inverter to obtain a $\overline{64V}$ signal. Connect that $\overline{64V}$ signal to the D inputs of the multiplexer and note the response on the screen. It turns out that $\overline{64V}$ inputs darken cells in the lower half of the rectangle, leaving those in the upper half unaffected.

Connect various combinations of logic 0, 64V, and $\overline{64V}$ to the D inputs of the multiplexer. Observe the response in each case, and continue experimenting in this fashion until you are convinced you understand the behavior of this valuable extended-matrix technique.

The general rules for designing figures using the extended-matrix technique go something like this:

- If a cell in the top half of the matrix and its extended counterpart in the bottom half are to be white, make no connections to that position on the multiplexer's D inputs.

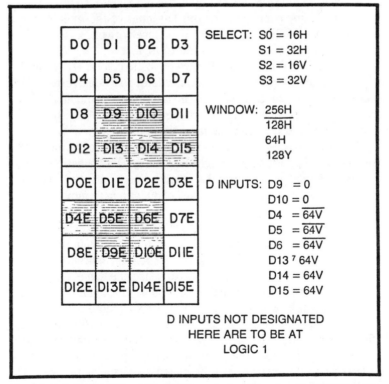

Fig. 4-9. Specifications for a stylized S figure built within a 4 × 8 extended matrix.

- If a cell in the top half of the matrix and its extended counterpart in the bottom half are to be black, connect that position on the multiplexer's D inputs to logic 0.
- If a cell in the top half of the matrix is to be black and its extended counterpart in the bottom half of the matrix is to be white, connect a noninverted 64V source to the appropriate D input on the multiplexer.
- If a cell in the top half of the matrix is to be white and its extended counterpart in the bottom half of the matrix is to be black, connect an inverted 64V source to the appropriate D input on the multiplexer.

This set of rules for designing static figures with the extended-matrix scheme might seem very complicated at first, but it can become rather obvious after playing with the circuits for a while.

Figure 4-9 shows the matrix pattern, select, window, and D-input specifications for generating a stylized S figure. Note that the specifications for the D inputs follow the general rules outlined above. Cells D0 and D0E, for example, are both white, so there is no need to make any connection to the D0 input of the multiplexer. Locations D9 and D9E, on the other hand, are both black, so the D9 input on the multiplexer is connected to logic 1.

Cell positions D13 and D13E have opposite colors: D13 is black and its extended counterpart, D13E, is white; so a noninverted 64V signal is applied to the D13 input of the multiplexer. And finally, D4 and D4E are to be white and black respectively, so an inverted 64V signal is fed to the D4 connection on the multiplexer.

The two figures in Fig. 4-10 are examples of some 4×8 extended-matrix designs you might like to try. The question-mark figure is especially fun to see on the screen. You might want to use it as a rather novel response to some sort of questionable move in a TV game later on.

After studying and applying this extended-matrix technique for a while, you will find it rather easy to design figures of your own. Just copy the matrix pattern in Fig. 4-8 and blacken the appropriate cells with a pencil. Of course you don't have to use the same select and window specifications shown in the examples here, but if you decide to change them, bear in mind that the matrix cannot be any larger than the one specified in these examples. Try it. You'll find it too tall to fit on the screen. So it is possible to make the matrix much smaller by reducing the horizontal- and vertical-count specifications. Then, too, you can shift the position of the matrix by changing the window specifications.

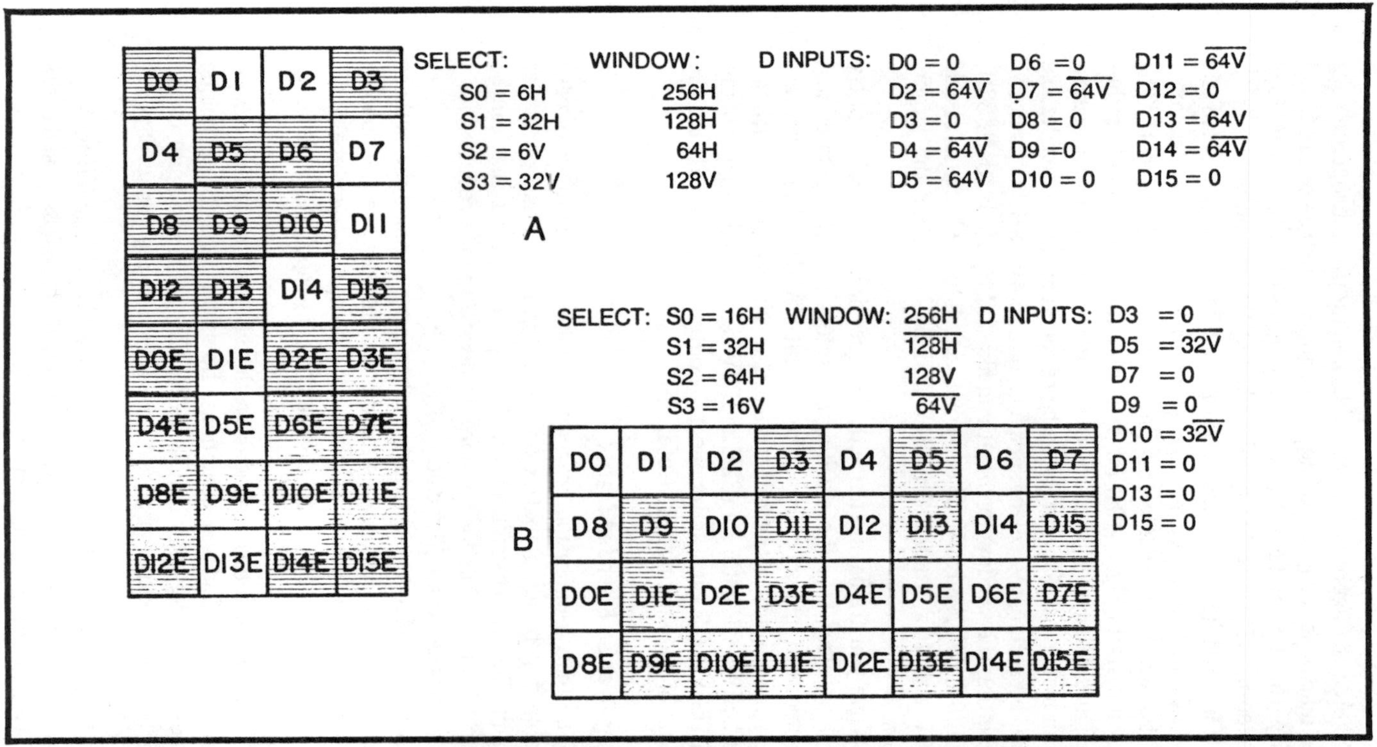

A

SELECT:

S0 = 6H
S1 = 32H
S2 = 6V
S3 = 32V

WINDOW:

256H
128H
64H
128V

D INPUTS:

D0 = 0	D6 = 0	D11 = $\overline{64V}$
D2 = $\overline{64V}$	D7 = $\overline{64V}$	D12 = 0
D3 = 0	D8 = 0	D13 = $64V$
D4 = $\overline{64V}$	D9 = 0	D14 = $\overline{64V}$
D5 = 64V	D10 = 0	D15 = 0

D0	D1	D2	D3
D4	D5	D6	D7
D8	D9	D10	D11
D12	D13	D14	D15
D0E	D1E	D2E	D3E
D4E	D5E	D6E	D7E
D8E	D9E	D10E	D11E
D12E	D13E	D14E	D15E

B

SELECT:

S0 = 16H
S1 = 32H
S2 = 64H
S3 = 16V

WINDOW:

256H
$\overline{128H}$
128V
$\overline{64V}$

D INPUTS:

D3 = 0	D10 = $\overline{32V}$
D5 = $\overline{32V}$	D11 = 0
D7 = 0	D13 = 0
D9 = 0	D15 = 0

D0	D1	D2	D3	D4	D5	D6	D7
D8	D9	D10	D11	D12	D13	D14	D15
D0E	D1E	D2E	D3E	D4E	D5E	D6E	D7E
D8E	D9E	D10E	D11E	D12E	D13E	D14E	D15E

Fig. 4-10. Further examples of extended-matrix figures. (a) A question mark in the 4 × 8 extended matrix. (b) Initials PH in an extended 8 × 8 matrix.

Sketch the figure you want by darkening the appropriate cells on the matrix pattern, adjust the select and window as desired, and specify the D inputs according to your sketch and the four extended-matrix rules described earlier in this section.

It is often helpful to build the original figure using a relatively large-scale matrix. After you are satisfied with the specifications, scale it down to size by lowering the order of the select inputs. The question mark in Fig. 4-10a, for example, turns out to be a rather large figure when built according to the select and window specifications shown in that diagram. It can be reduced in size a considerable amount by setting the select specifications to 4H, 8H, 4V, and 8V, then setting the window to something like 256H, $\overline{128H}$, 64H, 32H, 16H, 126V, 64V, and 32V. The V-count signal to the D inputs should be 16V and $\overline{16V}$, rather than 64V and $\overline{64V}$ used for the larger version.

While you are having fun with this question mark, why not try something else? Use the small-figure select and D inputs as just described. But instead of using the 8-input NAND gate to generate the little window, try replacing the NAND gate with an EXCLUSIVE-OR gate. Run 32H and 32V signals to the inputs of the EXCLUSIVE-OR gate, and connect the output of that gate to the $\overline{CE}$ terminal of the multiplexer. Cute, eh?

Folding Over an Extended Matrix

The matrix-extension procedure doubles the number of cells available for building matrix-oriented figures. That particular technique has no restrictions on the type of figures that can be generated, and it calls for no more hardware than is required for a basic matrix-generating circuit.

A matrix foldover scheme described here doubles the number of cells once again. A basic 4×4 matrix, for instance, can be doubled to a 4×8 pattern by means of the matrix-extension procedure, and it can then be doubled to an 8×8 matrix by applying a foldover technique.

There are some restrictions on the kind of figure that can be generated under foldover conditions, however, and the technique requires some additional EXCLUSIVE-OR gates. In spite of the restrictions and extra hardware, the foldover technique pays off quite often.

The diagrams in Fig. 4-11 show the 8×8 extended foldover matrix pattern as well as the extra circuitry that must be added to the basic 4×4 matrix generator in Fig. 4-5.

8 × 8 EXTENDED FOLDOVER MATRIX

D0	D1	D2	D3	D3F	D2F	D1F	D0F
D4	D5	D6	D7	D7F	D6F	D5F	D4F
D8	D9	D10	D11	D11F	D10F	D9F	D8F
D12	D13	D14	D15	D15F	D14F	D13F	D12F
D0E	D1E	D2E	D3E	D3EF	D2EF	D1EF	D0EF
D4E	D5E	D6E	D7E	D7EF	D6EF	D5EF	D4EF
D8E	D9E	D10E	D11E	D11EF	D10EF	D9EF	D8EF
D12E	D13E	D14E	D15E	D15EF	D14EF	D13EF	D12EF

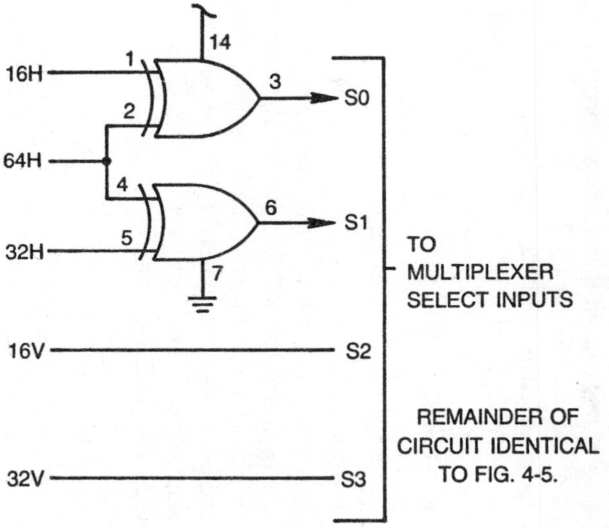

SELECT: S₀ = 16H F 64H   WINDOW: 255H   D INPUTS: 1, 0, 64V, 64V,
S1 = 32H F 64H   128H   AS REQUIRED
S2 = 16V   128V
S3 = 32V

Fig. 4-11. Matrix pattern and additional circuitry for creating an 8 × 8 extended foldover matrix from the basic 16-cell generator circuit. Select, Window, and D-input specifications are just examples.

97

A cursory study of the matrix pattern in Fig. 4-11 will show that the original 4×4 matrix is situated in the upper left-hand quadrant. The designations for each of the cells in this quadrant correspond exactly to the D inputs of the multiplexer in Fig. 4-5.

Then notice that the lower left-hand quadrant of this matrix is an extended version of the upper left-hand quadrant. The left-hand half of this 8×8 matrix, in other words, is simply the 4×8 extended matrix described in the previous section of this chapter.

The right-hand half of this matrix is the folded portion. The foldover cells all have an "F" suffix to clearly indicate they belong to the folded half of the matrix.

Compare the designations of the cells in the left-hand half of the matrix with those on the right and you will find that the right-hand half of the diagram is really a mirror image of the other half. The folded cell D3F, for instance, is one cell to the right of the center line, while its originating counter-part, D3 is just left of center. D0 is in one upper corner, while the folded version of it appears in the opposite upper corner.

The fact that the right-hand half of this 8×8 matrix is a mirror image of the left-hand half means that any figure using this format must be symmetrical around the vertical center line. While this might seem to be a rather severe restriction at first, it turns out that a great many interesting and useful figures do, indeed, have a symmetrical (mirror-image) quality. Look ahead to Fig. 4-12 for one good example.

All that is required for achieving the foldover effect in this case is to run the 16H and 32H signal through EXCLUSIVE-OR gates before applying them to the S0 and S1 select terminals of the multiplexer. One input of each of the EXCLUSIVE-OR gates is connected to 64H. So when 64H is at logic 0, noninverted versions of 16H and 32H appear at select inputs S0 and S1. When 64H switches to logic 1, however, S0 and S1 see inverted versions of 16H and 32H.

The circuit thus generates the normal matrix and extended-matrix patterns as long as 64H is at logic 0, but as soon as 64H rises to logic 1, it effectively reverses the horizontal scanning operation. Along the first row of cells, for instance, S0 and S1 see binary levels representing a normal count of 0, 1, 2, and 3. At the end of D3, though, the EXCLUSIVE-OR gates begin reversing the count: 3, 2 1, 0. A reversed image thus appears along the right-hand half of the matrix.

Connect the basic 4×4 matrix-generating circuit shown in Fig. 4-5, then add the two EXCLUSIVE-OR gates as shown in Fig. 4-10.

DO	DI	D 2	D 3	D3F	D2F	DIF	DOF
D 4	D 5	D 6	D 7	D7F	D6F	D5F	D4F
D8	D9	DIO	DII	DIIF	DIOF	D9F	D8F
DI2	DI3	DI4	DI5	DI5F	DI4F	DI3F	DI2F
DOE	DIE	D2E	D3E	D3EF	D2EF	DIEF	DOEF
D4E	D5E	D6E	D7E	D7EF	D6EF	D5EF	D4EF
D8E	D9E	DIOE	DIIE	DIIEF	DIOEF	D9EF	D8EF
DI2E	DI3E	DI4E	DI5E	DI5EF	DI4EF	DI3EF	DI2EF

SELECT:
S0 = 16H F 64H
S1 = 32H F 64H
S2 = 16V
S3 = 32V

WINDOW: 256H
$\overline{128H}$
128V

D INPUTS: D0 = $\overline{64V}$
D1 = 0
D2 = $\overline{64V}$
D3 = $\overline{64V}$
D6 = $\overline{64V}$
D9 = $\overline{64V}$
D12 = $\overline{64V}$
D13 = 64V
D14 = 64V

Fig. 4-12. Figure and specifications for a racing car, using the 8 × 8 extended foldover matrix circuit.

Finally, set the select and window specifications as shown. (The select statement S0=16H F 64H can be interpreted as meaning, "S0 equals 16H folded by 64H").

Using these specifications, you will find a large white square near the lower right-hand corner of the screen.

To begin getting a feeling for how this 8×8 extended foldover matrix works, connect the D inputs of the multiplexer to logic zero, beginning with D0 and working up toward D15. When you connect D0 to logic 0, you should see four black squares appearing at D0, D0F, D0E, and D0EF. In fact four black squares should appear anytime one of the multiplexer's D inputs is connected to a logic-0 source. The four squares represent the original D position, its extended counterpart, and foldover versions of both the original and extended squares.

Whenever any of the D inputs are connected to 64V, you should see a pair of black squares in the upper half of the matrix. The one on the right side is a mirror-image of the one on the left. And in the same fashion, connecting any of the multiplexer's D inputs to an inverted version of 64V creates a pair of black squares in the bottom half of the matrix.

The four rules for generating a 4×8 extended matrix pattern apply here; so if you have mastered the earlier procedure, you are fully prepared to begin building extended foldover patterns.

The diagram in Fig. 4-12 is one example of an 8×8 extended foldover figure. The idea here is to build a figure of a racing car for a couple of different TV games. Using the select, window, and D inputs specified in that figure generates a rather large version of the car; so after you've tried building it for yourself (and maybe making a few style modifications), reduce its size by scaling down all of the specifications a notch or two.

Why not try designing a few more interesting and potentially useful figures that are symmetrical about a vertical center line? Try a rocket, for instance, or some stars, squares with black centers, and triangles.

Figure 4-13 shows the matrix and circuitry for converting the 8×8 extended foldover matrix to one having symmetry about a horizontal center line. Three lower-order horizontal-count inputs go to select inputs S0, S1, and S2, while S3 sees a folded version of 16V. Note that the 32V signal that is used for generating the extended-matrix effect must also be folded before it is applied to the appropriate D inputs of the multiplexer circuit.

An example of an 8×8 extended, horizontally folded image is shown in Fig. 4-14. As with every matrix-generated figure in this chapter, it can be reduced in size by scaling down all the vertical- and horizontal-count inputs. Using the specifications given in Fig. 4-14, the airplane occupies most of the lower right-hand quadrant of the screen.

Figure 4-15 shows yet another version of the 64-cell extended foldover matrix built around the circuit in Fig. 4-5. In this instance the matrix is configured as a 4×16, with symmetry about the vertical axis. Using the select, window, and data specifications shown here, this particular matrix is quite useful for building missile images. See the suggested missile in Fig. 4-16.

See if you can apply your understanding of how the foldover principle works to generate a missile image that fits into a 16×4 matrix that is folded along the horizontal center line.

MATRIX OPERATIONS FROM A 32-CELL GENERATOR

The circuit in Fig. 4-5 is a basic 16-cell matrix generator. By applying extended-matrix and matrix foldover procedures, it is possible to build 32-cell and 64-cell matrices. The only restriction on the kinds of figures it can generate is that the 64-cell version is good only for making symmetrical figures.

And while it is a lot of fun to play with the system just described, personal experience with it shows that other people sometimes have

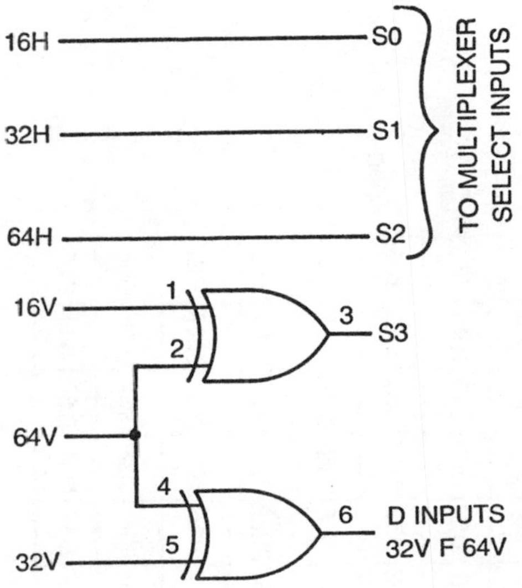

Fig. 4-13. Matrix configuration, circuit, and sample specifications for an 8 × 8 extended matrix that is folded horizontally.

101

D0	D1	D2	D3	D4	D5	D6	D7
D8	D9	D10	D11	D12	D13	D14	D15
D0E	D1E	D2E	D3E	D4E	D5E	D6E	D7E
D8E	D9E	D10E	D11E	D12E	D13E	D14E	D15E
D8EF	D9EF	D10EF	D11EF	D12EF	D13EF	D14EF	D15EF
D0EF	D1EF	D2EF	D3EF	D4EF	D5EF	D6EF	D7EF
D8F	D9F	D10F	D11F	D12F	D13F	D14F	D15F
D0F	D1F	D2F	D3F	D4F	D5F	D6F	D7F

SELECT
S0 = 16H
S1 = 32H
S2 = 64H
S3 = 16V F 64V

WINDOW: 256H
128H
128V

D INPUTS:

D0 = 0	D8 = 32V
D1 = 32V	D9 = 32V
D2 = 0	D10 = 32V
D3 = 0	D11 = 32V
D4 = 32V	D14 = 32V
D6 = 0	D15 = 32V
D7 = 32V	

Fig. 4-14. Figure and specifications for an airplane, using a horizontally folded, 8 × 8 extended matrix.

trouble identifying the object presented on the screen. Even with 64 cells available for building an image, the resolution is often so coarse that others might, indeed, have trouble seeing what the image is supposed to represent. When this is the case, it is time to move up to a matrix generator that yields a higher resolution.

The circuit in Fig. 4-17 uses two 16:1 multiplexer circuits. The basic system generates 32 cells. (Note that there are 32 D inputs, labeled D0 through D31.) If the matrix-extension technique is applied to this circuit, the number of available cells rises to 64. And if the foldover technique is also used, the system can generate a 128-cell symmetrical figure.

This system represents a 2:1 increase in image resolution over the basic 16-cell circuit in Fig. 4-5.

IC6 and IC6 are identical ICs. In fact they are the same multiplexer IC used for all of the complex-figure circuits already described in this chapter. Note, however, that this system has five select inputs, S0 through S4, while each multiplexer IC has input provisions for only four.

We can take care of the four basic select inputs on each multiplexer IC by connecting them in parallel: pin 15 of IC5 to pin 15 of IC6, pin 14 of IC5 to pin 14 of IC6, and so on. The parallel-connected select inputs on the two multiplexer ICs then go to system-select inputs S0 through S3.

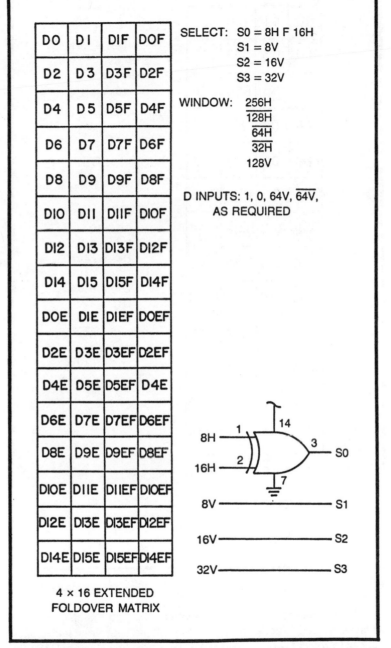

DO	D I	DIF	DOF
D2	D 3	D3F	D2F
D4	D 5	D5F	D4F
D6	D7	D7F	D6F
D8	D9	D9F	D8F
DIO	DII	DIIF	DIOF
DI2	DI3	DI3F	DI2F
DI4	DI5	DI5F	DI4F
DOE	DIE	DIEF	DOEF
D2E	D3E	D3EF	D2EF
D4E	D5E	D5EF	D4E
D6E	D7E	D7EF	D6EF
D8E	D9E	D9EF	D8EF
DIOE	DIIE	DIIEF	DIOEF
DI2E	DI3E	DI3EF	DI2EF
DI4E	DI5E	DI5EF	DI4EF

4 × 16 EXTENDED
FOLDOVER MATRIX

SELECT: S0 = 8H F 16H
         S1 = 8V
         S2 = 16V
         S3 = 32V

WINDOW: 256H
         $\overline{128H}$
         $\overline{64H}$
         $\overline{32H}$
         128V

D INPUTS: 1, 0, 64V, $\overline{64V}$,
          AS REQUIRED

Fig. 4-15. Matrix configuration, circuit, and sample specifications for a 4 × 16 extended, foldover matrix.

103

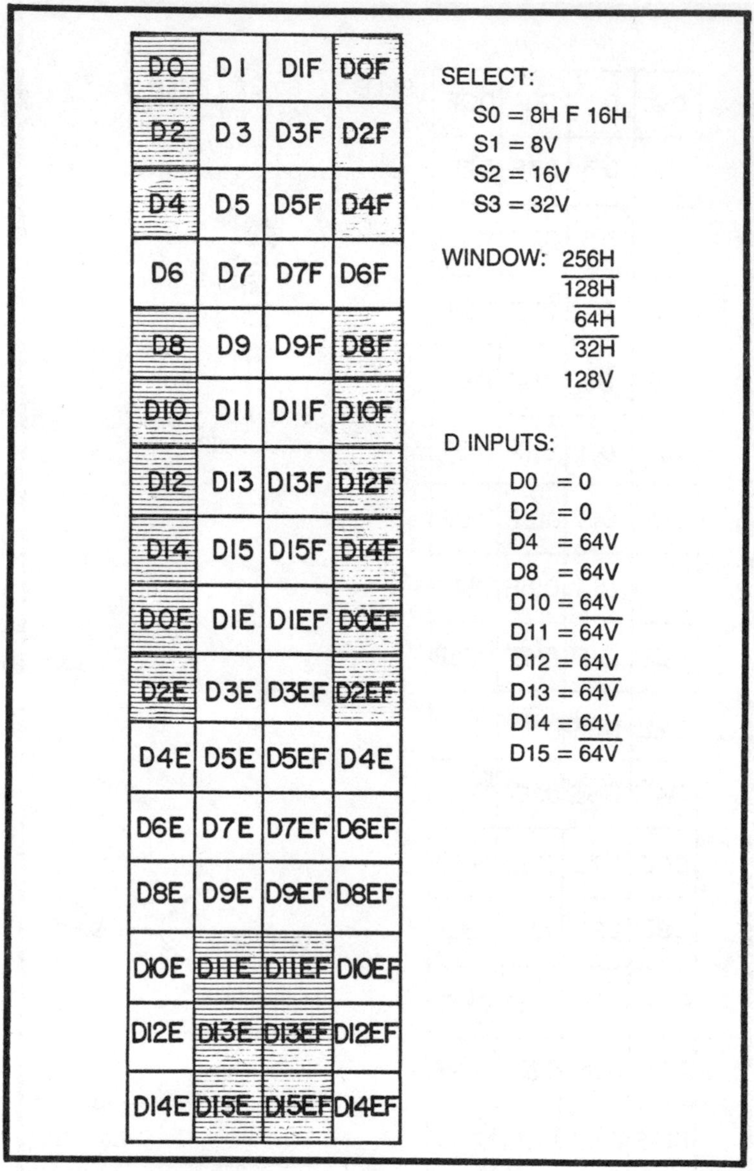

D0	D1	D1F	D0F	**SELECT:**
D2	D3	D3F	D2F	S0 = 8H F 16H
D4	D5	D5F	D4F	S1 = 8V
D6	D7	D7F	D6F	S2 = 16V
D8	D9	D9F	D8F	S3 = 32V
D10	D11	D11F	D10F	
D12	D13	D13F	D12F	**WINDOW:** 256H
D14	D15	D15F	D14F	$\overline{128H}$
D0E	D1E	D1EF	D0EF	64H
D2E	D3E	D3EF	D2EF	$\overline{32H}$
D4E	D5E	D5EF	D4E	128V
D6E	D7E	D7EF	D6EF	
D8E	D9E	D9EF	D8EF	**D INPUTS:**
D10E	D11E	D11EF	D10EF	D0 = 0
D12E	D13E	D13EF	D12EF	D2 = 0
D14E	D15E	D15EF	D14EF	D4 = 64V

D INPUTS:

D0 = 0
D2 = 0
D4 = 64V
D8 = 64V
D10 = 64V
D11 = $\overline{64V}$
D12 = 64V
D13 = $\overline{64V}$
D14 = 64V
D15 = $\overline{64V}$

Fig. 4-16. A vertical missile figure built within a 4 × 16 extended foldover matrix.

Using this kind of parallel selection, the two multiplexers are always selected exactly the same way. If the system-select inputs happen to select D2 on IC5 (pin 6), it must also be selecting D18 (pin 6) on IC6. As far as system-select inputs S0 through S3 are concerned, they select the same data input on both ICs at the same time. The scheme works very much like a two-deck rotary switch.

What, then, is the role of the S4 input? Ultimately, the purpose of the S4 input is to make certain the two multiplexers are never enabled at the same time. If this 5th-bit input happens to have a logic-0 level, for instance, it can enable multiplexer IC5 and disables IC6. Setting select input S4 to logic 1, on the other hand, makes it possible to disable IC5 and enable IC6.

ICs 5 and 6 are thus both disabled at the same time; or, according to the logic state of S4, one is enabled while the other is disabled. It is not possible to enable both multiplexers at the same time. (Both multiplexers are disabled by the window inputs, a circuit described a bit later in this section.)

Now consider all five system-select inputs at the same time. As long as the S4 select input is at logic 0, the status of the four lower-order select inputs (S0 through S3) select one of the 16 data inputs to IC5. An inverted version of that particular input to IC5 appears inverted at pin 10 of that IC. IC6, however, is disabled at that time. And though select inputs S0 through S3 might be selecting one of the 16 inputs to IC6, pin 10 of that IC remains fixed at logic 1, the disabled output condition.

IC5 and IC6 change roles when S4 goes to logic 1. IC6 then outputs its selected data to its pin-10 connection, and IC5 is disabled.

Data inputs D0 through D15 are thus relevant only as long as select input S4 is at logic 0. In a similar fashion, data inputs D16 through D31 are selected only as long as select input S4 is at logic 1.

There are effectively 32 different data inputs to this system. One of these 32 different inputs appears at the input side of the output NAND gate, IC2-C, depending on the 5-bit binary code appearing at the system's select inputs. There is a one-to-one correspondence between the 5-bit binary code presented at the select inputs and the data input being selected. Setting the select inputs to binary 20 (10100), for example, selects data input D20.

The window input works much the same way as all the other figure-windowing circuits described earlier in this chapter and in Chapter 3. In this instance, however, the window circuit keeps *both* multiplexers disabled until the proper horizontal and vertical count is reached. At that moment, on multiplexer IC or the other is enabled, depending on the logic level of select input S4.

Extended 64-Cell Matrices

The circuit in Fig. 4-17 is the starting point for a number of complex-figure matrix configurations. Connect this circuit on your

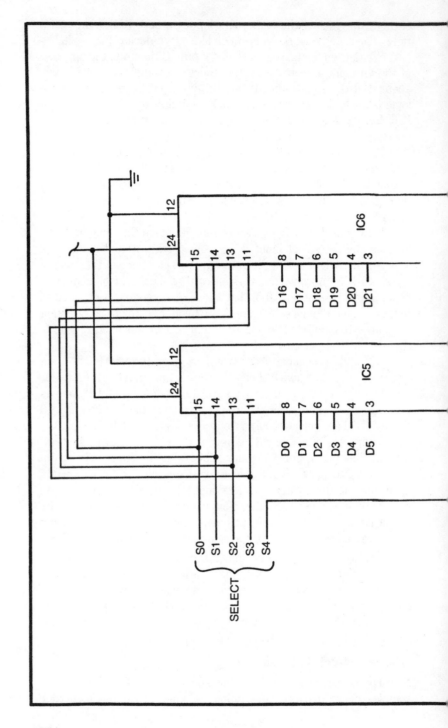

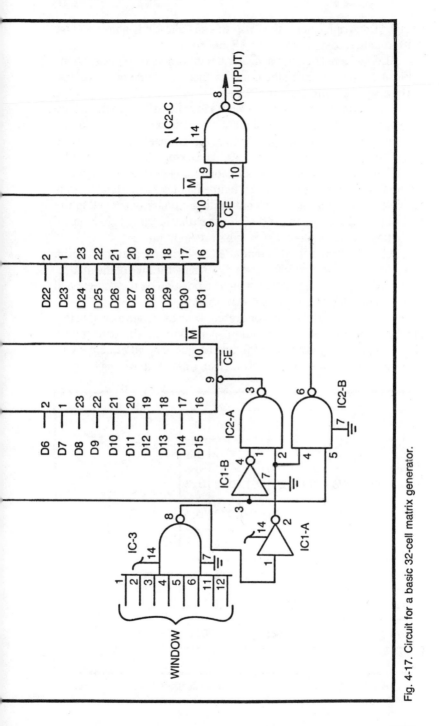

Fig. 4-17. Circuit for a basic 32-cell matrix generator.

breadboard arrangement, then use the specifications shown in Fig. 4-18 to generate an extended 8×8 matrix.

After assembling this particular circuit (using the specifications in Fig. 4-18, but leaving all the D inputs unconnected) you should see a white square pattern on the screen.

Connecting any one of the D inputs to logic 0 then creates a little black square at the corresponding matrix position. From this point, you can generate any complex figure you choose, using the same general procedures outlined for the 32-cell extended-matrix circuits.

Figure 4-19 shows the specifications for generating the figure of a little dog. This nonsymmetrical figure has far more detail than is possible with any of the figure-generating circuits described in the first part of this chapter. And of course that is the whole point of using this more complex matrix-generator circuit.

While working with this extended 8×8 matrix pattern, bear in mind that your select specifications determine the size of the matrix, the window specifications determine the position on the screen, and the D inputs determine the pattern itself.

You can have a lot of fun generating your own figures within this matrix. Spend a great deal of time playing with it, sharpening your ability to generate any desired figure as quickly and effectively as possible. Time spent on the project at this point will pay off big

DO	DI	D2	D3	D4	D5	D6	D7
D8	D9	DIO	DII	DI2	DI3	DI4	DI5
DI6	DI7	DI8	DI9	D20	D2I	D22	D23
D24	D25	D26	D27	D28	D29	D30	D3I
DOE	DIE	D2E	D3E	D4E	D5E	D6E	D7E
D8E	D9E	DIOE	DIIE	DI2E	DI3E	DI4E	DI5E
DI6E	DI7E	DI8E	DI9E	D20E	D2IE	D22E	D23E
D24E	D25E	D26E	D27E	D28E	D29E	D30E	D3IE

SELECT: S0 = 8H
S1 = 6H
SH
S3 = 8V
S4 = 16v

WINDOW: 256H
$\overline{128H}$
$\overline{64H}$
128V
$\overline{64V}$

D INPUTS: 1, 0, 32V, $\overline{32V}$
AS REQUIRED

Fig. 4-18. Matrix configuration and sample specifications for a 16 × 4 extended matrix.

108

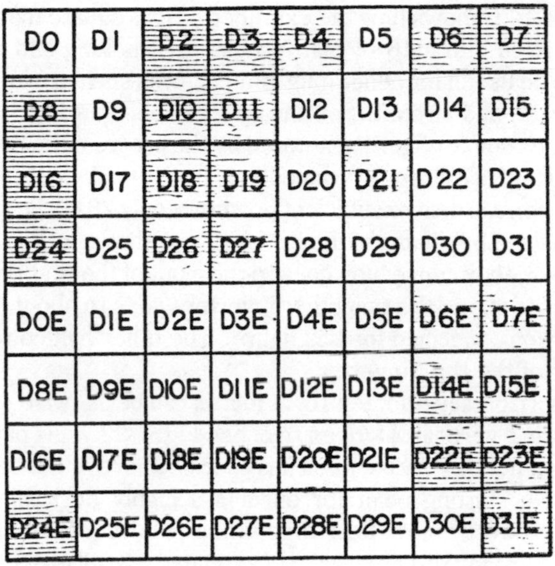

D0	D1	D2	D3	D4	D5	D6	D7
D8	D9	D10	D11	D12	D13	D14	D15
D16	D17	D18	D19	D20	D21	D22	D23
D24	D25	D26	D27	D28	D29	D30	D31
D0E	D1E	D2E	D3E	D4E	D5E	D6E	D7E
D8E	D9E	D10E	D11E	D12E	D13E	D14E	D15E
D16E	D17E	D18E	D19E	D20E	D21E	D22E	D23E
D24E	D25E	D26E	D27E	D28E	D29E	D30E	D31E

SELECT: S0 = 8H   WINDOW: 256H
$\qquad\qquad$ S1 = 16H $\qquad\qquad$ $\overline{128H}$
$\qquad\qquad$ S2 = 32H $\qquad\qquad$ $\overline{64H}$
$\qquad\qquad$ S3 = 8V $\qquad\qquad\quad$ 128V
$\qquad\qquad$ S4 = 16V $\qquad\qquad$ $\overline{64V}$

D INPUTS:
D2 = 32V	D16 = 32V
D3 = 32V	D18 = 0
D4 = 32V	D19 = 0
D6 = 0	D20 = 32V
D7 = 0	D21 = 32V
D8 = 32V	D22 = 32V
D10 = 32V	D23 = 32V
D11 = $\underline{32V}$	D24 = 0
D14 = $\overline{32V}$	D26 = 0
D15 = 0	D27 = 0
	D28 = $\overline{32V}$
	D31 = $\overline{32V}$

Fig. 4-19. Figure of a dog built within a 8 × 8 extended matrix.

109

dividends later on when you are attempting to design video games. Be sure to keep a careful record of your work, including drawings and specifications.

Figure 4-20 shows how the extended 64-cell square matrix can be transformed into a 16×4 matrix format. This long and narrow matrix can be useful for generating game figures such as side views of ships, cars, and aircraft. See the two examples in Fig. 4-21.

NOTE: The complex figure generated by the programming connections in Fig. 4-21a calls for 21 connections from the 8V source. Since the Sourcebox can deliver sufficient power for only 20 loads, the load must be divided by means of the buffer circuit shown in Fig. 4-21a. The 8V Sourcebox connection goes to the input of the first inverter. The output of one of the two other inverters goes to about half the 8V connections specified for this figure. The other half come from the output of the third inverter.

The horizontally oriented 16×4 matrix can be likewise restructured to form a vertical, 4×16 matrix. See Fig. 4-22. This particular matrix might not be very useful as it is specified here, but it becomes an invaluable starting point for building a highly desirable 8×16 extended foldover matrix described in the following section.

Before leaving this discussion of extended 64-cell matrices, it is important to see how they differ from the 64-cell extended foldover versions described in the opening sections of this chapter.

At first glance, 8×8 extended foldover matrix in Fig. 4-13 might appear identical to the 8×8 extended matrix in Fig. 4-18. Likewise, the vertical 4×16 extended foldover matrix in Fig. 4-15 looks much like the 4×16 extended matrix in Fig. 4-22.

Since these matrices have the same number of cells and the same general dimensions, why would an experimenter ever resort to the versions that use the more complicated circuit in Fig. 4-17? The simpler circuits are using a foldover technique to double the number of matrix cells, and that means the figures must be symmetrical about the foldover line. The matrices generated by the more complicated circuit in Fig. 4-17, on the other hand, do not use this foldover scheme; therefore, the figures are not limited to those having a symmetrical display. The nonsymmetrical figure of a dog in Fig. 4-19, for instance, cannot possibly be built within the 8×8 extended foldover matrix in Fig. 4-13. Figures using the matrix in Fig. 4-13 must be symmetrical about a horizontal line running through the middle of it.

A Useful 128-Cell, Extended Foldover Matrix

Adding a 7486 quad EXCLUSIVE-OR IC package to the circuit in Fig. 4-17 makes it possible to generate a large foldover matrix that

D0	D1	D2	D3	D4	D5	D6	D7	D8	D9	D10	D11	D12	D13	D14	D15
D16	D17	D18	D19	D20	D21	D22	D23	D24	D25	D26	D27	D28	D29	D30	D31
D0E	D1E	D2E	D3E	D4E	D5E	D6E	D7E	D8E	D9E	D10E	D11E	D12E	D13E	D14E	D15E
D16E	D17E	D18E	D19E	D20E	D21E	D22E	D23E	D24E	D25E	D26E	D27E	D28E	D29E	D30E	D31E

16 × 4 EXTENDED MATRIX

SELECT: S0 = 4H
         S1 = 8H
         S2 = 16H
         S3 = 32H
         S4 = 4V

WINDOW: 256H $\overline{32V}$
         $\overline{128H}$ $\overline{16V}$
         64H
         128V
         64V

D INPUTS: 1, 0, 8V, $\overline{8V}$, AS REQUIRED

Fig. 4-20. Configuration and sample specifications for a 16 × 4 extended matrix.

D0	D1	D2	D3	D4	D5	D6	D7	D8	D9	D10	D11	D12	D13	D14	D15
D16	D17	D18	D19	D20	D21	D22	D23	D24	D25	D26	D27	D28	D29	D30	D31
D0E	D1E	D2E	D3E	D4E	D5E	D6E	D7E	D8E	D9E	D10E	D11E	D12E	D13E	D14E	D15E
D16E	D17E	D18E	D19E	D20E	D21E	D22E	D23E	D24E	D25E	D26E	D27E	D28E	D29E	D30E	D31E

SELECT: S0 = 4H   WINDOW: 256H
S1 = 8H   128H
S2 = 16H   64H
S3 = 32H   128V
S4 = 4V   64V
                       32V
                       16V

BUFFER CIRCUIT

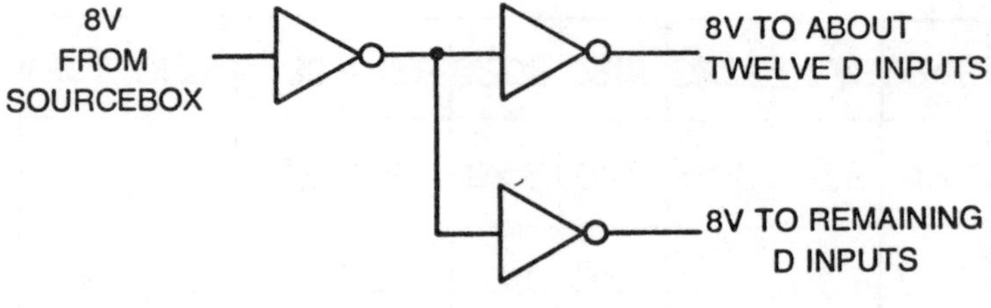

8V FROM SOURCEBOX

8V TO ABOUT TWELVE D INPUTS

8V TO REMAINING D INPUTS

D INPUTS: D0 = 8V   D8 = 0   D15 = 8V   D26 = 8V
D1 = 8V   D9 = 8V   D16 = 0   D27 = 8V
D2 = 8V   D10 = 8V   D17 = 8V   D30 = 8V
D3 = 8V   D11 = 8V   D18 = 8V   D31 = 0
D4 = 8V   D12 = 8V   D19 = 8V
D5 = 8V   D13 = 8V   D20 = 8V
D7 = 0   D14 = 8V   D21 = 8V

A

D0	D1	D2	D3	D4	D5	D6	D7	D8	D9	D10	D11	D12	D13	D14	D15
D16	D17	D18	D19	D20	D21	D22	D23	D24	D25	D26	D27	D28	D29	D30	D31
D0E	D1E	D2E	D3E	D4E	D5E	D6E	D7E	D8E	D9E	D10E	D11E	D12E	D13E	D14E	D15E
D16E	D17E	D18E	D19E	D20E	D21E	D22E	D23E	D24E	D25E	D26E	D27E	D28E	D29E	D30E	D31E

SELECT: $S0 = 4H$
$S1 = 8H$
$S2 = 16H$
$S3 = 32H$
$S4 = 4V$

WINDOW: $256H$
$\overline{128H}$
$\overline{64H}$
$128V$
$64V$
$\overline{32V}$
$\overline{16V}$

D INPUTS:

$D0 = 0$	$D16 = 0$
$D1 = 8V$	$D17 = 0$
$D2 = 8V$	$D20 = 8V$
$D5 = 8V$	$D21 = 0$
$D7 = 8V$	$D22 = 0$
$D3 = 8V$	$D23 = 0$
$D9 = 8V$	$D24 = 8V$
$D10 = 8V$	$D25 = 8V$
$D11 = 8V$	$D28 = 8V$
$D12 = 8V$	$D29 = 0$
$D13 = 8V$	$D30 = 0$
$D14 = 0$	$D31 = 0$
$D15 = 0$	

REMEMBER: D INPUTS
THAT ARE NOT LISTED
ARE TO BE AT LOGIC 1,
OR NO CONNECTION

B

Fig. 4-21. Sample figures built within the 16 × 4 extended matrix. (a) Figure of an aircraft carrier or submarine. Note the need for inverters acting as driver circuits. (b) Profile of a racing car and driver.

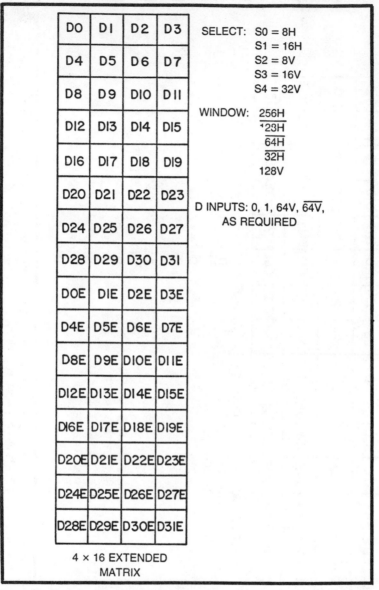

DO	DI	D2	D3
D4	D5	D6	D7
D8	D9	DIO	DII
DI2	DI3	DI4	DI5
DI6	DI7	DI8	DI9
D20	D21	D22	D23
D24	D25	D26	D27
D28	D29	D30	D3I
DOE	DIE	D2E	D3E
D4E	D5E	D6E	D7E
D8E	D9E	DIOE	DIIE
DI2E	DI3E	DI4E	DI5E
DI6E	DI7E	DI8E	DI9E
D20E	D2IE	D22E	D23E
D24E	D25E	D26E	D27E
D28E	D29E	D30E	D3IE

SELECT: S0 = 8H
S1 = 16H
S2 = 8V
S3 = 16V
S4 = 32V

WINDOW: 256H
$\overline{128H}$
$\overline{64H}$
$\overline{32H}$
128V

D INPUTS: 0, 1, 64V, $\overline{64V}$, AS REQUIRED

4 × 16 EXTENDED
MATRIX

Fig. 4-22. Configuration and sample specifications for a 4 × 16 extended matrix.

is perhaps one of the most useful of all. Connected to the basic 64-cell circuit as indicated in Fig. 4-23, the EXCLUSIVE-OR circuit expands the matrix to a 8×16 format.

The matrix in Fig. 4-23 is a folded matrix that requires symmetry about the vertical line running through its center, but in actual practice it turns out that an experimenter can generate a vast variety of interesting and useful video game figures with it. How about that cowboy figure specified in Fig. 4-24?

Turn your imagination loose on this matrix and see how many fascinating symmetrical figures you can generate. The principles for designing figures around this 8×16 extended foldover matrix with vertical symmetry are much the same as those for working out

DO	D1	D2	D3	D3F	D2F	D1F	D0F
D4	D5	D6	D7	D7F	D6F	D5F	D4F
D8	D9	DIO	DII	DIIF	DIOF	D9F	D8F
D12	D13	D14	DI5	DI5F	DI4F	DI3F	DI2F
D16	D17	D18	DI9	DI9F	DI8F	DI7F	DI6F
D20	D21	D22	D23	D23F	D22F	D2IF	D2OF
D24	D25	D26	D27	D27F	D26F	D25F	D24F
D28	D29	D30	D31	D3IF	D30F	D29F	D28F
DOE	DIE	D2E	D3E	D3EF	D2EF	DIEF	DOEF
D4E	D5E	D6E	D7E	D7EF	D6EF	D5EF	D4EF
D8E	D9E	DIOE	DIIE	DIIEF	DIOEF	D9EF	D8EF
DI2E	DI3E	DI4E	DI5E	DI5EF	DI4EF	DI3EF	DI2EF
DI6E	DI7E	DI8E	DI9E	DI9EF	DI8EF	DI7EF	DI6EF
D2OE	D2IE	D22E	D23E	D23EF	D22EF	D2IEF	D2OEF
D24E	D25E	D26E	D27E	D27EF	D26EF	D25EF	D24EF
D28E	D29E	D30E	D3IE	D3IEF	D3OEF	D29EF	D28EF

SELECT: S0 = 8H F 32H
S1 = 16H F 32H
S2 = 8V
S3 = 16V
S4 = 32V

WINDOW: 256H
128H
$\overline{64H}$
128V
64V

DATA IN: 1, 0, 64V, $\overline{64V}$, AS REQUIRED

8H — 1
2
32H
5
16H — 4
8V — S2
16V — S3
32V — S4
3 — S0
6 — S1

8 × 16 EXTENDED FOLDOVER MATRIX

Fig. 4-23. Configuration, circuit, and sample specifications for an 8 × 16 extended foldover matrix.

D0	D1	D2	D3	D3F	D2F	D1F	D0F
D4	D5	D6	D7	D7F	D6F	D5F	D4F
D8	D9	D10	D11	D11F	D10F	D9F	D8F
D12	D13	D14	D15	D15F	D14F	D13F	D12F
D16	D17	D18	D19	D19F	D18F	D17F	D16F
D20	D21	D22	D23	D23F	D22F	D21F	D20F
D24	D25	D26	D27	D27F	D26F	D25F	D24F
D28	D29	D30	D31	D31F	D30F	D29F	D28F
D0E	D1E	D2E	D3E	D3EF	D2EF	D1EF	D0EF
D4E	D5E	D6E	D7E	D7EE	D6EF	D5EE	D4EF
D8E	D9E	D10E	D11E	D11EF	D10EF	D9EF	D8EF
D12E	D13E	D14E	D15E	D15EF	D14EF	D13EF	D12EF
D16E	D17E	D18E	D19E	D19EF	D18EF	D17EF	D16EF
D20E	D21E	D22E	D23E	D23EF	D22EF	D21EF	D20EF
D24E	D25E	D26E	D27E	D27EF	D26EF	D25EF	D24EF
D28E	D29E	D30E	D31E	D31EF	D30EF	D29EF	D28EF

SELECT.
S0 = 8H F 32H
S1 = 16H F 32H
S2 = 8V
S3 = 16V
S4 = 32V

WINDOW: 256H
128H
$\overline{64H}$
128V
64V

D INPUTS:
D1 = 0
D2 = $\overline{64V}$
D4 = 0
D5 = $\overline{64V}$
D8 = 0
D9 = 64V
D10 = 64V
D11 = $\overline{64V}$
D12 = 0
D13 = 64V
D14 = 64V
D15 = 64V
D16 = 0
D17 = $\overline{64V}$
D19 = $\overline{64V}$
D20 = $\overline{64V}$
D21 = 0
D22 = 64V
D23 = $\overline{64V}$
D24 = $\overline{64V}$
D25 = 0
D26 = 64V
D27 = $\overline{64V}$
D29 = 64V
D30 = $\overline{64V}$
D31 = $\overline{64V}$

Fig. 4-24. A cowboy figure built within an 8 × 16 extended foldover matrix.

116

symmetrical figures in the earlier section entitled Folding Over an Extended Matrix. The only difference here is that you are working with twice as many cells.

Figure 4-25 shows the 128-cell extended foldover matrix oriented horizontally. The axis of symmetry in this case is a vertical line through the center of the image. Set up this matrix, using the EXCLUSIVE-OR circuit and specifications shown in Fig. 4-25. Then work out some figures of your own, bearing in mind that the right-hand half of the images must be mirror images of the left-hand half.

Further Experiments With the 32-, 64-, 128-Cell System

If you have been performing the experiments suggested in this chapter thus far, you most likely have the know-how and confidence necessary for generating other matrix formats. What's even more important is that you ought to be coming up with additional ideas you want to try, perhaps more-novel ideas than you have time to work on.

Suppose, for instance, you are thinking about putting more than one kind of complex figure on the screen. How do you go about it? Well, you certainly have to build two different figure-generating circuits, one for each figure you want to put on the screen. After that, you must effectively OR together their outputs before applying the signal to the GAME VID IN terminal of the Sourcebox unit.

Exactly how you should go about ORing together these signals depends on whether they emerge from the figure-generating systems as white on black or black on white. All of the multiplexers in this chapter generate inverted, black-on-white signals, but the inverter connected to the output of the multiplexer in Fig. 4-5 and the NAND gate at the outputs of the multiplexers in Fig. 4-17 reverse the image so that it is properly shown as a white matrix on a black background.

These "upright" signals can be ORed together (combined on the screen) by first running them to separate inputs of a common NOR IC. The output of that NOR gate can then be inverted to yield a composite video signal having the proper white-on-black format.

If you are confused about any procedure for combining complex figures on the screen, you ought to review the material in the section entitled COMBINING ANY NUMBER OF STATIC FIGURES ON THE SCREEN in Chapter 3. The procedures described there can be carried over to the circuits in this chapter.

MATRIX OPERATIONS FROM 64-CELL GENERATORS

The idea of expanding the cell-generating capacity by adding more multiplexer circuits can be extended indefinately. Each new multiplexer provides 16 more basic cell locations. Most experimenters, however, begin questioning the feasibility of expanding the complex-figure generating system beyond a certain point.

Is the ability to create a large and highly detailed pattern worth the trouble of working with all the multiplexer hardware? Only you can answer that question. It depends on what you are trying to do and what it's worth to you in the long run.

This section deals with an especially useful 64-cell generator. It is built around four 16:1 multiplexer ICs, thus giving the experimenter 64 data-input programming terminals. As described earlier in this chapter, any basic multiplexer-type figure generator can be easily modified to double the number of matrix cells. In this particular case, the experimenter has access to 128 cells. Then the user might elect to use a foldover scheme, thereby extending the number of cells to 256.

It turns out that this 64-, 128-, 256-cell matrix system is adequate for generating some of the most popular figures found on commercial TV games: cowboys, baseball players, tanks, aircraft of all sorts, an endless variety, really. Just look at some of the patterns used as examples through the remainder of the section.

The 64-Cell Generator Circuit

The 64-cell generator circuit in Fig. 4-26 uses four 16:1 multiplexer ICs. The 4 lower-order select inputs to the system, S0 through S3, select one of the 16 data inputs on each multiplexer. And the demultiplexer circuit, IC9, is responsible for enabling one of the four multiplexers, depending on the status of the two higher-order select inputs, S4 and S5.

The system is windowed and the outputs of the multiplexers are NANDed in a fashion identical to the 32-cell generator in Fig. 4-17.

The purpose of the four inverters, IC1-A through IC1-D, require some special explanation. It is a fact of TTL technology that most ICs in that family are capable of driving up to 20 other TTL-type circuits. Normally a gate drives far less than 20 others, so the problem of overloading the output never becomes an important design factor.

When using the matrix-extension technique (expanding the cell count from 64 to 128 in Fig. 4-26) one of the H- or V-count outputs from the Sourcebox unit might have to drive 20 or 30 D inputs at the same time. Whenever a particular complex-pattern circuit calls for driving more than about 15 D inputs from the same source, that source ought to be buffered. And that's the purpose of IC1.

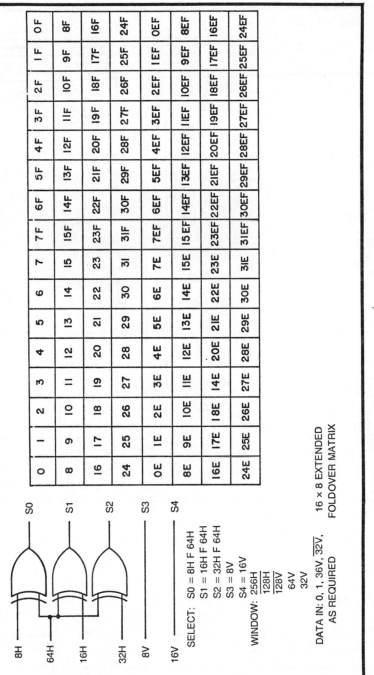

Fig. 4-25. Configuration, circuit, and sample specifications for a 16 × 8 extended fold over matrix.

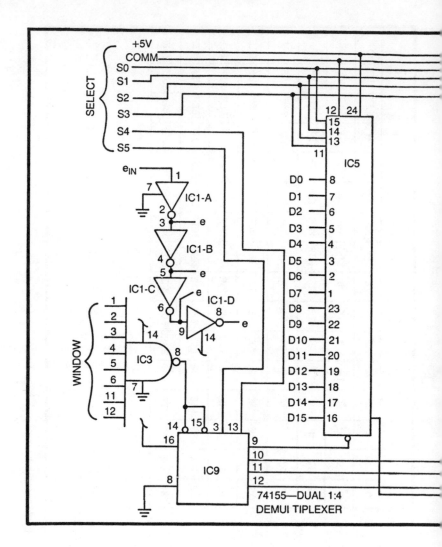

The e_{in} connection comes from the appropriate H- or V-count source. As far as that source is concerned, it has only one load connected to it. IC1-A inverts that signal, producing a useful $\bar{e}$ source that can drive up to 20 D inputs. The output of IC1-A is inverted by IC1-B to yield a noninverted "e" source that can likewise drive up to 20 D inputs. The last 2 inverters perform the same function as the first 2, providing 20 additional sources of inverted and noninverted figure-expansion signals.

Suppose, for example, a particular expanded matrix pattern calls for 25 32H inputs and 22 $\overline{32H}$ signals. The 32H signal from the

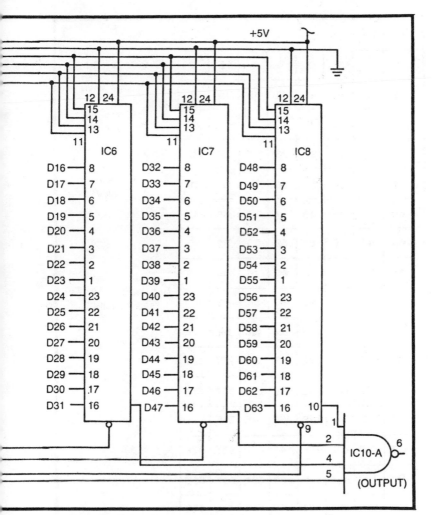

Fig. 4-26. Circuit for a basic 64-cell matrix generator.

Sourcebox unit can be connected to the e_{in} terminal. Then 11 of the 22 $\overline{32H}$ signals can be tapped off the output of IC1-A, 12 or 13 of the 32H signals can be tapped from the output of IC1-B, and the remainder of the $\overline{32H}$ and 32H signals can be taken from the outputs of IC1-C and IC1-D respectively.

Some 8x16 Expanded Matrices

Figure 4-27 shows a vertically oriented, 128-cell matrix that can be easily generated by the circuit in Fig. 4-26. If you build this circuit and use the SELECT and WINDOW data prescribed here, you will

121

0	1	2	3	4	5	6	7
8	9	10	11	12	13	14	15
16	17	18	19	20	21	22	27
24	25	26	27	28	29	30	31
32	33	34	35	36	37	38	39
40	41	42	43	44	45	46	47
48	49	50	51	52	53	54	55
56	57	58	59	60	61	62	63
0E	1E	2E	3E	4E	5E	6E	7E
8E	9E	10E	11E	12E	13E	14E	15E
16E	17E	18E	19E	20E	21E	22E	23E
24E	25E	26E	27E	28E	29E	30E	31E
32E	33E	34E	35E	36E	37E	38E	39E
40E	41E	42E	43E	44E	45E	46E	47E
48E	49E	50E	51E	52E	53E	54E	55E
56E	57E	58E	59E	60E	61E	62E	63E

SELECT: S0 = 8H
S1 = 16H
S2 = 32H
S3 = 8V
S4 = 16V
S5 = 32V

WINDOW: $\overline{256H}$
128H
64H
128V

DATA IN: 1, 0, 64V, $\overline{64V}$, AS REQUIRED

Fig. 4-27. Configuration and sample specifications for an 8 × 16 extended matrix.

find a rather large white rectangle occupying the lower right-hand quadrant of the screen. Connecting any of the D inputs to logic 0 creates a black cell in the corresponding matrix position and in its extended location as well.

The two examples in Fig. 4-28 include a rather novel footprint and the profile of a cowboy. While the footprint might not be very useful for building a TV game, it certainly illustrates some of the fun you can have creating video graphics with this system.

Figure 4-24 illustrated a way to build the image of a cowboy. The circuit was much simpler in that case, but it was using a foldover technique that demanded a symmetrical pattern. The profile in Fig. 4-28b, however, is a nonsymmetrical version of the same hombre.

It is possible to spend many, many hours playing with this matrix-generating scheme. If you want to make the figures smaller, simply scale down the SELECT, WINDOW, and D INPUT specifications one or two orders of magnitude. Cutting each of the specifications in half, for instance, cuts the size of the image in half.

Play with this system as long as you want. Just because you are having fun with it doesn't mean you aren't learning anything. Keep track of your experiments, noting both your failures and successes. That information will prove invaluable later on.

The extended matrix can be adjusted to form a horizontally oriented, 16×8 pattern. See the suggested specifications and pattern in Fig. 4-29.

The display in Fig. 4-30 merely shows one example of how the 16×8 extended matrix can be used. The image in this instance is a battleship or destroyer. Of course it can be modified slightly to transform it into a submarine or aircraft carrier.

This matrix is good for any sort of relatively complex, horizontal, nonsymmetrical figure.

A 256-Cell, Extended Foldover Matrix

The foldover scheme applied to the 128-cell matrix just described yields a 256-cell matrix. The example in Fig. 4-31 shows the rather simple additional circuitry and the left-hand half of an ever-popular tank image.

When you build the circuit and wire it to the specifications shown in Fig. 4-31, you will find a full tank image, with its right-hand half being a mirror image of the portion shown here. It is often advisable to show only the nonfolded half of such patterns, but for no reason other than drawing pictures with 256 cells becomes rather tedious. Besides, all the necessary information is contained in the original portion.

MULTIPLYING THE NUMBER OF IDENTICAL IMAGES ON THE SCREEN

While a single complex figure can play a vital role in most kinds of TV games, it is often desirable to display a number of identical complex figures on the screen. Take for example the mines for a minefield game or cars in an auto racing game.

0	1	2	3	4	5	6	7
8	9	10	11	12	13	14	15
16	17	18	19	20	21	22	23
24	25	26	27	28	29	30	31
32	33	34	35	36	37	38	39
40	41	42	43	44	45	46	47
48	49	50	51	52	53	54	55
56	57	58	59	60	61	62	63
OE	1E	2E	3E	4E	5E	6E	7E
8E	9E	10E	11E	12E	13E	14E	15E
16E	17E	18E	19E	20E	21E	22E	23E
24E	25E	26E	27E	28E	29E	30E	31E
32E	33E	34E	35E	36E	37E	38E	39E
40E	41E	42E	43E	44E	45E	46E	47E
48E	49E	50E	51E	52E	53E	54E	55E
56E	57E	58E	59E	60E	61E	62E	63E

SELECT:
S0 = 8H
S1 = 16H
S2 = 32H
S3 = 8V
S4 = 16V
S5 = 32V

WINDOW:
$\overline{256H}$
128H
64H
128V

D INPUTS:

D0 = 0	D33 = 64V
D1 = 0	D34 = 0
D2 = 64V	D35 = $\overline{64V}$
D3 = 64V	D37 = 64V
D4 = 64V	D38 = $\overline{64V}$
D5 = $\overline{64V}$	D39 = 0
D6 = $\overline{64V}$	D40 = 0
D7 = 0	D41 = 0
D8 = 0	D42 = 0
D9 = 0	D43 = $\overline{64V}$
D10 = 64V	D44 = $\overline{64V}$
D11 = 64V	D45 = $\overline{64V}$
D13 = $\overline{64V}$	D46 = $\overline{64V}$
D14 = $\overline{64V}$	D47 = 0
D15 = 0	D48 = 0
D16 = 0	D49 = $\overline{64V}$
D17 = 0	D50 = $\overline{64V}$
D18 = 64V	D51 = $\overline{64V}$
D20 = 64V	D52 = $\overline{64V}$
D21 = 0	D53 = 64V
D22 = 0	D54 = 0
D23 = 0	D55 = 0
D24 = 0	D56 = 0
D25 = 0	D57 = $\overline{64V}$
D27 = 64V	D58 = $\overline{64V}$
D28 = $\overline{64V}$	D59 = $\overline{64V}$
D29 = $\overline{64V}$	D60 = $\overline{64V}$
D30 = $\overline{64V}$	D61 = $\overline{64V}$
D31 = 0	D62 = 0
D32 = 0	D63 = 0

A

The procedure for generating a single complex figure can require quite a number of IC devices as clearly demonstrated throughout this chapter. There is no need, however, to build one complete matrix generator circuit for each figure that is to appear on the screen—at least not as long as the figures are all identical.

It turns out that one complex-figure generator is sufficient for creating any number of identical images on the screen. The general

0	1	2	3	4	5	6	7
8	9	10	11	12	13	14	15
16	17	18	19	20	21	22	23
24	25	26	27	28	29	30	31
32	33	34	35	36	37	38	39
40	41	42	43	44	45	46	47
48	49	50	51	52	53	54	55
56	57	58	59	60	61	62	63
0E	1E	2E	3E	4E	5E	6E	7E
8E	9E	10E	11E	12E	13E	14E	15E
16E	17E	18E	19E	20E	21E	22E	23E
24E	25E	26E	27E	28E	29E	30E	31E
32E	33E	34E	35E	36E	37E	38E	39E
40E	41E	42E	43E	44E	45E	46E	47E
48E	49E	50E	51E	52E	53E	54E	55E
56E	57E	58E	59E	60E	61E	62E	63E

SELECT: WINDOW:

SELECT	WINDOW
S0 = 2H	$\overline{256H}$
S1 = 4H	128H
S2 = 8H	64H
S3 = 2V	32H
S4 = 4V	128V
S5 = 8V	64V
	32V

D INPUTS:

D0 = 0	D38 = 0
D1 = 0	D39 = 0
D4 = 0	D40 = 0
D5 = 0	D41 = $\overline{16V}$
D6 = 0	D43 = $\overline{16V}$
D7 = 0	D45 = 16V
D8 = $\overline{16V}$	D46 = 0
D12 = $\overline{16V}$	D47 = 16V
D13 = $\overline{16V}$	D48 = 0
D14 = 0	D51 = $\overline{16V}$
D15 = 0	D52 = 0
D16 = 0	D53 = 16V
D17 = 16V	D55 = $\overline{16V}$
D20 = 0	D56 = 0
D21 = 0	D57 = 0
D22 = 0	D60 = $\overline{16V}$
D23 = 0	D62 = $\overline{16V}$
D24 = 0	D63 = 0
D25 = 0	
D29 = 0	
D30 = 0	
D31 = 0	
D32 = 0	
D33 = 0	
D34 = $\overline{16V}$	
D36 = 16V	
D37 = 0	B

Fig. 4-28. Sample complex figures in the 8 × 16 extended matrix. (a) Left footprint. Folding this figure by means of 64H creates a pair of footprints—left and right. See circuit in Fig. 4-31. (b) Profile of a cowboy.

idea is to first build the circuit for generating the desired figure, using the techniques already described in this chapter. Then some rather simple logic circuits can be added to the window inputs to create any number of the figures on the screen and in any desired pattern.

To get a first-hand, practical view of this procedure, build up any of the simpler complex-figure circuits and display the image on

0	1	2	3	4	5	6	7	8	9	10	11	12	13	14	15
16	17	18	19	20	21	22	23	24	25	26	27	28	29	30	31
32	33	34	35	36	37	38	39	40	41	42	43	44	45	46	47
48	49	50	51	52	53	54	55	56	57	58	59	60	61	62	63
0E	1E	2E	3E	4E	5E	6E	7E	8E	9E	10E	11E	12E	13E	14E	15E
16E	17E	18E	19E	20E	21E	22E	23E	24E	25E	26E	27E	28E	29E	30E	31E
32E	33E	34E	35E	36E	37E	38E	39E	40E	41E	42E	43E	44E	45E	46E	47E
48E	49E	50E	51E	52E	53E	54E	55E	56E	57E	58E	59E	60E	61E	62E	63E

SELECT: $S_0 = 8H$ $S_3 = 64H$
$S_1 = 16H$ $S_4 = 8V$
$S_2 = 32H$ $S_5 = 16V$

WINDOW: $256H$
$\overline{128H}$
$128V$
$\overline{64V}$

DATA IN: 1, 0, 32V, $\overline{32V}$,
AS REQUIRED

Fig. 4-29. Configuration and sample specifications for a 16 × 8 extended matrix.

the screen *without* any windowing. You will find that your figure is repeated a number of times in closely spaced rows and columns.

The pattern of images on the screen might be rather interesting without the benefit of windowing, but it is hardly useful in the context of a TV game. What remains to be done is selectively window some of those images, leaving some in place and eliminating the others.

As is so often the case in this TV-game business, there are several different approaches to selecting the figures that are to appear on the screen. Study all the approaches presented here, doing as much hands-on experimenting as possible.

Bar and Rectangle Windowing

Figure 4-32 shows in a block diagram fashion how the image-windowing circuitry is interfaced with a complex-figure matrix generator. The 8-input NAND gate normally shown as the window input for the complex-figure generators in this circuit is simply replaced with a different sort of windowing circuit.

0	1	2	3	4	5	6	7	8	9	10	11	12	13	14	15
16	17	18	19	20	21	22	23	24	25	26	27	28	29	30	31
32	33	34	35	36	37	38	39	40	41	42	43	44	45	46	47
48	49	50	51	52	53	54	55	56	57	58	59	60	61	62	63
0E	1E	2E	3E	4E	5E	6E	7E	8E	9E	10E	11E	12E	13E	14E	15E
16E	17E	18E	19E	20E	21E	22E	23E	24E	25E	26E	27E	28E	29E	30E	31E
32E	33E	34E	35E	36E	37E	38E	39E	40E	41E	42E	43E	44E	45E	46E	47E
48E	49E	50E	51E	52E	53E	54E	55E	56E	57E	58E	59E	60E	61E	62E	63E

SELECT:	WINDOW:	D INPUTS:			
So = 2H	256H	D0 _ 0	D13 = 0	D26 = 0	D47 = 0
S1 = 4H	128H	D1 = 0	D14 = 0	D27 = 0	D48 = $\overline{8V}$
S2 = 8H	64H	D2 = 8V	D15 = 0	D28 = 8V	D50 = $\overline{8V}$
S3 = 16H	32H	D3 = 8V	D16 = 8V	D29 = 8V	D52 = $\overline{8V}$
S4 = 2V	128V	D4 = 8V	D17 = 8V	D30 = 8V	D53 = $\overline{8V}$
S5 = 4V	64V	D5 = 8V	D18 = 8V	D31 = 8V	D54 = $\overline{8V}$
	16V	D6 = 8V	D19 = 0	D32 = 8V	D56 = $\overline{8V}$
		D7 = 0	D20 = 0	D33 = 8V	D58 = $\overline{8V}$
		D8 = 0	D21 = 0	D36 = 8V	D60 = $\overline{8V}$
		D9 = $\overline{8V}$	D22 = $\overline{8V}$	D37 = 8V	D62 = $\overline{8V}$
		D10 = 0	D23 = 0	D42 = 8V	D63 = $\overline{8V}$
		D11 = 8V	D24 = $\overline{8V}$	D45 = 8V	
		D12 = 8V	D25 = $\overline{8V}$	D46 = 8V	

Fig. 4-30. Figure of a battleship built in a 16 × 8 extended matrix.

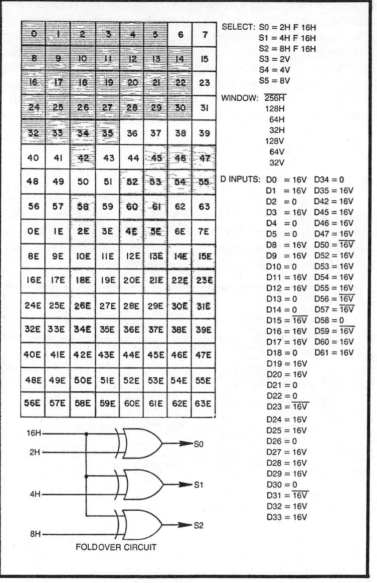

Fig. 4-31. Circuit, specifications, and half drawing of a tank figure. The half drawing is adequate for determining the specifications for any folded image.

Any of the circuits for generating broad bars and rectangles (see Chapter 3) can also serve as window generators for a complex-figure generator. The result is a regular pattern of identical complex figures on the screen. Use any of the bar or rectangle generators described in Chapter 3, but make certain they deliver a black-on-white signal to the $\overline{CE}$ input of your multiplexer in the complex-figure generator.

Let's look at that last statement a little closer. The multiplexer (complex-figure generator) is windowed ON whenever its $\overline{CE}$ input is pulled down to logic 0. This principle has been used in all of the examples thus far in this chapter. The multiplexer is thus enabled whenever the windowing circuit generates a logic 0. Or in other words, the complex figure will appear on the screen any time the windowing circuit shows a black bar or rectangle.

Of course the windowing black bar or rectangle must have a size equal to or greater than that of the figure it is controlling. Making the windows too small cuts off part of the figure, while making the windows too large allows two or more of the figures to appear hooked together. (The latter condition might be something of an advantage in certain instances, however).

You ought to be anxious to experiment with this idea now; so start by building the matrix generator circuit in Fig. 4-5, making *no*

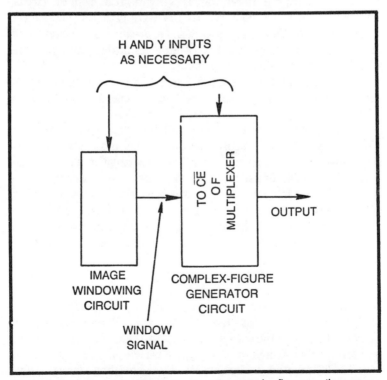

Fig. 4-32. Block diagram of circuitry for repeating complex figures on the screen.

connections to the window inputs for the time being. If you use the select and D-input specifications in Fig. 4-33a, you will find the screen filled with rows and columns of hooked-together Xs. (It gives the visual impression of a small checkerboard pattern, however).

If you are having trouble visualizing the Xs, window down to a single figure with 256H, 128H, 64H, 32H, 128V, 64V, and 32V. Now you should see a single X figure as shown in Fig. 4-33a. Remove all these window inputs before going on to the next step of this experiment.

Now the idea is to selectively eliminate some of the Xs, leaving behind a distinct pattern of them. First try applying 32H and 32V to the windowing NAND gate. You should find that half the Xs are eliminated, getting rid of the confusing, hooked-together feature. What is left is a regular pattern of horizontal and vertical X lines.

Including 64H and 64V with the 32H and 32V sources already connected to the window inputs increases the spacing between the rows and columns of Xs. See this particular set of window specifications in Fig. 4-33b.

Now remove the windowing NAND gate, IC3, from the circuit and replace it with a 2-input EXCLUSIVE-OR gate. As described in connection with Fig. 3-21, you will be creating a checkerboard pattern, a checkerboard pattern of little Xs in this case. See the circuit and specifications in Fig. 4-33c.

Try the windowing circuit in Fig. 4-33d for a touch of special interest, then try any of the other bar or line generators from Chapter 3.

When you think you have mastered the art of setting patterns of identical, square matrix figures on the screen, move on to figures built within rectangular matrices. Most rectangular matrices described in this chapter use the extension technique, or a combination of extension and foldover. Such figures can be repeated any number of times on the screen using the bar-and-rectangle windowing procedures. You will find, however, that you must be careful when selecting the H- and V-count specifications for the windowing circuitry.

As an example of repeating the image of an extended foldover matrix, try the racing car figure in Fig. 4-12. Reduce the size of the basic figure matrix two orders of magnitude as indicated in Fig. 4-34. With no windowing at all, the little car appears repeated a large number of times on the screen. But the figures are hooked together in a fashion that makes the image about useless.

The little figures can be separated by eliminating alternate rows and columns of them. The circuit in Fig. 4-34 shows the specifica-

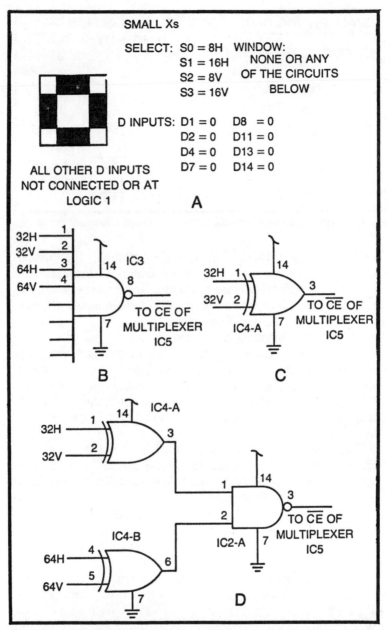

Fig. 4-33. Initial experiments with the line/rectangle pattern-repeating technique. (a) Matrix configuration and sample specifications for an X figure. (b) Windowing circuit for creating rows and columns of figures. (c) Circuit for generating checkerboard patterns of figures. (d) Circuit for generating an interesting pattern of figures.

```
┌─────────────────────────────────────────────────────────────┐
│  SMALL RACING CARS    (USE CIRCUITS IN FIGS. 4-5             │
│  ─────────────────                    AND 4-11)             │
│  SELECT:  S0 = 4H F 16H                                      │
│           S1 = 8H F 16H                                      │
│           S2 = 4V                                            │
│           S3 = 8V                                            │
│                                                              │
│  WINDOW: 32H, 32V    D INPUTS:  D0 = 16V̄    D9  = 16V        │
│                                 D1 = 0      D12 = 16V        │
│                                 D2 = 16V̄    D13 = 16V        │
│                                 D3 = 16V    D14 = 16V̄        │
│                                 D6 = 16V̄                     │
└─────────────────────────────────────────────────────────────┘
```

Fig. 4-34. Specifications for generating regular rows and columns of little racing cars.

tions for doing this particular windowing job. Note that the smallest H-count window input is one step larger than the largest H-count specification used for generating the figure. To be more specific, the figure-generating multiplexer circuit uses H-count inputs 4H, 8H, and 16H. The next larger H-count signal, 32H, is thus just large enough to cover the racing car figure.

By the same token, the V-count windowing should begin with the V-count signal that is one step larger than the largest V-count used for generating figure. The largest V-count for the figure in this instance is 16V, the extension inputs to the D connections. The 32V signal is thus the appropriate one for windowing the images horizontally.

The field of cars can be limited to one part of the screen by including $\overline{256H}$ and 128H at the windowing inputs. The two additional windowing inputs restrict the field of cars to a vertical "race track" situated just left of center.

A general rule for windowing complex figures is emerging from this discussion. Always begin windowing, using H- and V-count signals *one* step higher than the largest used for generating the basic figure.

If the basic figure is built within a 4×8 matrix, for example, and the largest H- and V-count signals used for generating that figure are 4H and 8V respectively, the windowing should begin with 8H and 16V.

Windowing for Irregular Patterns of Identical Figures

While the notion of windowing a basic complex figure to get a particular pattern of rows and columns serves some useful purposes for TV games, many other games call for patterns of identical figures that are not in regular rows and columns. It is often more desirable to create irregular, or even random, patterns of identical figures, something that cannot be done with the bar-and-rectangle windowing approach.

It is possible to generate a complex pattern of complex, but identical, figures by windowing a figure-generating multiplexer circuit with yet another multiplexer circuit. In other words, the window generator is, itself, a complex figure generator.

Figure 4-35 illustrates this particular approach to generating some complex patterns. IC5 and IC6 are both 16:1 multiplexer circuits. IC6 generates the basic complex figure as described in the first sections of this chapter. The inputs to S0 through S3 determine the dimensions of the complex figure, while information at the D inputs determine what the figure will be.

IC5 is a similar kind of circuit that generates a matrix of its own. The dimensions of this pattern matrix are determined by H- and V-count signals applied to pattern-select inputs WS0 through WS3, while the pattern, itself, is determined by the data applied to the field pattern data inputs W0 through W15.

Electrically speaking, the two multiplexer circuits are virtually identical. They play two entirely different roles in the pattern-generating process, however. IC6 generates the basic figure, while IC5 determines where and how many identical figures appear on the screen.

To see how this scheme works, program IC6 to generate the simple X pattern in Fig. 4-33a. As long as there are no connections to the inputs of IC5 and the pattern window NAND gate, you will see the basic X pattern repeated all over the screen.

Now connect the pattern select inputs to IC5 as specified in Fig. 4-35: WS0 = 32H, WS1 = 64H, WS2 = 32V, and WS3 = 64V. There will be no obvious change in the pattern on the screen, however, until one or more of the W inputs to IC5 is connected to logic 0. Every time you connect one of those W inputs to logic 0, you will find some of the figures eliminated from the screen.

IC5, itself, is serving the function of a complex figure generator. The "figure" in this instance is the desired pattern of cars on the screen. A logic 1, or no connection, to a W input allows the basic figure to appear at the corresponding matrix location. Setting a W input to logic 0, on the other hand, eliminates a figure at the matrix location. Using inverted or noninverted versions of 128H creates an extended window matrix. Figure 4-36 shows the specifications for

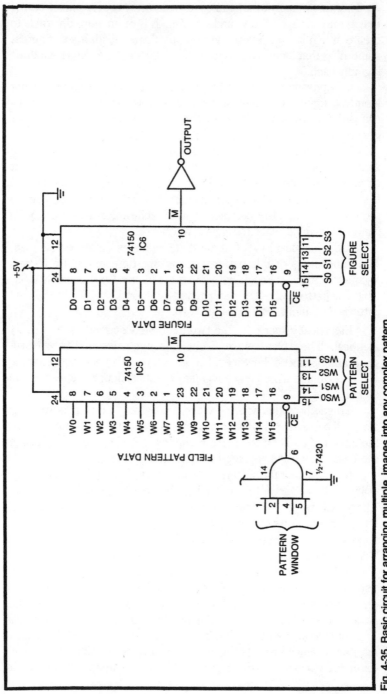

Fig. 4-35. Basic circuit for arranging multiple images into any complex pattern.

generating a large X figure that is, itself, made up of smaller X figures. Using the circuit in Fig. 4-35, IC6 generates the little Xs, and IC5 determines the big X pattern. The designated pattern window inputs restrict the pattern to a single large X on the screen.

If you understand how the basic complex-figure generators work, you can apply that knowledge to the complex-pattern generator. Any of the complex-pattern generators described in the first part of this chapter can be used as window generators. It is possible, if not altogether practical, to create a 256-cell figure matrix using the circuit in Fig. 4-26, and then repeat that figure anywhere within another 256-cell windowing matrix. The result would be a full-screen, complex pattern of identical complex figures.

SMALL X FIGURE (USE CIRCUIT IN FIG. 4-35)

SELECT:	S0 = 8H	WINDOW: FROM IC5
	S1 = 16H	
	S2 = 8V	
	S3 = 16V	

D INPUTS:	D1 = 0	D8 = 0
	D2 = 0	D11 = 0
	D4 = 0	D13 = 0
	D7 = 0	D14 = 0

LARGE X PATTERN

SELECT:	WS0 = 32H	WINDOW: $\overline{256H}$
	WS1 = 64H	$\overline{128H}$
	WS2 = 32V	$\overline{128V}$
	WS3 = 64V	

W INPUTS:	W1 = 0	W8 = 0
	W2 = 0	W11 = 0
	W4 = 0	W13 = 0
	W7 = 0	W14 = 0

Fig. 4-36. Example of arranging a complex figure into a complex pattern, a large X built from smaller Xs.

You must play with this scheme for a while to get a real understanding of how it works. Keep it simple at first, starting with the circuit in Fig. 4-35, then move on to one that uses two multiplexers for generating the basic figure and one for determining the repeated pattern.

It is important to master this technique now. Later chapters dealing with complete games, and the motion of figures assume an understanding of the complex-figure and pattern-generating schemes.

Chapter 5

Building Motion-Control Circuits

Motion makes TV games. Without some player-controlled and automatic motion, today's video game business would not exist. Given the choice between a system that only generates complex static figures and one that generates very simple figures that move, most people would choose the system that includes the motion feature.

The figures for the original table tennis, squash, and hockey games were exceedingly simple—merely rectangles and lines. But the player-controlled paddle motion and the automatic ball motion gives these games their real appeal. No one seems to care whether the ball is round or square. Motion makes the game.

You can build some good video games around the player-controlled and automatic motion circuits described in this chapter. There is no real need to generate the complex figures featured in Chapter 4.

At some point in your experience with custom video games, however, you will most likely find that adding one or two complex figures makes the games more fun and interesting.

Work through the descriptions and experiments in this chapter, carefully noting the special features of each one. There are a number of options offered here, and that implies that some motion-control circuits are better than others under certain circumstances.

Get a good understanding of all the motion circuits now, and you will be able to design more effective and efficient game circuits later on.

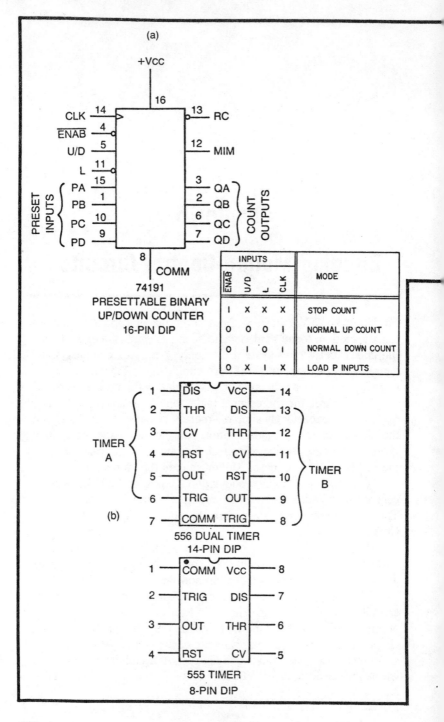

(a)

+VCC

16

CLK 14
ENAB 4
U/D 5
L 11

13 RC
12 MIM

PRESET INPUTS
PA 15
PB 1
PC 10
PD 9

3 QA
2 QB
6 QC
7 QD
COUNT OUTPUTS

8 COMM

74191
PRESETTABLE BINARY
UP/DOWN COUNTER
16-PIN DIP

INPUTS				MODE
ENAB	U/D	L	CLK	
1	X	X	X	STOP COUNT
0	0	0	1	NORMAL UP COUNT
0	1	0	1	NORMAL DOWN COUNT
0	X	1	X	LOAD P INPUTS

TIMER A

1 DIS   VCC 14
2 THR   DIS 13
3 CV   THR 12
4 RST   CV 11
5 OUT   RST 10
6 TRIG   OUT 9
7 COMM   TRIG 8

TIMER B

(b)

556 DUAL TIMER
14-PIN DIP

1 COMM   VCC 8
2 TRIG   DIS 7
3 OUT   THR 6
4 RST   CV 5

555 TIMER
8-PIN DIP

138

SPECIFIED	SUBSTITUTE	
	FIRST	SECOND
556	555	555
1 2 3 4 5 6	7 6 5 4 3 2	N. A.
7	1	1
8 9 10 11 12 13	N.A.	2 3 4 5 6 7
14	8	8

(c)

Fig. 5-1. Some ICs used for the first time. (a) Pinout and function table for the 74191 counter. (b) Pinouts for the 556 and 555 timers. (c) A chart showing how to substitute two 555 timers for a single 556 dual time. Numbers indicate pin numbers.

MOTION-CONTROL TINKERBOX

If you have been performing the experiments outlined in Chapters 3 and 4, you should have at hand a good assortment of NAND, NOR, and invert gates. You will need them for the motion-control Tinkerbox.

In addition, you will need some 555 monostable multivibrators (timers or the 556 dual timers), a few more 7493 counters such as those used in the Sourcebox, and some 74191 presettable up-down binary counters. Study the diagrams in this chapter, making up a list of ICs you might have to order now.

You will need the timers for performing the experiments in the first part of this chapter, but fortunately, they aren't difficult to find these days. You might have to send away for the 74191 counters, but here you have some lead time because they aren't required for a while.

Figure 5-1 shows the pinouts for the 555 and 556 timers and the 74191 counter. Most fo the circuits described in this call for using 556 dual timers. You can, however, substitute two 555s by making the changes in pin numbers as indicated on the chart in Fig. 5-1.

The counter in Fig. 5-1a is in its normal counting mode whenever the $\overline{\text{ENAB}}$ input is at logic 0, the load input, L, is at logic 1, and clock pulses are applied to the CLK input. The counter counts up or down, depending on the logic level applied at the U/D terminal. Setting U/D to logic 0 lets the counter count up, and setting it to logic 1 makes it count down, or backwards.

The counter can be preset to any desired count by applying the desired binary count at the preset inputs, PA through PD, and pulling the L input down to logic 0.

The counting operation can be stopped and held at any desired count by raising the $\overline{\text{ENAB}}$ input to logic 1. Counting then resumes from that point as soon as ENAB is returned to 0.

The ripple-clock, RC, and maximum/minimum, M/M, outputs perform special cascading and output control functions that will be described in detail when considering the actual circuits that use them.

SIMPLE PLAYER-CONTROLLED MOTION

Let's get some motion on the screen as quickly and simply as possible. To do this, tinker together the circuit shown in Fig. 5-2.

This circuit generates a narrow horizontal or vertical bar on the screen. The horizontal version can be moved vertically anywhere on the screen by means of the 500 kΩ potentiometer control, R1. And when you build the vertical version, you will find you can move that bar horizontally across the screen.

The heart of this system is a 555 timer. The circuit in Fig. 5-2 calls for using one-half of a 556 dual timer which, in essence, performs the job of a single 555 device.

The monostable timing is initiated by the HRST or VRST pulse from the Sourcebox unit, and the actual amount of timing is determined by R1, R2, and C2. When generating a movable horizontal bar, trigger the circuit from VRST and fix the values of R2 and C2 to 3.3 kΩ and 0.047 μF. To generate a movable vertical bar, initiate the timer from HRST and fix the values of R2 and C2 at 33 kΩ and 100 pF. Note that potentiometer R1, the motion control adjustment, is 500 kΩ in either case.

So here is what happens: A vertical or horizontal reset pulse initiates the monostable timing. It sets the pin-5 output terminal from logic 0 to logic 1, where it remains until the timing interval is over. If the circuit is triggered by HRST, this timing interval takes place with every horizontal scan line. Triggering the circuit from VRST causes the timing to take place once each vertical frame.

The NAND gate (IC3-A), inverter, and associated RC components make up a pulse-shortening circuit that functions exactly as

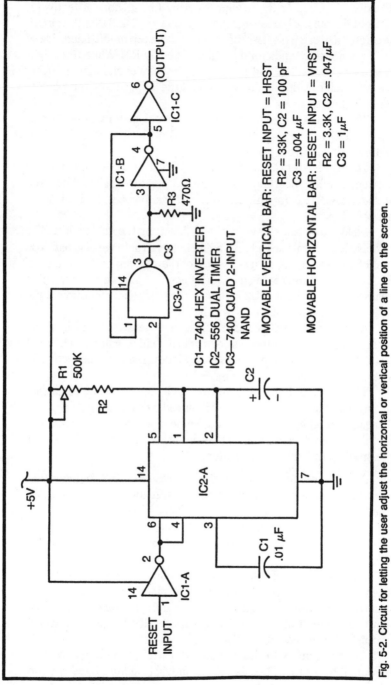

Fig. 5-2. Circuit for letting the user adjust the horizontal or vertical position of a line on the screen.

141

described in Chapter 3, Building Narrow Lines More Effectively. Without the pulse-shortening feature, you would find that the circuit generates a broad white bar that begins at the top or left-hand side of the screen and extends for a distance fixed by R1. While this might create an interesting, and perhaps potentially useful visual effect, the adjustable-width white bar has little application for player-controlled motion.

The pulse-shortening circuit effectively generates a narrow white bar that always occurs at the end of the broad, adjustable-width bar image from the timer.

Timing resistor R3 has a value of 470 ohms for both the movable horizontal and vertical line. Capacitor C3, however, should be fixed at about 0.004 μF for the movable vertical bar and at 1 μF for a horizontal bar.

Build the circuit shown in Fig. 5-2, setting the values first for a movable horizontal bar and then again for a movable vertical bar. You can, of course, adjust or modify any of the recommended values of R2, C2, and C3 to create any special position and size effects. Just bear in mind that R2 and C2 influence the position and motion of the bar, while C3 determines its width.

A movable line that spans the entire height or width of the screen has limited usefulness for ordinary video games. The next phase of the development, then, is to window the line, restricting its size a bit. Try the circuit in Fig. 5-3.

The circuit in Fig. 5-3 generates an image that is quite familiar to anyone who has observed or played with commercial video games. If you don't feel a bit of excitement when you see what you are creating on the screen with this circuit, you are probably missing the spirit of this whole enterprise.

All you have to do is rig up the circuit in Fig. 5-2 to generate a movable horizontal bar, then window it with some H-count signals. The NOR gate in this instance effectively ANDs together the movable bar and window signals, yielding an image that looks very much like the paddle devices for countless video games on the market today.

Note that the "paddle" is movable along a fixed vertical path. The vertical position of the image is determined by the setting of R1, while the window specifications determine the fixed horizontal position and width. Capacitor C3 and resistor R3 in the monostable circuit fix the height of the "paddle."

After playing with this circuit for a while, you might want to reorient it to create a "paddle" that is movable along a fixed horizon-

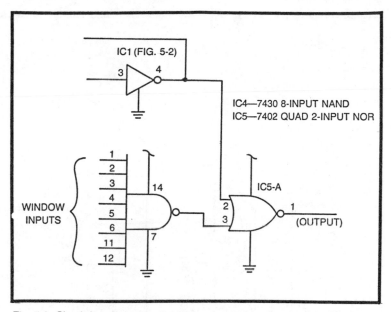

Fig. 5-3. Circuit for windowing the line generated by the circuit in Fig. 5-2.

tal path. What's involved in making that modification? Simply modify the circuit in Fig. 5-2 to create a movable vertical line, then window it with V-count signals from the Sourcebox Unit.

The circuit in Fig. 5-3, combined with the appropriate movable line generator in Fig. 5-2, is the basis for virtually all player-controlled motion of simple lines or rectangles along a fixed horizontal or vertical path.

Many video game designs, however, call for full horizontal *and* vertical control. The circuit in Fig. 5-4 is the basis for such a scheme.

The circuit in Fig. 5-4 is simply a composite of two motion control circuits. The portion of the circuit built around timer IC2-A is a vertical-line generator, while the portion built around IC2-B is a horizontal-line generator. Both lines can be positioned by means of their respective controls, R1 and R4.

The two movable lines are ANDed together to yield a rectangle signal that can be positioned anywhere on the screen. Control R1 moves the rectangle in a horizontal direction, while R4 moves it in the vertical direction.

Working with this relatively simple circuit ought to conjure up a whole lot of ideas for custom video games that require full control of motion by at least one player. In fact you are now in a position to develop the first and simplest sort of TV games—a game of tag.

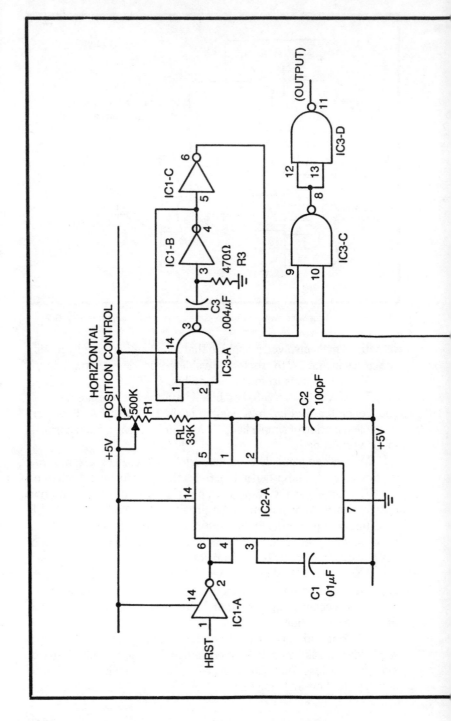

144

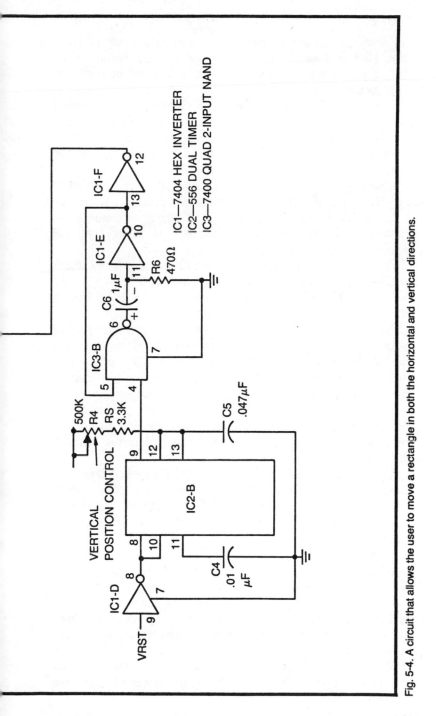

Fig. 5-4. A circuit that allows the user to move a rectangle in both the horizontal and vertical directions.

145

A GAME OF TAG

Pursuit games are among the most popular kinds of video games. Here is your chance to build one of them based on the player-controlled motion circuit described in the previous section of this chapter.

The game calls for building two independent player-controlled motion circuits, one for player A an one for player B. The outputs of the two circuits are essentially ORed together so that each player can see and control the motion of his own little rectangle on the screen.

Referring to the circuit in Fig. 5-5, player A's circuit consists of timers IC1-A and IC1-B, pulse-shortening circuits IC3-A, IC5-C, IC3-B, and IC5-D, and NOR gate IC6-A. Player A controls the horizontal position of his square by means of R1 and the vertical position by means of R3.

Player B's circuit is identical to that of Player A: timers IC2-A and IC2-B, pulse-shortening elements IC3-C, IC5-E, IC3-D, and IC5-F, and NOR gate IC6-B. The horizontal and vertical motion controls in this case are R5 and R7.

The outputs of the two players' circuits (player A from pin 1 of IC6-A and player B from pin 4 of IC6-B) are ORed together by means of the NOR/invert operation of IC6-C and IC4-A. The signal at that output point is a white-on-black signal containing the video information for positioning the little rectangles for both players.

Of course it would be possible to let the two players chase each other around the screen, counting on human judgement to determine when a "tag" is made. One additional IC lets the machine determine a "tag."

The "tag" detector in this instance is NAND gate IC4-B and one section of a dual J-K flip-flop, IC7-A. Now this contact-response circuit is the subject of a more detailed discussion later in this book, but since it adds a nice feature to the basic game, you ought to incorporate it at this point.

Briefly, you can see that IC4-B senses a condition where the players' little rectangles touch one another. The two inputs to this gate are positive-going pulses, each indicating the position of the two rectangles. When they are at least partially superimposed, the output of IC4-B suddenly drops from its normal logic-1 state to logic 0 (where it remains, incidentally, until the players move their rectangles apart).

The instant the output of IC-B, the contact detector, shows a transition from logic 1 to 0, it clocks the flip-flop to a condition where its Q output is set to logic 0. This Q output from IC7-A is connected to the reset inputs of all four timer circuits. And when Q is set to zero by the contact detector, it disables all four timers, sweeping the rectangles into the systems horizontal and vertical blanking regions.

Whenever the two rectangles touch, then, they both disappear from the screen. That is a clear indication that contact has been made. Resetting the game is a matter of first adjusting at least one of the motion controls to a different position, and then striking the RESET switch.

Striking the RESET pushbutton sets the Q output of IC7-A back to logic 1. This enables the timers to allow another "tag" play to begin. One of the controls must be changed before hitting the RESET button, however. Without changing one of the controls, the system would remain in its "tag" mode and the rectangles could not appear on the screen.

A somewhat refined and more challenging version of this tag game is presented in a later chapter.

The circuit in Fig. 5-5 uses only seven ICs. These ICs and the associated components (except the player controls) can be mounted on the standard plug-in board. (Radio Shack 276-153). Using the pin numbers specified in parentheses, the board can be plugged directly into the Sourcebox unit.

The two sets of player controls can be mounted in separate project boxes. Cables running between the circuit board and project boxes require only three wires: one for +5V and one to each of the two fixed timing resistors (R2 and R4 for player A, and R6 and R8 for player B).

The players can toss a coin to see who is "it," then that player chases the other around the screen until a "tag" is made. The players can then switch roles. Obstacle and timing circuits described later in this book can enhance the quality of the game quite a bit. This one, though, represents the simplest sort of TV game that has any real playing interest.

ADDING "INERTIA" TO THE PLAYER CONTROLS

The player-controlled positioning circuits described thus far in this chapter have an unrealistic quickness about them. It is possible to drive the rectangle across the screen in a mere fraction of a second. The simple modification described here gives the controls some inertia, lending a more realistic kind of motion to the rectangle.

The circuit in Fig. 5-6 is built around the monostable timer that is used in all previous player-controlled circuits. The timing interval, however, is adjusted in this instance by R7 instead of R1.

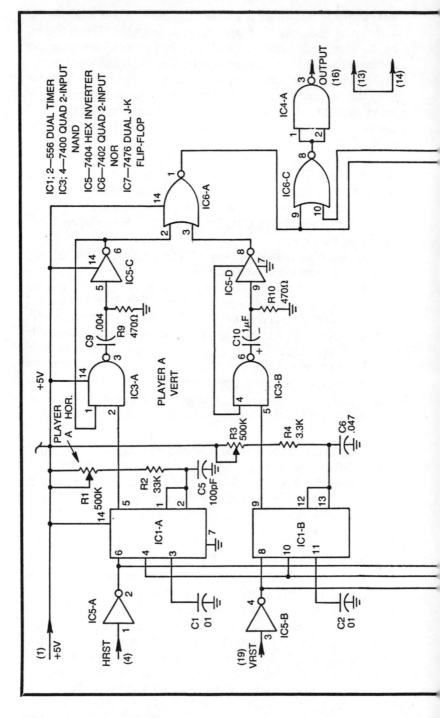

IC1; 2—556 DUAL TIMER
IC3; 4—7400 QUAD 2-INPUT
NAND
IC5—7404 HEX INVERTER
IC6—7402 QUAD 2-INPUT
NOR
IC7—7476 DUAL J-K
FLIP-FLOP

148

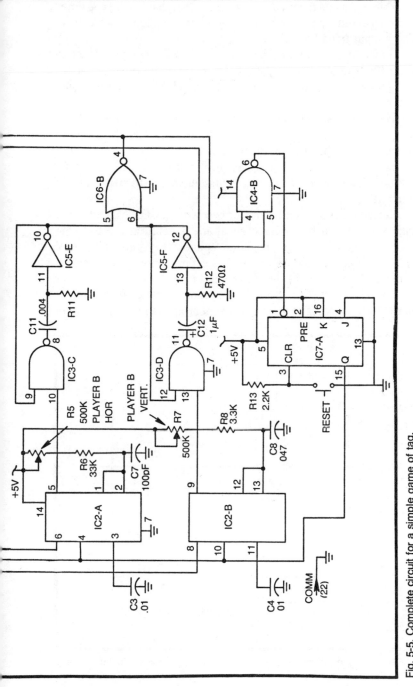

Fig. 5-5. Complete circuit for a simple game of tag.

149

This technique takes advantage of the fact that a 555-type timer can be adjusted by means of a voltage level applied to its control voltage input (pins 3 or 11 on the dual 556 version).

Generally speaking, pulling the control voltage input closer to the positive supply voltage potential lengthens the timing interval. Pulling it closer to ground, on the other hand, shortens the timing interval.

Thus it is possible to set the basic timing range by means of R1, R2, and C2, then vary the timing around that point by changing the voltage level to the control voltage input.

Set up the circuit in Fig. 5-6, omitting capacitors C7 and C8 for the time being. Connect a temporary jumper wire to the wiper arm of control R7.

Connect the loose end of the jumper wire to COMM, and adjust trimpot R1 so that the white vertical line appears at the extreme left-hand edge of the screen. Then connect the jumper to +5V instead of COMM. Adjust R1 until the vertical white line appears on the extreme right-hand side of the screen.

You might have to repeat this operation a couple of times to get a perfect response. The line should appear at the left-hand edge of

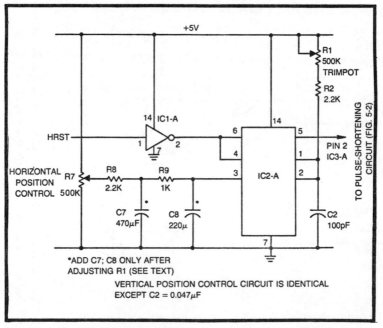

Fig. 5-6. Adding the impression of inertia to a horizontal or vertical positioning control.

the screen when the wiper arm of R7 is to COMM, and it should move to the extreme right-hand side when the wiper arm of R7 is to +5V.

Once you have set the position of R1 to your satisfaction, don't move it again. Remove the jumper from R7 and position the line on the screen by means of that control.

With this preliminary alignment job out of the way, insert capacitors C7 and C8 as shown in Fig. 5-6. As you adjust R7 now, you will find that the line responds as through it has some "slop" or inertia. The line's response, in other words, is not immediately coupled to changes at the position control.

While the values of "inertia" resistors R8 and R9 are critical to the alignment of the timer, the values of C7 and C8 are not. You can change the values of those capacitors to get the amount of inertia you want. The larger the values of C7 and C8, the more inertia the line seems to have.

The vertical positioning circuits can be modified in a similar fashion, triggering with VRST and changing the value of C2 from 100 pF to 0.047 μF. The initial alignment procedure is the same one already described for the "sloppy" horizontal position control circuit.

MANUAL CONTROL OF COMPLEX FIGURES

The material in this section describes one technique for moving complex figures to any desired point on the screen. This technique is an extension of the rectangle-motion scheme already discussed in this chapter. But rather than using a monostable multivibrator to generate the object itself, the monostable effectively "tells" a counter when to begin counting or when to reset to zero. The timer-controlled counter then provides select and windowing information for a matrix generator—any of the complex figure matrix generators in Chapter 4.

Figure 5-7 shows a simplified block diagram and a complete schematic for a circuit that lets the player move any complex figure in a vertical direction.

Monostable multivibrator IC2-A is triggered on each time a VRST pulse appears at its TRIG input. Or to put it in the context of the TV raster, this timer begins timing each time the raster reaches the bottom of the screen.

The timer's output remains at logic 1 through the vertical-blanking interval and into some portion of the vertical-scanning interval determined by the values of C2, R2, and R1. A very similar timing circuit in Fig. 5-2 generates a horizontal line that can be

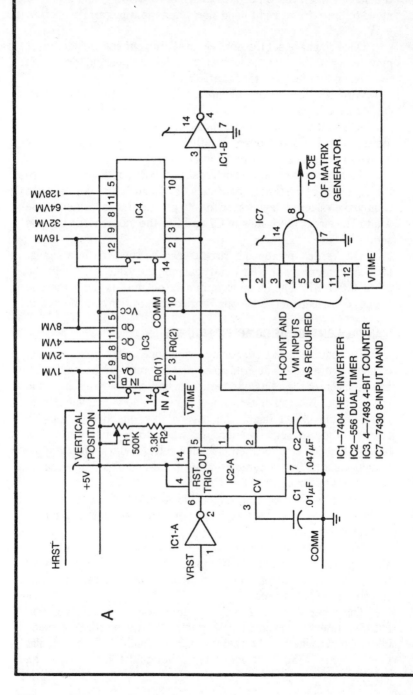

IC1—7404 HEX INVERTER
IC2—556 DUAL TIMER
IC3, 4—7493 4-BIT COUNTER
IC7—7430 8-INPUT NAND

TO CE
OF MATRIX
GENERATOR

H-COUNT AND
VM INPUTS
AS REQUIRED

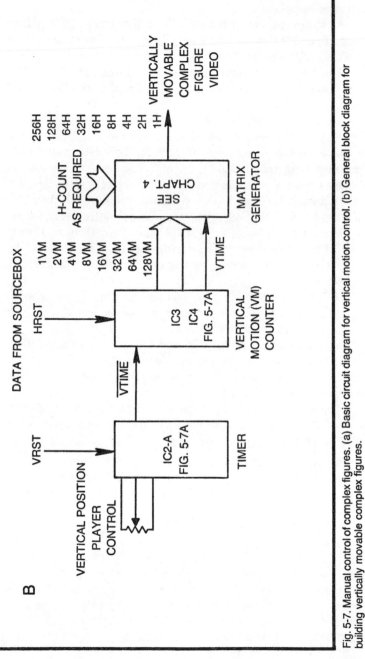

Fig. 5-7. Manual control of complex figures. (a) Basic circuit diagram for vertical motion control. (b) General block diagram for building vertically movable complex figures.

moved up and down the screen. The output of the timer in this instance, however, clears a set of two counters (IC3 and IC4) and holds the outputs at zero.

As soon as the timing interval is over, the output of IC2-A drops to logic 0, and the two counters are allowed to count in response to HRST signals from the Sourcebox unit.

The counters continue running through the remainder of the vertical-scanning interval—until a VRST signal marks the end of a frame.

The two counter ICs actually generate an alternate set of V-count pulses. These signals have the same frequency and counting format as the V-count signals from the Sourcebox. But rather than beginning their count from VRST, these motion-control V-count signals begin the moment IC2-A completes its timing interval. To distinguish these motion-control V-count signals from their counterparts from the Sourcebox, the motion-control vertical-count signals are labeled 1VM, 2VV, 4VM, and so on through 128VM. (256VM is not included in this format because 256V signals are rarely used in generating any of the complex figures described in Chapter 4.)

IC7, an 8-input NAND gate, is included in Fig. 5-7 only for experimental purposes. It is normally part of the windowing circuit for a complex-figure matrix generator.

Set up the circuit in Fig. 5-7a, and connect the output of IC7 to the CE connection of a multiplexer. You can then use this motion-control scheme to position any complex figure along a vertical line. See an example in Fig. 5-8.

The circuit in Fig. 5-8 generates the figure of a rocket that can be positioned and moved up and down on the screen by means of the VERTICAL POSITION control, R1.

Note from the complex-figure specifications in Fig. 5-8 that the matrix generator is seeing its S0 input as 4H folded by 8H. Both of these horizontal-count signals come directly from the Sourcebox. The vertical-select inputs, however, come from the vertical-motion control circuit, 4VM, 8VM, and 16VM.

The circuit thus generates a 4×16 extended foldover matrix that derives its horizontal components directly from the Sourcebox and its vertical components from the counters in Fig. 5-7a.

Once you get the vertical movable rocket image on the screen, you can adjust its range of motion by selecting alternate values of C2 and R2. You will also find that changing either or both of the inverted VM connections to the window section of the circuit modifies the range of vertical control.

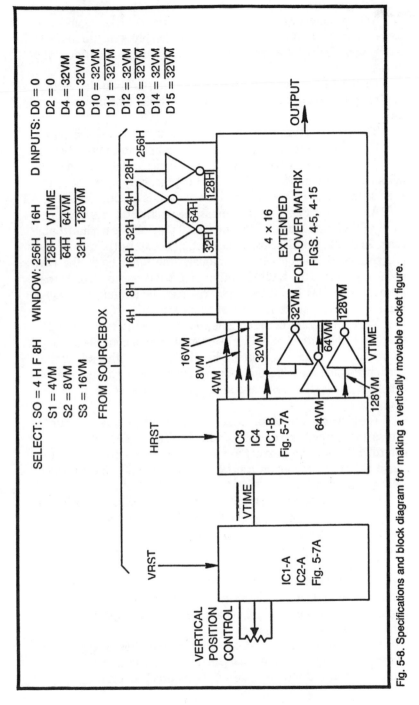

Fig. 5-8. Specifications and block diagram for making a vertically movable rocket figure.

You can actually build any of your favorite complex figures and move them vertically on the screen by simply substituting VM connections for the V-count specifications you specified for static complex figures.

Of course you can introduce some "intertia" into the vertical motion by modifying the timer circuit to work like that shown in Fig. 5-6.

The basic vertical-motion control circuit in Fig. 5-7 will play a vital role in all the table tennis games described later in this book.

The circuit for generating complex figures that are manually adjustable in the horizontal directions is practically identical to the vertical-motion circuit. The basic idea, in fact, is exactly the same.

As shown in Fig. 5-9a, a monostable multivibrator is triggered by the HRST signal, a pulse that occurs at the end of each horizontal scan. And although the horizontal-motion counters (IC's 5, 6, and 8A) receive HCLK pulses continuously, the timer holds the HM count at zero until the HTIME output of IC2-B drops to zero. At that moment, the HM counters begin running, generating a delayed version of the standard horizontal-count signals.

You can build any of the complex-figure generators described in Chapter 4, then attach it to this horizontal-motion control circuit as shown in the block diagram in Fig. 5-9b. Note that all of the horizontal-count specifications come from the horizontal-motion counters, while the vertical-count specifications come from the Sourcebox.

The player can adjust or move the complex figure back and forth across the screen by means of the HORIZONTAL POSITION control, R3. As in the case of the vertical-motion-control circuit, the range of horizontal motion can be modified by selecting alternate values of R4 and C4.

Figure 5-10 shows the block diagram and basic matrix specifications for generating a racing-car figure. The car in this instance is movable in the horizontal directions. You can use the same general scheme, however, to generate a horizontally movable version of any complex figure you choose.

Figure 5-11 is a complete schematic diagram for the movable racing car, including the matrix-generating circuit. This particular circuit will be used later in this chapter for making a popular racing game.

Using the pin numbers designated in parentheses, this circuit can be permanently mounted to a plug-in card (Radio Shack 276-153) and plugged into the receptacle on the Sourcebox Unit.

The HORIZONTAL POSITION control, R1, should be mounted to a small project box and wired to the main circuit at pins 5 and 6. If touching this little box causes distortion of the displayed figure, run an additional wire from the box, itself, to circuit COMM.

The figure can be viewed alone by connecting the inverted output of the multiplexer to card pin 16 (GAME VID IN). When this circuit is used as part of a larger game format, however, you will take the output from pin 15.

After mastering the technique for building circuits that allow vertical or horizontal motion of any complex figure, you should be able to generalize the procedure to build circuits having both vertically and horizontally controlled motion of any complex figure.

To achieve manual control over both vertical and horizontal positioning, simply build the two circuits in Figs. 5-7a and 5-9a, using their VM and HM outputs for the V- and H-count specifications. Any figure generated by the procedures outline in Chapter 4 can be moved in this fashion.

It is important to experiment with this motion-control scheme until you grasp some of its more subtle features and master them. Proper windowing and range of horizontal and vertical motion can cause some headaches for anyone who has not done their homework with this system.

The player-controlled motion circuits presented thus far in this chapter merely represent the simplest and most straight-forward approaches. There is yet another procedure for achieving player-controlled motion that will be described in the last sections of this chapter. The circuits you have worked with to this point are quite suitable for simpler games that reqire a low budget and not-too-close control over the figure being moved.

The motion-control scheme later has the disadvantages of higher cost and greater circuit complexity, but it has the distinct advantages of precision control and versatility, versatility in the sense that it can be used for both player-controlled and automatic motion. And what's more, the circuit yet to be described is most suitable for controlling motion from a stored program.

It is thus a good idea to study this entire chapter before deciding which kind of player-controlled motion circuit is most suitable for a particular custom TV game. A bit more time invested in study and experimentation will pay off in the long run.

AUTOMATIC FIGURE MOTION

A TV game without automatic motion isn't really a very good TV game at all. In fact it is automatic motion that separates tradi-

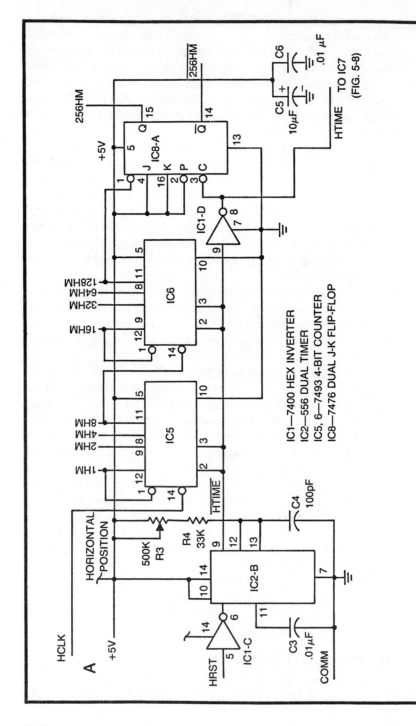

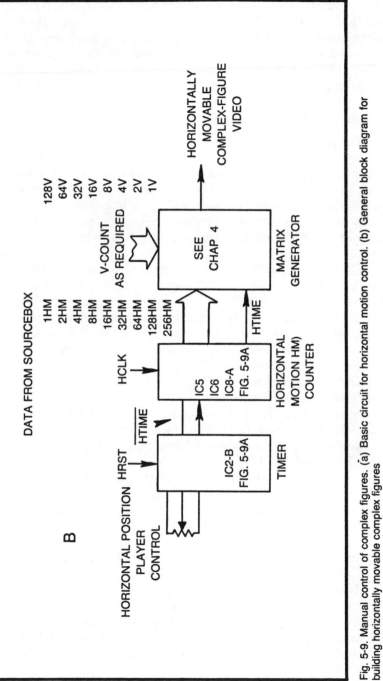

Fig. 5-9. Manual control of complex figures. (a) Basic circuit for horizontal motion control. (b) General block diagram for building horizontally movable complex figures

159

tional board games from video games. Consider, for example, some of the programmable TV game systems on the market today. They boast of hundreds of different video games; yet, a good many of those same games could be played equally well on a sheet of paper. Games relying on automatic motion give TV games the special popularity they enjoy today.

A Simple Circuit for Vertical Motion

The simplest kind of video-motion-control circuit is one that involves vertical motion only. The simplicity of this form of automatic motion belies its usefulness, however. This simple circuit, combined with some player-controlled motion and interesting complex figures leads the experimenter to a wide variety of interesting games. Follow the discussion and experiments carefully, and you will most likely get a good impression of what you might be able to do on your own.

The circuit in Fig. 5-12 allows the player to adjust the vertical direction and speed of a simple rectangular figure. The heart of the circuit is a free-running oscillator built around one section of a 556 timer. The values are selected so that the oscillator runs at approximately 60 Hz. There is no synchronization with the vertical-count sequence in the Sourcebox, so it is possible to vary the oscillator frequency above and below that 60-Hz rate.

The primary purpose of IC2 and IC3 is to window the vertically moving rectangle so that it appears as a rectangle, rather than a narrow horizontal bar. Build this circuit and note the video signal as it is taken from pin 2 of inverter IC2-A. You will find a white horizontal bar that moves upward or downward on the screen at a rate determined by the setting of R2.

You should be able to adjust R2 so that the bar stands still at any desired point on the screen. There might be a slight drift in one direction or another, but remember that this is the simplest, and not the most precise, vertical-motion circuit.

Whenever you make the bar stand still on the screen, the oscillator is running at the system's vertical framing rate, about 60-Hz rate.

Adjust R2 a bit one way or another and you will find the bar moving upward on the screen. The farther you move the control in that direction, the faster the motion. Whenever the bar is moving up the screen, the oscillator is running a bit slower than the 60-Hz vertical framing rate; and the faster the bar moves, the farther the frequency is from 60-Hz.

160

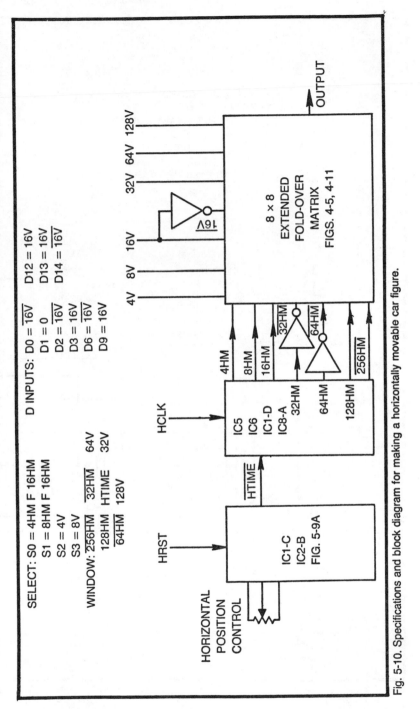

Fig. 5-10. Specifications and block diagram for making a horizontally movable car figure.

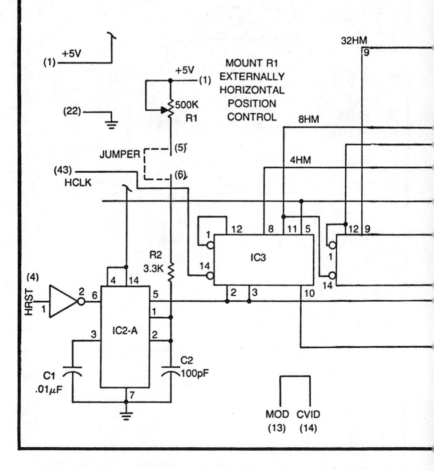

IC1—7404 HEX INVERTER
IC2—556 DUAL TIMER
IC3, 4—7493 4-BIT BINARY COUNTER
IC5—7476 J-K FLIP-FLOP
IC6—7430 8-INPUT NAND
IC7—7486 QUAD EXCLUSIVE-OR
IC8—74150 16:1 MULTIPLEXER

MOUNT R1
EXTERNALLY
HORIZONTAL
POSITION
CONTROL

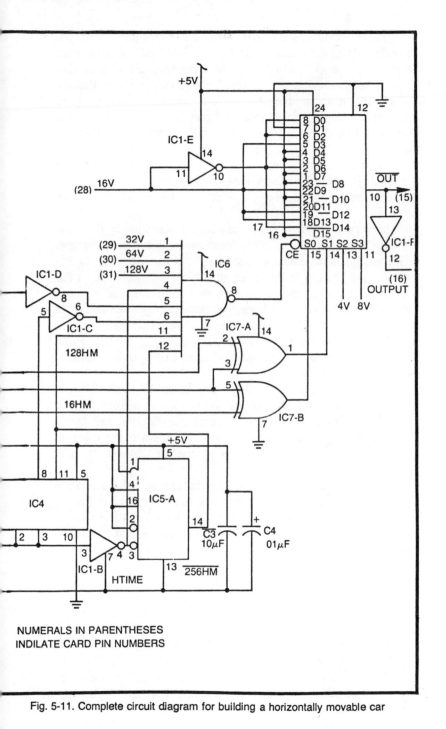

Fig. 5-11. Complete circuit diagram for building a horizontally movable car

Whenever you adjust R2 so that the bar moves downward, you are really setting the oscillator frequency above 60-Hz. The faster the downward motion, the farther the frequency is above 60-Hz.

So what you have here is a variable frequency oscillator that has a middle frequency of about 60-Hz. Varying the frequency either way from that 60-Hz point causes the figure to move up or down the screen at a rate determined by the deviation from the basic 60-Hz rate.

Use the windowing inputs to IC3 to narrow the bar in the horizontal direction. With the values shown in Fig. 5-12, you should be able to see a nice square if you window the bar with 256H, 128H, and 64H.

The vertical height of the rectangle is determined by the value of R7. Reducing the value of R7 reduces the height of the rectangle, and increasing its value increases the height of the rectangle. Unfortunately, any change in the value of R7 causes a change in the oscillator's frequency. So whenever you change the value of R7 to change the height of the rectangle, you must change the value of R6 by a proportional amount, but in the opposite direction.

Play with the values of R7 and R6 to alter the height of the rectangle and yet maintain complete control over the direction and speed of vertical motion.

Resistors R1 and R2 fix the range of speed control that is possible with R2. If these values are too small, you will find that the control is too sensitive, making the rectangle move so fast that it creates an unintelligible visual impression. Tinker with the values of R1 and R2 to get the range of speed control that seems most suitable.

If you would like to indulge in a bit of mathematics, consider the following equation: $s = 06-f$, where s is the time it takes the rectangle to make an excursion up or down the screen and f is the frequency of the oscillator. If s is a negative number, it means the figure moves downward, but if s is positive, the figure moves upward.

What, then, is the oscillator frequency if the figure is to move upward and cross the screen in about 1 second? Solving the equation and substituting +1 for s yields 59 Hz. What is the operating frequency if the rectangle is to move downward across the screen in 1 second? Rearranging the equation to solve for f: $f = 60-s$; and substituting -1 for s yields $f = 60-(-1)$ or 61 Hz.

The real reason for indulging in this bit of algebra is to show that most games require a maximum deviation of 1 Hz around the basic 60

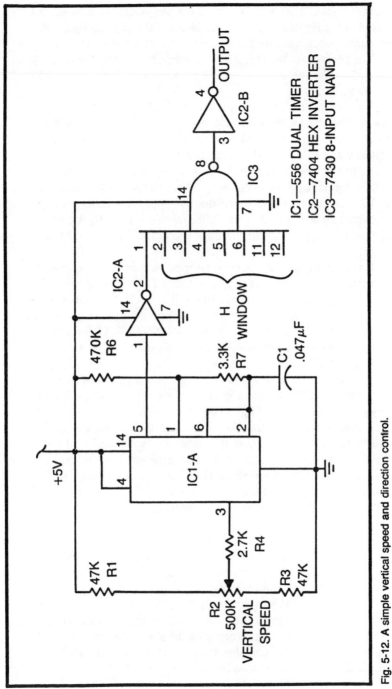

Fig. 5-12. A simple vertical speed and direction control.

Hz framing rate. That adds up to a 2 Hz bandwidth, or a maximum deviation of 2 Hz out of a possible 61 Hz. (Moving the figure any faster than one excursion per second is seldom necessary).

The percentage of change of frequency, then, is on the order of 3%, well within the guaranteed 2% frequency stability of the 556 timer device.

Now suppose you want to use the same kind of circuit for automatic horizontal control. That means you should build the same kind of circuit, but using timing values that set the oscillator's base frequency at 15,750 Hz, the basic horizontal scan rate.

As in the case of the vertical-motion-control circuit, the time required for making an excursion across the screen is given by s = 15,750-f, where f is the oscillator frequency. If s turns out to be a negative number, it means the figure moves to the left. A positive value for s means the figure moves to the right. But let's get to the point of all this.

If you should want a 1-second interval for moving the rectangle horizontally across the screen, you should be able to vary the oscillator frequency 1 Hz above or below 15,750 Hz—between 15,749 Hz and 15,751 Hz. The maximum percentage of change in this case is only slightly greater than one-tenth of 1%. Unfortunately the 556 timer and your regulated power supply cannot possibly hold that kind of tolerance.

Trying to build a horizontal-motion-control circuit around the scheme in Fig. 5-12 will be a great disappointment. It is virtually impossible to get a stable figure on the screen.

It is also difficult to use the circuit in Fig. 5-12 for generating complex figures as described in connection with the positioning controls (Fig. 5-9a, for instance). The problem here is that the oscillator would have to run at the HRST frequency of about 15,750 Hz, and we have just gone through the mathematical agony of showing that the oscillator isn't stable enough to get smooth control at that frequency.

Then, too, the vertical speed control does not lend itself to convenient digital control, the sort of control that is necessary when the speed and direction of vertical motion is to be determined by the game circuit, rather than by a player.

The circuit in Fig. 5-12 is thus wholly suitable for player-controlled motion of simple lines, bars, and rectangles in the vertical directions. It does not work very well for horizontal motion of any kind, vertical motion of complex figures, or vertical motion that is controlled by the game circuit itself.

Fortunately there is an alternate scheme that overcomes all three of these disadvantages. The principle involved here is commonly called *slipping-counter motion*. The idea is to build a horizontal- or vertical-counter circuit that is practically identical to those in the Sourcebox unit. The second counter circuit, however, runs out of sync with those in the Sourcebox. In effect, the images created by this slipping counter moves across the screen by virtue of the fact they are out of sync with the Sourcebox counters creating the raster pattern.

Slipping-Counter Vertical Motion Control

Figure 5-13 shows the basic circuit for vertical-slipping-counter motion. In a physical sense, it is a very simple circuit, composed of only three IC devices: two 74191 presettable 4-bit binary counters and a 7400 2-input NAND gate.

Recall from the discussions in Chapter 2 that the Sourcebox unit generates a vertical-scanning field composed of 261 lines. Sixteen of these lines are lost in the vertical retrace interval, but the point is that the vertical-count generator in the Sourcebox counts out 261 HRST pulses per vertical frame.

Now if you could build another vertical-count generator that counts out 261 HRST pulses per cycle, you would have a second source of vertical-count pulses. This new counter would run at the same rate as the one in the Sourcebox, but its reset point could occur anywhere in the vertical field. This circuit, in other words, would run at the same frequency as the one in the Sourcebox, but out of phase—out of phase anywhere between 0 and 260 HRST vertical-clocking intervals.

Next, suppose you use this out-of-phase vertical-count generator to create images on the screen. That image would be motionless on the screen, but it could be shifted up or down, depending on its phase relationship with the vertical-count generator in the Sourcebox. The greater the phase difference between the two counters, the greater the amount of shifting.

As an example, let the slipping counter in Fig. 5-13 run at the same frequency as the vertical-count generator in the Sourcebox. But let the slipping counter run out of phase to the extent that it reaches a count of 100 while the corresponding vertical counter in the Sourcebox is at count 150. The slipping counter would thus be cycling 50 HRST pulses behind the Sourcebox counter, and any image created from the vertical-count outputs of the slipping counter would appear 50 scan lines lower on the screen than the same image created from the vertical-count outputs of the Sourcebox.

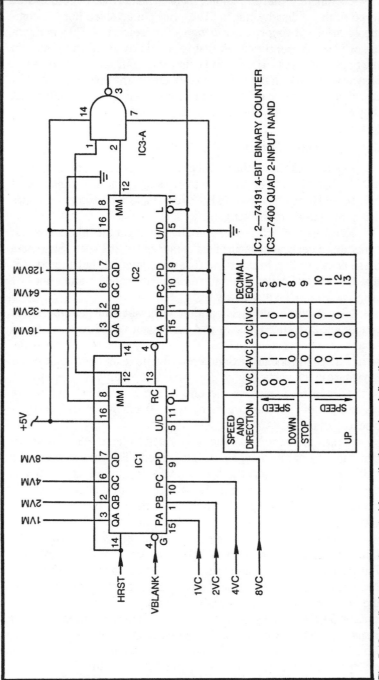

Fig. 5-13. A slipping-counter control for vertical speed and direction.

Alter the phasing so that the slipping counter reaches a count of 100 while the corresponding Sourcebox counter is at 50, and you will find the image shifted 50 scan lines higher on the screen. The slipping counter in this case is running 50 HRST pulses ahead of the Sourcebox vertical-count generator.

An image created by the VM outputs of the vertical slipping counter will be motionless on the screen as long as the frequency is identical to that of the vertical-count generator in the Sourcebox, but let the frequencies be different, and you will find the image moving up or down the screen.

Suppose the slipping counter has some provision for altering the number of HRST pulses it includes in one vertical frame. If this counter has a counting capacity of 262 instead of the usual 261, it resets one scan line later per frame. The overall effect is that any image created from the slipping-counter outputs moves down the screen at a slow but steady rate.

There are two ways to consider this kind of motion effect. Both lead to the same conclusion, an it is left to the reader to use the point of view that suits his own way of thinking.

One way to explain the steady downward motion just described is to consider that the slipping counter is running one HRST pulse farther out of phase each time one vertical frame is completed. And since the position of the image is determined by phase relationship between the slipping counter and Sourcebox, a continuous change in that phase relationship produces the effect of a steady motion.

Another way to look at the situation is to consider that the slipping counter runs at a slightly different frequency than its counterpart in the Sourcebox. If the slipping counter is cycling at 262 pulses per frame instead of 261, that means it is running at a slightly lower frequency. The slipping counter, in other words, is running out of sync with the Sourcebox counter. And since it is running at a slightly lower frequency, the image "rolls" downward on the screen.

Setting the slipping counter to count out 260 HRST pulses, instead of the 261 pulse-interval from the Sourcebox, the image will appear to move upward on the screen. The idea here is that the slipping counter is running at a higher frequency.

The direction of motion is thus determined by whether the slipping counter is cycling at a higher or lower frequency than the corresponding counter in the Sourcebox. If the slipping counter is running at a higher frequency (short counting) the image moves upward, and if the slipping counter is running at a lower frequency (long counting) the image moved downward . Of course the image is motionless as long as the two frequencies are the same.

Now the greater the frequency difference, the faster the apparent motion becomes. If the slipping counter is set so that it short-counts four pulses per frame, it moves upward about four times as fast as it does when short counting just one pulse per frame. Long counting four pulses per frame, by the same line of reasoning, makes the image move downward rather rapidly.

The table in Fig. 5-13 shows five 4-bit words that can be loaded into the vertical-motion-slipping-counter circuit. When that number is 1001 (decimal 9) the slipping counter runs at the same frequency as the vertical-count generator in the Sourcebox unit, and the result is a motionless image on the screen.

Loading decimal 8, 7, 6, or 5, however, forces the slipping counter to long-count by 1, 2, 3, or 4 HRST pulses per frame, yielding an image that moves downward at the rate of 1, 2, 3, or 4 scan lines per frame. (Since there are 60 frames completed each second, it is possible to calculate the time it takes the image to move down the screen.)

According to the table in Fig. 5-13, loading the decimal equivalents of 10, 11, 12, or 13 causes the image to move upward. The counter actually short-counts by 1, 2, 3, or 4 scan lines per frame in this instance.

All of this discussion merely indicates *what* the circuit in Fig. 5-13 does. Now it is time to investigate exactly *how* it does the job.

Anyone familiar with the fundamentals of digital electronics ought to recognize the two-counter portion of the circuit as an 8-bit synchronous binary counter. The counters are clocked by the HRST input to pin 14 of both IC's. Note, however, that the counters are disabled thrugh the VBLANK interval by means of the VBLANK signal applied to the G (enable) input of IC1. The circuit is thus allowed to count at the HRST rate only as long as VBLANK is at logic 0—at all times except through the VBLANK interval.

The 2-input NAND gate normally shows a logic-1 output, dropping to logic 0 only when the counter outputs reach a maximum count of 11111111. At that instant, the 2-input NAND gate sees a pair of logic-1 inputs, and its output drops to 0.

Whenever the output of IC3-A drops to logic 0, the two counter ICs are loaded with a certain set of binary numbers. IC2 is always loaded with 0000 virtue of the fact that its preset inputs are permanently tied to logic-0 common. IC1, however, is loaded with whatever 4-bit number appears at its preset inputs, PA through PD, and that number is the motion code described in the table accompanying the diagram in Fig. 5-13.

170

So what happens here is that the counter advances to its maximum count (11111111, or decimal 256) where it is immediately reloaded to the number appearing at the preset inputs of IC1, anywhere between 5 and 13. If the VC inputs show 1001, for instance, the counter replaces 11111111 with 00001001, or decimal 9. It then counts up to 11111111, with a 16-count pause whenever the VBLANK interval occurs. The total number of counting intervals in 1 complete cycle is thus 261, exactly equal to the number of counting intervals generated by the Sourcebox vertical-count circuit. An image using the VM outputs stands still on the screen.

If the VC inputs are altered to show a binary number other than 9, the slipping counter has more or fewer counts per cycle. Loading binary 8, for example, forces the slipping counter to work with one additional HRST pulse per cycle. In effect, this increases the cycle time, or in other words, decreases the frequency. The result in this instance is that images generated by the VM outputs appear to move upward on the screen.

Loading numbers larger than 9 shortens the counting cycle of the slipping counter, thereby making it cycle at a higher frequency. Any image using the VM outputs appears to move down the screen.

Construct the circuit in Fig. 5-13, and make your initial tests of taking the video from one of the higher-order VM outputs, 32VM or 64VM for instance. The horizontal bars on the screen should stand still when loading 1001 at the VC inputs. Then they should move upward rather slowly when loading 1010 or 1011. The bars move at the same speed, but upward, when loading 1000 or 0111 at the VC inputs.

You are now in a good position to generate bars, lines, rectangles, and complex figures that show continuous vertical motion. Use any of the procedures outlined in Chapters 3 and 4, substituting the VM signals where you would normally specify the Sourcebox V-count signals. Use the Sourcebox H-count signals in the usual fashion until you have built the horizontal slipping counter described in the section that follows.

If you have been conducting the vertical-motion experiments as recommended thus far in this chapter, you are probably acutely aware of the fact that the procedure for changing the speed and direction of motion for the slipping counter is somewhat more awkward that of the oscillator-controlled motion circuits.

The slipping-counter technique does not lend itself to direct control by means of a simple variable resistor, whereas the simpler control circuits do. The closing section of this chapter describes a rather simple circuit for achieving potentiometer control over slip-ping counters. But in instances where a player is to have manual control over vertical speed and direction, the control circuit in Fig. 5-12 is the better choice, assuming, of course, the image is a simple line, bar, or rectangle.

The digital speed and direction control feature of the slipping-counter circuit, on the other hand, is the better choice in games calling for automatic or machine control of vertical speed and direction. The slipping-counter technique is also the only option open when the figure is more complex than a simple line, bar, or rectangle.

Master the fundamentals of both vertical-control circuits and you will be fully prepared to handle any game-designing situation calling for vertical motion.

Slipping-Counter-Horizontal-Motion Control

While the experimenter might have several options when it comes to selecting vertical-motion-control circuits, no such options exist for controlling the speed and direction of horizontal motion.

One might think the vertical-motion circuits described in this chapter could be modified to suit the needs for horizontal motion. The idea might be to simply substitute HCLK for HRST and HBLANK for VBLANK. This is not the case at all. Merely substituting H-count parameters for V-count parameters creates an image on the screen that is, first, quite confusing and, second, practically useless.

The primary feature of horizontal counting is that the slipping counter must not be permitted to change its count length with every horizontal line. The horizontal-slipping counter must be loaded with its stop code for every visible scan line on the screen. If this is not done, the experimenter sees a series of diagonal lines, rather than straight vertical lines, moving across the screen.

The horizontal-slipping counter must see its stop code at all times except during one particular scan line, preferably one that occurs during vertical blanking.

If the horizontal-slipping counter is then loaded with a number that retards the horizontal timing, the vertical line will appear to move to the right. That retarded count, however, must occur only once during the scanning field.

On the other hand, shortening the count during one particular scan line makes the vertical line appear to move to the left. Again, the counter must see its stop code at any other time.

The circuit in Fig. 5-14 represents the basic horizontal-slipping counter. It is, indeed, the only horizontal-motion circuit used throughout this book.

ICs 1, 2, 3 and 5 in Fig. 5-14 perform the same general function as the vertical-slippng counter in Fig. 5-13. They are responsible for counting out a horizontal-count cycle of nine bits, four bits each for IC1 and IC2, and a ninth bit from the J-K flip-flop, IC5.

The 3-input NAND gate, IC5-A, senses the counter overflow of 111111111, or decimal 511. The starting point for the stop code in this case is binary 10010010, or decimal 137. Take the difference between these 2 figures and you end up with a counting cycle that is 374 pulses long. That is the number of pulses required for making a horizontally movable figures appear motionless on the screen.

An astute reader, however, might note that this number is quite different from the counting cycle of the horizontal-count generator in the Sourcebox unit. Recall that the Sourcebox generates a 454-pulse horizontal cycle.

The answer to this particular situation concerns the fact that HBLANK is applied to the enable input of IC1 in Fig. 5-14. The occurrence of this positive pulse disables the horizontal-slipping counter at the end of each scan line—for 80 HCLK pulses. So if you drop those 80 HCLK pulses from the Sourcebox interval, you end up with 374 HCLK pulses that occur while the horizontal lines are visible on the screen. That is the same number of pulses that emerge each cycle from the slipping counter set for a motionless figure.

Any figure having its horizontal components generated by the horizontal-slipping counter thus appears motionless on the screen as long as that counter is being loaded with a 374 HCLK cycle.

Now notice from Fig. 5-14 that the five higher-order bits are always loaded as 01000. The clearing input of IC3-A and the preset inputs of IC2 are always fixed for loading those values, no matter what the motion code might be.

The peculiar feature of the horizontal-slipping counter is that the stop code—the four lower order bits loaded at the preset inputs of IC1—must be loaded at the end of each horizontal cycle. If something other than the stop code is loaded each cycle, the circuit generates moving diagonal lines rather than moving, straight vertical lines.

A motion code other than the stop code is loaded only during one particular scan line that occurs during vertical retrace on the screen. IC4 and IC6 in Fig. 5-14 take care of this situation.

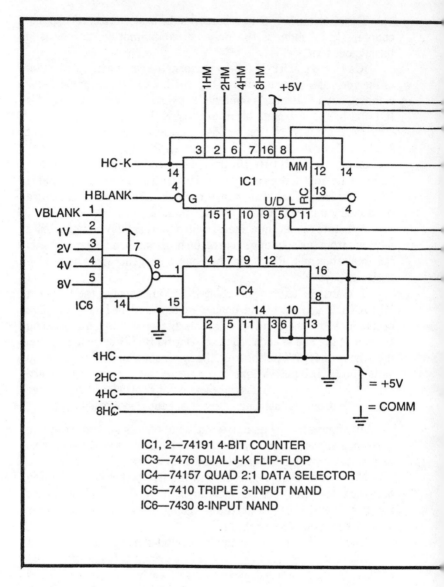

IC1, 2—74191 4-BIT COUNTER
IC3—7476 DUAL J-K FLIP-FLOP
IC4—74157 QUAD 2:1 DATA SELECTOR
IC5—7410 TRIPLE 3-INPUT NAND
IC6—7430 8-INPUT NAND

IC4 is a quad 2:1 multiplexer. It is a circuit that works very much like a 4-pole double-throw selector switch. When its input at pin 1 is at logic 1, the inputs at pins 3, 6, 10, and 13 appear at its outputs (pins 4, 7, 9, and 12 respectively). Note that these inputs are fixed at the circuit's stop code for the four lower-order bits: 1001. So as long as the signal at pin 1 of IC4 is at logic 1, the slipping counter is loaded with its stop code.

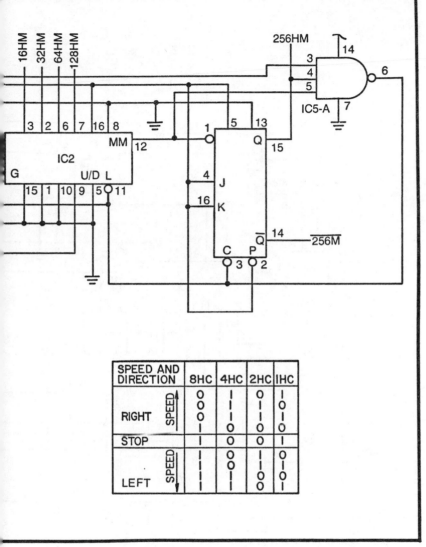

Fig. 5-14. A slipping-counter control for horizontal speed and direction.

Setting the pin-1 control at logic 0, however, shifts the outputs to the four inputs appearing at pins 2, 5, 11, and 14. Since the logic level at pin 1 is determined by the output of a NAND gate, IC6, it follows that the system sees something other than the stop code only when all inputs to the NAND gate are at logic 1. And these inputs come from VBLANK and a selection of V-count signals from the Sourcebox.

175

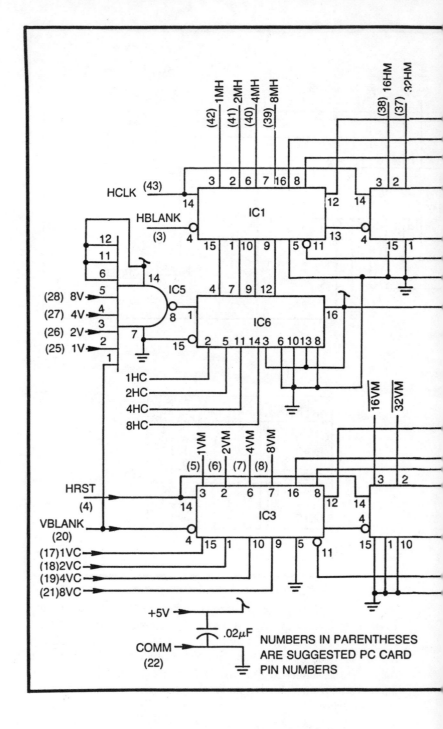

NUMBERS IN PARENTHESES
ARE SUGGESTED PC CARD
PIN NUMBERS

176

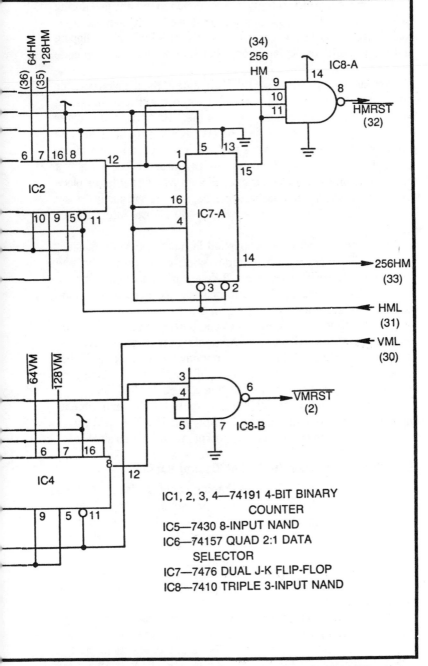

Fig. 5-15. Schematic diagram for a slipping-counter motion control circuit board

177

To make a long story short, IC6 responds to the one line during VBLANK where 1V, 2V, 4V, and 8V all at logic 1 at the same time. It is only during this one particular line that the horizontal-slipping counter can count a cycle that is longer or shorter than the stop-code cycle.

Now suppose you have set the HC inputs of the slipping counter to 1000, a code that makes the counter run one extra pulse. When that one critical scan line occurs during the VBLANK, the counter long-counts to set the reset point one HCLK pulse to the right. The system then automatically injects the stop code, creating a motionless vertical line that is shifted one HCLK interval to the right of where it was on the previous frame. Since this shifting takes place once during each frame, the vertical bar moves gradually to the right, one HCLK interval per frame, or 60 HCLK intervals per second.

Motion to the left is accomplished in much the same fashion, except the slipping counter is forced to short-count during that one critical line in the VBLANK interval. The table accompanying the schematic diagram in Fig. 5-14 summarizes the horizontal-motion codes for this system.

Construct the circuit in Fig. 5-14 and try it for yourself. You can create logic-0 at the HC inputs by connecting the points to COMM. You can create a logic-1 input by connecting a jumper to +5V, but that isn't really necessary with these TTL circuits, because no connection at all lets the inputs assume a logic-1 condition.

You can use any one of the HM outputs for this experiment, simply connecting one of them to GAME VID IN. The MM (max/min) output of IC2 makes a nice take-off point for a video signal too.

A Complete Slipping-Counter-Motion-Control Board

The vertical- and horizontal-slipping-counter circuits can be easily assembled on a single PC card, providing the experimenter with a universal digital-motion card. This card can be used for experiments aimed at getting a better understanding of slipping-counter motion control. But equally important, it can be used as a motion control board for any number of TV game circuits. A bit of time and effort invested in such a board will pay big dividends later in your work.

The universal slipping-counter motion board, shown in Fig. 5-15, has provisions for digitally controlling the speed and direction of both vertical and horizontal motion. Input connections to the Sourcebox unit include HCLK, HBLANK, HRST, VBLANK, and vertical-count signals 1V, 2V, 4V, and 8V. Of course +5V and COMM should be included on this list.

The control inputs are 1HC, 2HC, 4HC, and 8HC for horizontal motion, and 1VC, 2VC, 4VC, and 8VC for vertical motion. The motion-control codes for these two sets of inputs are included in Figs. 5-14 and 5-13 respectively.

The slipping-counter outputs are designated 1HM through 256HM for horizontal counting, and 1VM through 128VM for vertical counting. These outputs can be used for generating lines, bars, rectangles, and complex figures, as described in Chapters 3 and 4. Merely substitute the HM signals for H-count specifications and VM signals for the corresponding V-count specifications.

The scheme is left programmable to some extent. The idea here is to give the experimenter the greatest possible amount of flexibility with this one circuit board. To operate the system in the normal fashion, merely connect the $\overline{\text{HMRST}}$ output to $\overline{\text{HML}}$, and $\overline{\text{VMRST}}$ to $\overline{\text{VML}}$. (Leaving these points "programmable" allows the experimenter to insert other kinds of reset circuits that initialize the position of the movable figure.)

Chapter 6

Some Useful Game Control Schemes

Automatic motion is indeed the hallmark of video games, but automatic game sequencing runs a close second. Most TV games employ automatic start-up and stop features, for example. Then there are other kinds of events and sequences of events that occur during a game, some manually controlled and others automatic.

Consider the control schemes for a basic table tennis game. The game sequence is usually initiated manually by depressing a RESTART pushbutton, but it generally ends automatically as one player reaches a certain score. In some instances, the ball-serving sequence is initiated manually, while in other versions of the same game, the ball is served manually. But in either case, the serving sequence is terminated automatically as one player misses the ball. These operations are examples of game control schemes.

Study the circuits in this chapter carefully. A proper understanding of them will make it easier for you to understand the control features of sample games presented later in this book, and it will certainly make the process of designing your own games more fun, easier, and more efficient.

GAME START/RESET CONTROLS

Most TV games begin with some kind of initial action somewhere on the screen, and by the same token, most games include a critical point where the system is to be reset to begin another cycle of one game or begin a new game altogether.

These start and reset operations can be wholly manual, fully automatic, or a combination of the two. In any case, start and reset controls are generally built around a flip-flop circuit.

The flip-flop circuits in Fig. 6-1 are properly classified as R-S flip-flops. To be more precise, the circuit in Fig. 6-1a is an $\overline{R}$-$\overline{S}$ flip-flop, while the one in Fig. 6-1b is an R-S flip-flop. The outputs in both examples are compliments of one another, one is always at logic 1, while the other is at logic 0.

The $\overline{R}$-$\overline{S}$ flip-flop in Fig. 6-1a is set and reset by means of negative-going (active-low) input pulses. Whenever the $\overline{START}$ input is pulled down to logic 0 and $\overline{STOP}$ is held at logic 1. the PLAY output goes to 1 and the $\overline{PLAY}$ output switches to logic 0. As long as $\overline{STOP}$ remains at logic 1, the outputs hold, or remember, this condition, even after $\overline{START}$ returns to logic 1.

The outputs can then be reversed only by pulling STOP down to logic 0, while holding $\overline{START}$ at logic 1.

The R-S flip-flop in Fig. 6-1b works exactly the same way, but in this case the inputs are active high. The outputs are set and reset by means of positive-going pulses at the START and STOP inputs. Whenever START is pulled up to logic 1, for instance, the PLAY output responds by going to logic 1. At that same time, $\overline{PLAY}$ goes to logic 0. The circuit then remains in that particular output state as long as STOP remains at logic 0. The START input can switch between 1 and 0 any number of times, but PLAY remains at logic 1 as long as STOP is held at 0.

You will find the simple arrangements in Fig. 6-1 appearing one or more times in just about every full-scale TV game presented in this book. The only real difference between the two circuits is the polarity of their input waveforms. One uses negative-going pulses, while the other uses positive-going pulses. The choice of using one circuit or the other depends largely on the polarity of the input pulses that are available from the circuits that operate them.

Manual Start Switch Circuits

Many games begin with a player depressing a start pushbutton, and in some instances, cycles within a game are initiated that way. The circuits in Fig. 6-2 show how to interface a START pushbutton with the flip-flop circuits in Fig. 6-1.

The circuit in Fig. 6-2a is the simplest of the three. In this case, resistor R1 keeps the $\overline{START}$ logic level normally pulled up to logic 1. Depressing the $\overline{START}$ button pulls that logic level down to logic 0, where it remains until the button is released. Any contact bounce

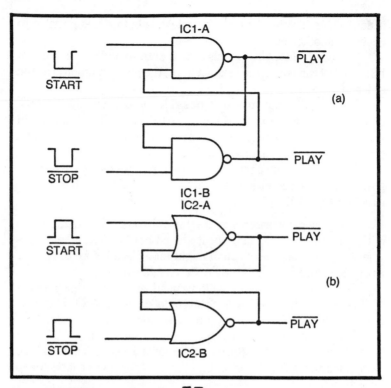

Fig. 6-1. Start/reset circuits. (a) A $\overline{R}$-$\overline{S}$ flip-flop triggered by negative-going pulses. (b) is R-S flip-flop triggered by positive-going pulses.

will appear at the output of this circuit, but it is effectively "filtered" by the flip-flop stage that follows it.

Since the signal from the circuit in Fig. 6-2a is an active-low, $\overline{START}$ level, it can be directly connected to the $\overline{START}$ input of the flip-flop in Fig. 6-1a.

The start circuit in Fig. 6-2b is a bit more complicated. In this case, however, depressing the START button generates a START pulse having a duration roughly equal to the time constant of R2 and C1. The button must be released before it is possible to generate another $\overline{START}$ pulse.

This circuit will show some contact-bouncing effects, but again, the flip-flop following that stage will eliminate these undesirable effects. The active-low nature of the pulse from this start circuit makes it directly compatible with the flip-flop in Fig. 6-1a.

The start circuit in Fig. 6-2c uses a 555-type timer to generate the START pulse. If the $\overline{LOCK}$ input is fixed at logic 1, this circuit generates a clean, positive-going pulse each time the START button is depressed. The button must be released before it is possible to generate another pulse.

The width of the pulse in this case is determined by the values of R3 and C2. Using the values shown here, the pulse duration is on the order of 10 ms.

The $\overline{\text{LOCK}}$ input makes it possible to lock out the START button action as long as $\overline{\text{LOCK}}$ is at logic 0. This is a handy feature in games where it is desirable to prevent a player from initiating a certain playing cycle until something else takes place.

The fact that the circuit in Fig. 6-2c generates an active-high, positive-going pulse makes it directly compatible with the flip-flop circuit in Fig. 6-1b.

Comparing the features of the three circuits in Fig. 6-2, the one in Fig. 6-2a is the simplest, but it should not be used in instances where an automatic reset action might take place before the player has a chance to release the START pushbutton.

The circuit in Fig. 6-2b should be used where there is a possibility that automatic reset will occur before the START button is released. It does not have any provision for automatic lockout.

The circuit in Fig. 6-2c has none of the disadvantages of the two other circuits, plus it features an optional lockout input. (If the lockout feature isn't to be used, that terminal should be connected to +5V.)

When selecting the circuit most appropriate for your game design, consider the complexity, polarity of the outputs, and requirements of the game.

These three circuits, incidentally, can be used in the same ways for manually resetting game operations. Simply switch the $\overline{\text{START}}$ and START labels to $\overline{\text{STOP}}$ and STOP respectively.

Automatic Stop Circuits

Games, or cycles within games, can be stopped or reset automatically by means of the circuits in Fig. 6-3. These are both pulse-generating circuits: The active-high STOP pulse from the circuit in Fig. 6-3b is directly compatible with the flip-flop circuit in Fig. 6-1b, while the active-low output from the circuit in Fig. 6-3a is compatible with that in Fig. 6-1a.

In both cases, the stopping action is initiated whenever a given set of *stop* conditions are met within the system. IC1-A in Fig. 6-3a, for example, normally shows a logic-1 output. Whenever all the inputs to this NAND gate find their way to a logic-1 state (presumably at the time all the conditions for automatic resetting are met), the

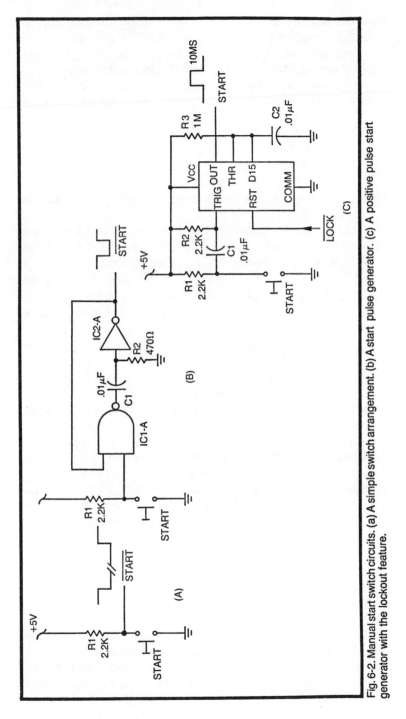

Fig. 6-2. Manual start switch circuits. (a) A simple switch arrangement. (b) A start pulse generator. (c) A positive pulse start generator with the lockout feature.

output of that gate suddenly drops to logic 0. This transition from 1 to 0 initiates a short, active-low pulse at the $\overline{STOP}$ output.

The STOP pulse from the circuit in Fig. 6-3a lasts only as long as the time constant of C1 and R1 allow. To get another pulse, one or more of the input parameters must return to logic 0. And after that, another pulse can be generated when all the inputs go to logic 1 once again.

The circuit in Fig. 6-3b uses a 555-type timer to generate an active-high STOP pulse. This pulse is initiated whenever the device's TRIG and RST inputs see a transition from logic 0 to logic 1. The pulse has a duration roughly equal to the product of R1 times C1. And for most purposes, the values shown in the diagram are suitable for generating a 10 ms pulse.

The input to the timer circuit makes the critical 0-to-1 transition whenever the two active-low stop parameters at NOR gate IC2-A are at logic 0 at the same time. The alternate circuit, made up of NAND gate IC2-A and an inverter, do the same job, with the advantage of being able to work with more than two input parameters at the same time. If you use the NAND/invert combination (instead of the NOR-gate version) the STOP pulse is initiated whenever all the active-low *stop* parameters go to logic 0 at the same time.

Both of these circuits generate an output pulse whenever the input stop parameters—conditions sensed within the game cycle—are met. Both generate a single pulse that can occur again only after the game has left the reset condition and enters it again.

The $\overline{RESET}$ output in Fig. 6-3a and the RESET terminal in Fig. 6-3b aren't used often, but they can be handy in a few instances. These logic levels merely indicate whether or not the system is in its reset condition, or to be more precise, whether or not the system is ready to enter its reset condition.

Either of the circuits in Fig. 6-3 can be used for automatic start operations as well. It's all a matter of connecting the pulse outputs to the appropriate START inputs in Fig. 6-1.

Delayed Start/Stop Operations

It is frequently desirable to insert a time delay between the moment a particular game response occurs and the initiation of a new game or game cycle. In a typical table-tennis game, for instance, there is a short time delay inserted between the time a player misses

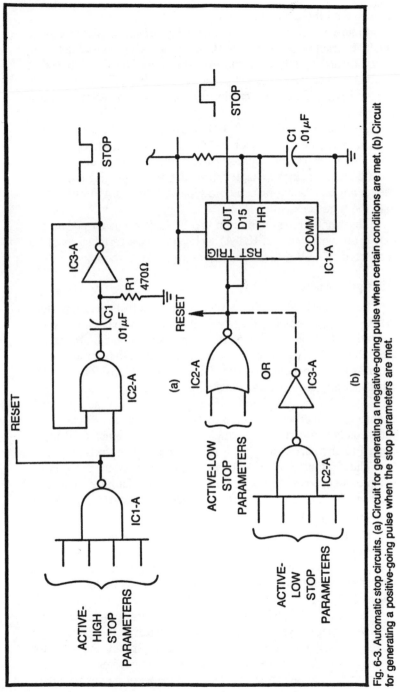

Fig. 6-3. Automatic stop circuits. (a) Circuit for generating a negative-going pulse when certain conditions are met. (b) Circuit for generating a positive-going pulse when the stop parameters are met.

the ball until the next serve begins.

Figure 6-4 shows a relaible time delay circuit. In this instance, a negative-going pulse at pin 6 of IC1-A initiates a monostable timing interval equal to 1.1 times the product of R1 and C1. When that interval is over, capacitor C2 passes a negative-going pulse to the trigger input of IC1-B which, in turn, generates a 10-ms positive pulse.

The positive pulse from IC1-B thus occurs at the end of the time delay interval, an interval set by the time constant of IC1-A.

The timing can be initiated by any of the start or stop circuits described thus far in this chapter, provided the trigger input of IC1-A sees a negative-going or active-low pulse that has a duration less than the time constant of R1 and C1.

The whole timing operation can be locked out by pulling the $\overline{\text{LOCK}}$ terminal (pin 4 of IC1-A) to logic 0. This terminal must be connected to +5V if the lockout feature is not to be used.

A Design Example

Before leaving the subject of start/stop controls, it is important to take a close look at how these circuits can be combined to yield the desired control effect. There are countless possibilities, using just the circuits described here. If you are willing to add a few more gates and passive components, you will find you are in a position to create just about any sort of control scheme you will ever want.

The following discussion is intended to lead the reader through a control design procedure, step by step. Although the discussion is built around one particular example, the methods employed can be applied to any sort of design situation for game controls.

The first step is to determine precisely what the control scheme is supposed to do. A flow chart is helpful here. The flow chart in Fig. 6-5a illustrates the operation of a start/stop control scheme that has the following characteristics.

The player is to initiate a game or game cycle by depressing a START pushbutton. As soon as the button is depressed, it should be locked out until the cycle is completed. The flow chart thus shows a manual start operation at the beginning of the cycle, followed immediately by a switch lockout operation.

As the START switch is locked out, the game begins. It isn't important what the game is at this point. Whatever the game might do, there always comes a time when it should be reset. Suppose, for example, the START switch launches a rocket figure on the screen. The moment the switch is depressed, the rocket begins to move,

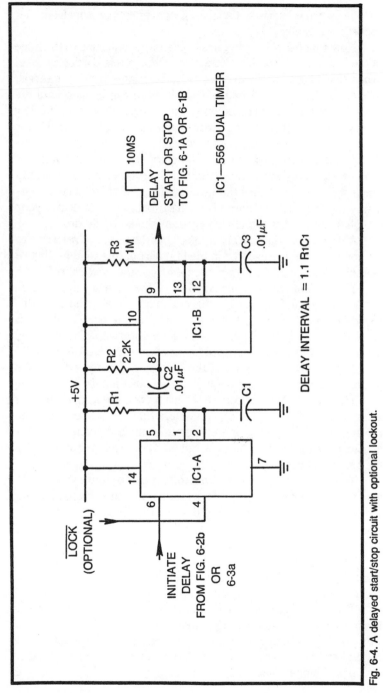

Fig. 6-4. A delayed start/stop circuit with optional lockout.

and the switch is locked out so that the player cannot launch another rocket for a while.

Now suppose the rocket misses its target and runs to the edge of the screen. That is the RESET condition in this particular case. When that happens, the control system initiates a delay interval, let's say a delay of 5 seconds. Nothing more can happen until the delay interval is over, but as soon as that time period lapses, the flow chart shows that the START switch is unlocked, thereby making it possible to restart another launch cycle.

Working out a good flow chart for start/stop controls can save a lot of hassle, time, and money later on. Time spent working out the simplest flow chart is thus time well spent. Perhaps equally important is the fact that building a flow chart forces you to clarify your thoughts about what the control system should really do.

After building the flow chart, block out the process, referring to the control circuits presented in the first part of this section. Figure 6-5b shows a block diagram generated from the flow chart.

The system calls for a manual START switch that can be locked out. The circuit in Fig. 6-2c fits this notion quite well. And since this particular start circuit generates positive-going pulses, the R-S flip-flop in Fig. 6-1b falls into place quite naturally. The inverted output of this flip-flop is then used for locking out the START switch.

The noninverted output of the R-S flip-flop stage enables the game, whatever that game might be. The exact nature of the game isn't relevant to the procedure at hand, but we can assume it eventually generates a set of parameters that call for resetting the controls. This reset parameter output from the game can thus initiate and automatically stop operation. The circuit in Fig. 6-3a fits the bill in this case.

The negative-going pulse from the auto stop circuit should then initiate a time delay of 5 seconds, and when that interval has lapsed, the positive-going pulse from Fig. 6-4 can reset the start-up flip-flop. The game is thus restarted and the START switch is enabled so the player can initiate another cycle.

The block diagram in Fig. 6-5b thus transforms the basic flow chart into a less abstract form. The next step is to make up a preliminary schematic diagram.

The preliminary schematic shown in Fig. 6-6 merely replaces the blocks in Fig. 6-5b with the circuits specified for those blocks. The primary objective is to see what types of semiconductors are needed and how many have to be used. There is no real need to assign pin numbers and component values other than those that are

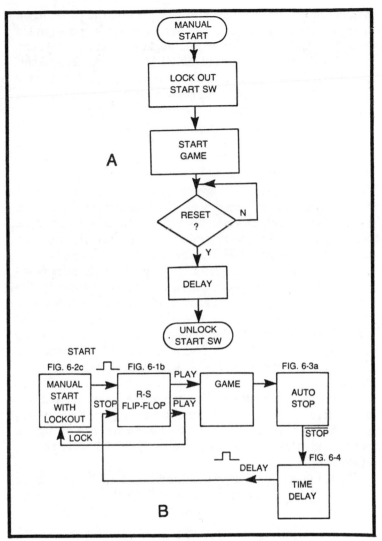

Fig. 6-5. Basic flowchart for control circuit designs. (a) A typical scheme using manual start and automatic reset with time delay. (b) Corresponding block diagram.

peculiar to the system being designed. In this case, the only unique control parameter is the length of the reset time delay. We have specified 5 seconds, so the preliminary schematic shows the values of R and C that are appropriate for this delay interval, 470 kΩ and 10 μF.

Another problem became apparent while setting up the preliminary drawing. This particular scheme ought to have a power-on initializing circuit. Without this power-on feature, the player might find he cannot initiate the game as soon as power is applied to the circuit. The flip-flop, in other words, might take on an initial state whereby the game is enabled and the START switch is locked out. This leads to the awkward possibility of never being able to get the game started. Of course different kinds of games present different start-up conditions, depending on the nature of the game, itself.

The little circuit in Fig. 6-6b shows a power-on reset circuit that can be inserted between the output of the time delay circuit and the STOP input of the R-S flip-flop. When power is first applied to the game, the 0.01-μF capacitor pulls the input of an inverter to logic 0 for several microseconds. The inverter's output thus rises to logic 1 for that interval, guaranteeing a logic-0 output from the NOR gate. This pulse is then inverted again and applied to the STOP input of the R-S flip-flop. Any reset pulses to that flip-flop come only from the delay circuit, once the system has been initialized after turn-on.

The most important reason for working out a preliminary drawing, however, is to give the designer an opportunity to optimize the number of IC chips required. As shown in the preliminary drawing in Fig. 6-6a, the circuit requires a total of 6 ICs: one package each of 2-input NORs, 2-input NANDs, 4-input NANDs and inverters, and two packages of 556 dual timers. Using so many different kinds of IC logic packages, however, leaves plenty of spares. See the table in Fig. 6-6.

Note that the circuit calls for only three inverters, and that there are three NAND gates left over. Why not replace the inverters with NAND-gate versions of them. That eliminates one package of inverters and makes more efficient use of the NAND gates already available.

Then, too, it is quite likely the game circuit will contain a spare 4-input NAND gate. That kind of gate at the input of the auto-stop circuit can be eliminated from the control circuit, leaving the job to be done on the game board, itself. That eliminates another IC package from the control circuit.

Now the circuit requires only four IC packages. The final step in the design procedure is to redraw the schematic, incorporating the modifications just described. The final circuit appears in Fig. 6-7.

After studying the flow diagram, block diagram, and preliminary schematic, you should have no trouble understanding the operation of the control circuit in Fig. 6-7. R8 and C6 make up the power-on initializing circuit, ensuring the START switch is enabled the moment power is first applied. Depressing the START switch then enables the game. And whenever the RESET input indicates a

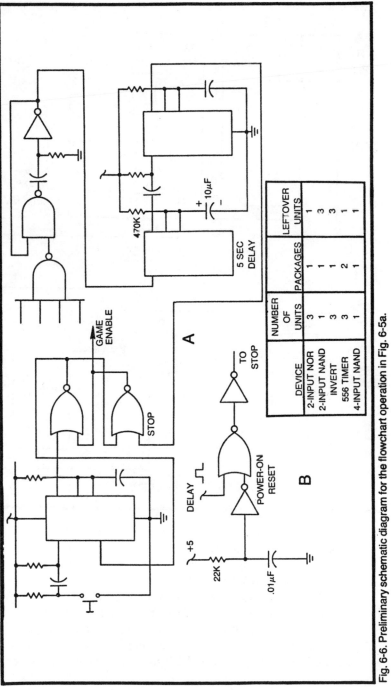

DEVICE	NUMBER OF UNITS	PACKAGES	LEFTOVER UNITS
2-INPUT NOR	3	1	1
2-INPUT NAND	1	1	3
INVERT	3	1	3
556 TIMER	3	2	1
4-INPUT NAND	1	1	1

Fig. 6-6. Preliminary schematic diagram for the flowchart operation in Fig. 6-5a.

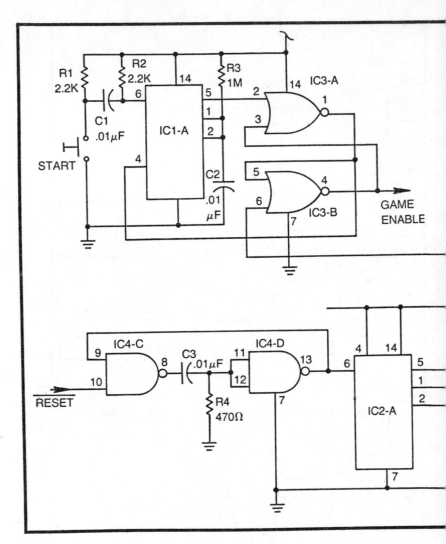

condition in the game that calls for resetting the system, it initiates the 5-second delay interval at IC2-A. After that interval is over, IC2-B generates a pulse that ultimately triggers pin 6 of IC3-B to disable the game and unlock the START switch circuit.

It would be a good idea to dream up a few control systems of your own, following the procedures outlined here. This same procedure, in a somewhat more elaborate form, is quite necessary for planning entire game systems. Get the procedure clear in your mind now, and you'll find you have a powerful design tool at your disposal later on.

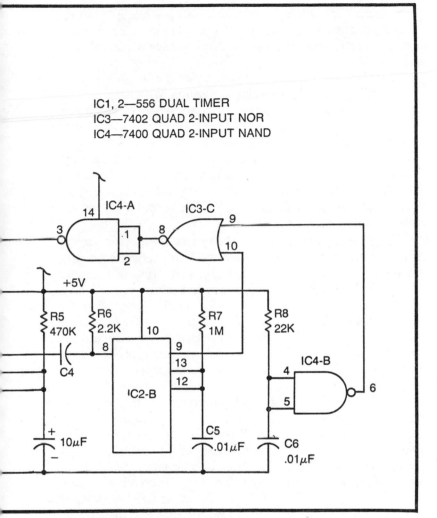

IC1, 2—556 DUAL TIMER
IC3—7402 QUAD 2-INPUT NOR
IC4—7400 QUAD 2-INPUT NAND

Fig. 6-7. Finalized schematic for the control operation described in connection with the flowchart in Fig. 6-5a.

FIGURE-CONTACT-SENSING CIRCUITS

Most TV games are designed so that they carry out an automatic operation whenever two or more figures come into contact with one another on the screen. Suppose you are working up an auto racing game. The cycle begins with your opponents' cars moving rapidly across the screen. And your job is to accelerate your car, moving into the traffic without touching any of the other cars. If you are setting up this game right, things will start getting a little hairy as

195

you begin moving your car faster than the others—one little slip and whamo!—you brush against one of the other cars, there is an explosion, and the game is reset so that you have to start all over again.

One of the key operations in this particular example is sensing contact with one of the other racing-car figures. What happens after that depends on the kind of control circuitry you devise. The important thing right now is providing a means for sensing a critical contact between two or more figures on the screen.

The figures on the screen are generally generated separately, using the schemes already outlined in Chapters 3 and 4. The images are ORed together to produce a composite video signal. Contact sensing must take place ahead of the last ORing operation, and it is basically an ANDing logic operation.

The little circuit in Fig. 6-8a shows how this contact-sensing AND operation can be applied when the figure generators output active-low (black-on-white) data. In this case, both inputs must be at logic 0 before the NOR gate outputs a logic-1 contact signal. This is an active-low, or negative-logic, AND operation. Whenever the images for A and B are not in contact with one another, the CON output in Fig. 6-8a rests at logic 0. When images A and B touch one another, however, the CON output begins generating positive-going pulses at the horizontal scan rate of the system (about 15,750 Hz).

The circuit in Fig. 6-8b shows how the contact-sensing circuit can be implemented. Images A and B are generated by the appropriate combinations of H- and V-count data applied to the inputs of IC1-A and IC1-B respectively. The outputs of these two NAND gates represent inverted, or black-on-white, versions of images A and B. These images are then ORed by means of a NAND gate, IC2-A. (Remember that inverted signals applied to a NAND gate yields an ORing effect.) The GAME VID output thus contains the video information for presenting both images A and B on the screen.

The inputs to IC3-A, however, are taken directly from the two image-generating NAND gates. IC3-A is the contact sensing circuit already described in connection with Fig. 6-8a. Whenever images A and B touch one another on the screen, their video data is lining up such that the CON output is showing positive active-high pulses. These pulses cannot occur at any other time.

In short, the circuit in Fig. 6-8b generates video information for two different images, combines them into a single composite game video signal and senses any contact between the two images.

The circuit in Fig. 6-8c performs the same function as that in Fig. 6-8a. In this latter example, however, the video data for the two

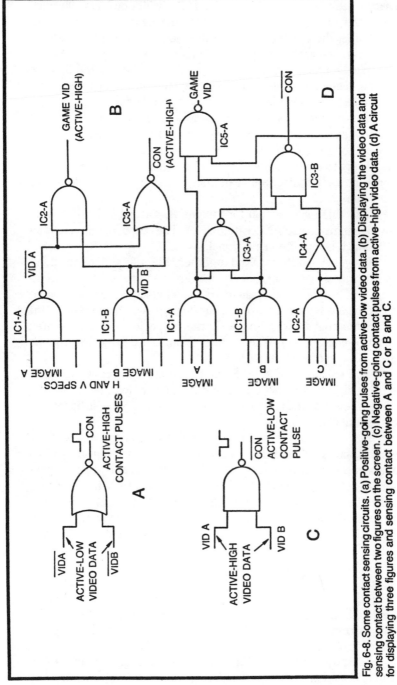

Fig. 6-8. Some contact sensing circuits. (a) Positive-going pulses from active-low video data. (b) Displaying the video data and sensing contact between two figures on the screen. (c) Negative-going contact pulses from active-high video data. (d) A circuit for displaying three figures and sensing contact between A and C or B and C.

images happens to have an active-high (white-on-black) format. Whenever the video data for these two images rise to logic 1 at the same time, the $\overline{CON}$ output generates negative-going (active-low) contact pulses at the horizontal-scanning rate.

Whether you should use the circuit in Fig. 6-8a or Fig. 6-8c for sensing contact between two figures depends on whether the available image information is active low or active high.

The circuit in Fig. 6-8d is simply another example of how contact-sensing circuits can be applied. In this instance, it is more efficient to use the NAND-gate sensing circuit from Fig. 6-8c. Here, the idea is to sense contact between images A and C or B and C. Apparently any contact between images A and B is not relevant to the game.

The video information for images A, B, and C is effectively ORed at the 3-input NAND gate, IC5-A. The output of this gate is an active-high composite game signal.

Images A and B are ORed together at IC3-A, and the resulting active-high signal is applied to one input of the contact-sensing circuit, IC3-B. The other input to this contact-sensing gate is an active-high version of image C. Thus if image A or image B (or both) come into contact with image C, the output of IC3-B generates negative-going pulses. When neither A nor B are touching image C, the $\overline{CON}$ output rests at logic 1.

The circuits in Figs. 6-8a and 6-8c are "universal" contact-sensing circuits. Figures 6-8b and 6-8d merely illustrate where the contact sensors are inserted into the game scheme and, incidentally, two specific applications.

Before leaving the subject of contact sensing, why not try working out a scheme that includes some contact sensing and an automatically controlled response. The flow chart in Fig. 6-9a represents a portion of a game where contact between two images causes one of them to be blanked from the screen. This might be part of a target game where the player launches a rocket at a moving target. If the rocket touches the target, the target is blanked from the screen until some reset action is initiated.

According to the flowchart, the target (image A) is reset so that it appears on the screen. The play then begins, and continues until image B touches the target. When the contact occurs, image A is blanked from the screen. The circles at the top and bottom of the flow chart imply that these operations are just part of a larger game and control scheme.

The flow chart is translated into a block diagram in Fig. 6-9b. The information for image A must pass through a gate before it is

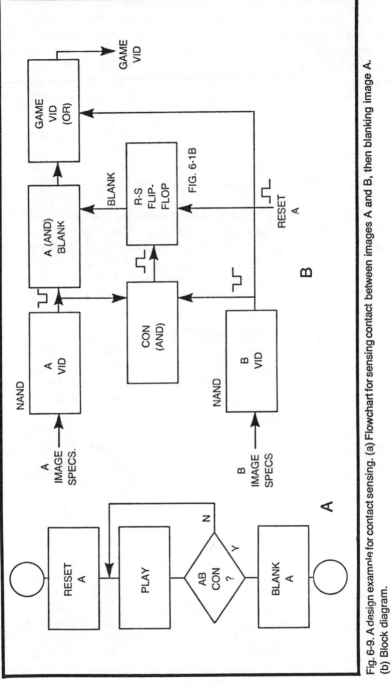

Fig. 6-9. A design example for contact sensing. (a) Flowchart for sensing contact between images A and B, then blanking image A. (b) Block diagram.

combined with the data for image B to produce a composite video signal. As long as this gate is open, both images can appear on the screen. Closing the gate, however, blanks image A from the screen, but lets image B remain.

The blanking operation is controlled by an R-S flip-flop circuit. In this instance, it is the circuit shown earlier in Fig. 6-1b. Now the flip-flop is controlled by positive-pulse inputs from the contact sensing circuit and some sort of outside reset circuit.

When the game is reset, the state of the flip-flop is set such that the A blank gate is open, allowing image A data to appear on the screen. The first contact-sensing pulse from the contact sensor, however, sets the flip-flop to a state where the A image is blanked off.

With the flow chart and block diagram completed, the next step is to work out a preliminary schematic diagram. This diagram, along with an analysis of the type and number of logic gates required, appears in Fig. 6-10a. See if you can properly relate the gate circuits in Fig. 6-10a with the operations specified in the block diagram.

The final schematic diagram in Fig. 6-10b shows how this whole operation can be implemented with three ICs.

INITIALIZING FIGURE MOTION CONTROLS

Games and game cycles often begin with certain figures placed at particular places on the screen. Such figures must be set to those initial positions whenever some critical event occurs. In the case of a table-tennis game, the ball is set to an initial position for serving purposes. It is then served, and if the player misses it, the ball travels to one side of the screen where it then disappears, being served again from the opposite side of the screen. The critical event in this case occurs when the ball reaches the opposite side of the screen. When that happens, it is first blanked and then initialized (set to a particular serving position).

Initializing operations are nearly always used in conjunction with figures that move around the screen automatically, although some manually controlled figures use initializing operations as well.

Figure 6-11 shows the basic initializing circuit. It is most often used with vertical- and horizontal-slipping counters, and the basic idea is to select one of two different sources of reset pulses for the counting operation. The two sources of reset pulses are labeled *slipping-counter reset* and *initializing reset* in this case. The slipping-counter reset pulses come from the slipping-counter circuit itself. These are the pulses that are normally used for resetting the counter to achieve the desired speed and direction of motion. They are directed to the loading inputs of the slipping counter whenever the *initializing control* input is at logic 1.

When the initializing control input is at logic 1, IC1-A is effectively opened so that inverted versions of the slipping-counter reset pulses emerge from its output. While the initializing control is at logic 1, however, inverter IC2-A switches that logic level to 0, as far as the pin-9 input of IC1-C is concerned. IC1-C is thus effectively gated off, thereby preventing any initializing reset pulses from reaching IC1-B. Setting the initializing control input to logic 1 blocks any incoming initializing reset pulses, but allows negative-going slipping-counter reset pulses to appear at the output of IC1-B. These pulses are applied to the loading line of the slipping-counter circuit, letting it operate in its normal, motion-generating mode.

Setting the initializing control input to logic 0 completely changes the situation. In this case, IC1-A is gated off by the logic-0 level appearing at its pin-2 input, but IC1-C is gated on by virtue of the logic-1 level now appearing at its pin-9 input. Inverted versions of the initializing reset pulses thus appear at the output of IC1-B.

In short, the circuit in Fig. 6-11 is simply a digital selector circuit. It selects one of two sources of reset pulses, depending on the logic level present at the initializing control input.

Note how this selector circuit is applied to a vertical-slipping counter in Fig. 6-12. As long as the INTC (initializing-control) input is at logic 1, IC3-B is gated on, and the normal reset pulses from IC3-A appear at the output of IC3-C and the load inputs of the counters. The circuit thus operates in its normal slipping-counter mode as long as INTC = 1.

Changing INTC to logic 0 gates off IC3-A, however, and delivers an alternate set of reset pulses to the load inputs of the counters. These reset pulses at the INTP input generally come from the Sourcebox unit, so they always occur at some particular vertical position on the screen. And when these pulses are applied to the slipping counter, it follows that the counter will be reset at that particular point on the screen.

There can be no motion effect from the slipping counter as long as it is being reset from INTP, even if the VC inputs are set for fast motion in either direction. Motion begins only when INTC is set to logic 1, thereby allowing the counters to be reset in the normal fashion from IC3-A.

Why not breadboard the circuit in Fig. 6-12 and try it for yourself. For the purposes of this experiment, connect VRST from the Sourcebox through an inverter to the INTP connection. Whenever the figure is to be initialized (INTC set to logic 0), the

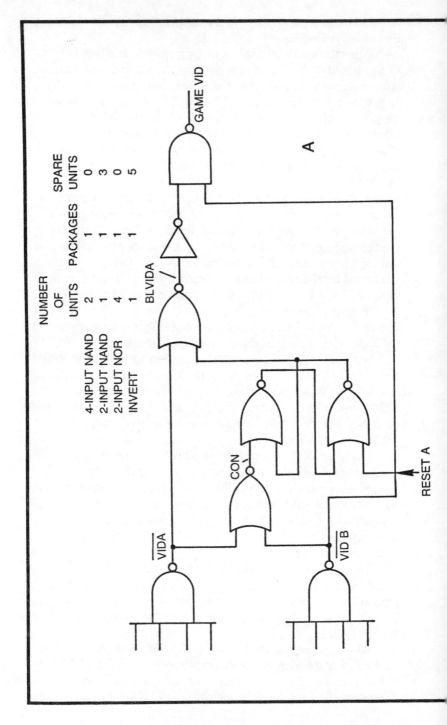

	NUMBER OF UNITS	PACKAGES	SPARE UNITS
4-INPUT NAND	2	1	0
2-INPUT NAND	1	1	3
2-INPUT NOR	4	1	0
INVERT	1	1	5

GAME VID

BLVIDA

CON

VIDA

VID B

RESET A

A

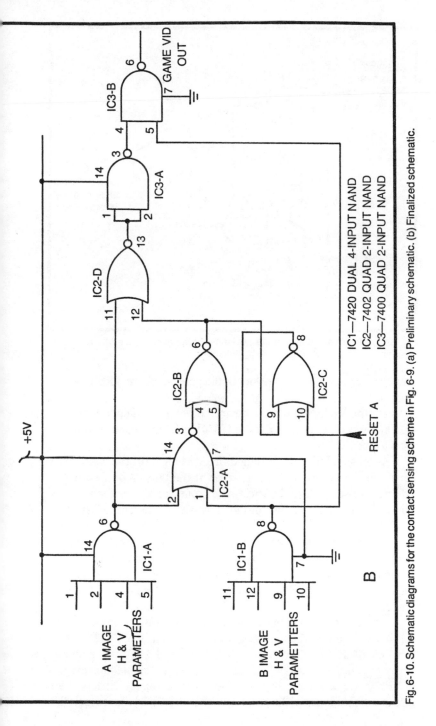

Fig. 6-10. Schematic diagrams for the contact sensing scheme in Fig. 6-9. (a) Preliminary schematic. (b) Finalized schematic.

IC1—7420 DUAL 4-INPUT NAND
IC2—7402 QUAD 2-INPUT NAND
IC3—7400 QUAD 2-INPUT NAND

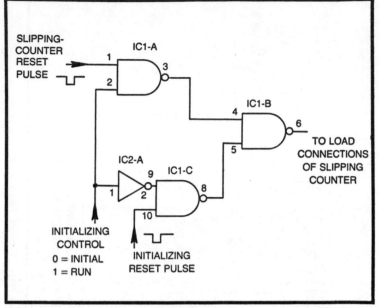

Fig. 6-11. Circuit for initializing the position of a figure generated by a slipping counter.

counters will reset at the bottom of the screen where VRST always occurs.

Set the VC inputs for any desired direction and speed (see the data in Fig. 5-13), feed VM128 to GAME VID IN, and use a jumper wire for grounding INTC.

As long as INTC is grounded (fixed at logic 0), the wide white bar on the screen should appear fixed at the bottom of the screen. Whenever INTC is disconnected from ground and connected to +5V (logic 1), the bar moves in a direction and at a speed determined by the VC inputs.

You can interrupt the motion and reset the position of the bar to the bottom of the screen at any time by simply connecting INTC to ground again. Connecting INTC to logic 0 initializes the position of the bar figure—initializes its position at the bottom of the screen in this case.

You can actually initialize the position of the bar anywhere on the screen you want by choosing a different source of INTP pulses. Try NANDing together 128V, 64V, 32V, and 16V, for example. Apply the output of this NAND gate to the INTP connection instead of VRST. You will find that the broad bar takes on an initial position just above the center of the screen whenever INTC is set to logic 0.

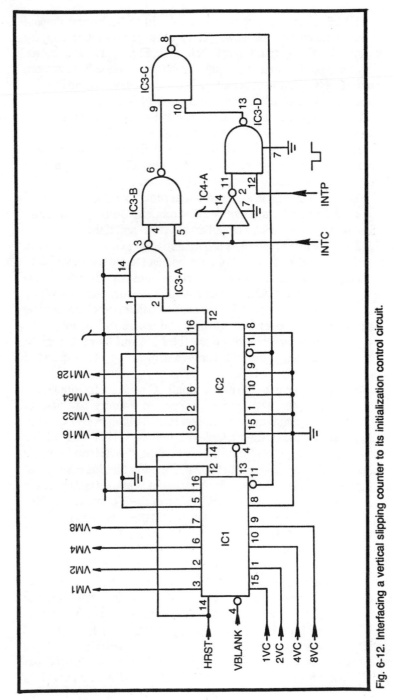

Fig. 6-12. Interfacing a vertical slipping counter to its initialization control circuit.

The initializing control can be used with a horizontal-slipping counter in much the same way it is used with vertical-slipping counters. See Fig. 6-13a. Using the circuit in Fig. 5-14 as a model for horizontal-slipping counters, simply break the connection between the output of IC5-A (the gate that signals a normal reset) and the load bus line to pin 11 of ICs 1 and 2 and pin 3 of IC3-A.

Any image generated by the horizontal-slipping counter will be initialized by INTP in Fig. 6-13a as long as the INTC input is at logic 0. Changing the status of INTP to logic 1 shifts the counter's reset operation to the output of IC5-A, thereby allowing the motion specified by the slipping counter's VC inputs.

Many TV games call for figures that move with both horizontal and vertical components of motion. The motion-control board in Fig. 5-15 is a natural choice for a circuit in this case; and if the circuit is to include an initializing feature, a pair of initializing controls, one each for horizontal and vertical motion, can be inserted in the reset line.

Using the initialization-control circuit described thus far requires three 2-input NAND gates and an inverter, and that would mean using a total of six NAND gates and two inverters for achieving initialization control over both vertical and horizontal motion of the same figure. It is possible to reduce the IC count by replacing the NAND-gate version of the initializing control with a 74157 quad 2:1 multiplexer. See Fig. 6-13b.

The circuit in Fig. 6-13b uses a single IC package for simultaneously controlling the initialization process of a figure having both vertical- and horizontal-motion components. As long as INTC in Fig. 6-13b is set to logic 0, the multiplexer selects VINTP and HINTP inputs (initializing pulses) for the vertical- and horizontal-slipping counters on the motion-control board. The effect in this case is that the figure generated by these slipping counters stands motionless in its initial position, regardless of the status of the VC and HC inputs.

Setting INTC in Fig. 6-13b to logic 1, on the other hand, lets the multiplexer deliver $\overline{HMRST}$ and $\overline{VMRST}$ pulses for the $\overline{HML}$ and $\overline{VML}$ inputs of the motion-control board. The figure thus moves in a direction and at a speed determined by the HC and VC inputs.

Serious experimenters might find it very instructive to breadboard the initializing-control circuit in Fig. 6-13b and attach it to the motion-control board in Fig. 5-15. Generate the desired figure from the VM and HM outputs of the slipping counters while the control circuit is initializing them. The most convenient source of initializing pulses is inverted versions of HRST and VRST from the Sourcebox. Simply apply an inverted version of HRST to the HINTP input in Fig.

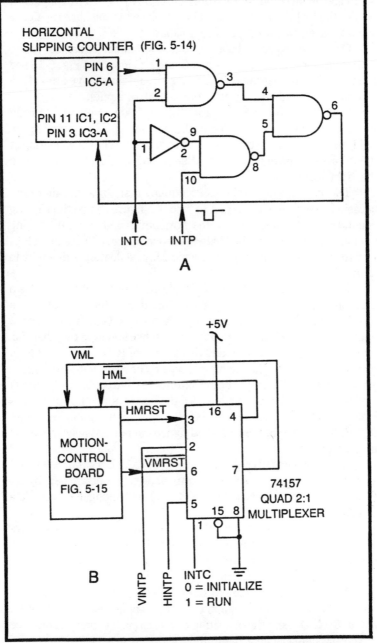

Fig. 6-13. More initialization controls. (a) Interfacing a horizontal slipping counter to an initialization control circuit. (b) Interfacing a complete motion control circuit to a horizontal and vertical initialization control that uses a quad 2:1 multiplexer.

6-13b and an inverted VRST from Sourcebox to the VINT input. Of course the INTC terminal should be grounded to initialize the figure and hold it steady while you are building it.

Once the figure is built to your own satisfaction, set some motion-control commands to the VC and HC inputs of Fig. 5-15 and remove INTC from ground. The figure should then move around the screen as prescribed by your motion-control inputs.

You should notice that the figure folds over very nicely whenever it reaches one edge of the screen. If it is moving to the right, for instance, the front part of the figure will begin appearing at the left-hand edge of the screen while the tail end is still moving into the right-hand edge.

This can be a desirable effect in many instances, but there are occasions where it is important to "hide" a figure. Since the slipping counters are disabled through the horizontal- and vertical-blanking intervals, figures cannot be hidden in those spaces. There must be a way to hide figures on occasions, especially while they are resting in their initial positions.

Figure 6-14 shows a rather simple control circuit that blanks a movable figure while it is resting in its initial position. You will note a flip-flop circuit composed of IC1-A and IC1-C. Whenever a negative-going $\overline{RESET}$ pulse occurs, the flip-flop is set so that the output of IC1-A is at logic 0 and the output of IC1-C is at logic 1. In this *reset* condition, the slipping counter sees the initializing reset arriving at the INTP input. For all intents and purposes, the figure is stationary in its initial position. At the same time, however, the logic-0 level from IC1-A gates off the figure-generating logic gate IC2-B. The image of the initialized figure cannot possibly appear on the screen.

Applying a negative-going pulse to IC1-A alters the operation, allowing the slipping counter to run at a rate determined by its control inputs (not shown in Fig. 6-14) and unblanking the image data from IC2-B.

Any figure generated by the slipping counter thus disappears from the screen the moment it is set to its initial position. It then remains invisible until a cycle is started; then it becomes a visible moving object on the screen.

An astute reader who has been following this discussion carefully might now be seeing some important applications of the circuit in Fig. 6-14. Doesn't the operation of this circuit remind you of some of the missile-launching operations included in some of the more popular commercial TV games?

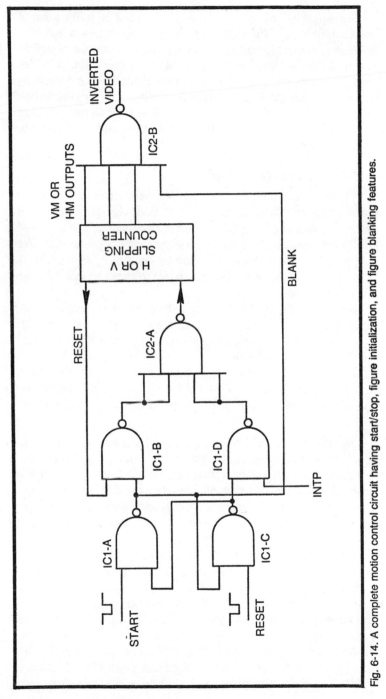

Fig. 6-14. A complete motion control circuit having start/stop, figure initialization, and figure blanking features.

Perhaps it is time to get off the pabulum and on to the meat of TV-game design. The following section describes a missile-launching game that incorporates all the control features described thus far in this chapter. You will find that the game action is rather nice, but the range of controls is somewhat limited. After describing this basic missile-attack game, we will return to a further discussion of more-elaborate initialization controls. These more sophisticated controls will then add an extra touch of interest and excitement to the basic missile game.

A BASIC MISSILE ATTACK GAME

The missile attack game described here uses two movable figures tentatively labeled image A and B. Image B is the attack missile that moves across the screen horizontally at a fixed speed and altitude (the altitude and speed will be made programmable later on.) Image B is the antiballistic missile that is launched vertically by the player. The object of the game is to hit the attack missile with the antiballistic missile.

Figure 6-15a is a flow chart for the basic missile attack controls. The cycle is started as the player launches the antiballistic missile, image A. Presumably, the attack missile is appearing at the left-hand side of the screen at the time.

If A = B (if the two images come into contact), the attack missile is blanked from the screen (BLANK B), and the antiballistic missile is reset to its initial position near the bottom center of the screen.

Whether B is hit or not, it continues its horizontal motion across the screen. If it has been hit, it is blanked (invisible). But in any case, the motion continues until it reaches the right-hand side of the screen (B = EDGE). As soon as B reaches the edge of the screen, it is unblanked so that it becomes visible; and since its left-to-right motion is continuous, it immediately appears in its attack position at the left-hand edge of the screen.

That's what happens if the player launches B so that it strikes the attack missile. But what happens if the player misses the missile?

If the player misses the attack missile, image B continues to move upward until it reaches the top of the screen (A = TOP). At that moment, the position of that missile is initialized (INITIALIZE A) and ready for the next attack. If missed, the attack missile remains visible as it moves to the right-hand edge of the screen.

Of course it is easy to begin beating this game every time since the attack missile flies at a fixed altitude and speed. You can,

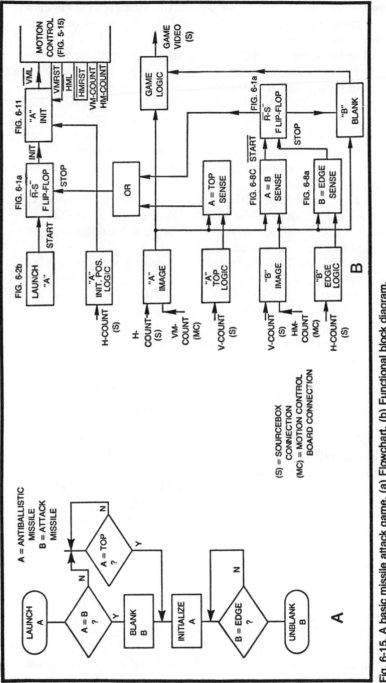

Fig. 6-15. A basic missile attack game. (a) Flowchart. (b) Functional block diagram.

211

however, add some interest by changing the attack missile's motion parameters. But that is the subject of the refinements described later in this chapter.

The block diagram in Fig. 6-15b shows the main control elements for this missile attack game. The circuit has only one control input, the LAUNCH "A" block in the upper left-hand corner of the diagram. The sole output is the GAME VIDEO terminal at the center right. Also note that the system uses the slipping-counter-motion-control board from Fig. 5-15. The vertical counter on that board fixes the speed and direction of the image A antiballistic missile, while the horizontal-slipping counter fixes the motion of the image B attack missile.

The purpose of most of the blocks in Fig. 6-15b can be related to the flow chart. Some of the blocks perform operations that are outside the realm of direct control operations, so we ought to take a moment to look at them a bit closer.

The "A" IMAGE block, for instance, generates the image of the antiballistic missile. Since this little rectangular figure moves in the vertical direction only, the only slipping-counter inputs required are those for generating the figure's vertical-position information—some VM count signals from the motion-control board. The figure's horizontal position is fixed by H-count pulses from the Sourcebox.

The "B" IMAGE block performs the same general function, generating the attack-missile image. In this case, the motion is in a horizontal direction, so this block must include HM inputs from the motion-control board. V-count signals from the Sourcebox fix the missile's vertical position, or altitude.

The game must include provisions for sensing a contact between the antiballistic missile and the top of the screen. Recall that this event occurs only when the missile is fired, but misses the attack missile. The "top of the screen" is defined by the "A" TOP LOGIC block, and is based purely on V-count data from the Sourcebox unit.

And finally, there must be some means for sensing a contact between the attack missile and the right-hand side of the screen. The "B" EDGE LOGIC block defines the right-hand side of the screen, and this is a simple matter of NANDing together the appropriate H-count signals from the Sourcebox.

A preliminary analysis of the circuit shows that two circuit boards are required for this particular game. One board is the motion-control board shown in Fig. 5-15, and the other is the game control scheme in Fig. 6-16.

Most of the circuitry in Fig. 6-16 can be related directly to the block diagram and then to specific control circuits described earlier in this chapter. The missile launching and initializing circuits, for example, appear at the top of the schematic diagram. The six NAND gates and two inverters are simply one-for-one combinations of the simpler circuits specified in the block diagram for LAUNCH "A", $\overline{\text{R-S}}$ FLIP-FLOP, and "A" INIT.

IC8-A defines the vertical information for the antiballistic missile. And using the three VM inputs specified at the input of IC8-A, it generates a movable horizontal bar that is 32VM pulses tall. The horizontal position of the antiballistic missile is taken from the point on the screen where 256H makes the transition from black to white, near the middle of the screen. This 256H signal from the Sourcebox is inverted by IC6-C to create a negative-going edge that triggers the pulse-shortening circuit composed of IC2-C and IC7-E. The value of C2 determines the width of the image. A value of 0.002 μF is specified here, but you might want to change that value to generate a figure width more suitable to your own ideas about how the figure should look.

The vertical and horizontal components for the antiballistic missile figure are effectively ANDed together in IC5-A, and an inverted (black-on-white) version of the figure is sent to a NAND gate (IC3-C), where it is uprighted and combined with the attack-missile figure.

The attack-missile figure is generated in a similar fashion. Its movable horizontal components are defined by the HM inputs to IC9-A. This particular set of HM inputs create an image that is 32HM pulses long in the horizontal direction. You might want to double its length by omitting the 32HM connection to IC9-A.

IC2-D is responsible for fixing the altitude of the attack missile. The inputs in this case are $\overline{128V}$ and 64V from the Sourcebox. These particular inputs, working in conjunction with the pulse-shortening circuit made up of IC3-A and IC7-B, create a thin horizontal line about one-fourth the distance from the top of the screen. This fixes the altitude of the attack missile. The vertical height of the attack missile can be adjusted by means of C3. IC5-B combines the horizontal and vertical components of the attack-missile figure.

The attack-missile figure must pass through IC4-D before it can be combined with the antiballistic missile at IC3-C. The image of the attack missile will indeed appear at GAME VID OUT as long as pin 14 of IC4-D is at logic 1. If there is ever a contact between the two missile images, as sensed by IC4-A, pin 14 of IC4-D drops to logic 0, thereby blanking the image of the attack missile from the screen.

The attack missile then remains blanked until its "invisible" image reaches the right-hand side of the screen, as defined by

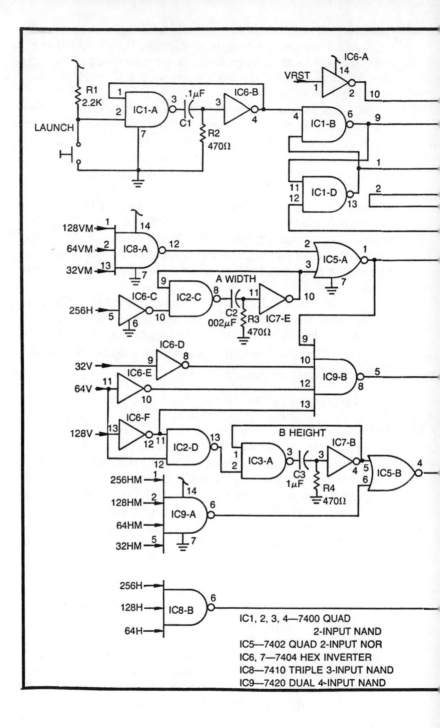

IC1, 2, 3, 4—7400 QUAD
2-INPUT NAND
IC5—7402 QUAD 2-INPUT NOR
IC6, 7—7404 HEX INVERTER
IC8—7410 TRIPLE 3-INPUT NAND
IC9—7420 DUAL 4-INPUT NAND

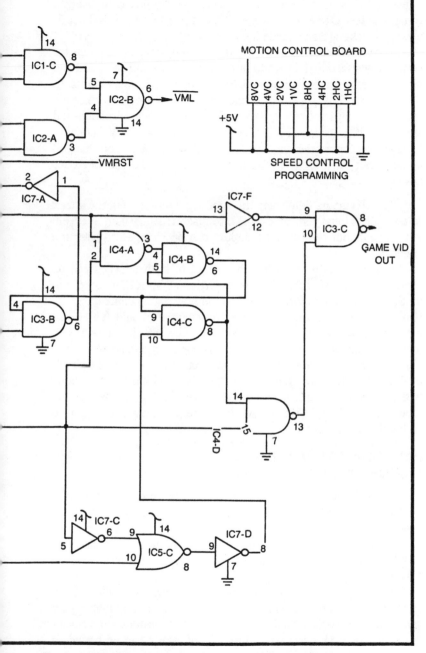

Fig. 6-16. Schematic diagram for the basic missile attack game.

215

IC8-B. IC5-C detects any contact between the attack missile and the right-hand side of the screen, resetting the flip-flop composed of IC4-B and IC4-C to a state where pin 14 of IC4-D returns to logic 1, unblanking the attack-missile image once again.

The insert in Fig. 6-16 shows a suggested set of connections for setting the speed and direction of the two missiles. The speed and direction of the antiballistic missile are set by the VC connections. In this case, 8VC must remain connected to +5V (logic 1) to make certain it always moves upward. (See the vertical direction and speed specifications in Fig. 5-13.) The three remaining VC connections are set for a rather high launch velocity. These can be changed to suit your own ideas about how fast the rocket should rise, however.

The HC inputs determine the speed and direction of the attack missile. 8HC must remain at logic 0 to make the missile move from left to right, but the other HC inputs can be changed to alter the speed.

Incidentally, the fact that the speed of both missiles can be changed by modifying the three lower-order VC and HC inputs to the motion-control board foreshadows some interesting control circuits to be described in the next section of this chapter. Wouldn't it be nice if the game were expanded so that two players can compete by manually adjusting the speed of their respective missiles?

The entire circuit in Fig. 6-16 çan be constructed on a 44-pin, 4-by 4-inch circuit board (Radio Shack 276-153). Then the board, along with the motion-control board described in Fig. 5-15, can be mounted in a simple Gamebox unit. The Gamebox can then be plugged into the plug receptacle on the Sourcebox.

PROGRAMMING VARIABLE INITIAL POSITIONS, SPEED AND DIRECTION

Virtually all of the motion-control circuits described thus far in this chapter have fixed initial-position parameters as well as a fixed speed and direction program. It turns out to be rather simple, however, to make the initial positions, figure speed, and direction programmable, either by a player or by the internal game-control system.

Take, for example, the missile-attack game described in the last section. It is possible to add a lot more interest by making the attack missile programmable as far as the attack altitude and velocity are concerned. Of course the direction of attack can be varied as well, but that wouldn't be altogether appropriate in this case.

Then consider the typical table-tennis game. Whenever the ball is served, the machine ought to be able to set the ball's vertical position and direction just before the serving operation takes place.

The circuits described in this chapter show how to program a wide variety of initial positions, speeds, and directions. The examples are oriented toward manual, or player, controls, but it turns out that the schemes for automatically setting these parameters aren't much different.

Programming the Initial Position

The circuit in Fig. 6-17 shows four SPDT switches, labeled A through D, each connected to one input of an EXCLUSIVE OR gate. The second input to each of the gates goes to a source of count pulses from the Sourcebox, 32H, 64H, 128H, and 256H in this particular example. The outputs of the four EXCLUSIVE OR gates are NANDed together at a 4-input NAND gate, IC2-A.

One of the most useful properties of an EXCLUSIVE OR gate is that it can operate as an inverter or noninverter, depending on the logic level presented to the second input. Consider IC1-D in Fig. 6-17. Whenever the A switch is set to its "1" position, the 32H signal applied to the other input emerges from the gate with the same phase as the input. Setting switch A to its "0" position, however, causes IC1-D to invert its 32H input.

An EXCLUSIVE OR gate thus passes a noninverted version of its signal input whenever the control input is at logic 1, but it inverts the signal whenever the control input is at logic 0.

The circuit in Fig. 6-17 is capable of generating vertical bars on the screen that are 32H wide and positioned at any 1 of 16 different locations. The table accompanying the schematic shows all possible combinations of switch settings and the output specifications that result. If, for example, $D = 0$ while $C = B = A = 1$, the effect would be the same as applying $\overline{256H}$, 128H, 64H, and 32H directly to the inputs of the NAND gate.

If you want to check out this circuit in a rather simple fashion, run the output of the NAND gate through an inverter and to the GAME VID IN connection on the Sourcebox. You will indeed find that you can create a white vertical bar that has a position on the screen determined by the settings of switches A through D. In a sense, this circuit is a switch-programmable line generator. Of course you can apply any combination of H- and V-count inputs to the four signal inputs to create horizontal and vertical lines. You can also expand the circuit to accommodate eight signal inputs by using eight switches, four more EXCLUSIVE OR gates, and a 7430 8-input NAND gate.

The circuits in Fig. 6-18a and 6-18b show how this circuit can be applied to the missile-attack game. The circuit in Fig. 6-18a lets the player adjust the horizontal position of the antiballistic missile. The 256H and 128H inputs to IC10-A fix the positions to a region spanning the middle half of the screen. The player has control over the position of the antiballistic missile within that range by manipulating switches SA, SB, and SC. Using three switches in this manner offers eight different launch positions.

To use this circuit in conjunction with the missile game drawn up in Fig. 6-16, disconnect IC6-C in that circuit, and connect the output of IC11-A in its place. Now you will be able to program the horizontal position of the antiballistic missile, giving you a better chance of shooting down the attack missile. If you manipulate the switches quickly enough, you can actually steer the antiballistic missile while it is in flight.

The circuit in Fig. 6-18b can also be added to the basic missile-attack game. This circuit, however, controls the altitude of the attack missile. The altitude is fixed within the upper third of the screen by the 128V signal that is always inverted by IC12-A before it is applied to NAND gate IC11-B. A player can vary the altitude of the attack missile to any one of eight different positions within that range by means of switches SA through SC.

Incorporating this altitude-programming circuit into the missile-attack game is a matter of disconnecting IC2-D in Fig. 6-16 and connecting the output of IC11-B to pin 2 of IC3-A.

Of course these are merely two specific examples of how the position-selection scheme in Fig. 6-17 can be applied. This circuit is quite useful in any case where you would like to have program control over the horizontal or vertical position of an object on the screen.

The same circuit can also be used for defining the initial position of a movable figure. In this case, the output of the NAND gate is used as the source of initializing pulses. See the block diagram in Fig. 6-18c.

If you would like to check out the operation of this circuit, construct the circuit shown back in Fig. 6-13a, then couple the output of IC2-A in Fig. 6-17 to the INTP input of Fig. 6-13a.

Setting INTC to logic 0, you will find you can program the initial position of any figure generated by the slipping counter. The figure can then be "launched" from that initial position by setting INTC to logic 1.

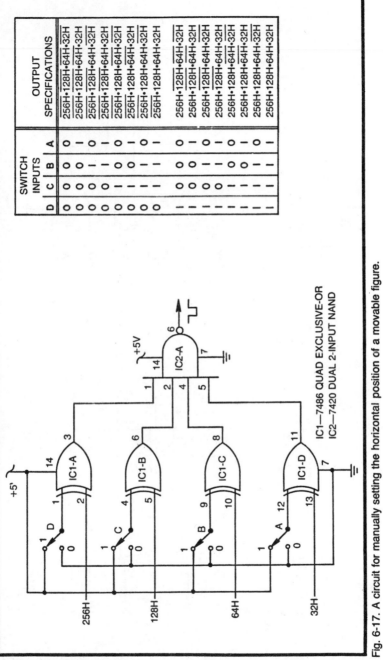

Fig. 6-17. A circuit for manually setting the horizontal position of a movable figure.

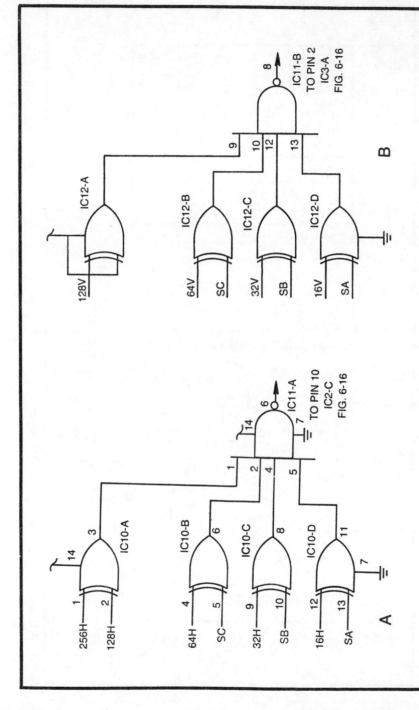

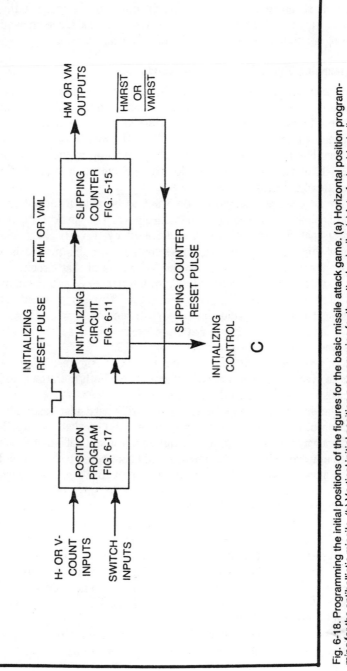

Fig. 6-18. Programming the initial positions of the figures for the basic missile attack game. (a) Horizontal position programming for the antiballistic missile. (b) Vertical initial position programming for the attack missile. (c) Interfacing block diagram.

As described thus far, the circuit in Fig. 6-17 can serve two purposes: It can be used for adjusting the position of a figure on the screen by means of some programming switches, and it can be used for programming the initial position of a movable figure.

Programming Figure Speed and Direction

The circuit for programming the speed and direction of a movable figure is somewhat simpler than the one used for programming initial positions. As indicated in Fig. 6-19a, a set of four SPDT switches can be connected to the VC or HC inputs of a slipping counter. The appropriate motion codes are listed in the tables in Figs. 5-13 and 5-14. All this simple switch circuit does is allow the player to adjust those codes manually.

As an example, suppose you want to be able to adjust the vertical speed and direction of a movable figure. The vertical component of that figure's motion is generated by a vertical-slipping counter (Fig. 5-13). Obtaining some control over this motion is a matter of connecting switches to the VC inputs of that circuit.

If switch A is connected to 1VC, switch B to 2VC, and so on, as illustrated in Fig. 6-19B, the player can set the figure for a rather fast downward motion by adjusting the switches for $A = 1$, $B = 0$, $C = 1$ and $D = 0$. These settings correspond to the fast-downward-motion code specified in Fig. 5-13.

This switch circuit can be used with the basic missile attack game to give the player a choice of speeds for both the attack and antiballistic missiles. See the diagram in Fig. 6-19b.

The directions cannot be changed in this particular case. The direction of the two missiles ought to be fixed so that the attack missile always moves from left to right and the antiballistic missile moves upward. Thus 8VC is permanently connected to logic 1 and 8HC is always connected to logic 0. The other three inputs in each case, however, give one or two players a wide range of speeds— eight different speeds, to be exact.

The speed of the antiballistic missile, for example, is programmable by switches SA, SB, and SC. In a similar fashion, the attack velocity is adjustable by means of switches SD, SE, and SF.

Incorporating this speed-programming circuit into the missile-attack game is a matter of making the switch connections designated in Fig. 6-19b to the corresponding VC and HC slipping counter inputs shown in the insert in Fig. 6-16.

If you have been following these discussions carefully, you ought to be getting at least a mental impression of some incredibly

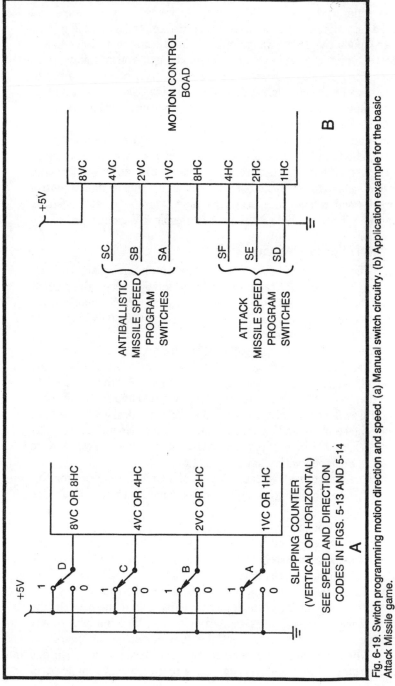

Fig. 6-19. Switch programming motion direction and speed. (a) Manual switch circuitry. (b) Application example for the basic Attack Missile game.

interesting and exciting TV games. Unlike any of the commercial fixed or programmable games on the market today, building your own games gives you a range of game interfacing that grows to any degree of interest and excitement you choose. You certainly aren't limited to a couple of joysticks and one or two pushbuttons. You can devise games having elaborate control terminals sporting a variety of programming switches, launch and firing buttons, blinking warning lights, sirens—the whole works.

You can build your own custom games that are as realistic or far-fetched as your imagination allows. And as clearly demonstrated so far in this chapter, it is possible to begin with a rather simple game format and expand it almost without limit, adding more control circuits and refining the action as time, knowledge and finances permit. Try that with a $200 programmable TV game set!

A Simple Program Memory

The prospect of being able to switch-program initial positions, speeds, and directions can soon lead to a situation where the players face a bewildering array of switches. While it might be neat to work with a lot of switches, having to set a lot of switch positions slows down the action in some cases.

Suppose you devise a game calling for programming the initial position, direction, and speed of a figure that moves in both the horizontal and vertical directions. If the player is allowed complete freedom to choose these parameters, that adds up to 16 different control switches, 4 each for vertical motion, vertical initial position, horizontal motion, and horizontal initial position. Now you might like that idea, but it can be expensive, especially if there are two or more players equipped with such a control panel.

One way to reduce the number of switches required for this sort of game is by using a simple switch-position memory circuit. See Fig. 6-20.

ICs 2 through 5 in this circuit are quad D latches. Any combination of 1s and 0s applied to the four input terminals (pins 2, 3, 6, and 7) will appear immediately at the corresponding outputs (pins 16, 15, 10 and 9) whenever the control inputs (pins 4 and 3) are pulled up to logic 1. When the control input is then returned to logic 0, the outputs retain the same logic levels written into them while the control was at logic 1. The memory circuit is then immune to any changes in the inputs as long as the control remains at logic 0.

Whenever there is a need to switch-program more than one motion parameter, then, it is possible to do the job with a single set of four switches. As shown in the example in Fig. 6-20, a player can enter vertical-motion data by first setting the positions of the data select switches (SA through SD) to the desired combinations of 1s and 0s and *then* depressing the LOAD V MOTION pushbutton for a moment. Depressing that particular button ultimately applies a logic-1 level to the control inputs of IC2, thereby writing that combination of 1s and 0s into the memory. The VC outputs of IC2 then retain that data until the LOAD V MOTION button is depressed again.

Vertical-position data can be entered in the same fashion, depressing LOAD V POSITION in this case.

The data from the select switches can be loaded into the output latches in any desired sequence and at any time. Some specific examples cited later in this book include some special automatic controls for locking out the programming operations through certain critical phases of the game.

THE TAGALONG FEATURE

You might be familiar with commercial TV games that have a movable figure that can be positioned anywhere on the screen by means of a player control. This figure, however, also carries a "missile" of its own. The missile goes wherever the primary figure goes—at least until the player "launches" it.

For our purposes here, we will refer to this notion of one figure being carried along by another as a *tagalong* feature. In a sense, a secondary figure tags along with a primary movable figure until the player somehow indicates the secondary figure should "fly" on its own.

The block diagram in Fig. 6-21a shows how the tagalong feature can be incorporated with a primary figure that moves in a horizontal direction. You can see that this particular circuit calls for two horizontal-slipping-counter circuits, one for the primary figure and another for the secondary, or tagalong, figure.

For the sake of simplicity, the primary figure has no initialization circuitry. And since this is the case, the primary slipping counter generates HM outputs that define a continuous horizontal motion. (Of course the speed and direction of that motion is determined by the primary counter's HC inputs.)

As long as the INTC input to the secondary-figure initialization circuit is set at logic 0, the secondary slipping counter takes its reset pulses from $\overline{\text{HMRST}}$ output of the primary-figure counter. The secondary counter is thus synchronized to the primary counter,

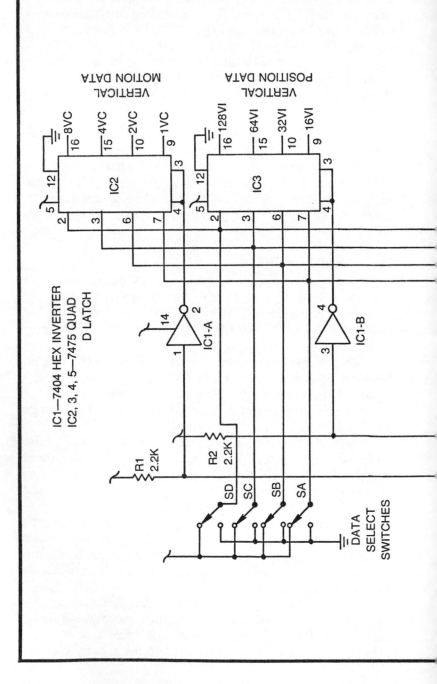

VERTICAL
MOTION DATA

VERTICAL
POSITION DATA

IC1—7404 HEX INVERTER
IC2, 3, 4, 5—7475 QUAD
D LATCH

DATA
SELECT
SWITCHES

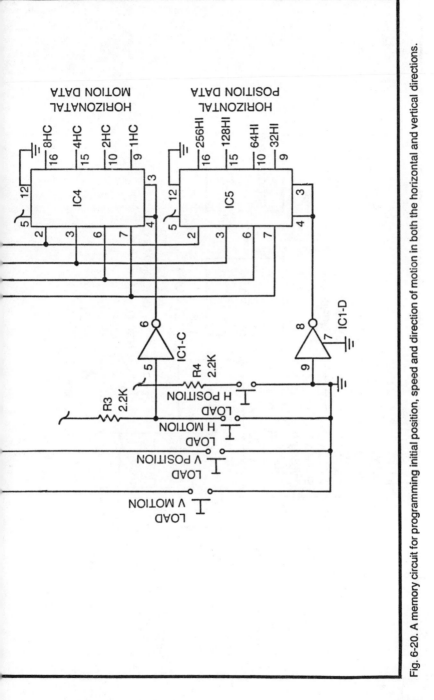

Fig. 6-20. A memory circuit for programming initial position, speed and direction of motion in both the horizontal and vertical directions.

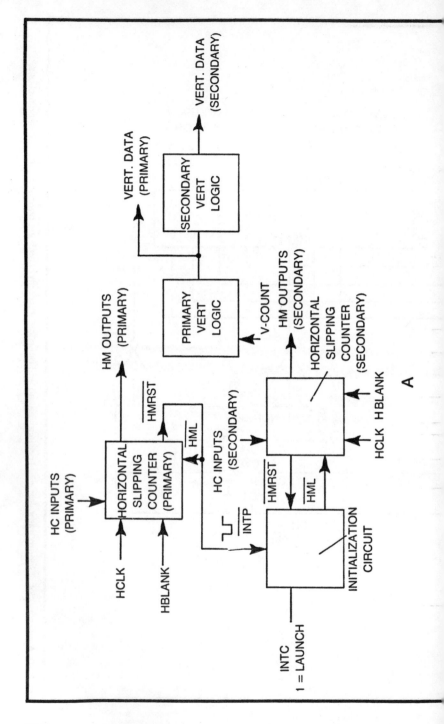

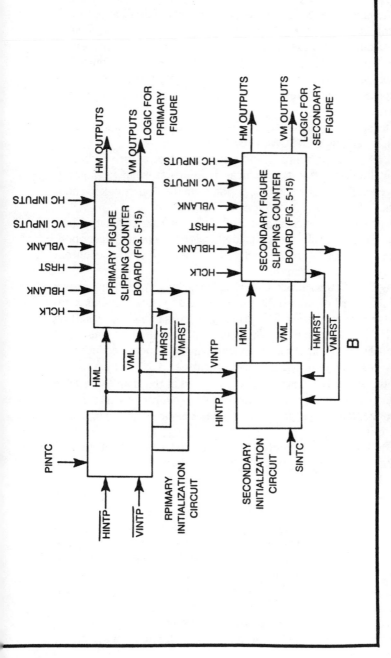

Fig. 6-21. Tagalong block diagrams. (a) The secondary figure follows its primary figure in a horizontal direction until launched by INTC = 1 (b) A complete tagalong control scheme, including initialization circuitry for the primary figure

forcing the secondary figure to follow the primary figure wherever it goes. And that is the main feature of the tagalong scheme—force the secondary counter to work in step with the primary-figure counter.

Whenever the INTC input to the secondary initialization circuit is set to logic 1, however, the secondary horizontal-slipping counter begins taking reset pulses from its own reset circuit, thereby letting it run independent of the primary counter. The secondary figure thus takes off on its own, running away from the primary figure at a direction and speed determined by the HC inputs to the secondary counter.

The secondary figure can be "reattached" to the primary figure by simply returning INTC to logic 0 once again.

Since both the primary and secondary figures are locked to horizontal motion only, the vertical data for determining their respective lengths can be taken direction from the Sourcebox V-count outputs.

A scheme for launching a secondary figure from a primary figure moving in the vertical direction is identical to the one just described. The only practical difference is that one should use vertical counters and vertical-count parameters.

Figure 6-21b is a block diagram of a tagalong system that allows two-dimensional motion (both horizontal and vertical) for the primary and secondary figures. The primary figure is initialized by setting the PINTC input to logic 0. When this happens, the horizontal- and vertical-slipping counters in the primary figure slipping-counter circuit are reset by external initialization pulses, $\overline{\text{HINTP}}$ and $\overline{\text{VINTP}}$. And if the secondary figure is also initialized at the time (by setting SINTC to logic 0), the secondary slipping-counter board is seeing both horizontal- and vertical-reset pulses from the primary initialization circuit.

The two slipping-counter boards are thus synchronized, and the initial position of the primary figure is determining the position of the secondary figure.

Once PINTC is set to logic 1, the primary slipping counter begins taking reset pulses from its own reset-pulse system, causing the primary figure to begin moving in directions and at speeds determined by the VC and HC inputs to the primary figure slipping-counter board. Since SINTC is still at logic 0, the secondary figure slipping counter is still taking reset pulses from the primary circuit. The secondary figure is thus locked to the primary figure, following it wherever it goes.

Whenever SINTC is set to logic 1, the secondary figure slipping counter is finally released from the primary circuit. The secondary figure thus departs from its home, moving away in a direction and at a speed determined by the VC and HC inputs to the secondary figure slipping counter.

Returning SINTC to logic 0 returns the secondary figure to its "home" at the primary figure, whether the primary figure has been initialized or not.

The speed and direction of the secondary figure can be totally independent of the speed and direction of the primary figure. The relationships between the speed and direction of the two figures are strictly determined by the HC and VC inputs of the two pairs of slipping counters. In some instances, however, you might want the secondary figure to depart at a faster speed, but in the same direction as the primary figure. In this case, connect together the 8VC and 8HC inputs to the two slipping counters. This will lock together their directions of travel. The settings of their three lower-order VC and HC inputs then determine the relative speeds after the secondary figure is launched.

The Torpedo Attack and Dogfight games in Chapter 7 illustrate the application of tagalong circuits.

Chapter 7
A Collection of War Games

It would be possible to devote at least several more chapters to all sorts of special game controls, first presenting some basic control circuit and then demonstrating a specific application. But this is a good time to change the form of presentation, describing a game first, and then showing some of the special controls it uses.

Although you can certainly build any of the games in this chapter without referring to anything else in this book but Chapter 2, it would be wise to complete your study of the entire book first.

For instance, you will notice that the figures used in the war games described here are more rectangles, and not interesting, complex figures. You have the option of using the material in Chapter 4 to generate such figures from the simpler ones used here.

For the sake of overall simplicity, the games in this chapter do not include any audio and scoring circuits. These, too, can be added with great effect later on, but of course, you must complete a study of the material relating to audio effects and scoring first.

And finally, you ought to be aware of figure-rotation effects. None of the figures in this chapter can be rotated on the screen; so if you want to add the rotation features, you must study the more advanced chapter dealing with that particular subject.

Don't be mislead into thinking the games in this chapter are overly elementary, however. While these games are, indeed limited with respect to the finer niceties of video-game technology, their control schemes are as complex and meaningful as any you will find anywhere.

This chapter strikes at the very heart of TV games, demonstrating the essential control features without confusing the issue with a lot of added features (intended by others to make you buy the product or to keep on shoving quarters in the slot). You can add the razzle-dazzle later on it you want.

MISSILE ATTACK II

Here is an extended version of the Missile Attack game already described in Chapter 6. This version requires two players, one for controlling the attack missile and another for controlling the antiballistic missile. Player B's task is to program the path of the attack missile, then launch it toward a target. The attack missile is always launched from the left-hand side of the screen and at an initial altitude programmed by Player B. The target is located at the lower right-hand corner of the screen, and Player B can strike that target using a wide variety of programmable velocities, initial altitudes, and rates of descent.

Player A's task is to protect the target by launching antiballistic missiles. The antiballistic missile can be launched only from the bottom of the screen, but Player A can program the horizontal position of his missile just prior to launching it.

Neither player has any control over their respective missiles once they are launched.

This game features a pair of program panels that add special interest to the whole affair. The players get the impression they are working with a computerized system in a fashion that is not found on any commercial TV games. This is not an easy game to play. It is a challenging game bound to spark the interest of players who like to think clearly, act quickly, push buttons, and throw switches.

The Basic Game Plan

The flow chart in Fig. 7-1 outlines the automatic control scheme for Missile Attack II. Under normal conditions, Player B launches the attack missile first, presumably setting it on its path toward the target. Player A then responds by launching the antiballistic missile.

Assuming both missiles are launched and set, the system enters a 4-point-decision-making mode. Suppose the antiballistic missile strikes the attack missile before anything else happens. (This would be a score for Player A.) Whenever A = B, the image of the attack missile flashes on the screen for about one-half second before it is reset to its initial position again. The antiballistic missile is immediately reset the moment A = B.

234

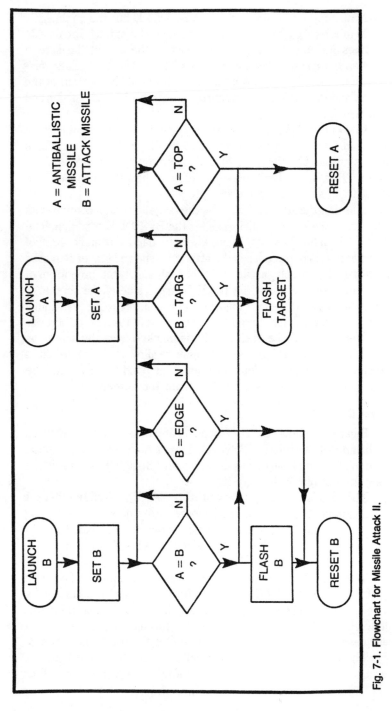

Fig. 7-1. Flowchart for Missile Attack II.

A = ANTIBALLISTIC MISSILE
B = ATTACK MISSILE

LAUNCH A → SET A

B = TARG ? — N
B = TARG ? — Y → FLASH TARGET

A = TOP ? — N
A = TOP ? — Y → RESET A

B = EDGE ? — N
B = EDGE ? — Y

LAUNCH B → SET B

A = B ? — N
A = B ? — Y → FLASH B → RESET B

Now suppose both missiles are launched, but the antiballistic missile misses the attacker. In this instance, the antiballistic missile continues its upward path until it reaches the top of the screen (decision A = TOP). The moment A = TOP, the antiballistic missile is immediately reset to its initial position at the bottom of the screen, and Player A is free to reprogram the horizontal position and launch again.

One of two things happen to the attack missile if the antiballistic missile misses it. The best thing, as far as Player B is concerned, is that his missile hits the target in the lower right-hand corner of the screen. This is the B=TARG condition. When that happens, the target flashes to indicate a clean hit.

Whether the attack missile hits the target or not, it continues its path across the screen until it reaches the B=EDGE condition. The "EDGE" is defined as a line along the right-hand side and bottom of the screen. If Player A misses the attack missile and Player B misses the target, the attack missile will either fall short (hit the bottom of the screen) or overshoot (hit the right-hand side of the screen.)

In any case, the attack missile is immediately reset to its initial position upon reaching the right-hand edge or bottom of the screen.

The attack missile, incidentally, is blanked from the screen as long as it is in its initial position. This feature allows Player B to adjust the initial launch altitude without tipping his hand to Player A. The antiballistic missile is never blanked from the screen.

Player Controls

Figure 7-2 shows the control panel and other relevant features for the antiballistic missile, Player A. Player A adjusts the horizontal position of the antiballistic missile anywhere in 16 different positions along the bottom of the screen.

The idea is to set switches SF through SI to 1 of 16 different combinations of 1s and 0s, then momentarily depress the LOAD pushbutton. The figure of the antiballistic missile responds by moving to the position specified by the switches. A bit of work with these switches will show exactly how they work.

The antiballistic missile can be launched from its initial position by depressing the LAUNCH pushbutton. Once the missile is launched, all switches and buttons are locked out, making it impossible to change the path of the antiballistic missile until it is automatically reset (by striking the attack missile or the top of the screen).

The attack missile control panel is somewhat more complex because Player B has more initial parameters to control. See Fig. 7-3.

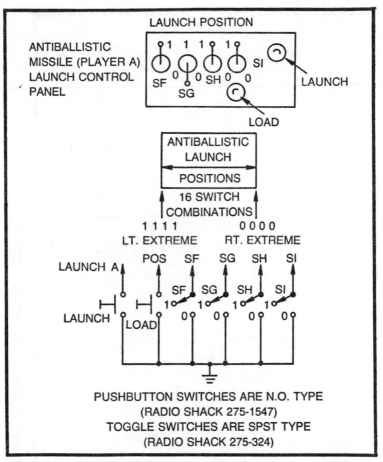

Fig. 7-2. Player A control panel, range of launch positions, and panel schematic.

Player Bs controls are enabled only while the attack missile is in its blanked, initial position. Player B can set the initial attack altitude to any one of eight positions in the upper half of the screen by setting the positions of switches SC, SD, and SE. Setting all three INITIAL ALTITUDE switches to their 1 positions fixes the maximum altitude, while setting them all to their 0 positions fixes the minimum altitude. There is no need to depress any sort of loading button in this particular case.

Player B also sets the attack velocity and rate of descent. There are four possible velocities and rates of descent set by switches SA and SB. See the chart in Fig. 7-3. Setting the attack velocity is a matter of first setting SA and SB to the desired positions, then depressing the VELOCITY pushbutton. The same two switches,

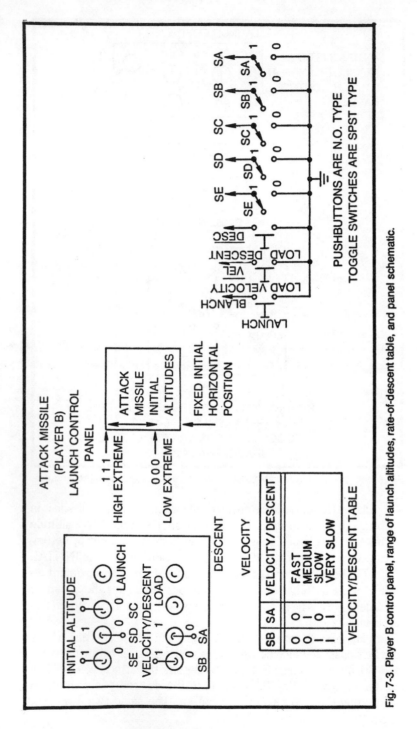

Fig. 7-3. Player B control panel, range of launch altitudes, rate-of-descent table, and panel schematic.

SA and SB, are used for setting the rate of descent, but that parameter is loaded into the system by depressing the DESCENT pushbutton.

The attack missile is then launched by depressing the LAUNCH pushbutton. Once the LAUNCH button is depressed, Player B is committed to the path he programmed just prior to the launching operation. All controls are locked out until the attack missile is blanked and reset to its initial position.

There are a number of different attack velocities, rates of descent and initial altitudes that direct the attack missile to the target. Player B's task is to come up with one of these proper combinations that avoids the antiballistic missile. Part of Player B's strategy, however, might be to throw Player A out of position with a false run, then make a deadly strike the next time around.

The Flashing Image Circuit

The only portion of this game that has not beem considered in some detail in earlier chapters is the one that causes the images to flash when they are hit. The attack missile flashes whenever the antiballistic missile hits it, and the target flashes whenever the attack missile hits it. In either case, the flashing effect serves as positive confirmation of a score.

Figure 7-4 illustrates the basic image-flashing circuit that will be used in a number of different games throughout this book. The IC in this case is a 556 dual timer. Section IC1-A is connected as a monostable multivibrator that is triggered into action by a brief negative-going signal, FLASH START.

The output of IC1-A can be used for resetting or timing other game operations, but more importantly, this timing allows a free-running multivibrator to generate a pulsing output signal. Whenever this oscillator, IC1-B, is gated off, it delivers a logic-0 level to one input of IC2. In the case of a NOR gate, this means the gate is open, allowing an inverted version of an IMAGE signal to pass through uninterrupted.

The moment the oscillator is gated on, however, it generates sequences of 1 and 0 outputs, thereby interrupting the IMAGE signal at the same rate. The overall effect is that the IMAGE is flashed on and off at a rate determined by the values of R2, R3, and C2, and for a period of time determined by the values of R1 and C1.

Game Block Diagram

Figure 7-5 shows the three major portions of the Missile Attack II game. The first diagram, Fig. 7-5a, represents the main control portion for the antiballistic missile, Player A. Player B's control circuitry is blocked out in Fig. 7-5b. The overall game control scheme is shown in Fig. 7-5c.

Referring to the block diagram in Fig. 7-5a, assume the antiballistic missile is in its reset condition, resting at the bottom of the screen. The ALAUNCH signal is in a logic-1 condition at this time and the R-S flip-flop is allowing two things to happen. First, it is enabling the horizontal position logic circuit so that Player A can manually adjust the horizontal position of his missile via the switches on his control panel. Second, the reset flip-flop is in a condition where the initialization-control circuit is feeding VRST pulses to the vertical-slipping counter. The significance of this latter condition is that the slipping counter is synchronized to the vertical-counting system in the Sourcebox. There is no vertical motion of the antiballistic missile.

The figure logic block is responsible for combining the antiballistic missile's horizontal data (from the horizontal-position logic block) and its vertical data (from the VM outputs of the slipping counter) to create the image on the screen. The antiballistic missile's figure signal is designated AFIG in Fig. 7-5a.

As long as the antiballistic missile is in its reset condition, then, it cannot move in a vertical direction because its vertical slipping counter is synchronized to the 60-Hz VRST signal from the Sourcebox, but it can be manually moved in the horizontal direction by the control panel and horizontal-position logic circuit.

Player A launches the antiballistic missile by depressing his LAUNCH pushbutton. This action generates a brief negative-going pulse at ALAUNCH, setting the R-S flip-flop to its launch mode. Two things happen then: The horizontal-position logic is locked out so that the player no longer has control over the missile's horizontal position, and the initialization-control circuit is set to allow the slipping-counter action to take place. The antiballistic missile thus rises from the bottom of the screen at a rate determined by the VC programming of the vertical-slipping counter. (The programming for this counter is not shown in Fig. 7-5a because it is internally fixed at a relatively fast rate).

All of the circuits blocked out in Fig. 7-5a can be found in earlier chapters of this book. Look for the R-S flip-flop, horizontal-position logic, and initialization-control circuits in Chapter 6. The vertical-slipping counter is found in Chapter 5, and the figure logic is a simple variation of the basic figure-generating circuits in Chapter 3.

Figure 7-5b outlines the main control circuits for the attack missile. This system includes elements that are nearly identical to

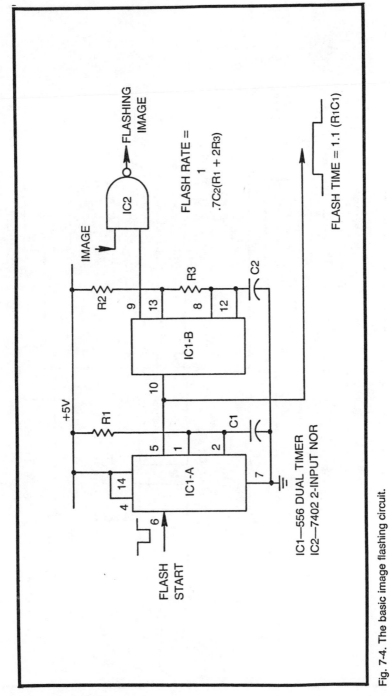

Fig. 7-4. The basic image flashing circuit.

241

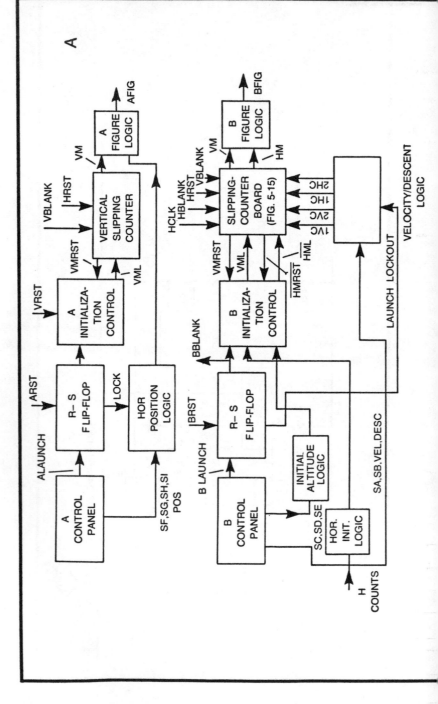

A

242

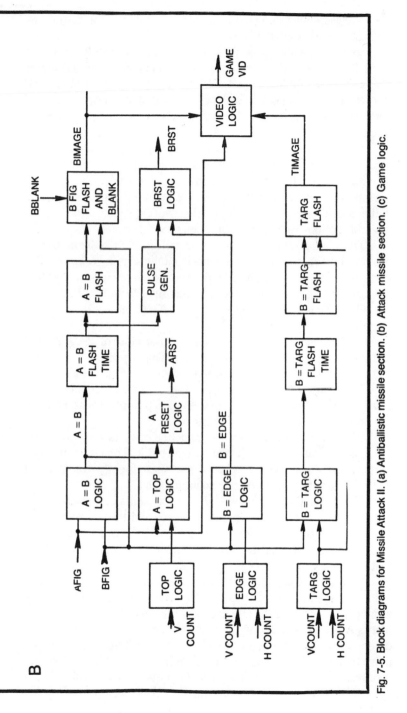

Fig. 7-5. Block diagrams for Missile Attack II. (a) Antiballistic missile section. (b) Attack missile section. (c) Game logic.

the antiballistic missile system as well as a scheme for setting the vertical and horizontal speeds.

Suppose the attack missile has been reset to the left-hand edge of the screen. The R̄-S̄ flip-flop is then in a condition that (1) allows Player B to set the horizontal velocity and vertical rate of descent and (2) fixes the initialization control so that the horizontal- and vertical-slipping counters are synchronized with the Sourcebox counts.

The velocity and rate of descent parameters actually control the 1VC, 2VC, 1HC, and 2HC controls of the slipping-counter board (see Fig. 5-15). The other speed/direction controls for this counter are internally wired to assure right-to-left and top-to-bottom motion of the attack missile. Player B, in other words, can control only the rates of motion, and not the directions.

The initial position of the attack missile is fixed in the horizontal position by the signal from the horizontal-initial-logic block. The vertical position is determined by the setting of control switches SC, SD, and SE, assembled by the initial-altitude-logic block.

Once Player B depresses his LAUNCH pushbutton, a brief negative-going pulse at BLAUNCH switches the condition of the R̄-S̄ flip-flop, thereby locking out any further control of the missile and switching the synchronization of the slipping-counter board for automatic motion across the screen.

The attack missile remains in motion until a brief positive-going pulse occurs at the BRST input of the R̄-S̄ flip-flop. At that moment, the entire system is returned to its reset state.

Whether the attack missile is launched or in its reset state, its image is generated by the "B" figure logic block. The horizontal- and vertical-counting data for this figure are taken directly from the HM and VM outputs of the slipping-counter board.

The block diagram in Fig. 7-5c represents the main game-control system. The top-logic, edge-logic, and target-logic blocks simply generate information regarding the positions of those objects. The target-logic data, however, is the only one of these three that is actually displayed on the screen.

Note that an inverted version of the antiballistic missile figure (AFIG) is directed to both the A=B and A=TOP logic blocks, while an inverted version of the attack-missile figure (BFIG) is directed to blocks A=B, B=EDGE, and B=TARG. These are simply contact-detection blocks described generally in Chapter 6. A=B generates a pulse whenever the two missiles come into contact with one another, A=TOP generates a pulse whenever the antiballistic missile reaches the top of the screen, B=EDGE generates a pulse whenever the attack missile contacts either the bottom or right-hand edge of the screen, and B=TARG generates a pulse whenever the attack missile hits the target.

Much of what remains to be explained in Fig. 7-5c can be determined from the flow chart in Fig. 7-1. The A-reset logic block, for instance, is responsible for resetting the position of the antiballistic missile whenever A=B or A=TOP. This reset pulse is designated ARST.

Whenever A=B occurs, the pulse from that block also initiates a flash-time timer in the A=B flash-time block. This block, in turn, generates a logic-1 level that entables the A=B flasher. And when the timing is over, the pulse generator produces a brief pulse that ultimately resets the position of the attack missile.

The attack missile is also reset the instant it reaches the bottom or right-hand edge of the screen. The BRST logic block thus generates a negative-going attack missile reset pulse (BRST) whenever the A=B flash timing is over or the missile contacts the edge of the screen.

Whenever the B=TARG block senses a contact between the attack missile and the target, it also initiates a flash timer. This timer enables the B=TARG flashing circuit which, in turn, switches the target-image data off and on in the target-flash block.

Returning to the attack-missile figure for a moment, note the B-figure flash and blank block has two separate control inputs. The image data for the attack missile (BFIG) can be completely blanked off the screen while it is in its reset position. The BBLANK signal from the attack-missile control system is responsible for this blanking effect.

The same attack missile image, however, is also blanked on and off by the A=B flash circuit. In either case, the unblanked, blanked, or flashing image data emerges as the BIMAGE signal.

The BIMAGE, AFIG, and TIMAGE signals are all combined into the game's composite figure video at the video-logic block.

The flashing circuits in Fig. 7-5c are all described in connection with the circuit in Fig. 7-4; the top-, edge-, and target-logic blocks are variations of the figure generators in Chapter 2. The contact-sensing circuits are generally described in Chapter 6.

If you have been studying this book diligently, you will find nothing new here at all.

Circuit Diagrams

Figures 7-6, 7-7, and 7-8 show the circuit diagrams for the Missile Attack II game. The game calls for four circuit boards, the three just mentioned and a slipping-counter board from Fig. 5-15. Of course there are two separate control panels that have already been described in Figs. 7-2 and 7-3.

After studying the game's flow chart and block diagrams in some detail, there is little need for a highly detailed description of the circuits themselves. The overall wiring block diagram in Fig. 7-9 will prove invaluable when analyzing the operation of the system at the circuit-board level.

Figure 7-6 shows a board containing most of the control elements for the antiballistic missile system. ICs 1-A and 6-F, along with C1 and R7, merely transform the negative-going launch signal into a brief, negative-going pulse. IC2-A and IC2-C make up the $\overline{R}$-$\overline{S}$ flip-flop that is set so that pin 3 is at logic 1 and pin 8 is at logic 0 whenever that pulse occurs.

ICs 2-B, 2-D, and 1-B make up the initialization control circuit. Whenever the antiballistic missile is in its reset position, this circuit delivers an inverted VRST pulse to the loading input of the vertical-slipping counter, IC7, and IC8. Whenever the missile is launched, however, the initialization-control circuit delivers the output of IC1-D back to the load input of the slipping counter.

The four sections of IC3 determine the pattern of inverted and noninverted H-count signals for determining the initial horizontal position of the antiballistic missile. See details in connection with the circuit in Fig. 6-17. These position-determining signals pass directly through IC9, a quad D latch, as long as the system is in its reset condition and the LOAD button is depressed. IC4-A is responsible for ANDing the launch status information from the $\overline{R}$-$\overline{S}$ flip-flop and the $\overline{POS}$ logic level from the player's LOAD button.

Whenever the LOAD button is released or the missile is launched, pins 4 and 13 of IC9 go to logic 0, thereby placing the latches into their memory modes. The horizontal-position data that existed the moment the circuit is latched then remains fixed at the inputs of IC5-A.

The position of the antiballistic missile in the horizontal plane is actually defined by IC5-A. Since this pluse is too wide for generating the horizontal width of the antiballistic missile, it is shorted in the circuit made up of IC1-C, IC6-C, R6, and C2. The value of C2 can be changed to suit the designer's own impression of how wise the antiballistic missile figure ought to be.

The height and vertical position of the antiballistic missile are both determined by the pin-12 output of the higher-order vertical-slipping counter, IC8. This output is inverted by IC6-D and effectively ANDed with the horizontal portion of the image at IC4-B. The noninverted version of the missile figure is then inverted by IC6-E before applying it to other portions of the system.

The circuit in Fig. 7-7 deals mainly with the control aspects of the attack missile. The launching pulse is formed by IC1-A and IC4-A in a fashion identical to the launching circuit for the antiballistic missile. The $\overline{R}$-$\overline{S}$ flip-flop, composed of IC1-B and IC1-C, is set to its launch condition by the negative-going launch pulse from IC4-A, and it is reset by a negative-going version of the BRST pulse from the output of IC4-B.

The initialization-control portion of the attack missile circuit is embodied in IC8, actually a quad 2:1 multiplexer. Only two of the four sections are used here, but that is adequate for shifting the operation of the slipping-counter board (Fig. 5-15) between the initializing pulses and motion-generating pulses.

The attack-missile system is initialized as long as the output from IC1-B is at logic 0, thereby directing vertical-synchronizing pulses to the $\overline{VMRST}$ and horizontal-synchronizing pulses to $\overline{HMRST}$ inputs of the slipping counter.

The vertical-synchronizing pulses are taken from the initial-altitude circuit, IC7 and IC3-A. Switches SC, SD, and SE on Player B's control panel determine the pattern of V-count signals that reach the inputs of IC3-A. The output of IC3-A then determines where vertical reset for the attack missile takes place on the screen during reset.

IC3-B determines the horizontal position of the attack missile through the reset phase of the operation. This is a position that is fixed by the inverted H-count inputs to IC3-B, a position at the extreme left-hand edge of the screen. This position-determining signal from IC3-B is shortened by IC1-D and IC4-F before it is applied to the initialization-control circuit, IC8.

As long as the attack missile is in its reset condition, then the slipping-counter board holds its position as determined vertically by the output of IC3-A and horizontally by the output of IC4-F.

When the missile is launched, the output of IC1-B changes to a logic-1 condition, and the vertical- and horizontal-loading signals for the slipping counter are taken from the $\overline{VML}$ and $\overline{HML}$ sources. The figure is thus free to move across the screen in a direction and at rates determined by the VC and HC inputs of the slipping-counter board.

Player A has access to only the two lower-order speed control inputs for horizontal and vertical motion. The key to this part of the circuit lies in the operation of the quad D latch circuit, IC9. As long as

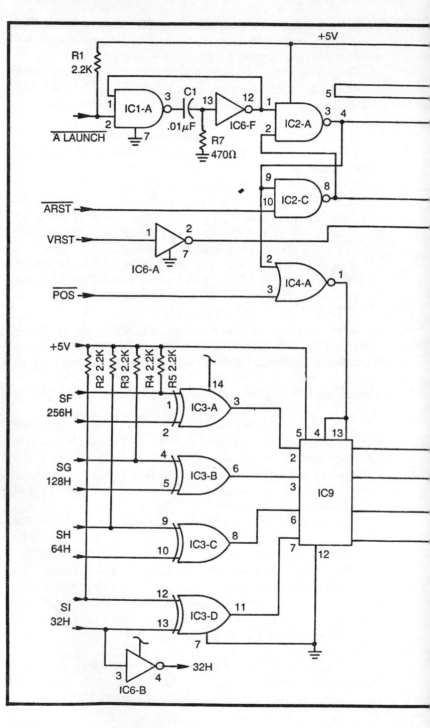

248

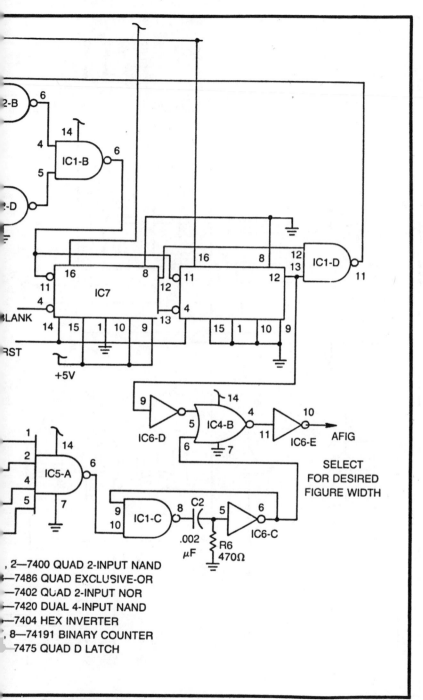

Fig. 7-6. Schematic diagram for the antiballistic missile control circuit board.

249

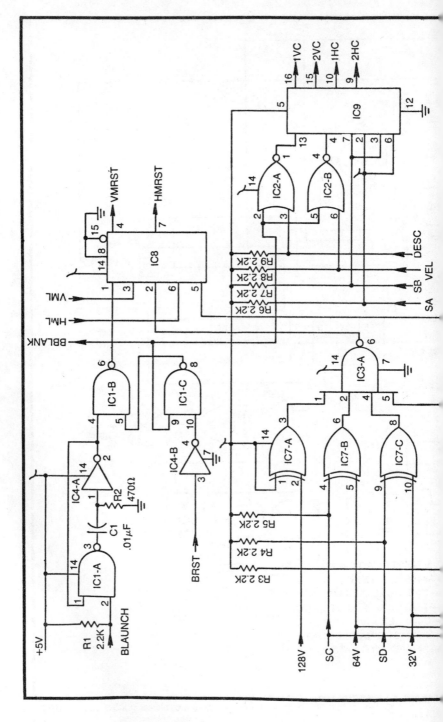

250

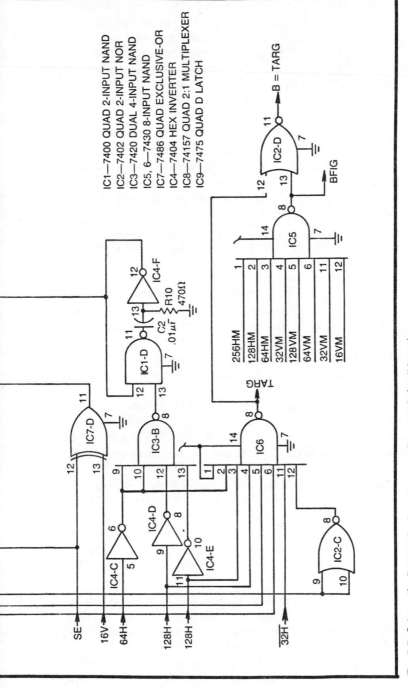

Fig. 7-7. Schematic diagram for the attack missile control circuit board.

251

the attack missile is in its reset condition, the player can load data from switches SA and SB into this latch by depressing either the VELOCITY or DESCENT LOAD pushbuttons.

Depressing the VELOCITY button, for example, feeds the logic levels from SA and SB into IC9 and through that set of latches to the 1HC and 2HC outputs. Releasing the VELOCITY button then latches that 2-bit data in place by allowing the output of IC2-B to fall to logic 0.

Depressing the DESCENT button, on the other hand, feeds the logic levels from SA and SB into IC9 and to outputs 1VC and 2VC. This data is latched the moment Player B releases the DES CENT pushbutton.

The entire latch circuit is fixed in its memory mode whenever the attack missile is launched. Launching the missile feeds a logic-1 level to pin 2 of IC2-A and pin 5 of IC2-B, placing both halves of the latch circuit into the memory mode and disabling the effect of the velocity- and descent-control switches.

Once launched, the attack missile falls at a rate determined by the data latched at the 1VC and 2VC outputs of IC9, and it travels horizontally at a rate determined by the 1HC and 2HC outputs of that same latch. The initial altitude was originally determined by the settings of switches SC through SE.

While most of the circuitry in Fig. 7-7 deals with controlling the operation of the attack missile, there is room on the board for a couple of other circuits.

IC6 fixes the position and size of the target image, while IC5 determines the position and size of the attack missile, itself.

The information from these two 8-input NAND gates is effectively ANDed together in IC2-D to sense contact between the target and attack-missile images.

The circuit in Fig. 7-8 is mainly responsible for sensing contact between the images and taking the appropriate action. IC1-A, for instance, defines the right-hand edge of the screen, while IC1-B defines the bottom. These two edge-parameters are combined in IC3-A to yield an active-high (noninverted) definition of EDGE for the attack missile. These three ICs are embodied in the block labeled "edge logic" in Fig. 7-5c.

IC8-A defines the top of the screen for the antiballistic missile. Its active-low (inverted) output is combined with an inverted version of the AFIG signal in IC4-A to detect contact between the antiballistic missile and the top of the screen.

IC5-A and IC5-C detect contact between the attack missile, the edge of the screen, and the antiballistic missile, respectively. If there is contact between the attack missile and the edge of the screen, the output of IC5-A goes to logic 1 and ultimately through IC3-B as a pulse for resetting the position of the attack missile.

If, on the other hand, there is contact between the two missiles, the output of IC5-C goes to logic 1. This signal is inverted by IC5-D and applied to the trigger input of flashing-timer IC7-A. The output of that timer enables the missile-flashing IC, IC7-B. This rectangular waveform is inverted by IC2-E and applied to the attack-missile-logic circuit, IC1-C. When the flashing interval is over, the negative-going edge of the timing pulse at pin 5 of IC7-A is shaped and applied as one of two attack-missile-reset pulses to IC3-B.

Contact between the attack missile and the target is sensed by IC2-D in Fig. 7-7. This pulse is inverted by IC4-C in Fig. 7-8 and used for enabling the target-flashing timer, IC6-A. The flashing output from IC6-B modulates the target image from $\overline{\text{TARG}}$ at IC4-D, where it is then inverted and ORed with the image information for the two missiles in IC8-B.

A complete slipping-counter board is an integral part of the system, as shown in the wiring block diagram in Fig. 7-9. This board is already described in connection with the circuit diagram in Fig. 5-15. Figure 7-9 merely shows how it is interfaced with the three game boards just described.

Note carefully the programming of the 4HC, 8HC, 4VC, and 8VC connections to the slipping-counter board in Fig. 7-9. These connections must be made in order to make the attack missile move in the proper directions at all times.

Construction and Assembly Hints

Each of the boards described in this section can be built on a 4-by 4-inch plug-in boards (Radio Shack 276-153) and interconnected by means of edge-card connectors (Radio Shack 276-1551).

The connections on an additional mother board can be used for interfacing the game circuits with the Sourcebox unit.

The slipping-counter board should take its +5V source from the GAME-A power supply in the Sourcebox. The three other boards can then operate most effectively from the GAME-B power supply.

The two control panels can be built into small aluminum project boxes.

TORPEDO ATTACK

Here is another two-player war game. One player controls the motion of an attack craft (AC), and his goal is to lob a torpedo at a

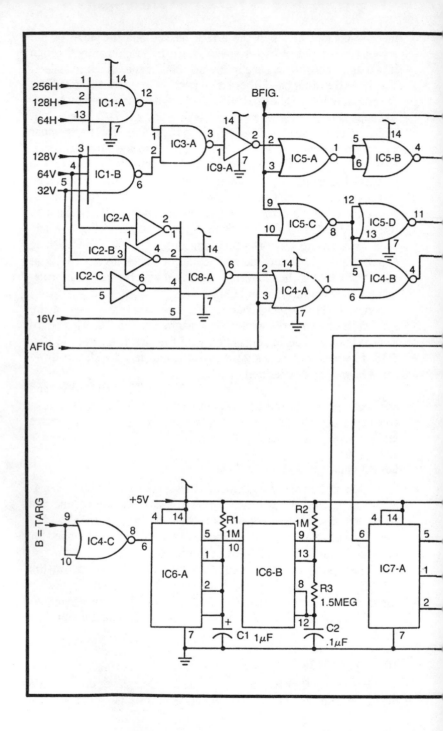

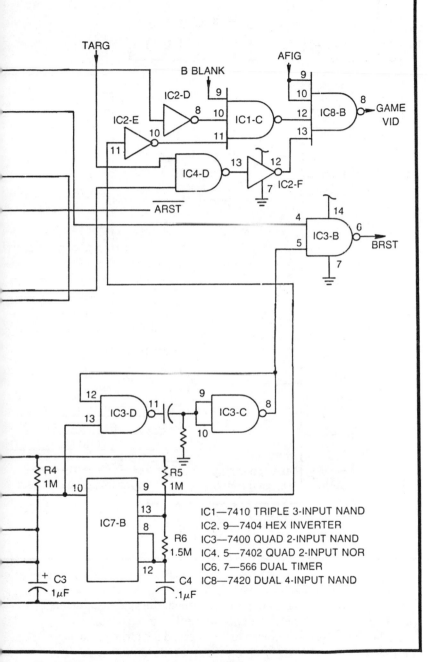

Fig. 7-8. Schematic diagram for the game logic circuit board.

255

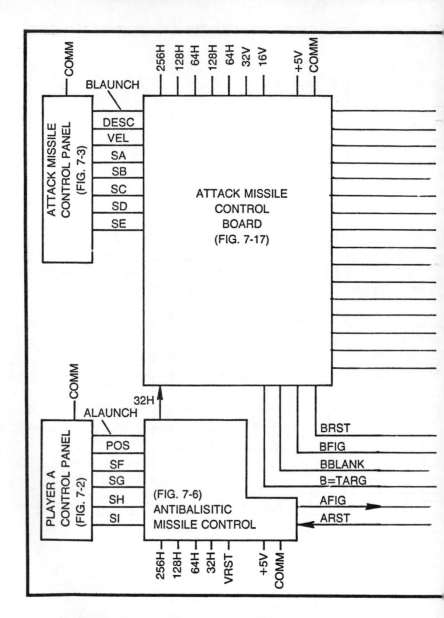

target image located in the lower right-hand corner of the screen. Unlike the Attack Missile game just described, the aggressor in this case has full control over his craft during the torpedo run.

The second player's objective is to defend the target by launching defense torpedos (DT) at the aggressor's attack craft. The horizontal positions of the four defense torpedoes are fixed, but the

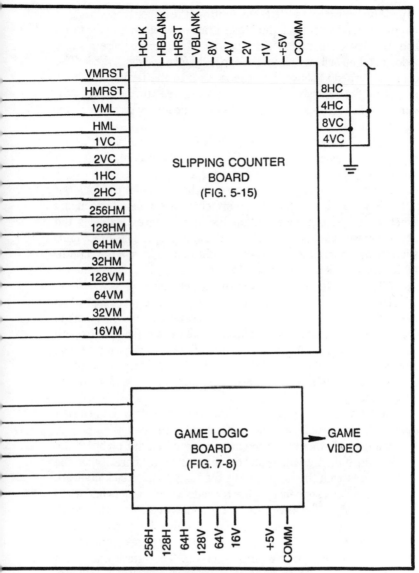

Fig. 7-9. Wiring diagram for the Missile Attack II game.

DT player can launch them one at a time in any sequence and any number of times.

The really unique feature of this Torpedo Attack game, however, is that it marks our first application of the tagalong feature described briefly in Chapter 6. The attack craft carries the attack torpedo in the tagalong fashion. When the aggressor launches his torpedo by depressing a FIRE pushbutton, the attack torpedo is free to move along the path that the attack craft was following at the time. The AC player must head directly toward the target, fire his torpedo, and then pull away from the target before colliding with it. The launched torpedo follows the original path to the target.

While the defensive player can, indeed, destroy the attack craft with a defense torpedo, he cannot destroy the attack torpedo after it has been fired.

Figure 7-10c shows the four different images that can appear on the screen at any given moment: DT (defense torpedo), AC (attack craft), AT (attack torpedo), and the target.

The defense torpedoes can be launched at any time along the paths shown by dashed lines. The attack craft can be moved in any direction and at any speed within the viewing area, carrying the attack torpedo until it is launched by the aggressor. The attack craft is free to move through the left- and right-hand edges of the screen, but it "crashes" if it touches the top or bottom. The dotted lines in Fig. 7-10c indicate one particular AC attack run.

The aggressor has full control over the attack craft except when one of three reset conditions occur. According to the flowchart in Fig. 7-10a, the attack craft is automatically reset (and destroyed) when AC=EDGE1, AC=TARG, or DT=AC. Translating these choice-point operations into plain English, DT=AC means one of the defense torpedoes strikes the attack craft, a score in favor of the defensive player.

AC=TARG means the attack craft itself collides with the target image. This represents a draw or a score for the defensive player, depending on whether or not the attack torpedo is still on board the attack craft. If the torpedo is still on board the attack craft when the latter collides with the target, both the target and attack craft are destroyed, a draw sequence. If the torpedo has been launched when the attack craft collides with the target, however, only the attack craft is destroyed. Another point for the defensive player.

AC=EDGE1 is a condition where the aggressor steers the attack craft too high or low on the screen. The attack craft must remain between the top and bottom of the screen. Touching either of these two boundaries destroys the attack craft and represents a default score for the defensive player.

So according to Fig. 7-10a, the attack craft is flashed on and off, and reset to a starting position whenever it is hit by one of the defense torpedoes, hits the top or bottom of the screen, or collides with the target. The AC reset position, by the way, is at the left-hand edge of the screen, about halfway between the top and bottom. The attack player has no control over the reset position and timing.

Now suppose the defensive player launches a defense torpedo. Once launched, a defense torpedo continues its rather rapid upward motion until one of two events occur: the DT strikes the attack craft (DT=AC) or the DT images reaches the top of the screen (DT=TOP). In either case, the DT image is reset immediately and the defensive player is ready to launch another one.

Figure 7-10b is the flow chart for the attack torpedo. One of two things must happen after the aggressor launches a torpedo. The torpedo can strike the target (AT=TARG), causing the target image to flash and then returning the torpedo to the attack craft. The other thing that can happen after launching the attack torpedo is that it misses the target and moves to the top, bottom, or right-hand edge of the screen. These three edges, designated EDGE2, represent the limits of the AT's travel. Hitting any one of them immediately resets the position of the AT to the attack craft. There is no score for either player.

Torpedo Attack Game Panels

Figure 7-11 shows the general layout of the two control panels for the Torpedo Attack game. The panel for the DT player consists of four pushbuttons switches, labeled 1 through 4, that launch defense torpedoes. The numerals represent the four torpedoes located in the relative positions indicated in Fig. 7-10c.

The defense player can launch any one of the torpedoes at any time and in any sequence. But a launched torpedo must complete its cycle (either hitting the top of the screen or the attack craft) before another can be launched.

The control panel for the attack player, Fig. 7-11b, includes a pair of controls for steering the attack craft and a FIRE pushbutton for launching the attack torpedo. The attack player can control the motion of his craft as indicated by the arrows on the control panel. A serious experimenter might want to replace the two AC motion controls with a single two-dimensional joystick control, thereby making the steering and firing operations somewhat less awkward.

Potentiometer Control of Speed and Direction

All of the slipping-counter speed and direction controls described thus far call for inserting a 4-bit binary number that determines the direction and speed of the apparent motion. The Missile Attack II game, for example, lets the player controlling the attack

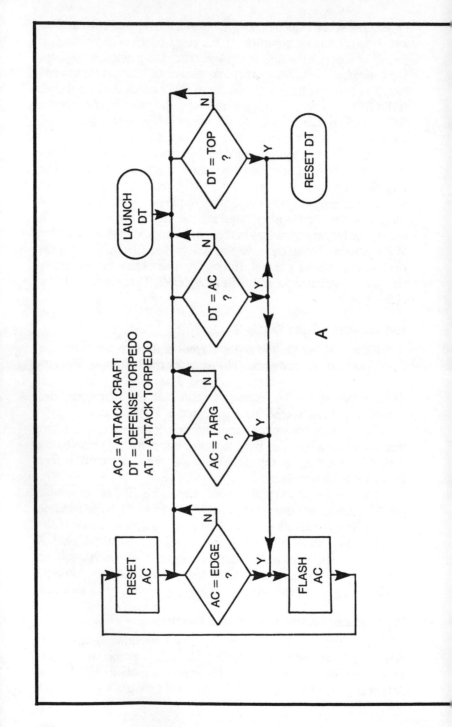

AC = ATTACK CRAFT
DT = DEFENSE TORPEDO
AT = ATTACK TORPEDO

A

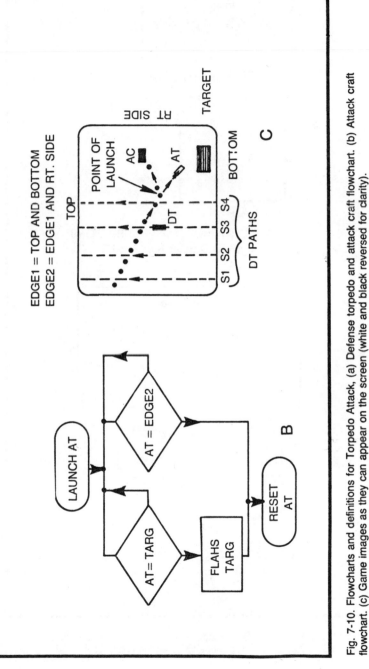

Fig. 7-10. Flowcharts and definitions for Torpedo Attack. (a) Defense torpedo and attack craft flowchart. (b) Attack craft flowchart. (c) Game images as they can appear on the screen (white and black reversed for clarity).

261

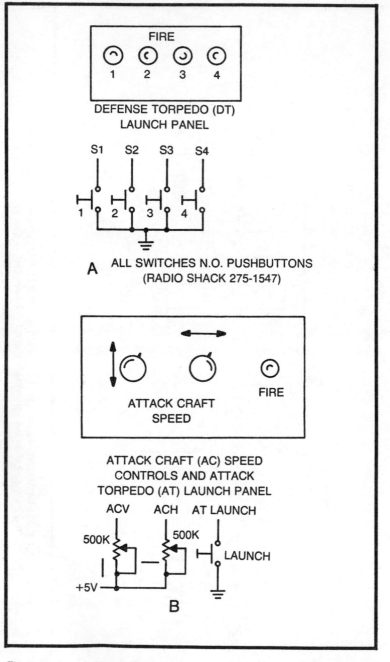

Fig. 7-11. Control panels for Torpedo Attack. (a) Defense torpedo panel and schematic. (b) Attack system panel and schematic diagram.

missile's path enter motion data via a set of switches. The control input in this case is purely digital.

Digital speed and direction controls, however, are not always the most appropriate. It is often more helpful and realistic to control the motion of a figure by means of dials—potentiometers, to be more specific.

Figure 7-12 shows a relatively simple circuit that converts the digital motion-control input into an analog format. In essence, this circuit converts the setting of a potentiometer into a 4-bit binary number for controlling the count length of a slipping counter. Using this scheme, a player controls the speed and direction of an image by turning the shaft of the variable resistor, R2.

This elementary sort of A/D converter includes a 4-bit binary counter (IC4), a monostable multivibrator having an adjustable output timing interval (IC3), a clock-pulse gating circuit (IC2-B), and a synchronizing-pulse generator (IC2-A and IC1-B). The inputs to the circuit are a 128V count pulse from the Sourcebox, a 2V count from Sourcebox, and the main control resistor, R2. The output is a 4-bit binary word that ultimately determines the speed and direction of motion of a figure on the screen. The 4-bit output is the one required for setting the count length of a slipping-counter circuit.

Two such circuits are required where the player is to have control over both the horizontal and vertical components of motion. The horizontal control includes the components shown in the main schematic in Fig. 7-12. IC5, shown in the insert in Fig. 7-12, must be added for potentiometer control of the vertical-motion component.

The waveforms in Fig. 7-12 illustrate the operation of the circuit. Whenever 128V makes a transition from logic 0 to logic 1 (near the middle of the screen), the pulse generator (IC2-A and IC1-B) generates a negative-going pulse, designated $\overline{128P}$ throughout the remainder of this book.

The monostable multivibrator is programmed such that its output timing interval is initiated on the trailing edge of the $\overline{128P}$ pulse. See the second waveform in Fig. 7-12. With the pin-3 output of the monostable circuit thus set to logic 1, 2V pulses at pin 5 of IC2-B are allowed to pass to the clocking input of the counter circuit, IC4. The counter then increments at the 2V rate until the timing interval is over.

When the timing interval is completed, the counter holds its last 4-bit output count until another $\overline{128P}$ pulse occurs. That brief pulse clears the output of the counter to zero, letting the next counting interval begin from zero.

The timing interval of the monostable multivibrator is determined by the values of R2, R3, and C3. Normally the controls are adjusted so that the count reaches any number between 5 and 15, the normal operating range for the binary numbers fed to the speed and direction control inputs of the slipping counters.

So let's suppose the player wants to stop the motion of a figure on the screen. All he has to do is adjust the value of R2 so that the counter increments to the binary equivalent of 9 (the stop code) during the monostable's timing interval. When the $\overline{128P}$ pulse occurs, then, the counter is cleared to zero, then allowed to count at the 2V rate until the timing interval is over. To stop the motion of the figure, the counting interval should be terminated with the counter showing an output of 1001 (decimal 9).

The counter then holds that number until $\overline{128P}$ occurs once again. And if the player has not changed the position of the control, the counter repeats its count-to-9 sequence.

If the player then wants to move the figure to the right at a relatively high speed, he adjusts the control so that the monostable's output timing is a bit shorter, short enough to stop the counting operation at a number such as 0101 (decimal 5).

If, on the other hand, the player wants to move the figure to the left, he adjusts R2 for a slightly longer timing interval from IC3, letting the counter run to perhaps 1101 (decimal 13).

Recall that the horizontal-slipping counter samples its speed and direction codes during the vertical-blanking interval. This circuit has its 4-bit output established before vertical blanking occurs, and it holds that number through blanking and, in fact, all the way to the end of $\overline{128V}$.

The vertical-slipping counter samples its 4-bit control input continuously. And since the output of IC4 in Fig. 7-12 spends some of its time counting, it yields some undesirable and confusing vertical-motion effects on the screen. It is thus necessary to load the output of IC4 into a temporary memory circuit when it is being used in conjunction with a vertical-slipping-counter circuit. IC5 shown in the insert in Fig. 7-12 is a quad D latch that performs this function.

The outputs of IC4 are connected to the corresponding inputs of IC5 for vertical-motion control. The latch is normally in its memory mode, keeping the four VC outputs stable through the counter's up-counting functions. The count output is then updated whenever the VRST pulse occurs.

The TRIM potentiometer in Fig. 7-12 is used for adjusting the control range of the main control potentiometer. First set the main

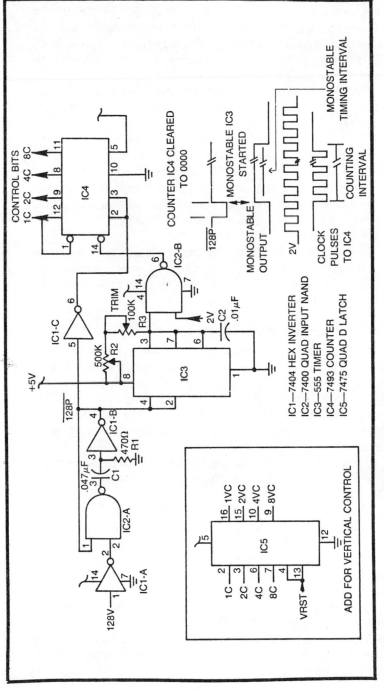

Fig. 7-12. Circuits for potentiometer control of speed and direction.

control to one extreme position, then adjust R3 for the desired maximum speed in that direction. Then set R2 to its opposite extreme and adjust R3 again for the desired maximum speed. Work R2 back and forth between its extremes, gradually adjusting the trimpot for the most useful control range.

The main control, R2, is normally mounted externally on a separate control panel. The trimpot, however, is mounted to the circuit board.

Figure 7-13 includes a pair of these motion-control circuits: one for the horizontal and another for the vertical motion of the attack craft. Note that the two monostable multivibrators, IC1-A and IC1-B, share the same 128P inputs, and that R1 controls the horizontal component of motion and R3 controls the vertical component. Also note that the vertical-speed counter (IC4) is followed by the latch circuit, IC5.

This potentiometer-controlled motion interface circuit is an integral part of the attack craft control in the Torpedo Attack game. It will also be used a number of times in other game systems through the remainder of this book.

A Complete Tagalong Motion Control System

The attack craft in this game is to carry along an attack torpedo until the aggressor launches it, presumably toward the target image. Chapter 6 includes a general description of the tagalong process, but now it is time to look at one such system in much greater detail.

The schematic diagram in Fig. 7-13 shows the tagalong-control portion of the system. Eventually we will show that this circuit interfaces with a pair of slipping-counter-control boards, one for the primary figure (the attack craft) and another for the secondary figure (the attack torpedo). See the slipping-counter schematic in Fig. 5-15.

Most of the circuitry in Fig. 7-13 is simply a pair of potentiometer-controlled elements that generate binary speed and direction codes. IC1-A and IC3, of instance, translate the setting of R1 into a 4-bit binary number representing the speed and direction of a figure in the horizontal plane. IC1-B, IC4, and IC5 do the same sort of job for motion in the vertical directions.

Now bear in mind that this circuit controls two separate slipping-counter boards. All of the input and output designations that include a P character indicate signals to or from the primary-figure slipping counter, while those including an S character indicate signals concerned with the secondary figure.

Suppose the secondary figure (the attack torpedo in this case) is supposed to be taging along with the primary figure (the attack craft). In this instance, the $\overline{\text{FIRE}}$ input to IC6, IC7, and IC9 is at logic 1. This particular logic level sets memory latches IC6 and IC7 to their "read" modes—they are passing any 4-bit words at their inputs directly to their outputs. In other words, any change in the 4-bit words from IC3 and IC5 appears immediately at the outputs of IC6 and IC7 respectively.

The output designations from IC6 and IC7 imply they are 4-bit motion-control words for the horizontal- and vertical-slipping counters on the secondary-figure slipping-counter-motion board. 1SHC through 8SHC from IC6, for instance, are connected to the 1HC through 8HC control terminals of the horizontal counter, while 1SVC through 8SVC go to their respective vertical-counting-control inputs, 1VC through 8VC.

The two 4-bit motion-control words for the primary-figure slipping-counter board are taken ahead of ICs 6 and 7. These outputs are designated 1PVC through 8PVC and 1PHC through 8PHC.

As long as $\overline{\text{FIRE}}$ is at logic 1, then, both motion-control boards see the same sets of motion-control codes, and whatever changes in motion are prescribed for the primary figure are likewise delivered to the secondary figure.

The 2:1 multiplexer, IC9, also works under the control of the $\overline{\text{FIRE}}$ signal. As long as $\overline{\text{FIRE}}=1$, slipping-counter synchronizing pulses for the primary and secondary figure are identical: $\overline{\text{PHML}}=\overline{\text{SHML}}$, $\overline{\text{PVML}}=\overline{\text{SVML}}$. The primary and secondary figures thus appear at the same place on the screen.

As long as $\overline{\text{FIRE}}=1$, the player has complete control over the motion of both the primary and secondary figures by means of controls R1 and R3. And what's more, the secondary figure is always superimposed on the primary one. The latter follows the former, wherever it might go.

The picture changes completely, however, when $\overline{\text{FIRE}}$ is set to logic 0. The player still has complete control over the primary figure as before, but now latches IC6 and IC7 are set to their memory modes. The 4-bit motion-control words appearing at their outputs are fixed at the values present the moment $\overline{\text{FIRE}}$ changed from 1 to 0.

The result is that the secondary figure continues moving in the direction and at a speed specified at the moment $\overline{\text{FIRE}}$ is changed from 1 to 0. The player has no control over the motion of the secondary figure then.

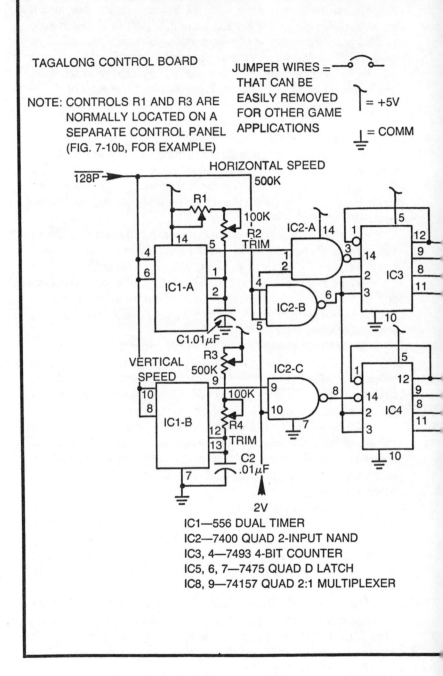

TAGALONG CONTROL BOARD

JUMPER WIRES = THAT CAN BE EASILY REMOVED FOR OTHER GAME APPLICATIONS

NOTE: CONTROLS R1 AND R3 ARE NORMALLY LOCATED ON A SEPARATE CONTROL PANEL (FIG. 7-10b, FOR EXAMPLE)

= +5V

= COMM

HORIZONTAL SPEED

128P

500K

R1

100K

R2 TRIM

14

4

6

5

1

2

IC1-A

IC2-A 14

1

3

14

2

3

5

12

9

8

11

IC3

10

C1.01μF

IC2-B

4

6

5

VERTICAL SPEED

10

8

R3 500K

9

100K

R4 TRIM

12

13

IC1-B

7

C2 .01μF

IC2-C

9

10

7

8

1

14

2

3

5

12

9

8

11

IC4

10

2V

IC1—556 DUAL TIMER
IC2—7400 QUAD 2-INPUT NAND
IC3, 4—7493 4-BIT COUNTER
IC5, 6, 7—7475 QUAD D LATCH
IC8, 9—74157 QUAD 2:1 MULTIPLEXER

268

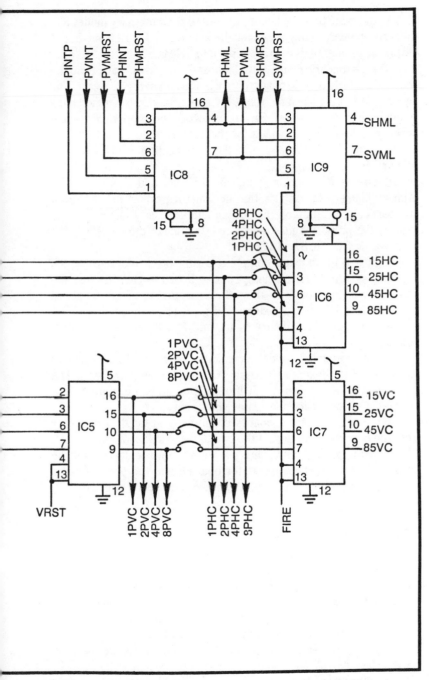

Fig. 7-13. Schematic diagram for a complete tagalong control circuit board.

269

At the same time the latches are set to their memory mode, IC9 shifts the synchronizing pulses for the secondary figure from that of the primary figure to its own set of pulses, $\overline{SHMRST}$ and $\overline{SVMRST}$.

The secondary figure thus flies under its own set of motion codes and synchronizing pulses until $\overline{FIRE}$ is set to logic 1 again. The instant $\overline{FIRE}$ is returned to logic 1, the secondary figure immediately snaps back to the primary figure, following the motion codes and synchronizing pulses specified for the primary figure.

IC8 in Fig. 7-13 is simply the initialization control for the primary figure. As long as $\overline{PINTP}$ is at logic 0, this 2:1 multiplexer circuit directs initial-position pulses, $\overline{PHINT}$ and $\overline{PVINT}$ to the primary-figure's reset inputs, thus holding the primary figure fixed at one particular position on the screen. As soon as $\overline{PINTP}$ is set to logic 1, the primary figure is free to "fly" under the control of the 4-bit words from IC3 and IC5.

Figure 7-14 shows a complete wiring block diagram for the tagalong system. The tagalong control board is the one just described in connection with the schematic in Fig. 7-13. The two slipping-counter boards are identical (Fig. 5-15), although board No. 1 is reserved for the primary figure and No. 2 for the secondary figure.

All the wiring between the tagalong-control board and the two slipping-counter boards is necessary in any tagalong operation. The experimenter is free to use only those slipping-counter outputs that are required for a particular game, however.

The slipping-counter boards consume a great deal of power from the power supply. In fact the two of them in Fig. 7-14 run a 5V, 1A regulator to its limits. One power supply regulator must be dedicated to these slipping-counter boards, and the power for the tagalong-control board must be taken from a second regulator circuit.

Torpedo Attack Block Diagram

We have had to depart from a detailed description of the torpedo game in order to discuss the operation of potentiometer-controlled speed and direction circuits as well as the basic tagalong control. It would probably be a good idea to refresh your ideas about the torpedo game, reviewing the action of the control panels and flow chart, before resuming this particular discussion.

Figure 7-15a shows the basic block diagram for the defense torpedo system. A command to launch any one of the four DTs comes from the DT launch panel goes to the DT horizontal position logic circuit, which determines the DT figure to be displayed. The same firing pulse from the DT launch panel goes to a simple pulse generator and releases the initialization operation on a vertical-slipping counter. The vertical component of the selected DT figure thus begins moving upward from its initial position at the bottom of the screen. The rate of motion is internally fixed at a moderately high speed.

The DT horizontal-position-logic circuit thus determines which one of the four DTs are fired, while the DT initialization logic and vertical-slipping counter determine when and how rapidly the DT figure moves up the screen. The horizontal and vertical components of the selected DT figure are combined in the DT figure logic block to form a complete image.

The DT figure continues moving up the screen until a negative-going $\overline{DTRST}$ pulse appears at the initialization-logic block. At that moment, the DT figure is blanked from the screen and the whole DT system is re-initialized until the defensive player launches another one.

The attack craft and attack torpedo block diagram is somewhat more involved. Note first in Fig. 7-15b that this system includes the tagalong scheme represented by the tagalong control board, the primary figure slipping counter, and the secondary figure slipping counter. The video information for the two figures are taken from their respective slipping counters and formed into images by the AC and AT figure logic blocks.

A pulse generator taking its input from 128V generates both the $\overline{128P}$ and $\overline{PVINT}$ pulses required for the tagalong scheme. Whenever the position of the primary figure is to be initialized, its vertical position is thus fixed at the point where the 128V count makes a transition from 0 to 1, near the middle of the screen.

The $\overline{HINTP}$ pulse generator merely fixes the horizontal position of the primary figure whenever it is initialized. In this case, the figure is initialized at the end of HBLANK, or at the left-hand edge of the screen.

The attack control panel provides horizontal and vertical information from a pair of potenitometers or a joystick. These signals control the motion in the same fashion as R1 and R3 in Fig. 7-13.

The AT flip-flop circuit determines whether the secondary figure, the attack torpedo, is synchronized with the primary figure or free to move on its own accord. An $\overline{ATLAUNCH}$ pulse from the attack-control panel sets this flip-flop to a condition that allows the attack torpedo to leave the primary figure. This is accomplished by setting $\overline{FIRE}$ to logic 0. The secondary figure then remains indepen-

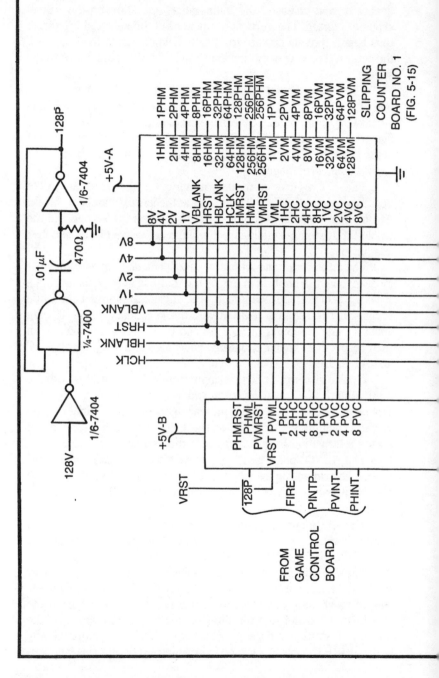

SLIPPING COUNTER BOARD NO. 1 (FIG. 5-15)

FROM GAME CONTROL BOARD

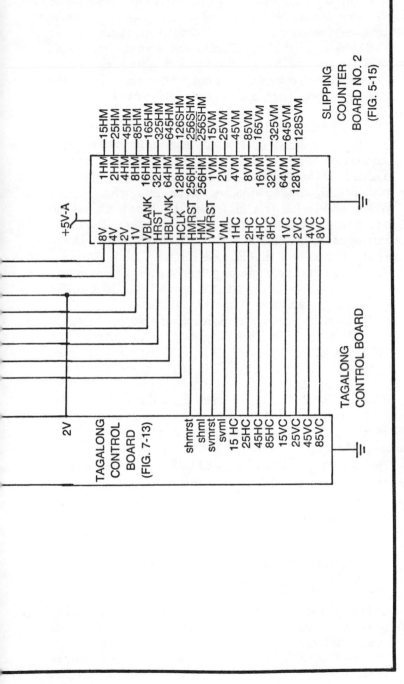

Fig. 7-14. Wiring diagram for a complete tagalong system.

dent of its primary counterpart until an $\overline{\text{ATRST}}$ pulse occurs. The ATRST pulse resets the flip-flop and returns $\overline{\text{FIRE}}$ to logic 1, thereby superimposing the AT figure onto the AC figure.

The block diagram in Fig. 7-15c represents the game logic portion of the system. Studying this block diagram in conjunction with the two previous block diagrams and the flow chart in Fig. 7-10 should lead to a good understanding of what this part of the system does.

The target figure, located in the lower right-hand corner of the screen, is fixed by a set of H- and V-count inputs from the Sourcebox unit. An inverted version of the target image is then directed to the AT=TARG logic block which generates a set of pulses whenever the attack craft figure (AFT) touches the target figure.

Whenever AT=TAGR in this fashion, the logic block sets the target flash time to indicate a score for the aggressor. The target image is flashed at a rate determined by the TARG FLASH block and for an interval fixed by TARG FLASH TIME.

At the end of the target flashing time, a pulse generator produces a pulse that resets the attack-torpedo image back to the attack-craft image—wherever it might be at the time.

EDGE2 is not displayed on the screen, but it plays a vital role in the game. Recall that EDGE2 is defined as the top, bottom, and right-hand edge of the screen. The EDGE2 logic block generates this set of invisible boundaries from VBLANK (top and bottom) and HRST (right-hand edge).

AT=EDGE2 LOGIC compares EDGE2 with ATFIG. Whenever they coincide, indicating the attack torpedo is running out of bounds, this block generates a pulse that ultimately resets the position of the attack torpedo back to the attack-craft figure.

The EDGE1 LOGIC block uses VBLANK to define the invisible top and bottom boundaries. Whenever the attack-craft figure (ACFIG) touches one of these two boundaries, the AC=EDGE1 LOGIC block generates a pulse that initiates a flashing time for the attack-craft image. This represents a default score for the defensive player. The aggressor has run his craft out of bounds.

The attack-craft figure is also flashed whenever the AC=TARG block senses contact between the attack craft and the target. Again, this represents a default score for the defensive player.

And finally, the attack-craft figure is flashed when AC=DT (a defense torpedo strikes the attack craft). The AC=DT LOGIC block takes care of this operation.

The AC FLASH TIME is thus set under any one of three conditions: AC=EDGE1, AC=TARG, and AC=DT. All three instances can represent a score for the defensive player because they lead to a destruction of the attack craft.

A defense torpedo that has been fired is reset under either of two conditions: AC=DT or DT=TOP. In the first case, the defensive player has successfully stopped an attack by hitting the attack craft with a torpedo. If a defense torpedo misses its target, however, it continues its steady upward motion until it reaches the top of the screen as defined by DT=TOP LOGIC. The TOP in this case is determined by VBLANK and a TOP PULSE GENERATOR.

The four figures to be displayed (the target, attack craft, attack torpedo, and defense torpedo) are combined in the GAME VID OUTPUT LOGIC block to yield a composite game-video signal.

Torpedo Attack Schematics

The complete Torpedo Attack game system requires three circuit boards for the tagalong feature, three special game-control boards, and two player-control panels. As described earlier in this section, the tagalong feature is made up of a pair of identical slipping-counter boards (Fig. 5-15) and a tagalong-control board (Fig. 7-13). Figure 7-14 shows the complete wiring detail for these three tagalong boards.

The three special control boards for Torpedo Attack are shown in schematic form in Figs. 7-16, 7-17, and 7-18. The control panels are described in connection with the schematics and layouts in Fig. 7-11.

The wiring block diagram in Fig. 7-19 shows the wiring detail between the tagalong assembly, the three special control boards, and the control panels.

The circuit board in Fig. 7-16 contains all the components for the DT (defense torpedo) figures. The defense player's four firing buttons are connected to inputs S1 through S4. These inputs are normally pulled up to logic 1 by the four 2.2-kΩ resistors connected to +5V. Whenever the defense player depresses one of his four firing buttons, the logic level at the corresponding S input to the DT control board is forced to logic 0.

IC4-A in Fig. 7-16 functions as an OR gate when used with this active-low input format. Its main job is to sense the fact that the defense player has depressed any one of the four firing buttons.

Depressing any one of the four DT firing buttons thus causes IC4-A to generate a positive-going logic level which is then inverted to a negative-going level by inverter IC5-C. This negative-going logic level is then transformed into a brief negative-going pulse by

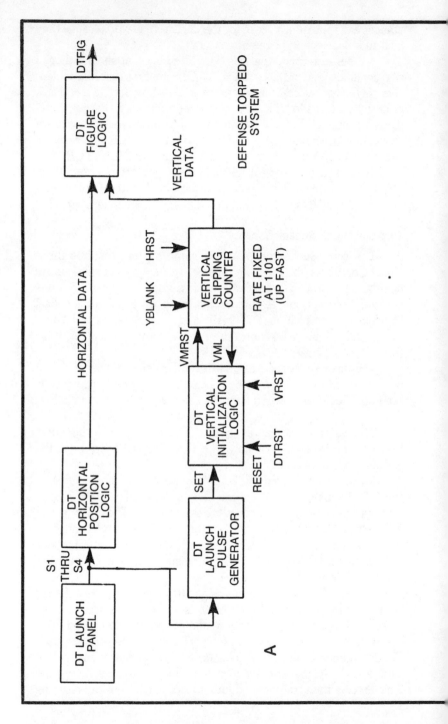

276

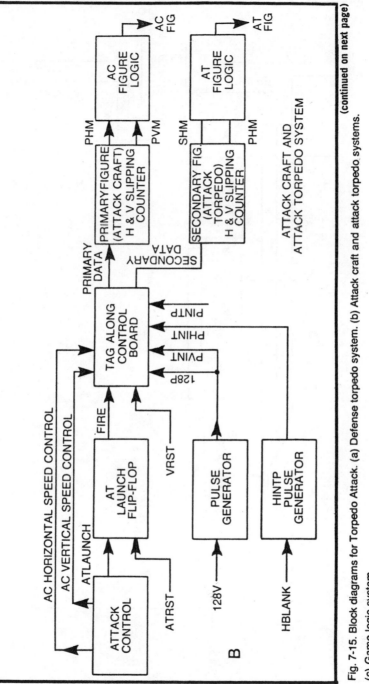

Fig. 7-15. Block diagrams for Torpedo Attack. (a) Defense torpedo system. (b) Attack craft and attack torpedo systems. (c) Game logic system.

(continued on next page)

277

(continued from previous page)

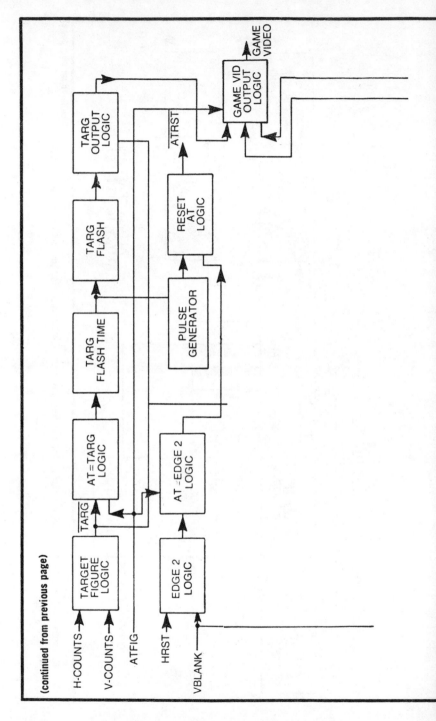

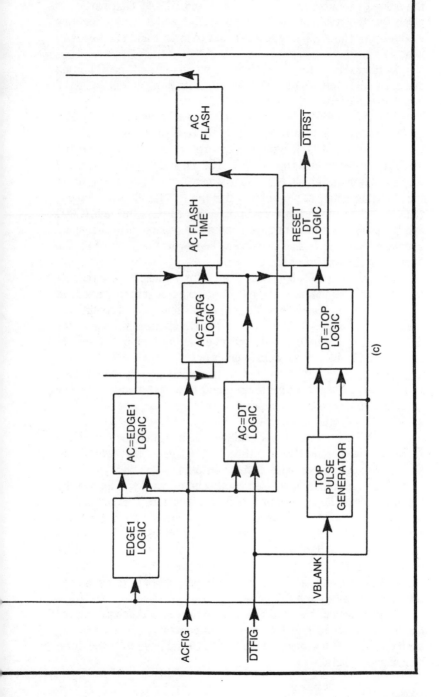

(c)

the pulse generator, made up of IC1-A and IC5-A. That particular pulse sets the status of a $\overline{R}$-$\overline{S}$ flip-flop (IC2-A and IC2-B) to its firing mode—one where pin 3 of IC2-A is set to logic 1 and pin 6 goes to logic 0.

Putting this all together, depressing any one of the DT firing switches ultimately sets the DT system to its firing mode, and a DT figure is launched.

The DT system is reset to its initial condition whenever the $\overline{R}$-$\overline{S}$ flip-flop receives a negative-going DTRST pulse at pin 5 of IC2-B.

The output of the $\overline{R}$-$\overline{S}$ flip-flop controls the operation of a figure initialization circuit made up of IC2-C, IC2-D, and IC3-A. This part of the circuit is in the initialization mode whenever a DT figures is not in flight. In this instance, pin 6 of IC2-B in the $\overline{R}$-$\overline{S}$ flip-flop is at logic 1, thus allowing an inverted version of VRST to pass through IC2-D and IC3-A to the loading or reset inputs of a pair of vertical-slipping counters, IC8 and IC9. This forces the vertical positon of all DT figures to the bottom of the screen.

Whenever a DT figure is fired, the initialization circuit is switched to a condition whereby the slipping counters are loaded with reset pulses from IC3-B. Under this particular set of conditions, the slipping counters let the DT figure move up the screen at a rate determined by the hard-wired logic leveis at preset inputs (pins 15, 1, 10, and 9) of the two slipping counters.

The DT circuitry described to this point merely determined whether or not a DT figure is fired and how fast it moves up the screen. The next part of the problem is to see how one of the four possible DT figures is selected.

The DT figure selection circuitry is built around the four EXCLUSIVE OR gates in IC6, the three NAND gates that feed them, and the 4-input NAND gate at their outputs.

To see how this figure-selection scheme works, suppose the defensive player depressed the FIRE 1 pushbutton. This action pulls the logic level of S1 input down to logic 0, causing a logic-1 level to appear at the output of IC4-A as described previously. The output of this gate is returned to pins 4 and 13 of IC10, the gate inputs of a 4-bit data latch. The pattern of logic levels present at the S inputs is thus latched in IC10, and remains fixed at the outputs of IC10 even after the player releases the firing button.

In this particular example described here, the defensive player has depressed the FIRE 1 button on his control panel, so the 4-bit latch is loaded with a logic 0 at pin 9 of IC10 and logic 1s at the three remaining outputs.

NAND gates IC1-C and IC1-D now see logic-0 levels at one of their two inputs, thereby guaranteeing logic-1 levels from those two gates. The output of IC1-B remains at logic 0 because its two inputs from the latch are still fixed at logic 1.

The EXCLUSIVE OR gates in IC6 then produce a pattern of inverted and noninverted H-count signals. IC6-B and IC6-C both yield inverted versions of their respective H-count inputs, while IC6-A produces a noninverted version of 128H. Since IC6-D is permanently wired to invert its 32H input, it follows that the EXCLUSIVE OR configuration is producing H-count signals of $\overline{256H}$, 128H, $\overline{64H}$, and $\overline{32H}$. NANDing these four signals together in IC4-B produces a DT image having its horizontal position determined by the four H-count parameters just described. That's true if the player depresses the FIRE 1 button.

The following list summarizes the H-count parameters from this DT selection circuit whenever the defensive player fires any one of the four defense torpedoes:

- S1—$\overline{256H}$, 128H, $\overline{64H}$, $\overline{32H}$
- S2—$\overline{256H}$, $\overline{128H}$, $\overline{64H}$, 32H
- S3—256H, $\overline{128H}$, $\overline{64H}$, $\overline{32H}$
- S4—256H, $\overline{128H}$, 64H, $\overline{32H}$

The output of IC4-B determines the horizontal position, or to be more specific, it determines which one of the four DT figures are fired. The output of IC3-B at the vertical-slipping counter then determines the vertical position of the DT figure. These two figure parameters are first transformed into pulses by a set of pulse generators, then applied to IC7-B where they are molded into the DT figure itself. The value of C2 fixes the vertical height of DT, while C3 sets in width.

The complete DT figure from IC7-B is inverted by IC7-C and sent to yet another NOR gate which, in effect, actually functions as a blanking gate for the DT figure. Some sort of DT figure data appears continuously at pin 3 of IC7-A, but the logic level at pin 2 is determined by whether the system is in a firing or DT initializing mode.

A NOR gate of this type is effectively switched off whenever one of its inputs is at logic 1, a condition that occurs whenever the $\overline{R}$-S flip-flop shows a logic-1 level from pin 6 of IC2-B. Recall that this condition signifies the DT figure is reset to its initial position. The DT figures are thus blanked from the screen until they are fired.

The circuit in Fig. 7-17 is basically a figure generating board. IC8 generates the target figure from the selection of H- and V-count signals shown at its inputs. The ACFIG signal from IC3-A is the

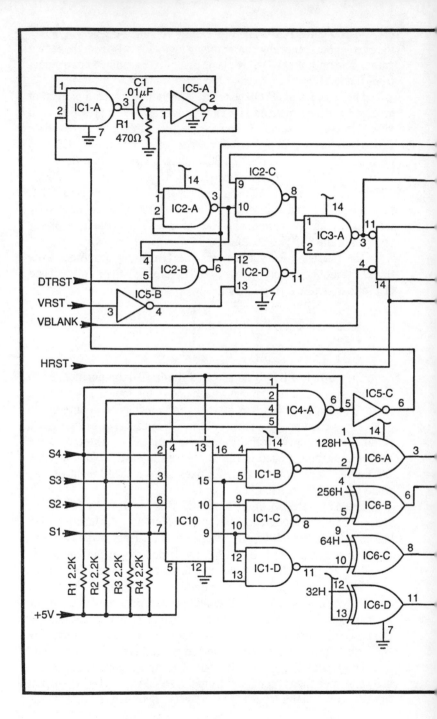

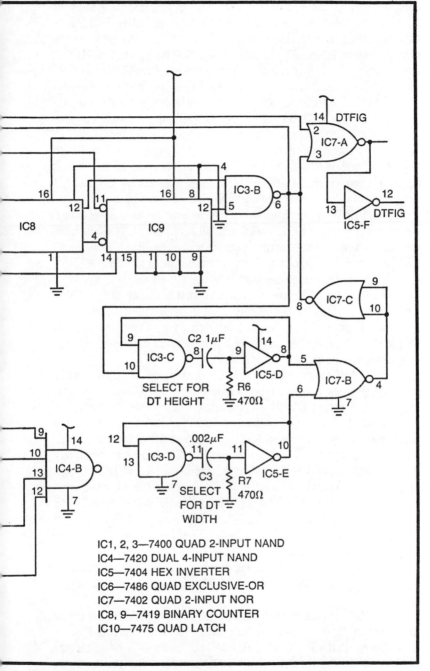

IC1, 2, 3—7400 QUAD 2-INPUT NAND
IC4—7420 DUAL 4-INPUT NAND
IC5—7404 HEX INVERTER
IC6—7486 QUAD EXCLUSIVE-OR
IC7—7402 QUAD 2-INPUT NOR
IC8, 9—7419 BINARY COUNTER
IC10—7475 QUAD LATCH

Fig. 7-16. Schematic diagram for the defense torpedo circuit board.

283

composite image for the attack craft. The horizontal component of this movable figure is determined by the primary-figure HM inputs to IC5-A. And in a similar fashion, the vertical component comes from the primary-figure VM inputs to IC5-B. The signals from IC5-A and IC5-B are sent through pulse generators before they are effectively ANDed by IC3-A. The value of C1 fixes the horizontal length of the attack-craft figure, while C2 determines its vertical height.

ATFIG from IC3-B is the attack-torpedo figure, which is generated in a manner identical to that of the attack-craft figure. IC6-A determines the horizontal component from the secondary-figure HM data, and IC6-B fixes the vertical component of the attack torpedo from secondary-figure VM data. Capacitors C3 and C4 determine the horizontal and vertical size of this figure.

The $\overline{\text{FIRE}}$ output from IC2-C is a logic level that equals 0 whenever the attack torpedo is fired. The $\overline{\text{ATLAUNCH}}$ signal from the aggressor's control panel sets the $\overline{\text{R}}$-$\overline{\text{S}}$ flip-flop (IC2-B and IC2-C) so that $\overline{\text{FIRE}}$ goes to 0 and remains there until the ATRST (attack torpedo reset) pulse occurs.

The final Torpedo Attack control board is shown in Fig. 7-18. This circuit performs most of the game-control functions shown in the block diagram in Fig. 7-15c. Comparing these two figures, you should have little trouble matching block diagram functions with the logic components in the schematic.

AT=TARG logic, for instance, takes place at IC1-B, while timers IC9-A and IC9-B are responsible for target-flashing effects. EDGE2 is generated by IC4-D, and the AT=EDGE2 function is performed by IC5-C. The outputs of IC9-A or IC5-C are ultimately responsible for producing an ATRST pulse at the output of IC7-B.

EDGE1 is present at the output of IC6-C, where it is effectively ANDed with ACFIG in IC3-D to perform the AC=EDGE1 logic function. AC=TARG takes place at IC4-A, while the AC=DT function takes place at IC3-C. The three inputs to the AC FLASH TIME block in Fig. 7-15c appear at IC5-A in Fig. 7-18, and the output of that particular NOR gate goes to flash timer IC8-A where it initiates the AC flashing interval.

The figures to be displayed on the screen are combined at IC5-B and IC1-C. Pin 8 of IC1-C is the game's composite video output.

The $\overline{\text{PINTP}}$ logic level from IC6-E is responsible for resetting the attack craft to an initial position determined by outputs $\overline{\text{PVINT}}$ (IC7-F) and $\overline{\text{PHINT}}$ (IC7-C). IC1-D and its associated inverters produce both the $\overline{\text{PVINT}}$ pulse $\overline{\text{128P}}$ required for the tagalong system.

284

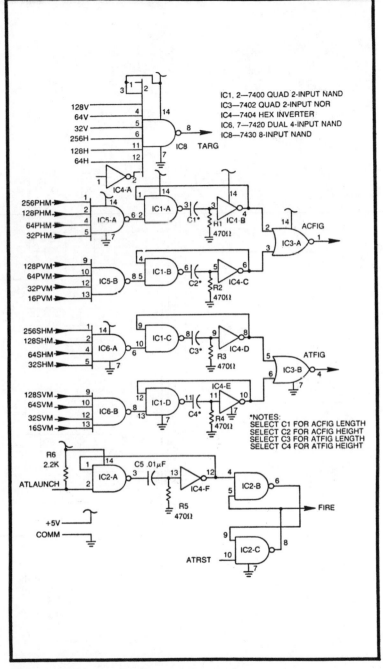

Fig. 7-17. Schematic diagram for the figure board.

285

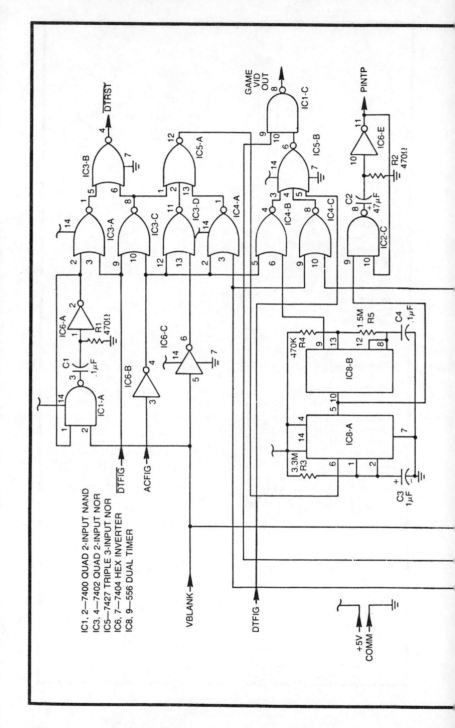

IC1, 2—7400 QUAD 2-INPUT NAND
IC3, 4—7402 QUAD 2-INPUT NOR
IC5—7427 TRIPLE 3-INPUT NOR
IC6, 7—7404 HEX INVERTER
IC8, 9—556 DUAL TIMER

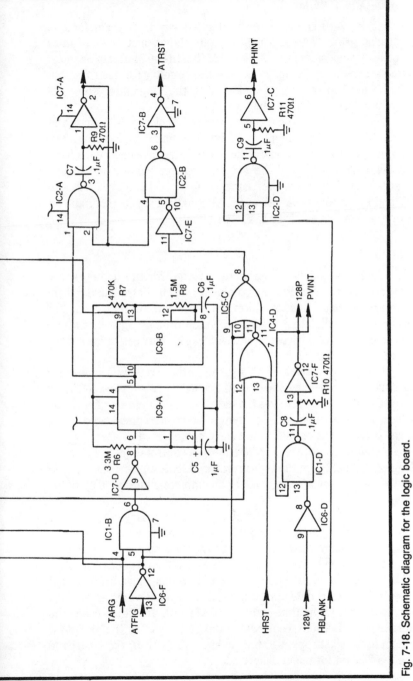

Fig. 7-18. Schematic diagram for the logic board.

Torpedo Attack Wiring Diagram

Figure 7-19 shows a recommended wiring diagram for this particular game. The tagalong system shown in this diagram is actually a composite of the three circuit boards and interconnections detailed previously in Fig. 7-14. Half the circuitry for this game can thus be used in other games, including the Dogfight system described in the section that follows.

Using six circuit boards and two control panels pushes the system's main power supply a bit beyond maximum capacity. Try operating one slipping-counter board and the tagalong board from the Game-A supply, and the second slipping-counter and Figure Boards (Fig. 7-17) from the Game-B supply. That leaves only the DT and Logic boards as well as the two control panels that must be operated from an auxiliary 5-V, 1-A supply.

DOGFIGHT

Here is a popular video game adapted for the home experimenter. The game requires two players, each controlling the flight of an aircraft that is capable of firing a missile at the other's craft. The players have complete freedom to fly their primary figure anywhere on the screen. This particular version has no barriers or borders to restrict the flight.

The special wrinkle in this game is the circuitry required for making the missile leave the craft at twice the craft's speed and in the same direction. This involves the use of a 2× vector multiplier circuit which, at first thought, might seem to be rather complicated, but it turns out that the circuitry isn't very complicated at all.

The flow charts in Fig. 7-20 show the control sequences for this Dogfight game. Since the two charts are identical, a careful study of one of them automatically leads to a complete understanding of the other.

Suppose both players are piloting their primary figures (their respective "C" figures) around the screen, carrying their missiles in a tagalong fashion. Now let Player A trigger his missile. According to the flow chart on the left-hand side of Fig. 7-20, this action sets the AM (Player A's missile) mode. One of two things can happen: that missile figure can come into contact with Player B's craft (AM=BC) or A's missile flight time expires (AMT=0). In either case, the missile is immediately returned to the primary craft (RESET AM) but if the missile happens to hit the opponent's craft, the destroyed craft is flashed for about 1 second.

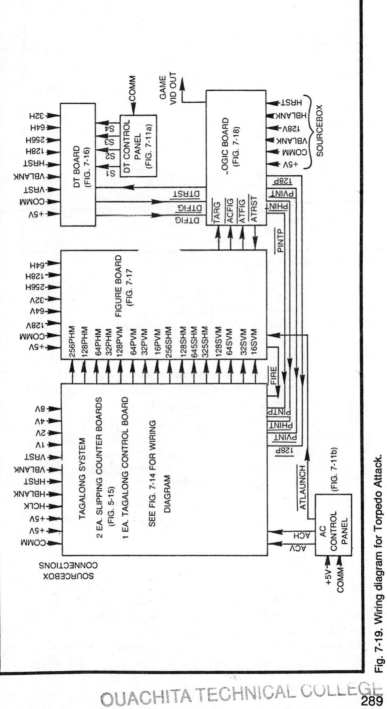

Fig. 7-19. Wiring diagram for Torpedo Attack.

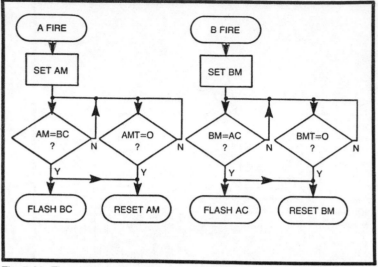

Fig. 7-20. Flowcharts for Dogfight.

So the overall picture looks something like this. There are two aircraft flying freely around the screen. A player can fire a missile from his craft, and that missile figure leaves the primary craft in the same direction, but at twice the speed. The missile can fly for about 1 second before it is blanked from the screen and returned to the primary craft. If that missile happens to strike the opponent's craft enroute, the opponent's craft is destroyed (flashed) and the missile is returned to its primary figure once again.

The game can go on indefinitely because this particular version has no provisions for keeping score and automatically resetting the game. These features can be added at a later time.

The two identical control panels are quite simple, consisting only of a firing button and a set of flight-path controls. The two potentiometers shown in Fig. 7-21 can be replaced with a joystick control to produce simpler and more realistic interaction between the control panels and activity on the screen.

Vector Logic

This Dogfight game is built around two identical sets of tagalong systems, one set for each player. And that means the experimenter must be prepared to install four slipping-counter boards (Fig. 5-15) and two tagalong-control boards (Fig. 7-13).

The secondary figures in both systems tagalong with the primary figures in the usual fashion until a player launches his missile. The secondary figure then leaves the primary figure, taking on a speed and direction that is dictated by the set of control data present the moment the missile is fired. In the case of the Missile and Torpedo Attack games described earlier in this chapter, the missile leaves the primary figure with the same speed and direction the primary figure had at the moment of launching. In this case, however, the missile leaves in the same direction, but at a faster speed. And that means the secondary-figure controls must be loaded with speed and direction data that is entirely different from that of its primary figure.

Figure 7-22 shows a complete analysis of control data that is entered into any of the slipping-counter schemes described thus far. There are two relevant mathematical equations that show how fast a figure moves across the screen and, alternately, how long it takes to move across the screen.

The velocity (v) is expressed in rather unusual units of screens per second. It is possible to use other, more conventional units of speed, such as inches per second, but such units vary with the size of the experimenter's TV screen. The screens-per-second unit of speed on the screen.

The velocity of a figure, in either the horizontal or vertical direction, is determined by the first equation in Fig. 7-22. Note that

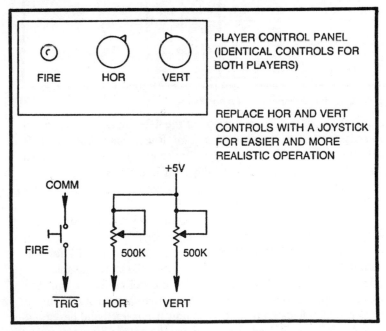

Fig. 7-21. Control panel and schematic for each player.

$$v = \frac{60(9-M)}{C} \qquad t = \left| 1/v \right|$$

v = FIGURE VELOCITY IN SCREENS/SECOND
M = DECIMAL VALUE OF SPEED CODE ENTERED INTO THE SLIPPING
    COUNTERS
C = HORIZONTAL OR VERTICAL COUNT TOTAL
    C = 245 FOR VERTICAL MOTION
    C = 374 FOR HORIZONTAL MOTION
t = TIME REQUIRED FOR FIGURE TO CROSS THE SCREEN IN A
    HORIZONTAL OR VERTICAL DIRECTION IN SECONDS

CODE	M	VERTICAL		HORIZONTAL	
		v	t	v	t
0000	0	1.4	0.7	2.2	0.45
0001	1	1.3	0.8	1.9	0.51
0010	2	1.2	0.9	1.7	0.58
0011	3	0.96	1.0	1.5	0.68
0100	4	0.8	1.2	1.2	0.82
0101	5	0.64	1.6	0.98	1.0
0110	6	0.48	2.1	0.73	1.4
0111	7	0.32	3.1	0.49	2.0
1000	8	0.16	6.2	0.24	4.1
1001	9	0.0	00	0	00
1010	10	−0.16	6.2	−0.24	4.1
1011	11	−0.32	3.1	−0.49	2.0
1100	12	−0.48	2.1	−0.73	1.4
1101	13	−0.64	1.6	−0.98	1.0
1110	14	−0.8	1.2	−1.2	0.82
1111	15	−0.96	1.0	−1.5	0.68

v > 0 = MOTION DOWN
OR RIGHT
v < 0 = MOTION UP OR
LEFT

Fig. 7-22. Vector motion equations and table.

the M variable is a decimal version of the 4-bit binary control word entered into the slipping-counter system. Recall that the stop code is 1001, or decimal 9. In this instance, M=9 and v turns out to be equal to 0, a clear indication that entering 1001 into the slipping counter yields a figure speed of 0. The figure does not move in that particular up/down or left/right direction.

Variable C is a constant number that reflects the maximum counting capacity of the slipping-counter circuit. C is thus equal to 245 for the vertical component of motion and it is 374 for the horizontal component. The v columns in the table show the solutions to this equation for all possible motion control codes in both the horizontal and vertical directions. Note that a velocity having a negative value indicates motion in an upward or left-hand direction. Positive values of v indicate motion down the screen or to the right.

So if a figure happens to be moving with M=6 in the horizontal direction, it is moving downward and to the left. And since the downward velocity is 0.48 screens/second and the left velocity is −0.73 screens/second, it follows that it is moving at a relatively sharp downward angle. If you are familiar with the mathematical procedures for drawing vectors and solving them, you can determine the exact angle and speed.

It is, in fact, quite tempting to digress from the main topic and indulge in some vector analyses of the data in Fig. 7-22. The results could be quite useful, but the matter is better left to reader's who have the knowledge and initiative for doing the job.

Returning to the matter of multiplying the speed components of the secondary figure, look at the table and circuit in Fig. 7-23. The left-hand side of the table shows 10 different slipping-counter controls that might be present at the control inputs of the primary-figure-motion-control board. There are actually as many as 16 possible motion-control codes, but many of them are invalid in the context of our 2× vector logic system. The 8 valid codes are for M values from 5 through 12. The values of 4 and 13 are shown on the table to illustrate the nature of the invalid conditions, but the list also should include 13 through 15 and 0 through 3.

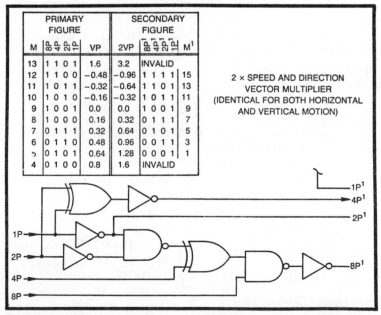

PRIMARY FIGURE			SECONDARY FIGURE		
M	8P 4P 2P 1P	VP	2VP	8P 4P 2P 1P	M¹
13	1 1 0 1	1.6	3.2	INVALID	
12	1 1 0 0	−0.48	−0.96	1 1 1 1	15
11	1 0 1 1	−0.32	−0.64	1 1 0 1	13
10	1 0 1 0	−0.16	−0.32	1 0 1 1	11
9	1 0 0 1	0.0	0.0	1 0 0 1	9
8	1 0 0 0	0.16	0.32	0 1 1 1	7
7	0 1 1 1	0.32	0.64	0 1 0 1	5
6	0 1 1 0	0.48	0.96	0 0 1 1	3
5	0 1 0 1	0.64	1.28	0 0 0 1	1
4	0 1 0 0	0.8	1.6	INVALID	

2 × SPEED AND DIRECTION
VECTOR MULTIPLIER
(IDENTICAL FOR BOTH HORIZONTAL
AND VERTICAL MOTION)

Fig. 7-23. Vector table and circuit for achieving launch velocities twice that of the primary figure.

293

The primary-figure control codes are translated into velocities in the VP column. This data is taken directly from the table in Fig. 7-22. The 2VP column then shows the VP figure multiplied by 2. Multiplying a velocity vector changes only the speed and not the direction, so the 4-bit binary words on the right-hand side of the table in Fig. 7-23 show the control codes that suit the 2VP velocity figures. Again, this data is taken directly from Fig. 7-22. The M' column merely translates the control codes into their corresponding decimal values.

What this table is saying is that when any primary figure is carrying along a secondary figure with one velocity component of $M=12$, the secondary figure should be launched with a velocity component of $M=15$. The secondary figure will move away in the same direction, but with twice the speed of the primary figure.

Primary-figure M figures greater than 12 or less than 3 are considered invalid because the $2\times$ transformation calls for M' values that are greater or less than a 4-bit binary format allows. A figure cannot go any faster than 1111 or 0000.

The circuit in Fig. 7-23 shows how the primary-figure data is translated into a $2\times$ format for its secondary figure. As long as the primary control data stays within its valid operating range of $M=5$ through $M=12$, the circuit performs the prescribed transformations.

Interfacing this $2\times$ vector circuit with the tagalong control system is a matter of removing the jumpers specified in Fig. 7-13 and connecting the PVC outputs of that circuit to the corresponding P inputs of the $2\times$ vector circuit. The four outputs of the vector circuit are then connected to their respective PVC' connections in Fig. 7-13.

A second $2\times$ vector circuit can then be interfaced with the PH connections in a similar fashion.

The secondary figure then tags along with its primary figure as long as the $\overline{\text{FIRE}}$ terminal in Fig. 7-13 is at logic 1. Even though the secondary figure is receiving control data that is different from the control data for the primary figure, the secondary figure is effectively initialized at the primary figure's position.

Setting $\overline{\text{FIRE}}$ to logic 0, however, loads latches IC6 and IC7 in Fig. 7-13 with the $2\times$-transformed-control data, and as a result, the secondary figure flies away at twice its host's speed.

Dogfight Block Diagram

The block diagram in Fig. 7-24 represents the Dogfight game described in this section. The PLAYER A CONTROLS block gener-

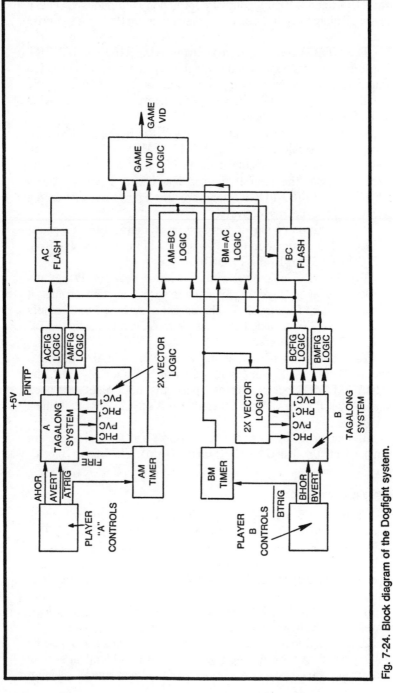

Fig. 7-24. Block diagram of the Dogfight system.

295

ates AHOR and AVERT control information continuously. These lines are simply the potentiometer connections on Player A's control panel.

The A TAGALONG system transforms the AHOR and AVERT signals into motion-control codes for the slipping counters included in that system. The primary-figure motion codes are taken directly from the input data, while the secondary-figure codes are modified by the 2× vector logic block.

Whenever Player A depresses his FIRE button, $\overline{ATRIG}$ initiates a monostable timer circuit, AM TIMER. This timer immediately releases the secondary figure from its host, causing the missile to leave the aircraft figure. The blocks labeled ACFIG LOGIC and AMFIG LOGIC generate the figures for Player A's aircraft and missile respectively.

The operation of Player B's system is identical to this point, with the video information for his aircraft and missile coming from BCFIG LOGIC and BMFIG LOGIC.

The AM=BC logic block senses contact between Player A's missile and Player B's craft. Whenever such a contact occurs, it indicates a score for Player A. The output of AM=BC both resets the AM TIMER (returning the A missile to AC) and causing the BC figure to flash on the screen.

The same sort of operations are involved in the BM=AC scheme. Whenever Player B's missile strikes Player A's craft, the BM=AC LOGIC block generates a pulse that both resets the position of Player B's missile and makes Player A's aircraft figure flash on and off.

All four game figures, the two aircraft and two missiles, are combined into the final GAME VID in the GAME VID LOGIC block.

Dogfight Schematics

Figures 7-25 and 7-26 show the two special control circuit boards required for this Dogfight game. Most of the circuitry in Fig. 7-25 is dedicated to performing the 2× vector multiplying operations for both players. This particular circuit board also contains the firing logic for both players and the 128P generator for the tagalong systems.

The circuit in Fig. 7-26 contains all the figure-generating logic as well as the contact and figure-flashing logic.

Before explaining the theory of operation of these two boards, it is important to realize they are used with two identical sets of tagalong systems, one system for each of the two players. All input and output designations carrying an "A" prefix denote connections to Player A's systems, while those carrying a "B" prefix indicate connections in Player B's system.

It might be helpful at this point to look ahead a bit to the wiring block diagram in Fig. 7-27. You can see the two special Dogfight boards, the vector and figure boards, servicing two complete tagalong systems.

Now notice that the vector board in Fig. 7-25 has four of the $2\times$ vector multiplier circuits described previously in Fig. 7-23. Each receives a set of four primary-figure-motion-control bits from the tagalong control boards.

The first of these four $2\times$ vector circuits accepts bits A1PHC through A8PHC. These are Player A's primary figure horizontal-motion codes. The outputs from this same circuit, designated A1PHC' through A8PHC', are the $2\times$-corrected motion codes for Player A's secondary figure horizontal-slipping counter.

The vector circuit having inputs A1PVC through A8PVC gets its data from Player A's primary figure vertical-motion control circuit; and the outputs (A1PVC' through A8PVC') go to his secondary figure vertical-control circuit.

The two remaining vector circuits in Fig. 7-25 perform exactly the same operation on Player B's motion-control codes.

IC8-A in Fig. 7-25 is a timer that is programmed for monostable operation. Whenever Player A despresses his FIRE button, a negative-going pulse at ATRIG initiates a 1-second output pulse from IC8-A. This output, labeled AFIRE, is responsible for separating Player A's missile from his aircraft. As noted in Fig. 7-27, AFIRE is connected to the FIRE input on Player A's tagalong control board.

The timing operation continues until the monostable completes its normal 1-second interval or a negative-going AMRST pulse occurs at pin 4. As described in connection with the circuit in Fig. 7-26, this AMRST pulse occurs whenever Player A successfully shoots down his opponent.

Player B's firing circuit, built around IC8-B, works the same way. BTRIG is taken from Player B's control panel FIRE button, the BFIRE output separates his missile from aircraft B, and the timer can be reset immediately by a negative-going pulse at BMRST.

The compact pulse generator made up of IC7-E, IC9-A, and IC7-F merely generates the 128P pulse required for any tagalong motion control system. In this case, the 128P pulse services the tagalong systems for both players.

Since this Dogfight game runs continuously, there is no need for any sort of game resetting operations, and as a result, it is possible to

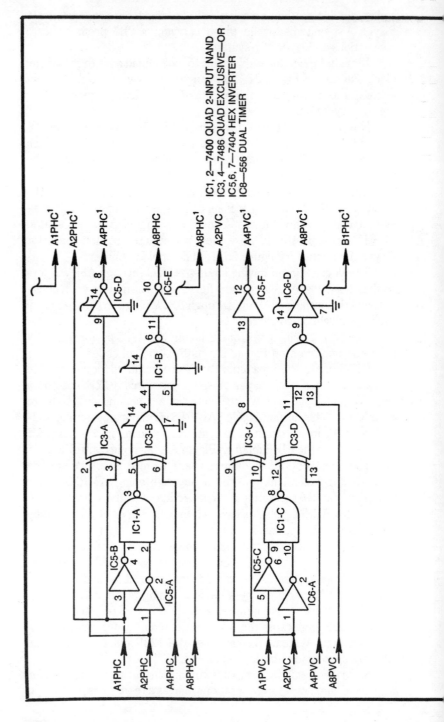

IC1, 2—7400 QUAD 2-INPUT NAND
IC3, 4—7486 QUAD EXCLUSIVE—OR
IC5, 6, 7—7404 HEX INVERTER
IC8—556 DUAL TIMER

298

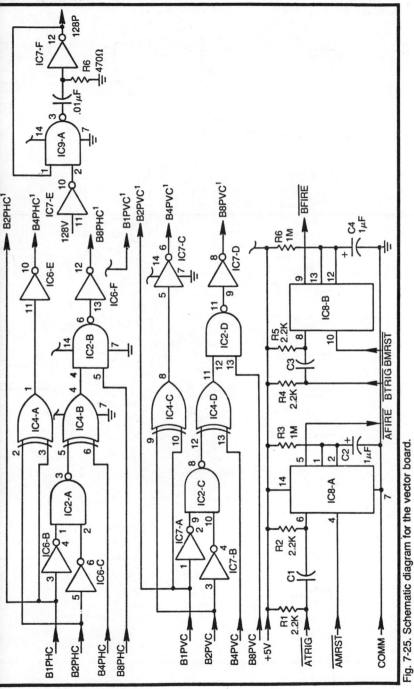

Fig. 7-25. Schematic diagram for the vector board.

299

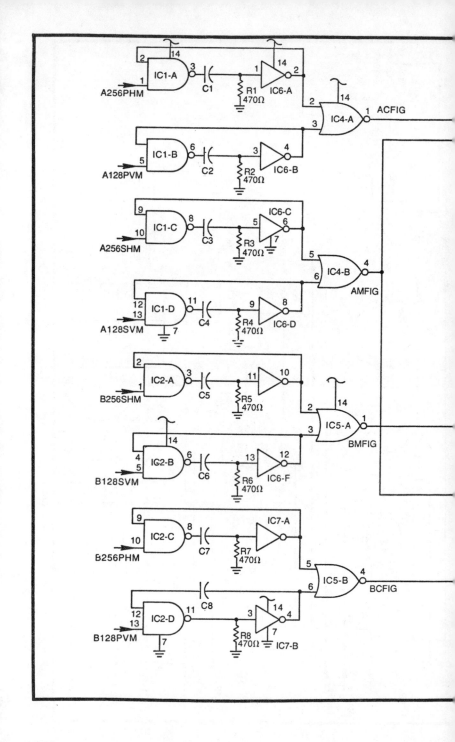

300

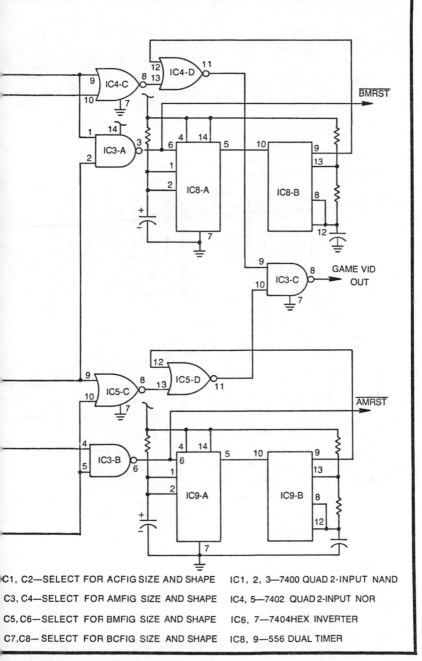

Fig. 7-26. Schematic diagram for the figure board.

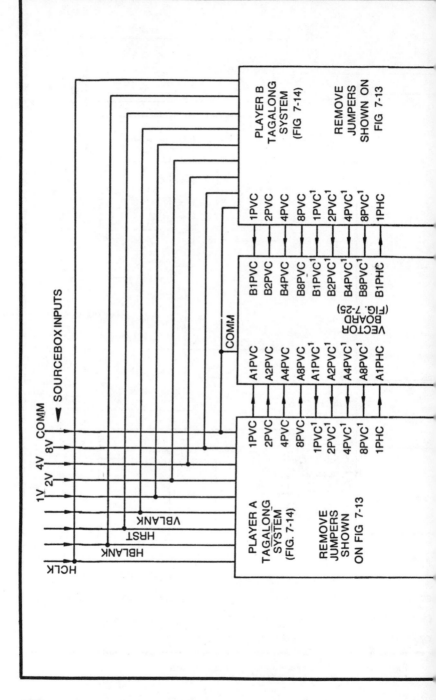

302

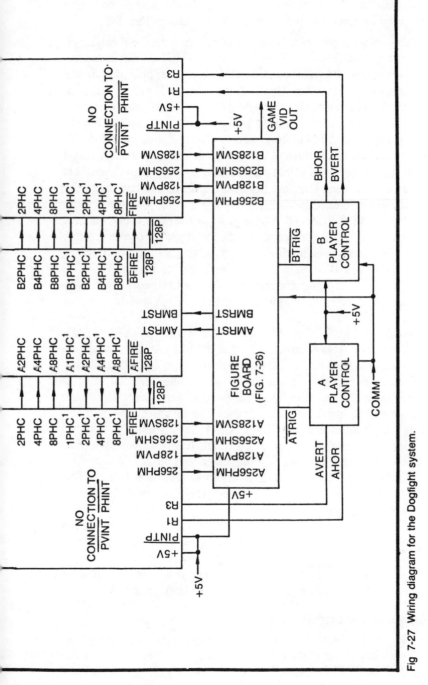

Fig 7-27 Wiring diagram for the Dogfight system.

build the figures from the negative-going edges of the high-order bit on all four slipping counters. This rather simple procedure is implemented by the eight pulse generator circuits in Fig. 7-26.

The trickiest part of this circuit is interpreting the meaning of the input designations. A256PHM at pin 1 of IC1-A, for instance, represents the 256HM output of Player A's primary figure horizontal-slippng counter. By the same token, A128PVM is Player A's 128VM signal from his primary-figure vertical-slipping counter.

The outputs of these two pulse generators are effectively ANDed together in IC4-A to generate Player A's primary-aircraft figure. The selected values of C1 and C2 determined the horizontal and vertical dimensions of that particular figure. The experimenter is free to select values that suit his own impression of how large the aircraft figures should be.

Inputs A256SHM and A128SVM are the high-order counter outputs from Player A's secondary-figure slipping counters. After shortening these pulses with a set of pulse generators, they are combined in IC4-B to yield the missile figure for Player A.

Player B's slipping-counter signals are handled in the same fashion, producing his missile figure from IC5-A and his aircraft figure from IC5-B.

IC3-A in Fig. 7-26 senses contact between Player B's missile and A's aircraft. This is, in other words, the BM=AC LOGIC shown in the block diagram in Fig. 7-24. In the same way, IC3-B signals any contact between Player B's aircraft and A's missile.

A contact between a missile and the opponent's aircraft initiates a timer circuit which, in turn, causes the image of the stricken aircraft to flash on and off. Timer IC8-A, for instance, is initiated whenever B's missile contacts A's aircraft. IC8-B is then allowed to oscillate, alternately gating A's images on and off at IC4-D.

IC9-A is another timer that controls oscillator IC9-B. The action of these two devices is initiated whenever there is contact between A's missile and B's aircraft.

The two pairs of images (Player A's aircraft and missile, and B's aircraft and missile) are combined at IC3-C to yield the games video-output signal.

$\overline{AMRST}$ and $\overline{BMRST}$ are set to logic 0 whenever a missile scores, thereby returning the missle to its host aircraft.

Dogfight Wiring Diagram

Figure 7-27 shows the wiring diagram for the Dogfight game. One very important feature that might be easily overlooked is the fact that the PINTP connections on the two tagalong systems are connected directly to logic 1, or +5V. This connection disables the primary-figure-initializing circuit so that the game procedes continuously. There is never any condition that calls for initializing the positions of either primary figure.

This system uses a total of eight circuit boards and two control panels: two slipping counter and one tagalong control for each player, as well as a vector and figure board. The tagalong system for Player A should be operated from the +5V source for Game A, and the tagalong system for Player B should operate from the Game-B supply. The vector board, figure board, and two control panels must then be powered from an auxiliary +5-V, 1-A supply. Of course all COMM connections should be connected together.

Chapter 8

Programmable Position and Motion Controls

It is possible to realize some overall savings of time and money by using programmable figure-generating and motion-control circuits. The initial investment is larger because programmable circuits are generally more complicated than those designed for specific game applications. Being able to use the same circuitry for a number of different video game formats, however, soon lets the circuit pay for itself a number of times over.

The circuits described here are close cousins of the fully programmable TV game computer systems on the market today. The experimenter isn't bound to a set of fixed game formats; yet, the scheme goes a long way toward simplifying game design procedures and reducing the amount of new hardware for each game. It also turns out that these little programmable circuits can do some things that are terribly difficult to do with the motion-control circuits described thus far.

The digital device at the heart of this programmable-figure scheme is the 7485 4-bit magnitude comparator shown in Fig. 8-1. Basically, the circuit accepts two 4-bit binary words or numbers, compares their magnitudes, and generates an output specifying whether one is equal, greater or less than the other.

One of the two input numbers is designated number A, and is composed of bits A0 through A3, with A0 being the least-significant bit. The second input number is designated number B, and is composed of bits B0 through B3, with B3, with B0 being the least-significant bit.

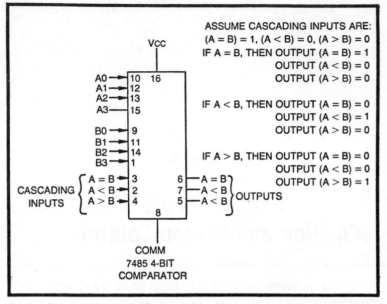

Fig. 8-1. Pinout and operating features of the 7485 4-Bit magnitude comparator.

When these two 4-bit numbers are applied to their respective inputs of the comparator, one of the three outputs switches to a logic-1 level. If the two numbers are exactly equal, output A=B goes to logic 1. If number A happens to be greater than B (A=1001 and B=0101, for example), output A > B goes to logic 1. And finally, if input A is less than B, output A < B goes to logic 1.

The cascading inputs are used only when the comparator IC is being used with an identical unit to compare words having eight or more bits. Otherwise, cascading input A=B should be connected to logic 1, and the inequality cascading inputs should both be grounded. Circuits in the following sections of this chapter illustrate all these operating modes.

A PROGRAMMABLE FIGURE POSITION CONTROL

Chapter 3 deals with the basic circuitry for generating lines, bars, and rectangles on the screen. The logic-circuit designs in those instances determine both the size and position of the figures. Such figures can be placed anywhere on the screen by using the appropriate set of H- and V-count inputs from the Sourcebox, but once they are fixed, it is difficult to change them on a finished circuit board.

The circuit described here is generally more complicated than any in Chapter 3, but it is rather easy to change the parameters determining the size and position of the figure. In a manner of speaking, it is a programmable-figure size and position control.

The circuit in Fig. 8-2 shows a complete figure-programming circuit for either the horizontal or vertical parameters for fixing the position and size of a line/bar figure on the screen.

The circuit has two sets of inputs. The inputs labeled 1, 2, 4..., 256 go to their respective connections from the H- or V-count terminals of the Sourcebox unit. If the circuit is being used to generate horizontal parameters, for example, input 1 goes to 1H, input 2 goes to 2H, and so on.

A second set of nine inputs labeled 1P through 256P generally go to fixed 1 or 0 logic levels.

These inputs are continuously compared in IC1, IC2, and IC4-A. IC1 compares the four lower-order bits, and when they are equal, it delivers an A=B logic level to IC2 where the 16, 32, 64, and 128 bits are compared. If the first eight pairs of inputs are equal, IC2 then generates an A=B output from its pin-6 connection.

IC1 and IC2 are 4-bit magnitude comparators that are cascaded to perform 8-bit comparison. The two IC's compare the eight lower-order H- or V-count signals with the eight corresponding logic levels at the P inputs. IC4-A, in conjunction with an inverter function at IC4-B, make up a 1-bit magnitude comparator for the 256 bit. If the 256 bit from the Sourcebox is the same as the 1 or 0 logic level at the 256P input, the output of IC4-B goes to logic 1.

IC3-A thus sees two comparison signals. If all eight of the lower-order bits are equal and the 265-bit inputs are equal, IC3-A generates a logic-0 level as long as that condition exists.

Putting this information all together, the circuit in Fig. 8-2a works as a 9-bit magnitude comparator, generating a logic-0 output only when the signals from the Sourcebox have logic levels that are identical to those set at the nine P inputs.

Use the circuit in Fig. 8-2a as the basis of an experiment with the magnitude comparator scheme. Connect the Sourcebox inputs to the H-count signals and make provisions for either grounding or connecting the P inputs to +5V. If the PP output is connected directly to the GAME VID IN connection on the Sourcebox, you will be working with a fine, black horizontal line on a white background. Running PP through another inverter before applying the signal to Sourcebox will generate a white line on a black field.

In any event, you will find you are working with a vertical line that is 1H wide. To get the experiment started, connect the P inputs to the following pattern of 1s (+5V or no connection at all) and 0s (ground connection): 100001010, where the bit on the left is the

256P input and the one on the right is the 1P bit. You should find a 1H line running down the center of the screen.

What is happening here? By programming the P inputs to 100001010, you are asking the circuit to look for that particular pattern of 1s and 0s from the H-count outputs of the Sourcebox. And since that particular H-count occurs at the center of the screen, it follows that the comparator circuit generates its output at that particular moment. See the master counting table in Chapter 2 for other program patterns.

There are two conditions that will not show a line on the screen. If the program inputs specify an H-count in the horizontal blanking region, the comparator generates a line figure, but it is lost in the blanking region. In the other case, you can program counts that are larger than the number of H-counts in a line—larger than binary 111000110 or decimal 454. In this instance, you are asking the circuit to look for a number that Sourcebox never generates, and as a result, the line is never generated at all.

The same basic ideas apply when using this comparator scheme with V-count inputs. Here the circuit generates a horizontal line that is 1V wide and in a position determined by the pattern of logic levels at the P inputs. As in the case of the horizontal-comparison experiment, programs calling for a line in the vertical-blanking region or any calling for a line at 100000101 (decimal 261) or more do not generate visible lines.

So if the circuit in Fig. 8-2a is wired for H-count programming, you can fix the position of a 1H vertical line anywhere on the screen between 000000000 (extreme left side) and 11100101 (extreme right side). The pattern of 0s and 1s at the P inputs correspond exactly to the inputs to a NAND gate as specified in Chapter 3. In essence, this comparator circuit works as a 9-input NAND gate for fixing the size and position of a line on the screen. The only difference here is that the programming can be changed much easier than for a hard-wired NAND gate.

Once you have built this comparator circuit and you are certain you understand how to program the P inputs to set the position of the 1H-wide vertical line, set the position to some convenient viewing place on the screen, and connect the 1P input to the 1H input. Now input 1 and 1P are both operating from 1H. They are always equal. The result is a line that is 2H-clock-pulses wide. You can still adjust the position of the line from program inputs 2P through 256P, but now the line is wider.

Then connect 2P to input 2 and 2H. With the two lower-order program inputs thus connected to their respective H-count inputs,

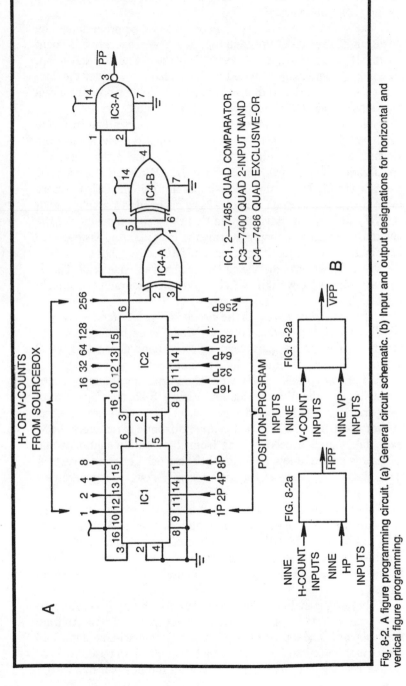

Fig. 8-2. A figure programming circuit. (a) General circuit schematic. (b) Input and output designations for horizontal and vertical figure programming.

311

you will find the line is now 4H wide. Its position is then programmed by inputs 4P through 256P.

The width of the line can thus be adjusted or programmed by connecting lower-order program inputs to their respective H-count inputs: 1P to 1 and 1H, 2P to 2 and 2H, 4P to 4 and 4H, and so on. The more program inputs wired in this fashion, the wider the line. The position of that line is then adjusted by the higher-order program inputs not connected to their respective H-count sources.

As a design example, suppose you want a vertical line 16H wide just left of center of the screen. The NAND-gate specifications from Chapter 3 would be $\overline{256H}$, 128H, and 64H, but in this case, the specifications are as follows: 1P=1=1H, 2P=2=2H, 4P=4=4H, and 8P=8=8H. To be sure, the comparator scheme calls for more more circuitry (the circuit in Fig. 8-2a as opposed to a simple 3-input NAND gate), but the advantage is that the size and position of the line can be changed by simply altering the P inputs. And as described later in this chapter, the P inputs can be altered by other circuitry — the size and position of the line can be changed automatically. That is virtually impossible with the NAND-gate line-generating scheme in Chapter 3.

After experimenting with the circuit in Fig. 8-2a for a while, you will find you can generate sets of parallel lines by fixing certain program inputs to one particular logic level and connecting the P inputs on either side of it to their respective H-count signals.

All of this applies equally well when orienting the comparator circuit around the V-count inputs. Figure 8-2b shows a pair of comparator circuits in block diagram form. The circuits are identical in every respect. The one generating horizontal parameters, however, takes its Sourcebox inputs from the nine H-count lines and generates an active-low $\overline{HPP}$ signal. The block generating vertical data takes its Sourcebox information from V-count and generates a $\overline{VPP}$ output signal.

The simple circuits in Fig. 8-3 show several suggested techniques for combining the horizontal- and vertical-equality signals. In Fig. 8-3a, the $\overline{HPP}$ and $\overline{VPP}$ signals are effectively ANDed together to yield a white rectangle. The size and position of this rectangle is determined by the horizontal- and vertical-program inputs.

The circuit in Fig. 8-3b uses a pair of pulse generators to overcome a certain disadvantage inherent in the simple ANDing operation of Fig. 8-3a. Using the bar-positioning scheme described earlier in this section, you will find that it is difficult to position larger bars or rectangles exactly where you want them. A bar that is 64H wide, for example, can appear only in one of six different positions, the same six positions indicated for black and white 64H bars in Fig. 3-1.

The circuit in Fig. 8-3b, on the other hand, allows maximum precision and flexibility as far as positioning a rectangle of any size is concerned. The whole business of determining the horizontal and vertical dimensions of the rectangle is taken from the programming of the comparators and shifted to the values of the capacitors, C1 and C2. The programming of the comparators fixes the position of the rectangle with 1H and 1V precision.

While it is difficult to alter the size of a rectangle generated by the output circuit in Fig. 8-3b, the experimenter (or the game circuit

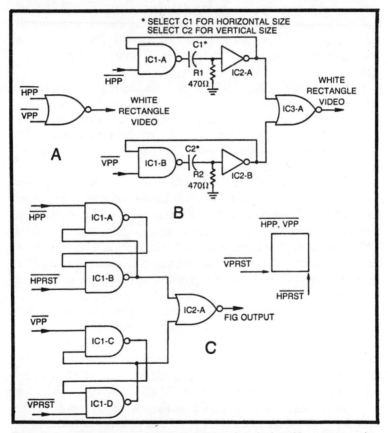

Fig. 8-3. Combining outputs from horizontal and vertical position programming circuits. (a) Forming a rather small rectangle figure by effectively ANDing active-low inputs to a NOR gate. (b) Adjusting the dimensions of a rectangle by selecting capacitor values in a pair of pulse generators. (c) Using R-S flip-flops to extend the dimensions of a comparator-programmed rectangle.

itself) can have precise control over the position via the comparators' program inputs. This feature will become especially valuable when working with ultra-slow-motion controls later in this chapter.

The purpose of the most complex comparator output circuit in Fig. 8-3c might seem rather obscure at this point, but it is shown here for the sake of completeness. The circuit is composed of two R-S flip-flops, each having one input taken from a comparator circuit. The flip-flops are reset by PRST pulses from an external source, and their outputs are effectively ANDed together by IC2-A.

The flip-flop composed of IC1-A and IC1-B is set to its active state whenever it sees an HPP pulse from the horizontal-program comparator. Presumably, the occurrence of this pulse indicates the starting point of a figure's horizontal dimension. That particular flip-flop then remains active until an external HPRST pulse occurs. If that reset pulse happens to be an inverted version of HRST from the Sourcebox, the bar begins at the point HPP occurs and ends at the right-hand side of the screen.

The vertical portion of this flip-flop circuit, built around IC1-C and IC1-D, is set in a similar fashion from the VPP signal from a vertical comparator. It is then reset by an external source such as an inverted VRST from the Sourcebox. The result in this instance is a vertical bar that begins when VPP occurs and runs to the bottom of the screen.

ANDing the outputs of the two flip-flop sections then yields a rectangular figure having its upper left-hand corner fixed at a point where HPP and VPP occur at the same time. If the flip-flops are then reset as described in the foregoing examples (inverted versions of HRST and VRST) the figure extends to the right and bottom of the screen. Of course it is possible to use alternate sources of HPRST and VPRST pulses to adjust the position of the figure's right and bottom edges.

This particular circuit will be used for programming the size and position of complex figures as described in Chapter 4.

Figure 8-4 is a suggested circuit for a complete programmable-position-control circuit. IC1 and IC2 accept horizontal-counting and programming information, while IC3 and IC4 handle the vertical programming. The outputs are delivered to pulse generators where the horizontal dimension of the rectangle is determined by the value of C1 and the vertical dimension by the value of C2.

The circuit can be assembled on a 40-pin board (Radio Shack 276-153) with plenty of room to spare. The arrangement calls for using all 40 pins, however.

The program inputs can be selected by means of 18 different toggle switches, one to each of the P inputs. Certainly this would be a rather awkward scheme for programming the position of the figure, but it is an alternative that is suitable in some circumstances. See the suggested input switch circuit in Fig. 8-6.

Figure 8-5 shows an alternative to the comparator positioning board in Fig. 8-4. The primary advantage of this alternate circuit is that it requires only 23 pins as opposed to the full complement of 40 pins for the circuit in Fig. 8-4. The trick is to eliminate virtually all of the H- and V-count inputs by building a set of counters on the position-control board, itself.

The horizontal counters are IC5 and IC6, and since they are clocked by 1H and reset by HRST from the Sourcebox, they follow the basic counting pattern of the H-count system in the Sourcebox. IC7 and IC8 perform the same function for the vertical-positioning circuit, being clocked by HRST and reset by VRST from the Sourcebox.

Using on-board H- and V-count generators thus eliminates a lot of wiring between the board and Sourcebox. There are some trade-offs though. The H-count generator (IC5 and IC6) generates counting signals between 2H and 256H. The lower-order 1H bit is not included in the comparison process in the horizontal section. Omitting the 1H comparison, however, only means that the figure is positioned with 2H precision. And that doesn't pose many problems, in most instances.

There are also only eight bits available for vertical positioning. In this case, the 256V bit is omitted. Since that particular signal is seldom useful at all, there is little lost by leaving it out of the comparison operation.

Also note that the circuit in Fig. 8-5 requires eight ICs, rather than the seven in Fig. 8-4. And furthermore, you can see that the alternate circuit generates active-high HPP and VPP signals, rather than a composite-figure signal. Even so, these are rather minor compromises, considering how much easier it is to wire the circuit in Fig. 8-5 into a game system.

Switch Inputs for Figure Positioning

Figure 8-6 is a sketch of a circuit that can be used for entering as many as 18 position-control bits into either of the circuit boards in Figs. 8-4 and 8-5. The circuit is drawn specifically for the circuit in Fig. 8-4, but it can be interfaced with the simpler circuit in Fig. 8-5 by omitting the 1HP position (S9 and R9) and the 256VP position (S10 and R10).

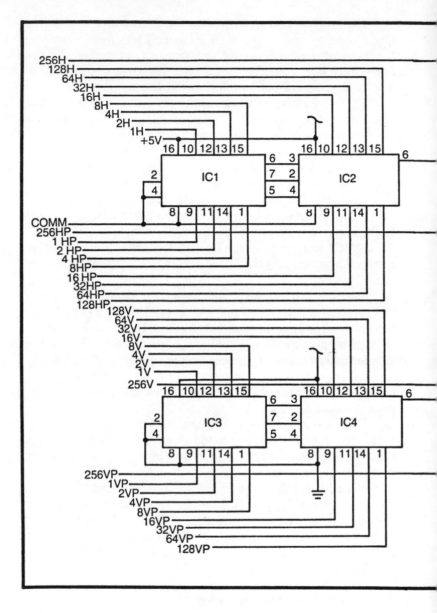

Position Programming From Counters

In the context of the comparator positioning circuits described thus far in this chapter, it is possible to specify the positioning information from a switch panel (Fig. 8-6, for example) or from any other source of logic levels. Some of those "other sources" include

316

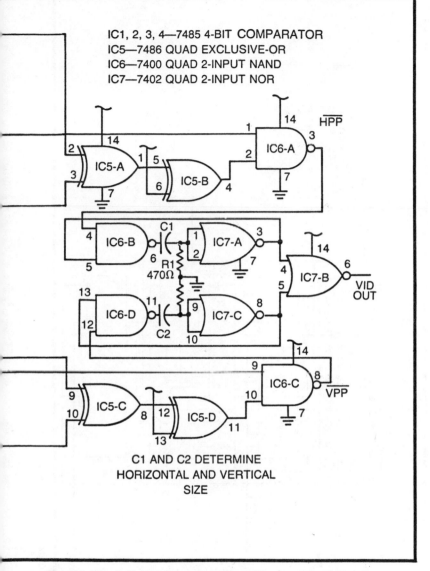

Fig. 8-4. Circuit diagram for a complete position programming system.

counters, data latches, multiplexer pattern generators, or random access memories.

Figure 8-7 shows how a set of binary counters can be used for specifying position data. The essential idea in this case is to vary the position of a figure each time the circuit is clocked. One phase of the

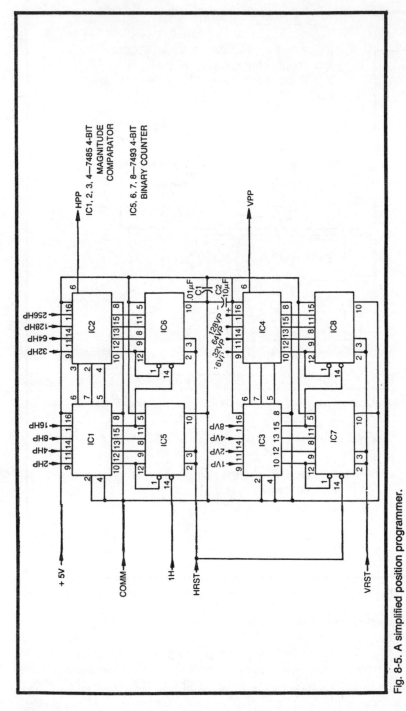

Fig. 8-5. A simplified position programmer.

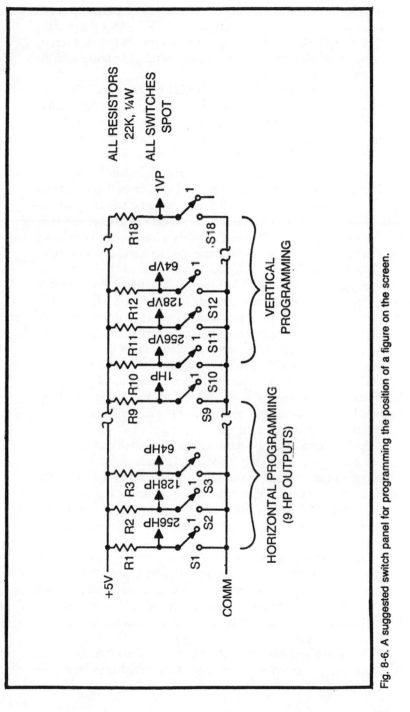

Fig. 8-6. A suggested switch panel for programming the position of a figure on the screen.

game sets the counters' outputs to zero and fixes the position of a figure at some particular place on the screen. When that phase of the game is completed, a clock pulse advances the counters, thereby changing the position information and, ultimately, the position of the figure on the screen.

This counter input scheme has a wide variety of possible configurations, and the one shown here specifies position information for just two 4-bit magnitude comparitors, IC1 and IC2. The whole business can be expanded to accommodate the more complex and complete position programmers in Figs. 8-4 and 8-5.

IC1 in Fig. 8-7 compares only the four higher-order bits from the H-count section of the Sourcebox. The horizontal bar it generates is thus fixed at the 32H width. By the same token, IC2 compares only 16V, 32V, 64V, and 128V from the Sourcebox unit, thereby generating a VPP signal that is 16V wide. Let me repeat that the comparator circuitry can be expanded to handle eight or nine signals from both the H- and V-count outputs from the Sourcebox. The idea is limited to four each in this case to (1) make the discussion simpler and (2) make the point that one does not have to use a full 8- or 9-bit comparison to do every sort of pattern-programming job.

The counters, sources of positioning information, are IC3 and IC4 in Fig. 8-7. The counters are cascaded so that they can count anywhere from 0000 0000 (decimal zero) through 1111 1111 (decimal 255). There are thus 256 possible combinations of positioning information for the comparators. Any number of counters can be cascaded in this fashion to accommodate an equal number of inputs to an expanded comparator scheme.

The J terminals indicate hard-wire jumper positions. The state of the counters determine the sequence of positions, but the jumper wires connected between the output of the counters and the inputs of the comparitors determine what those positions will be.

Capacitors C1 and C2 are merely de-glitching capacitors that eliminate any transient spikes generated by this particular type of counter circuit.

The figures in the inserts in Fig. 8-7 suggest some ways for controlling the counters. The manual clock option provides a simple and reliable means for debouncing a manual pushbutton input. Each time the CLK pushbutton is depressed, a monostable multivibrator, built around IC5, generates a 10-ms pulse that advances the counters.

The normally closed pushbutton in the manual clear option can be depressed to clear both counters to their initial zero configuration.

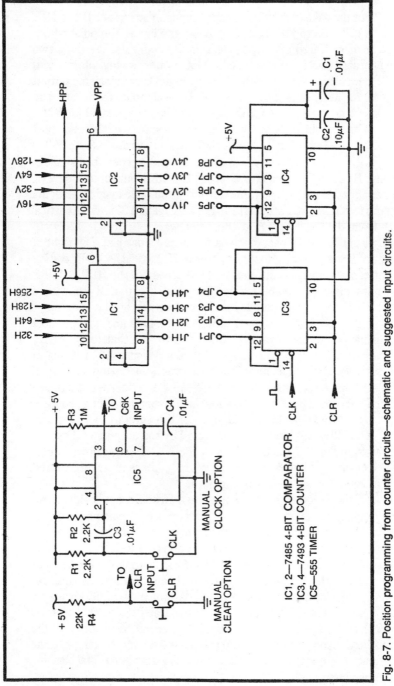

Fig. 8-7. Position programming from counter circuits—schematic and suggested input circuits.

IC1, 2—7485 4-BIT COMPARATOR
IC3, 4—7493 4-BIT COUNTER
IC5—555 TIMER

321

For the sake of this discussion, suppose you jumper JP1 to J1H, JP2 to J2H, JP3 to J3H, and so on down the line to the point where you connect JP8 to J4V. Upon clearing the counters, then, the two comparator circuits see 0000 and 0000 as positioning information. HPP, in other words, will show a logic-1 comparison output whenever 32H, 64H, 128H, and 256H are all equal to logic 0. The same is true in this case for the V-count signals specified for IC2.

What should you expect to see on the screen in this example? Nothing at all. Beginning the horizontal and vertical bars at 0000 places them in the system's horizontal- and vertical blanking regions. But suppose you now depress the CLK pushbutton several times (or advance the counter in any other suitable fashion) until the inputs to IC1 and IC2 are both 1001. This means a 32H-wide vertical bar from HPP will appear at the point where 256H=1, 128H=0, 64H=, and 32H=1. That happens to specify a bar just a bit right of center. The same set of four bits going to IC2 would let VPP position a horizontal bar across the middle of the screen. If the HPP and VPP outputs are effectively ANDed together, you end up with a 32H×16V rectangle located just right of center on the screen.

Figure 8-8 indicates the positions of the bars under all possible combinations of comparator inputs. It turns out that there are 14 uninterrupted vertical positions. (Out of a possible 16, 1 is lost in vertical blanking and another is split between the bottom and top of the screen.) As far as horizontal positioning is concerned, there are 11 uninterrupted positions (3 are lost in horizontal blanking and 2 are split by the right- and left-hand sides of the screen).

The 32H×16V rectangle generated by the outputs of the comparators in Fig. 8-7 and combined by the NAND gate shown in Fig. 8-8 can be positioned in any one of 154 different, uninterrupted positions in the screen's viewing area.

The correspondence between these 154 different positions and the clocking of the circuit in Fig. 8-7 depends on the arrangement of jumpers between the counters and comparators. If the jumpers are connected as specified earlier in this section (JP1 to J1H, JP2 to J2H, and so on in that order through JP8 to J4V), clearing the counters to zero places the figure in the horizontal- and vertical-blanking regions. Clocking the counters causes no noticeable difference until the count reaches 0010 and IC1 and 0001 at IC2. At that point, a corner of the rectangle appears in the upper left-hand corner of the screen. Subsequent clocking operations moves the rectangle to the right across the top of the screen until it is lost in horizontal blanking once again.

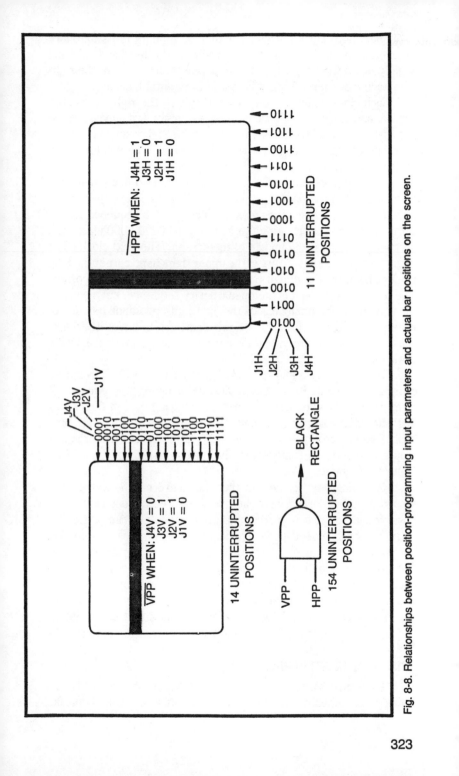

Fig. 8-8. Relationships between position-programming input parameters and actual bar positions on the screen.

Four more clock pulses after that, it appears in its full glory (uninterrupted by the top of the screen) at the left-hand side and slightly down from the top. The rectangle then moves to the right with each clock pulse until it is lost in horizontal blanking.

Each clock pulse carries the rectangle to the right across the screen, and at the end of each of these excursions, it appears at the left again, but in a lower position. Out of the 256 possible positions available from the counters, 154 of them expose an uninterrupted rectangular figure.

The only problem with this scheme is that so many combinations are lost in the blanking regions, but this is where the jumper option in Fig. 8-7 becomes an asset. The jumper sequence can be scrambled such that clearing the counters to 0000 0000 places the rectangle very near the middle of the screen. The next clock pulse might then position the figure in the upper right-hand corner, and the clock pulse after that might take it to the lower right-hand corner. The counters still count in their usual binary sequence, but mixing up the jumper programming places the figure into positions that do not necessarily follow an orderly, stepwise pattern. In effect, the figure can be made to skip around the screen and even disappear from view at times.

Designing any game around this particular sort of counter/comparator scheme is a matter of first determining the sequence of comparator inputs you want, then connecting jumpers in such a way that an orderly sequence of counts is transformed into your prescribed sequence of positions. The Golf game described later in this chapter uses this technique for placing the holes and tees of an 18-hole golf game.

Returning now to the fact that the figure can be moved in a stepwise and orderly fashion across the screen, doesn't it seem possible this sort of counter/comparator combination can be used for motion control? Indeed it can. The idea is to set up the programming so that the figure moves in very small increments across the screen. The rate of motion is determined by the frequency of the clocking operation, and the direction of motion is determined by whether the and comparators for generating figure motion on the screen.

The section that follows deals with circuits that use counters and comparitors for generating figure motion on the screen.

UNIVERSAL POSITION PROGRAMMERS

The universal position programmer circuit shown in Fig. 8-9 includes all the features of position programmers described thus far,

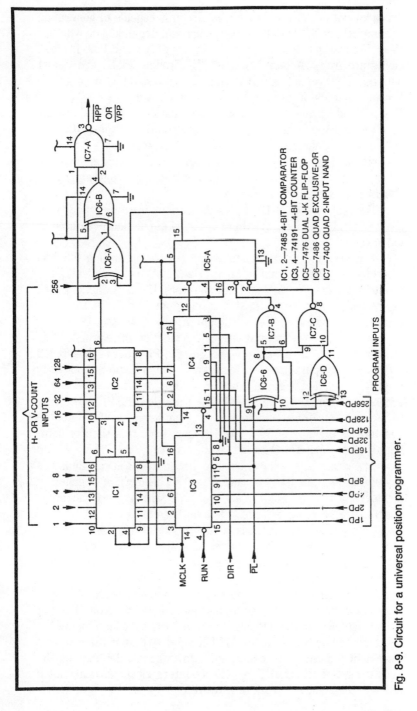

Fig. 8-9. Circuit for a universal position programmer.

plus a lot, lot more. As shown, the circuit is capable of generating either a HPP or VPP black bar on the screen, depending on whether H- or V-count data is applied to the inputs of IC1 and IC2. If these inputs are from H-count sources 1H through 256H, the circuit outputs a HPP vertical bar. If the inputs to IC1 and IC2 are from the V-count sources, it outputs VPP horizontal bars.

IC1 and IC2 are 4-bit magnitude comparators that are basically used in the same fashion described earlier in this chapter. IC3 and IC4, used in conjunction with flip-flop IC5-A, make up a 9-bit pre-settable up/down binary counter system. These counters, among other things, can be used for counter-position programming as described in the previous section.

The table in Fig. 8-10 shows the various operating modes for the counters and interprets them in terms of position-programmer functions.

The first line of the function table shows a loading function whereby any 9-bit combination of PD inputs is loaded into the counters and fed directly to the comparators. If the PD inputs are all set to logic 0, for instance, this loading operation tells the comparators to respond to H- or V-count inputs 0000 0000 0.

As indicated on the first line of the function table, the loading function is established by simply setting the PL input to logic 0. All other control inputs are then irrelevant. This function is normally used in conjunction with the program memory function listed on the second line. Here the RUN input is fixed at logic 1 and $\overline{PL}$ is returned to logic 1. Any 9-bit combination of logic levels loaded into the counters and comparators while PL is at logic 0 is then remembered" when $\overline{PL}$ is set to logic 1. You can change the PD inputs and clock the circuit if you want, but the stored data will remain in the system as long as RUN=1 and $\overline{PL}$=1. This sort of register of memory function is not readily available with any of the other position-programming schemes described to this point.

Before investigating the real implications of this combination of loading and memory functions, it would be a good idea to preview the other two possible operating modes, the ones listed on the last two lines of the function table.

The system is taken from its loading mode by setting $\overline{PL}$ to 1, and then it can be taken from its memory mode by setting RUN to logic 0. With RUN=0 and $\overline{PL}$=1, the counters can be incremented or decremented by pulses at the MCLK input. Whether the counters increment (up count) or decrement (down count) depends on the logic level at DIR. If DIR=0, the counters clock upward, but if DIR=1, the counters clock downward.

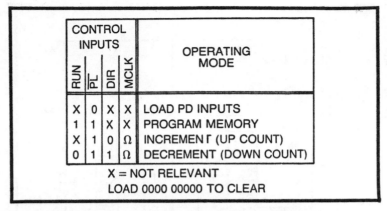

CONTROL INPUTS				OPERATING MODE
RUN	PL	DIR	MCLK	
X	0	X	X	LOAD PD INPUTS
1	1	X	X	PROGRAM MEMORY
X	1	0	Ω	INCREMENT (UP COUNT)
0	1	1	Ω	DECREMENT (DOWN COUNT)

X = NOT RELEVANT
LOAD 0000 00000 TO CLEAR

Fig. 8-10. Function table for the universal position programmer.

A particular count can be stopped and "remembered" by simply setting RUN to logic 1 at the appropriate time. If desired, the count can be resumed from that point by simply setting RUN to logic 0 again.

Perhaps the best way to get a good feeling for how the universal position programmer works is by building the circuit in Fig. 8-9 onto a circuit board and interfacing it with the input controls shown in Fig. 8-11. Building the position programmer onto a circuit board will not be a waste of time and effort because it will prove useful in some TV-game designs later on. The input circuits can be built in a breadboard fashion so that the parts can be used for other game purposes.

For the sake of a preliminary set of experiments, connect the comparator inputs 1 through 128 to their respective H-count signals from the Sourcebox unit. This will provide an HPP output signal that ultimately appears as a fine, black vertical line on the screen. The simple circuit in Fig. 8-12 shows a technique for widening the bar and changing it to white on black for easier viewing.

Experiments With a Position Programmer

To begin the experiments, set the STOP/RUN switch to the logic-1 STOP position. Then set the nine PD input switches for some desired bar position. In the context of the presentation in Chapter 3, a logic-1 PD input is tantamount to a noninverted H-count signal, while a logic-0 input yields the effect of using an inverted H-count input.

Note there is no response on the screen while adjusting the settings of the PD switches. This feature allows the experimenter to

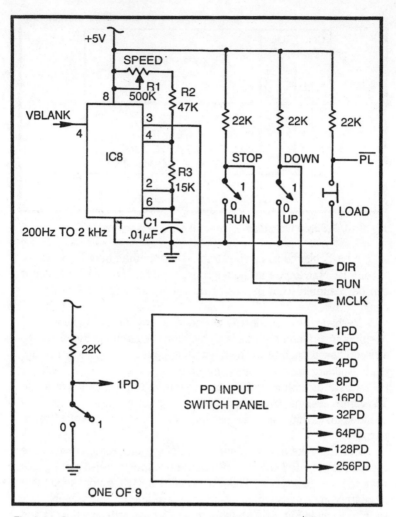

Fig. 8-11. Suggested input interface for experiments with the universal position programmer.

set up the position-programming codes without having the figure jumping all over the screen. With the PD switches now set to a desired program combination, momentarily depress the LOAD pushbutton. You will see the bar on the screen jump immediately to the position you specified on the PD input switches.

Try a few more positions, first setting the codes on the PD switch panel and then depressing the LOAD pushbutton. The bar can indeed be set to any desired position on the screen with 1H precision.

Once you are satisfied you understand the function of the load and memory scheme, position the bar close to the middle of the screen, set the UP/DOWN switch to its UP position, and then set the RUN/STOP switch to RUN. IC8 in Fig. 8-11 is connected as a free-running multivibrator, and if it is operating properly, you should see the bar moving to the right across the screen.

The speed of motion depends mainly on the value of R1. If the multivibrator is running at its lower frequency limit (about 200 Hz) the bar drifts across the screen rather slowly. If, on the other hand, R1 is set so that the multivibrator runs in the neighborhood of 2 kHz, the bar makes a complete cycle across the screen in about 4 seconds.

IC8, itself, is enabled only through the VBLANK interval. Note the VBLANK connection to pin 4 of IC8. While this multivibrator is enabled, it produces clocking pulses for the counters in Fig. 8-9, effectively changing the position information for the bar. The changes take place in an orderly fashion, giving the impression of rather smooth and continuous motion across the screen. The faster the multivibrator runs through the VBLANK interval, the faster the bar advances across the screen.

The direction of motion is determined by the UP/DOWN switch, a switch that ultimately sets the DIR control input to logic 1 or 0. The bar thus moves to the right across the screen when UP/DOWN is set to UP, and then the bar moves to the left when that switch is set to DOWN.

The motion can be stopped, holding the bar at some particular point on the screen, by setting the RUN/STOP switch to STOP. The multivibrator continues producing clocking pulses through every VBLANK interval, but the bar remains motionless on the screen because the counters are disabled.

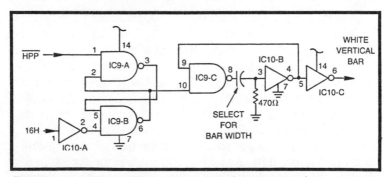

Fig. 8-12. A circuit for widening the bar generated by the universal position programmer.

Figure 8-13 shows a set of curves that translate the multivibrator's operating frequency into numbers indicating the speed of the bar. Those numbers indicate the length of time required for making one complete cycle of motion across the screen. If, for example, the system is operating from H-count signals from the Sourcebox, and the multivibrator is operating at 1 kHz, the Horizontal Motion curve shows that the bar will complete one cycle of horizontal motion across the screen in about 7.6 seconds.

If the inputs to the comparators in Fig. 8-9 are taken from the V-count signals from the Sourcebox, the bar moves vertically at a rate shown by the Vertical Motion curve. In the case of vertical motion, setting the UP/DOWN switch to UP causes the bar to move downward, while setting that switch to DOWN causes the bar to move upward. (If this seems to cause some confusion, simply bear in mind that the UP and DOWN designations on the direction switch indicate the direction of the counter, and not the direction of motion.

A Slow-Motion Figure Generator

A thoughtful reader ought to be asking some relevant questions at this pont. Why should I ever build a figure-motion-control circuit around a set of counter/comparator circuits when the slipping counters are simpler? What can this universal position programmer do that cannot be done with the simpler positioning circuits described earlier in this chapter?

Both questions can be answered in the following terms. The universal position programmer is, indeed, a more complicated system than any slipping counter and position programmer. The fact of the matter is, however, that this universal programmer can perform some operations that are virtually impossible with the simpler circuits.

The case in point is the speed of motion that can be generated by the programmer circuit in Fig. 8-9. The slipping-counter-motion-control circuit is analyzed in terms of its operating speeds in Fig. 7-22. According to that table, the circuit cannot generate figure speeds less than 6.2 seconds per screen. The minimum cycle time for the figure is either infinity (figure motionless) or 6.2 seconds.

Using the universal programmer as a motion-control circuit, however, allows figure-cycling times on the order of 20 seconds. In essence, the universal programmer can be used as an ultra-slow-motion generator. Having a figure move across the screen in 6.2 seconds (the greatest amount of time possible with a slipping-counter arrangement) might be too fast for many game applications.

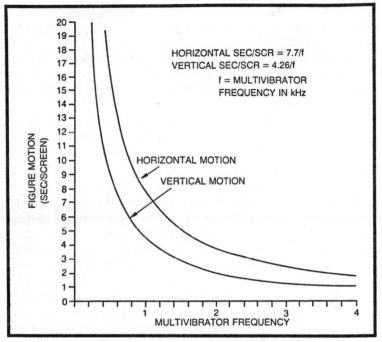

Fig. 8-13. Curves and equations for determining the screen cycle time of a slow motion figure generator.

Where this is the case, the universal programmer comes to the rescue.

The circuit in Fig. 8-14 shows a practical motion-control circuit built around a pair of universal-position programmers. Two of the circuits in Fig. 8-9 are required in this case, one for controlling vertical motion and another for controlling the horizontal component of figure motion.

Both motion circuits are clocked from their own multivibrators: IC1-A for generating vertical-speed pulses and IC1-B for generating MCLK pulses for the horizontal-position programmer. The two position programmers share a common position-initializing circuit built around IC2-A and IC2-B. The idea here is to load some pre-scribed position codes into the position programmers whenever a negative-going pulse occurs at the INT input, pin 1 of IC2-A. All counting action stops as long as the system remains in this initializing mode, and the position programmers take their positioning information directly from their respective PD inputs.

A negative-going pulse at the system's MOVE input, however, sets the $\overline{PL}$ inputs of the two programmers to logic 1, thereby switching the circuits from their loading mode to their counting mode. The figure is thus free to move on the screen at speeds determined by the settings of R1 and R4.

The direction of horizontal motion is set by the logic level at the H DIRECTION input: 1= left and 0= right. By the same token, the direction of vertical motion is set by the V DIRECTION input: 1= up and 0 =down.

The figure can be stopped at any point on the screen by setting the STOP input to logic 1. This action merely stops the motion. It does not initialize the position of the figure. Setting the STOP input to logic 1 is tantamount to entering the stop code (1001, or decimal 9) into a slipping-counter motion-control circuit.

As shown in Fig. 8-14, the motion-control circuit is a hybrid analog and digital system. The speed of motion is determined by the setting of two potentiometers, a feature that is quite convenient for many game applications. The direction, stopping, and initializing controls, however, are purely digital in nature. This, too, is a nice feature in most instances.

As demonstrated in earlier chapters, however, it is frequently necessary to control the speed of a figure from some internal circuitry. Automatic speed control of this sort ought to be digital in nature. The circuit should be able to accept a binary word that determines the figure speed.

Compare this situation with the speed-control scheme for a slipping counter. In the case of a slipping counter, the most natural way to control the speed of the figure is by entering a 4-bit binary word. The circuit is basically a digital one. Converting the slipping-counter motion-control system to one having potentiometer control is a tricky process calling for an analog-to-digital (A/D) converter circuit.

The situation is just reversed for the universal position programmer. This circuit most naturally accepts potentiometer speed controls. And where it is necessary to control the speed in a digital fashion, it is necessary to add a digital-to-analog (D/A) converter. The circuit in Fig. 8-15 shows a simple D/A converter scheme that is most appropriate for setting the motion speed.

The D/A converter in this case is a binary ladder network composed of resistors R7 through R12. The PC inputs are eight possible combinations of 1s and 0s, as shown in the table accompanying the circuit. IC1-A is the same multivibrator having that designation in Fig. 8-14. Two such circuits are thus required for full vertical- and horizontal-motion control.

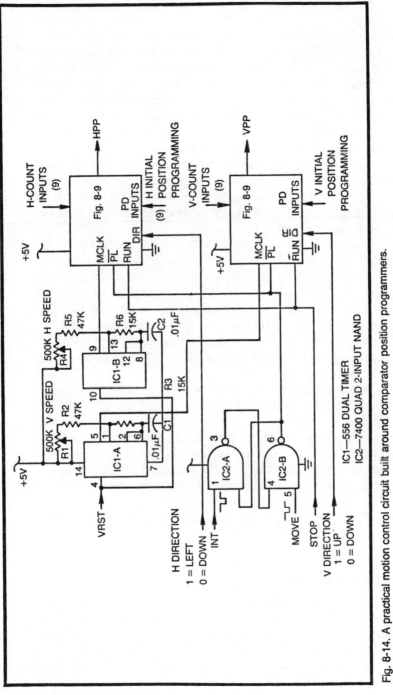

Fig. 8-14. A practical motion control circuit built around comparator position programmers.

The important point, however, is that the D/A converter translates any one of eight possible combinations of three binary inputs into a voltage level proportional to the size of the binary number. A 3-bit input of 0000, for example, yields a relatively low voltage at pin 3 of IC1-A, thereby making the multivibrator run at a rate faster than that determined by the setting of R1 alone. As the 3-bit input is incremented upward toward the slowest speed code (111, or decimal 1), the voltage at pin 3 of IC1-A increases toward +5V, thereby causing the multivibrator to run at a correspondingly slower speed.

If a figure is to be manually controlled, potentiometer speed controls are most appropriate, and the circuit in Fig. 8-14 can be constructed as shown there. If, on the other hand, the figure speed is to be controlled from some source of 3-bit binary numbers, the multivibrators in Fig. 8-14 should have control voltage inputs as modified by the circuit in Fig. 8-15.

When using the circuit in Fig. 8-15, set the PC inputs to 111 and carefully adjust the speed-trim resistor for the slowest motion you want to see. Then set the PC inputs to 000 and, if necessary, readjust the speed-trim resistor for the fastest speed you want. Switch the PC inputs back and forth between 000 and 111, fine-tuning the speed-trim potentiometer until you get the two extremes of motion speed appropriate for the game at hand. Once the speed-trim resistor is set, it should not be accessible for readjustment from any of the players' controls.

Two more bits can be added to this 3-bit speed-control scheme. One additional bit, designated PC3 in Fig. 8-15 can go to the DIR connection to control the direction of motion. A fifth bit, PC4, can go to the STOP connection for determining whether the figure will move or be stopped on the screen. The 5-bit digital word that results is thus capable of controlling both the speed and direction of motion. Of course two sets of these control words are required for both horizontal- and vertical-motion control.

The three video games described in the remainder of this chapter illustrate applications of all the position-programming schemes.

NINE HOLES OF GOLF

The Golf game featured in this section exemplifies the application of a counter/comparator circuit as a game programmer. The game consists of nine different patterns, each setting a different position of a golf green, hole, and tee. Every time the player depresses a TEE pushbutton, a different hole, green, and tee configuration appears on the screen.

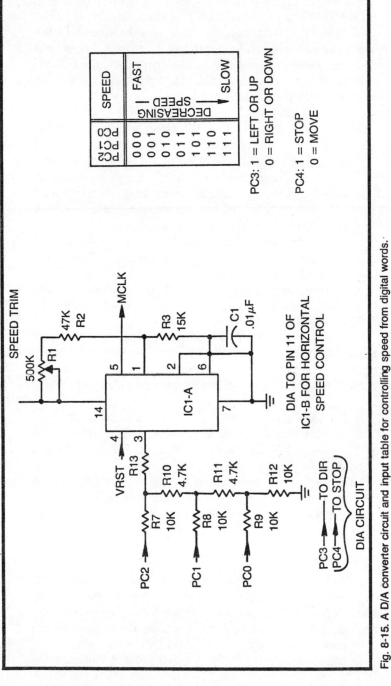

Fig. 8-15. A D/A converter circuit and input table for controlling speed from digital words.

As shown in Fig. 8-16, the player has a set of adjustments labeled UP/DOWN and LEFT/RIGHT. After teeing up the ball by depressing the TEE pushbutton, the player sets the controls for the relative speed and direction he wants the ball to take. When he is satisfied with those adjustments, he then depresses the SWING pushbutton. That action launches the ball, and it travels across the screen—presumably toward the green and hole—for a fixed period of time.

When the ball comes to a stop, the player adjusts the controls again, then depresses the SWING button. He continues this sequence until the ball "falls into the hole." When he makes the hole, the game is locked out, and can be resumed only by depressing the TEE pushbutton again. This action brings the programming feature into play: the position of the ball is initialized on a new tee position, and the player faces an entirely different situation.

The screen diagram in Fig. 8-16 shows just one of the nine different initial positions for the ball and green. After making the ninth hole, the 9-hole cycle begins all over again.

Besides demonstrating a compelling application of the position-programming circuits, this game includes some new ideas about figure-speed control.

As stated earlier, the ball travels for a fixed period of time after the player depresses the SWING pushbutton. As long as the ball is not on the green, it travels at a relatively high velocity, but once on the green, its speed is cut in half and it moves for a shorter period of time.

The ball color also changes as it moves onto the green. Normally the ball appears as a small white square. The green is also white. But when the ball reaches the green, the ball color changes from white to black.

The golf game, as described here, has no obstacles on the course, but the circuit boards include some terminals for adding obstacles later on. Numerals indicating the hole and score can also be added at a later time.

Golf Block Diagram

The basic block diagram for this Golf game is shown in Fig. 8-17. When the player operates the TEE switch, the program counter advances to set up a new position for the green and hole. The ball position is also initialized at a point determined by the program counter and BALL H INITIAL POSITION logic.

The ball then remains initialized until the player depresses the SWING switch. Depressing the SWING switch starts the BALL

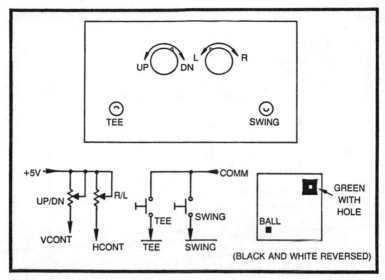

Fig. 8-16. Control panel diagram and schematic, and screen diagram for Golf.

TRAVEL TIMER and allows the slipping counter to move the ball in a direction and at a speed determined by the settings of the player's controls. When the ball timing interval is over, the BALL SPEED CONTROL sets the speed to zero, effectively stopping the ball on the screen. The ball then moves from that point when the player depresses the SWING button.

When the ball reaches the green, the BALL ON GREEN circuit generates logic levels that both change the color of the ball from white to black and slow down the ball speed and travel time.

The ball can be putted on the green, presumably toward the hole. And once the SCORE block senses contact between the ball and hole, it resets the BALL TRAVEL TIMER to stop ball motion and lock out the SWING switch. The ball cannot be moved then until the whole system is reinitialized by depressing the TEE switch.

Circuit Boards for Golf

The golf game described in this chapter requires four circuit boards: those shown in Figs. 8-18, 8-19, 8-20, and a slipping-counter board from Fig. 5-15. The functional block diagram in Fig. 8-17 and the wiring diagram in Fig. 8-22 can be quite helpful for learning about the circuit boards shown here.

The logic board in Fig. 8-18 includes the program counter, ball initialization control, ball travel timer, and A/D converter blocks shown on the functional block diagram.

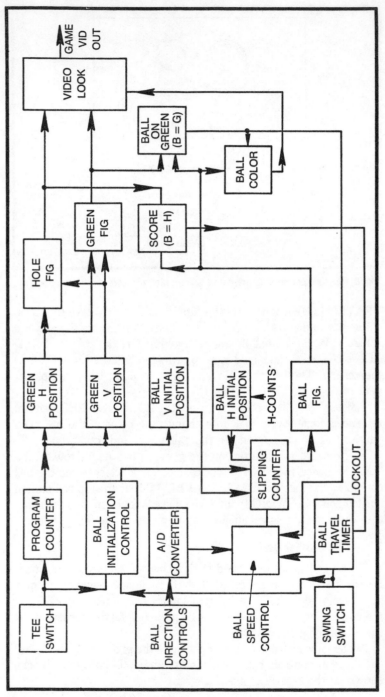

Fig. 8-17. Function block diagram for Golf.

Depressing the TEE pushbutton on the control panel generates a logic-0 level that is wired to the TEE input of this logic board. This action initiates a 10-ms monostable multivibrator action from IC5-A. The brief pulse from that IC increments the count of the program counter, IC9.

IC9 is simply a 4-bit binary counter that is wired to count nine different binary states, 0000 (decimal 0) through 1000 (decimal 8). Each time the player depresses his TEE pushbutton, IC5-A generates a pulse that increments that counter. The program counter's outputs are labeled CA through CD, where CA is the least-significant bit.

Depressing the TEE switch also sets an $\overline{R}$-$\overline{S}$ flip-flop, composed of IC2-A and IC2-B, to a state where the output of IC2-A goes to logic 0. This point is wired to the select input of a 2:1 multiplexer, pin 1 of IC6. As long as pin 1 of IC6 is at logic 0, $\overline{HINTP}$ and $\overline{VINTP}$ initializing pulses are directed to the $\overline{HML}$ and $\overline{VML}$ outputs of that IC. Since these outputs eventually find their way to the slipping-counter board, it follows that depressing the TEE switch initializes the slipping counter which, in turn, initializes the position of the ball on its tee. This circuitry represents the ball initialization control section of the system.

The ball-travel timer is built around IC5-B in Fig. 8-18. This is a monostable multivibrator that is initiated by a negative-going logic level from $\overline{SWING}$. If the $\overline{RST}$ input at pin 10 of IC5-B is at logic 1, depressing the SWING switch starts the timing action.

The SWING input is also connected to the reset input of the R-S flip-flop, IC2-A, and IC2-B. So when the player depresses the SWING button on his control panel, the output of IC2-A switches to logic 1, altering the state of IC6 in such a way that the slipping counter takes its loading information from $\overline{HMRST}$ and $\overline{VMRST}$. In other words, if the position of the ball has just been initialized by depressing the TEE switch, depressing the SWING switch releases the ball so that it can move across the screen.

Returning to the ball-travel timer, IC5-B, the time of travel is mainly determined by the values of R11 and C8. The input at pin 11 influences the travel time as well, however. The BG input to this logic board goes to logic 1 only when the ball is touching the green. That logic-1 level is inverted to logic 0 by IC3-D and applied to pin 11 of IC5-B through the BGT TRIM potentiometer, R12. Lowering the voltage at pin 11 in this fashion shortens the timing interval of the monostable, thus giving the impression the ball slows down when it touches the green.

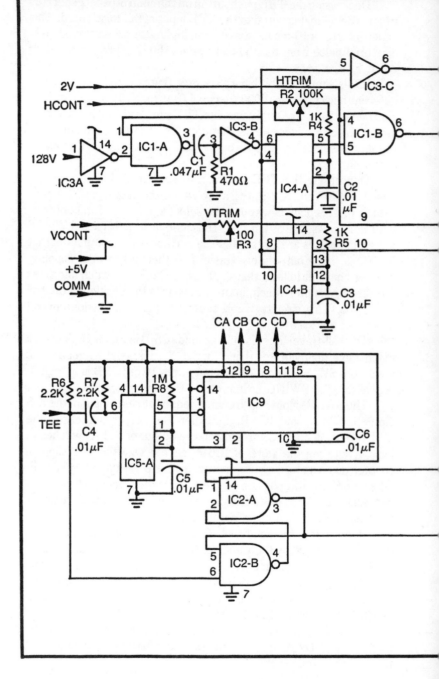

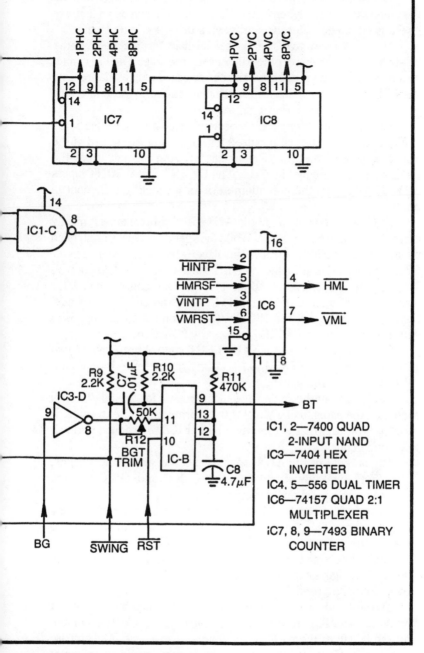

Fig. 8-18. Logic board schematic for Golf

341

The ball, in other words, travels for a longer period of time off the green than it does when it is on the green. R12 can be adjusted to give a good speed difference between a drive and putt swing.

The $\overline{\text{RST}}$ input to IC5-B is responsible for locking out the ball-travel timer whenever the ball touches the hole. The ball cannot be moved once it is in the hole. It can be released only by depressing the TEE switch, an action which reinitializes the system at a new point determined by the program counter.

The A/D converter circuitry occupying most of this logic board in Fig. 8-18 is simply that required for controlling the speed of the ball from potentiometers. The circuit is taken directly from the discussion surrounding Fig. 7-12. The HCONT and VCONT inputs come directly from the potentiometers (or joystick) on the control panel.

The horizontal portion of the A/D speed control is built mainly around IC4-A and counter IC7. While the speed is actually controlled by the RIGHT/LEFT control on the player's panel, trimmer resistor R2 is used for calibrating the speed. To adjust this HTRIM control, set the RIGHT/LEFT potentiometer on the control panel for maximum right speed, then trim HTRIM for the desired maximum right speed. Then set the RIGHT/LEFT control to the opposite extreme and readjust HTRIM for good left motion.

Continue working the RIGHT/LEFT control between its two extremes, adjusting HTRIM as necessary to get smooth right-and-left control from the panel.

Work through the same set of adjustments for the UP/DOWN control on the panel, using VTRIM to calibrate the two extremes. It is IC4-B, you see, that works with counter IC8 to produce vertical-ball-motion codes.

The outputs of the A/D converter section are 1PHC through 8PHC (horizontal speed and direction codes) and 1PVC through 8PVC (vertical speed and direction codes).

The circuit in Fig. 8-19 is called the Figure Board on the wiring block diagram. This board includes circuitry for converting the output of the program counter into position information for the hole and green, detecting contact between the ball and green or ball and hole, and changing the color of the ball from white to black as it moves onto the green.

The size and position of the green is determined by comparator circuits IC7 and IC9, where IC7 determines the horizontal component and IC9 fixes the vertical component. These two ICs compare board inputs CA through CD with horizontal- and vertical-count signals from the Sourcebox unit. Recall that the "C" inputs come from the program counter on the logic board in Fig. 8-18.

These two comparators are programmed so that the horizontal positions of the green can be in any one of seven positions on the right-hand side of the screen. The vertical positions can be any one of four possible between the top and bottom. That all figures out to 28 possible positions, but the program counter allows only nine of them. It is left to the reader to analyze the programming as shown in Fig. 8-19, and perhaps alter it to suit his own notions of where the green should appear.

IC8 uses the "C" states from the program counter to position the ball when it is first set on the tee. There are seven possible positions between the top and bottom of the screen, but only one horizontal position that is determined by the H-count inputs at IC5-C.

The initial position information for the ball is transformed into a brief pulse by sets of pulse generators, and then leaves the board as slipping-counter initializing pulse BHINTP and BVINTP.

The foregoing discussion summarizes the purpose and application of the comparator-type programming circuits. Recall that the holes are counted by the program counter circuit in Fig. 8-18. The outputs of that counter, CA through CD, are then used as program inputs to three comparator circuits. The comparators then determine the relative positions of the green and the initial position of the ball. All that remains as far as the circuit in Fig. 8-19 is concerned is to see how the figures themselves are formed.

The horizontal component of the green figure emerges from pin 6 of comparator IC7, and the vertical component of that same figure comes from pin 6 of IC9. These two outputs are NANDed together in IC2-B to form an active-low version of the green figure.

The outputs of the comparators also go to an input of two 3-input NAND gates, IC5-A and IC5-B. These two gates are responsible for generating the little black hole that always appears near the center of the green. IC5-A generates the horizontal component of the hole, while IC5-B generates the vertical component.

These two hole components are effectively ANDed together in IC3-B to generate an active-high version of the hole figure. The green and hole figures are then combined at IC3-C to produce the image of a white green with a black hole in the center of it. Of course the position of this composite green-and-hole figure is determined by the programming of comparators IC7 and IC9.

The ball figure is formed by the most-significant-bit outputs of the slipping-counter board. Each time the horizontal-slipping

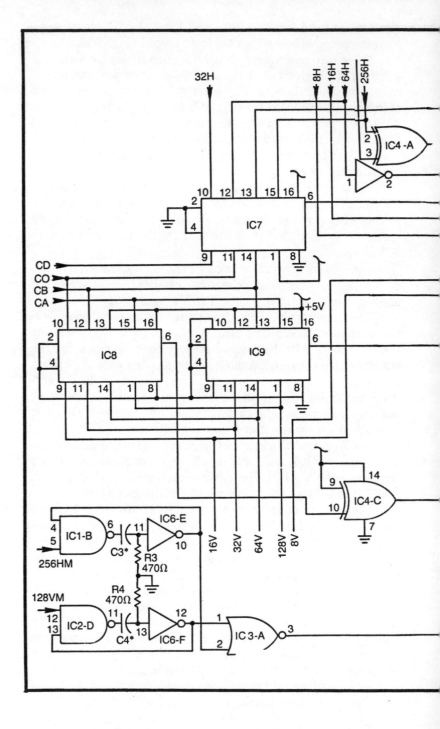

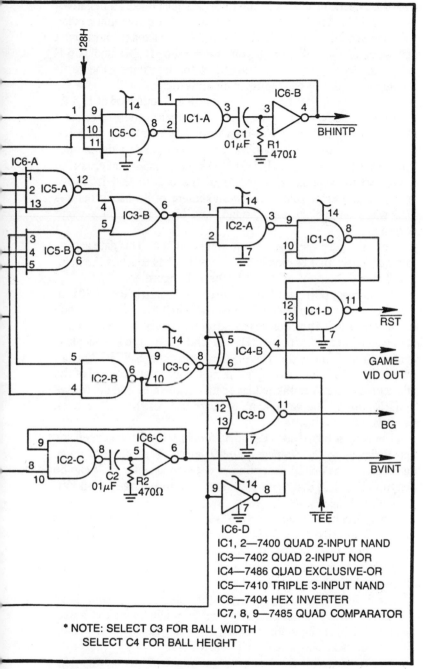

Fig. 8-19. Figure board schematic for Golf

345

counter is reset, for instance, the 256HM signal makes a negative-going transition that is transformed into a brief negative-going pulse by the action of IC1-B and IC6-E. This little pulse fixes the horizontal component of the ball's image on the screen. IC2-D and IC6-F perform the same pulse-generating function, determining the vertical component of the ball figure from 128VM.

The two components of the ball image are combined at IC3-A, producing an active-high ball figure. This figure goes to several different gates, including IC6-B where it is combined with the green-and-hole image to create the game's composite video-output signal. That particular EXCLUSIVE-OR gate, incidentally, is also responsible for switching the color of the ball so that it always appears with a color that is the complement of its background—white when on a black background, and black when on a white background.

The ball figure also goes to one input of IC2-A. This gate acts as a contact sensor that responds whenever the ball touches the hole. (Recall that the output of IC3-B is the hole figure.)

The primary purpose of the game control board in Fig. 8-20 is to control the ball motion once it leaves the initial tee position. When the ball is in its initial position, it is held motionless by the synchronizing effects of initializing pulses ($\overline{\text{HINTP}}$ and $\overline{\text{VINTP}}$) to the slipping-counter circuit. Once the player depresses the SWING button, however, the ball can move and it is no longer under control of the initialization circuitry until the player makes the hole and depresses the TEE button. The game-control board handles the ball's motion once it is off the initial tee.

The control board does its job by feeding HC and VC speed and control signals to the slipping-counter board. The action of these control signals has been described in detail in Chapter 5. It can be seen from Fig. 8-20 that a complete set, 1HC through 8HC and 1VC through 8VC, leaves this board.

This circuit is unique among slipping-counter control-word generators described thus far inasmuch as it can generate any one of four sets of control words. It can generate a stop code (1001), a full-speed code, a half-speed code and a special rebound code that will be used in a later version of this golf game.

ICs 6, 7, 8, and 9 in Fig. 8-20 are the selector circuits for these four speed codes. They are actually dual 4:1 multiplexers that select one of four different input logic levels, according to the status of 2-bit selector inputs at pins 2 and 14 in each case.

The output of IC2-A goes to one input of an $\overline{\text{R}}$-$\overline{\text{S}}$ flip-flop composed of IC1-C and IC1-D. The $\overline{\text{RST}}$ output of that flip-flop is set

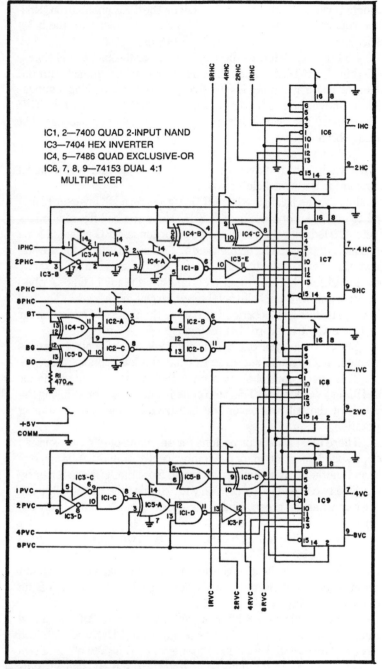

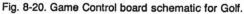
Fig. 8-20. Game Control board schematic for Golf.

347

to logic 1 whenever the player depresses the TEE pushbutton. $\overline{RST}$ then remains at logic 1 until the ball makes contact with the hole, indicating the completion of one hole of golf.

$\overline{RST}$ is connected to the reset input of the ball travel timer, IC5-B in Fig. 8-18. So when the ball figure makes contact with the hole, the ball-travel timer is effectively locked out, making it impossible to move the ball by depressing the SWING pushbutton. This lack of action is a clear indication the player has been successful at hitting the hole.

The only way to unlatch the $\overline{RST}$ signal is by depressing the TEE switch, which moves the ball off the hole and to the initial position for the next hole of golf.

Finally, the ball figure from IC3-A goes through inverter IC6-D and to one input of NOR gate IC3-D. Here the ball figure is effectively ANDed with the green figure to produce a BG signal, a logic level indicating the ball is on the green. This signal is used for slowing down the speed of the ball and shortening the travel time. Exactly how this signal shortens the travel time has already been described in connection with the ball-travel timer circuit in Fig. 8-18. The ball slowing effect will be described as part of the theory of operation for the Game Control board that follows.

Before seeing *how* one of four different sets of control words is selected, we ought to see exactly what the four options are.

This speed control system must include stop-code words for the HC and VC outputs. This stop code is necessary for stopping the motion of the ball whenever the ball-travel timer ends its timing operation.

There must also be provisions for selecting one of two sources of ball-speed information, one coming directly from the A/D converter and another that multiplies the speed from the A/D converter by two. The two speeds are necessary for running the ball at full speed until it reaches the green, where the speed should be effectively cut in half.

Some circuitry in Fig. 8-20 handles the two-speed information in the same way it is handled for the Dogfight game in Chapter 7. The idea is to automatically change the speed of the ball vector without changing its direction, and that is accomplished by means of the circuit first described in Fig. 7-23.

The circuit in Fig. 8-20 includes two of these 2× speed and direction multipliers. One of these handles the PHC input data and the other works with PVC data. Whenever the outputs of these two circuits are directed through the selectors to the HC and VC outputs, the ball travels twice as fast as it does when these circuits are not selected.

In this particular Golf game, the ball's speed data is taken from the 2× vector multiplier circuits until it touches the green. As soon as the ball touches the green, the speed and direction data is selected directly from the PHC and PVC inputs, giving the impression the ball speed is cut in half.

These three sources of speed and direction information—the stop code, 2× vector speed, and normal speed—are the only ones used in this particular game. There are provisions on the board, however, for a fourth option.

The fourth option is a rebound effect that is called up whenever the ball strikes an obstacle on the course. Since the obstacles are not included in this game format, the rebound circuitry is not used. A later chapter, however, takes up the subject of rebound effects, and the obstacle feature will be added to the Golf game at that time.

For the time being, it is sufficient to say that the ball speed and direction selectors can take their information from the RHC and RVC inputs. The obstacle contact input, BO, is normally pulled down to logic 0 by R1; so as long as no connection is made to that input, the obstacle rebound inputs (the RHC and RVC inputs) are never selected.

The circuit in Fig. 8-20 thus has provisions for selecting one of four sources of speed and direction information, but only three are used in this version of the Golf game.

The sources of ball speed and direction information that reach the HC and VC outputs are determined by the BT and BG inputs. For the present time, the special rebound-selecting input, BO, will be ignored. The function table in Fig. 8-21 shows the relationship between the BT and BG inputs and the ball-speed and direction information selected at the HC and VC outputs.

Recall that the BT signal is an active-high logic level that stands at logic 1 as long as the ball-travel timer is activated. This logic-1 level indicates the ball is supposed to be in motion. The ball is not supposed to be moving as long as BT=0.

The BG input to the control board is a logic level that indicates whether or not the ball is on the green. When the ball is NOT on the green, BG=0, but as soon as the ball makes contact with the green, BG switches to logic 1.

According to the function table in Fig. 8-21, then, the circuit selects the slipping-counter stop code (1001) whenever BT=0. The ball, in other words, should stop moving whenever the ball-travel timer is not timing a SWING operation.

BT BG	HC OUTPUTS	VC OUTPUTS	BALL MOTION
0 0	STOP CODE	STOP CODE	STOP
0 1	STOP CODE	STOP CODE	STOP
1 0	2X PHC CODE	2X PVC CODE	FAST—BALL NOT ON GREEN
1 1	PHC CODE	PVC CODE	SLOW—BALL ON GREEN

NOTE: THESE FUNCTIONS ASSUME THE REBOUND SELECT
INPUT, BO, IS FIXED AT LOGIC 0

Fig. 8-21. Functions for Golf speed control.

The circuit then selects the $2\times$ vector-multiplier function whenever BT=1 and BG=0. Interpreting this in terms of game operations, that means the ball is in flight, but has not yet touched the green. The ball travels in a direction, but at twice the speed, dictated by the outputs of the A/D converter.

The selector circuit then takes its data directly from the A/D converter whenever BT=1 and BG=1. This status occurs whenever the ball is moving and touching the green. The overall effect is that it travels in the same direction, but at half the speed, it has during free flight off the green.

Golf Wiring Block Diagram

Figure 8-22 shows the wiring block diagram for this particular Golf game. The system requires four circuit boards of the type specified throughout this book (Radio Shack's 276-153 40-pin plug-in boards).

The power-supply loading can be balanced reasonably well by operating the slipping-counter board from one supply and the three remaining boards and control panel from another 1-A supply.

The obstacle inputs are not shown here because they should be left unconnected for this version of golf. A later chapter will show how to use these RHC and RVC connections on the control board.

AMBUSH

Ambush is a one-player game that takes advantage of position programming in a rather unique way. The game is a variation of the old arcade game where the player is supposed to shoot at bad guys

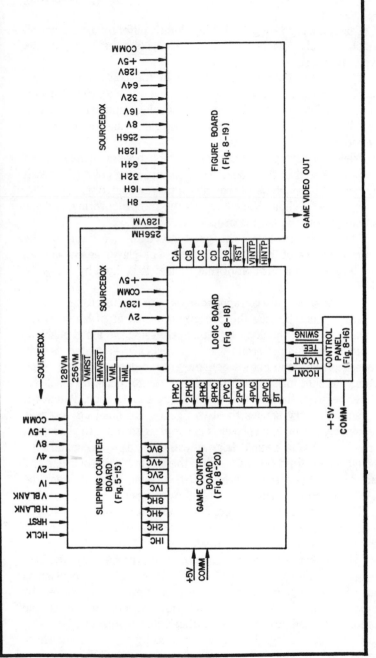

Fig. 8-22. Wiring block diagram for Golf.

popping up at various places in the game area. Scoring is based on the number of bad guys that are hit during a specified game-playing time interval.

This Ambush video game is only slightly different in that the bad guys shoot back. And if one of these villians hits the good guy (the player, of course), the game is over.

The unique feature of this game in the context of position programming is that the positions of the bad guys are purely random. The position information is selected from a high-speed counter that is "read" only during a brief time when the game calls for displaying a new bad guy.

While the playing is rather tricky, Ambush is one of the simplest games presented in this book. From a hardware point of view, it requires only two circuit boards and a player control panel.

Figure 8-23 shows the control panel, the panel wiring, and one example of how the playing area looks.

The player can move the good-guy figure vertically on the screen by means of the MOVE control. The player has no control over the horizontal position of that figure. It is fixed by the game logic.

The bad-guy figure can appear anywhere on the left-hand half of the screen, and shooting the bad guy is a matter of lining up the vertical position of the good guy and depressing the FIRE pushbutton. If the two figures aren't lined up vertically—situated directly across from one another—when the player depressed the FIRE button, the shot misses, and the player cannot chalk up a score.

Remember, though, that the bad guy shoots back. Whenever the game circuitry senses the two figures are lined up vertically (presumably because the player is attempting to shoot the bad guy), there is a fixed 1/10 second delay before the bad guy fires; and if the good guy hasn't fired yet and is still in the bad guy's line of fire, it's all over. The bad guy scores a hit and the player must depress the START button to begin the game all over again.

The general strategy, then, is to shoot at the bad guy while on the run up or down the screen. Don't take more than 1/10 second to line up and shoot, or you'll be dead.

Whenever the player manages to shoot the bad guy, the bad-guy figure flashes on the screen for a couple of seconds. The flashing figure then disappears from view, immediately being replaced by another bad guy at some randomly determined position on the screen. If the bad guy isn't shot within about 4 seconds, he disappears without flashing, only to be replaced by another somewhere else on the screen.

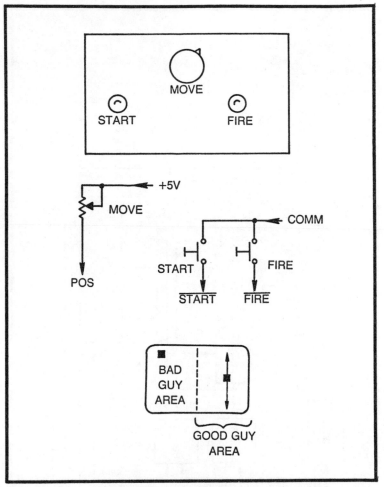

Fig. 8-23. Control panel diagram and schematic, and screen diagram for Ambush.

Providing the good guy isn't hit, the game runs for about 3 minutes before it is reset. The player then totals up the number of successful shots, and depresses the START button to begin another game.

Ambush Block Diagram and Schematics

The block diagram and schematics for the two special circuit boards are shown in Figs. 8-24 through 8-26. The wiring block diagram is in Fig. 8-27. Use all of these figures when studying the theory of operation of this particular video game.

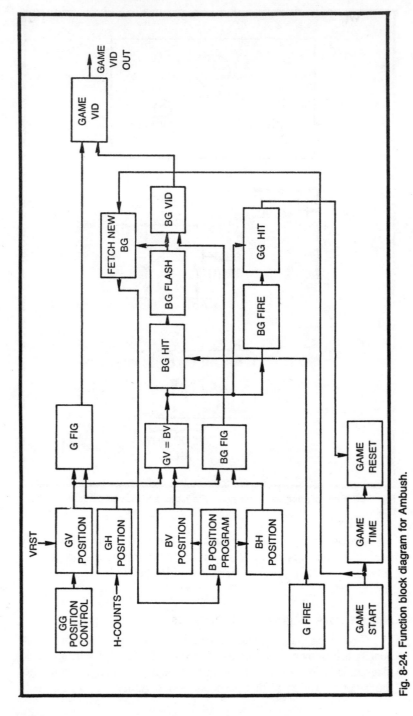

Fig. 8-24. Function block diagram for Ambush.

354

Whenever the player depresses the START button on the control panel, a negative-going logic level at pin 5 of IC1-B in Fig. 8-25 sets the state of a R-S flip-flop. The flip-flop responds by showing a negative-going edge at pin 3 of IC1-A. That edge-triggers a pulse-generator circuit composed of IC1-C and IC4-A. The brief negative-going pulse from that pulse generator triggers IC6-A, the game's 3-minute master timer circuit. Depressing the START button thus initiates a 3-minute monostable timing interval that can be interrupted only by a logic-0 level to pin 4 of that timer device. Of course that $\overline{GHIT}$ input indicates the good guy has been hit.

Now note that the output of the master game timer (IC6-A, pin 5) goes to a pulse generator and then to the resetting input of the $\overline{R}$-$\overline{S}$ flip-flop (pin 1 of IC1-A). The game is thus reset whenever the output of IC6-A makes a transition from logic 1 to 0. And that occurs when (1) the 3-minute game time expires or (2) the good guy is shot.

Depressing the START button also sends a logic 1 level to pin 8 of IC6-B. This enables the monostable so that the good guy can fire a shot by depressing the FIRE button. The shot is timed by IC6-B so that it lasts only about 1/10 second, but if GV=BV (good-guy vertical equals bad-guy vertical), the output of IC1-D registers a hit in favor of the good guy.

The pulse from IC1-D initiates a 1-second timing interval (monostable IC7-A) which, in turn, enables the bad-guy flashing action of IC7-B. A pulse generator connected to the pin-5 output of the flash timer generates a negative-going pulse and the *end* of the flashing time, indicating it is time to call up a new bad guy figure.

Once the game is started, then, the player can fire at any time by depressing the FIRE pushbutton. If the bad-guy figure happens to be in the line of fire at the time, the bad-guy figure flashes on the screen and is replaced by another bad guy a second later.

All of this assumes the good guy isn't hit first. Whenever the good guy is hit, the resulting logic-0 level at pin 10 of IC6-B locks out the good guy's firing circuit. A dead man can't fire a gun, you see.

IC8-A and its associated components in Fig. 8-25 are responsible for setting the vertical position of the good guy by means of the MOVE control. A complete description of this "sloppy" control appears in conjunction with the circuit in Fig. 5-6. The value of C11 in this particular circuit can be selected to fix the vertical size of the good-guy figure.

IC5-A fixes the horizontal part of the good-guy figure. Capacitor C12 can be selected to scale the width of that figure. The vertical and horizontal components of the good-guy figure are thus available from pin 6 and pin 8 of IC4.

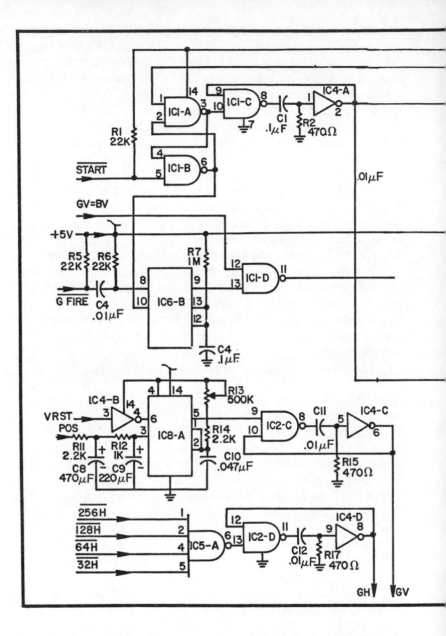

IC5-B in Fig. 8-25 determines when a new bad-guy figure is to be selected. The input connections to this IC show the new figure is selected under any one of three game conditions: when the game is first started, after a dead bad guy goes on to the hereafter, and after a bad guy has managed to survive on the screen for about 5 seconds.

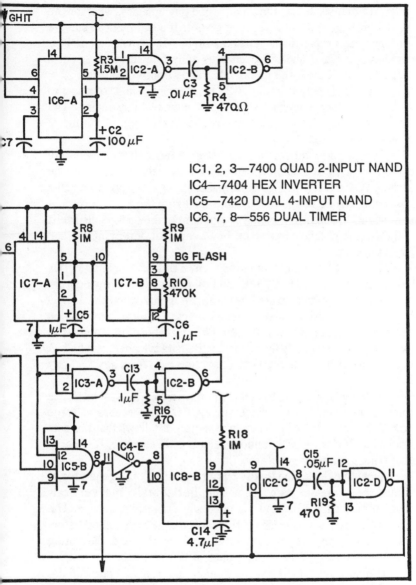

Fig. 8-25. Control board schematic for Ambush.

The circuits for indicating the start of a new game and the end of a bad guy's death scene have been described already.

IC8-B is responsible for keeping a bad guy on the screen for no more than 5 seconds. This timer is initiated whenever a new bad guy appears on the screen, but since it is connected as an interruptable

357

timer, it can be reset anytime a new bad guy appears, whether the old one managed to live 5 seconds or not. If a bad guy can survive through the normal timing interval of IC8-B, a pulse generator composed of IC2-C and IC2-D creates a brief negative-going pulse that ultimately resets the monostable action once again.

The LOAD output in Fig. 8-25 is normally at logic 0, rising to logic 1 only long enough to call up a new bad-guy figure. The remainder of the Ambush circuitry is shown on the Ambush-figure board in Fig. 8-26.

The special feature of the Ambush game is its ability to generate bad-guy figures at random positions on the left-hand side of the screen. IC4 and IC5 in Fig. 8-26 make up a pair of programmable position controls. IC4 is responsible for fixing the vertical component and IC5 sets the horizontal component of the bad-guy figure. It is the 4-bit logic levels from IC6, however, that determine the bad guy's position.

IC6 is a 4-bit latch, or memory, circuit. The data input in this case comes from the 1V, 2V, 4V, and 8V connections of the Source-box. This 4-bit data is loaded into the latch only when the LOAD input to pins 4 and 13 is at a logic-1 level. This loading condition occurs only for a brief interval when the control board operations call for seeing a new bad-guy figure. Once the data is loaded, it is held at the outputs of IC6 until the control system calls for a new bad-guy figure.

Since the data inputs to IC6 come from a counter system that is running continuously, and since the LOAD pulse occurs at some time that is determined by the game action, it follows that the data loaded into IC6 is virtually random in nature. In essence, IC6 works as a random-number generator.

Accepting the notion that IC6 is a random-number generator, it should become apparent that the horizontal- and vertical-programming data to IC5 and IC4 occurs in a random sequence. The bad-guy figure thus appears on the screen at some position determined strictly by the random number from IC6 and the wiring between IC6 and the program inputs of IC4 and IC5.

The horizontal and vertical components from IC4 and IC5 are NANDed together in IC1-A to create a bad-guy figure that measures 16V×16H. This image is passed through IC2-A, where it can be flashed whenever the good guy scores a hit. The horizontal and vertical components of the good-guy figure are combined in IC2-C. And after that, the two figures are effectively ORed together by IC2-B and IC1-B to create the game's video output.

All that remains to be discussed is the way the bad guy knows he is lined up with the good guy so he can fire a shot. IC1-C senses the alignment of the two opposing figures and generates a negative-going pulse that initiates monostable timer IC7-A. This particular timer is set for 0.1 second. And at the end of that time, a second 0.1-second timer (IC7-B) is initiated.

IC1-C senses alignment of the two figures on the screen, IC7-A inserts a 0.1-second delay, and IC7-B is responsible for making the bad guy fire a shot. IC1-D in Fig. 8-26 normally shows a fixed logic-1 output, but if the bad guy fires while he is lined up with the good guy, IC1-D senses this fact and generates a $\overline{GHIT}$ output.

Recall that a $\overline{GHIT}$ pulse resets the entire game system, making it impossible for the good guy to fire another round until the player depresses the START pushbutton. Without the 0.1-second delay inserted by IC7-A, the good guy wouldn't stand a chance of shooting anyone.

Ambush Wiring Diagram

The wiring diagram in Fig. 8-27 indicates this is a rather simple and inexpensive game to set up. The only calibration adjustment is fixing the value of R13 in Fig. 8-25. This trimpot works with the MOVE control to set the range of motion of the good-guy figure.

R13 should be adjusted so that moving the MOVE control between its two extremes moves the good-guy figure to the top and bottom of the screen.

The figure board should be operated from one of the +5V supplies, while the control board and panel can take their supply voltage from the second source.

STORMTROOPER ATTACK

You are the sole defender of a spacecraft. Eight enemy stormtroopers begin slowly advancing on your position, and you are all armed with deadly ray-gun weapons. You must defend your position, wiping out all eight stormtroopers before they reach your position.

The screen diagram in Fig. 8-28 shows the initial formation for this Stormtrooper game. You, the good guy, are located at the bottom of the screen, and your motion is limited to that part of the screen. The eight stormtroopers move straight down the screen toward you at the rate of about one-screen-per-71 seconds. In other words, you have only about 60 seconds to kill them off.

The control panel includes a MOVE control that lets the player move the good guy back and forth along the bottom of the screen, a

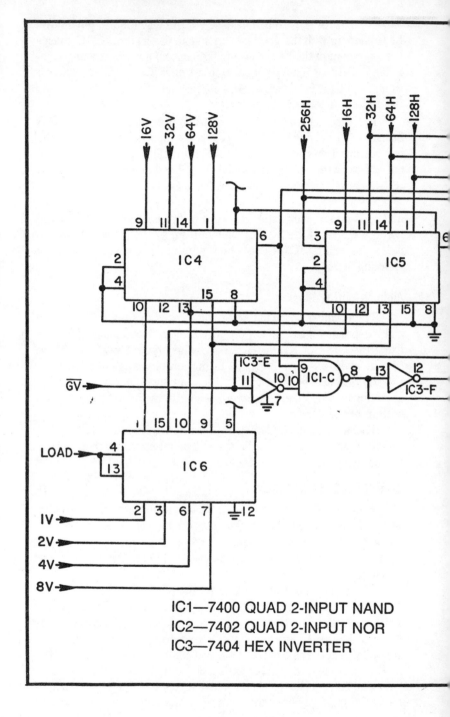

IC1—7400 QUAD 2-INPUT NAND
IC2—7402 QUAD 2-INPUT NOR
IC3—7404 HEX INVERTER

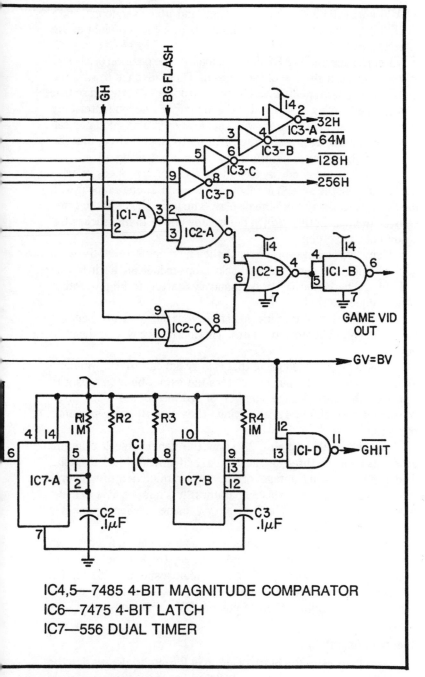

IC4,5—7485 4-BIT MAGNITUDE COMPARATOR
IC6—7475 4-BIT LATCH
IC7—556 DUAL TIMER

Fig. 8-26. Figure board schematic for Ambush

START button for beginning a new game and attack sequence, and a FIRE button that makes the good guy shoot a beam of light at the stormtroopers.

Depressing the START button initializes the position of all eight stormtroopers at the top of the screen. Their advance toward the good guy begins immediately. The stormtroopers are rigged so that they all fire a volley of shots at the good guy 0.1 second after they sense one of them is lined up with the good guy. The good guy can fire at any time by depressing the FIRE button, but he, too, must be lined up with one of the stormtroopers before scoring a kill.

Whenever the good guy hits one of the stormtroopers, they all disappear from the screen for about 0.5 second, then reappear with the dead guy missing from the display. The main object of the game is to kill them all in this fashion before any one of them reaches the bottom of the screen.

If any live stormtroopers reach the end of the screen, the good guy's position, the game automatically stops to indicate a win for the bad guys. The game has to be manually started to begin another attack sequence.

The game is also terminated in the event the good guy manages to wipe out all eight stormtroopers. This indicates a win for the good guy.

This is a fast-paced game that is very difficult to win without a lot of practice. Until a player masters the game, he might want to score on the basis of the number of stormtroopers killed in 10 consecutive attack sequences, trying to beat this 10-game sequence of scores.

Figures 8-29 through 8-33 show the general block diagram, schematics for the three circuit boards, and a wiring block diagram. The game takes advantage of the slow-motion feature of programmable position-control comparators. It is not possible to make the stormtroopers advance so slowly using a slipping-counter motion-control scheme.

A second feature of this game is its ability to blank figures from the screen when they are "hit," and then keep track of the number of remaining stormtroopers. Both of these features, extra-slow motion and selective elimination of figures from the screen, can be developed into a number of other custom TV-game systems.

Theory of Operation

As indicated on the block diagram in Fig. 8-29, depressing the START button both starts S MOTION and resurrects all previously

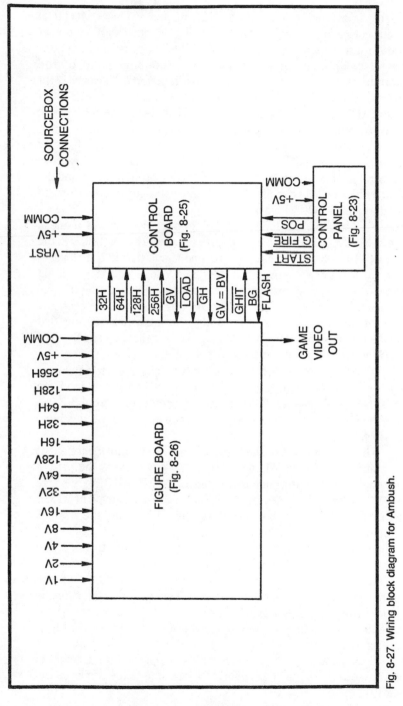

Fig. 8-27. Wiring block diagram for Ambush.

363

killed stormtroopers from the S KILL memory. The S MOTION control block is responsible for generating the downward motion of the stormtroopers, while the SH LOGIC block generates the horizontal component of those figures. Assuming none of the stormtroopers have been shot yet, S KILL memory allows all eight figures to appear on the screen. Outputs from the S MOTION CONTROL AND S KILL memory are combined in the S FIG logic block to generate the complete set of stormtrooper figures.

The good guy's position at the bottom of the screen is fixed by V-count inputs and G POSITION logic. Motion back and forth across the screen is controlled by the MOTION control on the panel and the G MOTION control circuit. The complete good-guy figure is formed by the G FIG LOGIC block.

Now suppose the good guy is lining up for his first shot at one of the stormtroopers. The player depresses the FIRE button, and the G FIRES block generates a 0.5-second signal that is transformed into the image of a narrow beam by G BEAM logic. This logic circuit makes the beam appear to come from the good-guy figure and extend to the advancing front of the stormtroopers. If the good guy is lined up properly with one of the stormtroopers during that 0.5-second interval, the SH=GH block senses that fact and the HIT block generates a scoring pulse for the good guy.

A pulse from the HIT block both blanks the stormtrooper figures at S HIDE (they all seem to take cover when the good guy fires, and eliminates the figure of the stricken enemy from S KILL MEMORY. The stormtrooper images reappear with the dead one missing.

The trickiest part of the game is that the stormtroopers shoot back at the good guy. Whenever the good guy crosses the path of any one of the live stormtroopers (sensed by SH=GH), they pause for 0.1 second before they all fire a beam at the good guy. The TIME DELAY block inserts this brief delay before initiating the S FIRE interval. S BEAM LOGIC generates the stormtroopers' beam image that appears to come from each of the live stormtroopers and toward the good guy's position on the screen.

GHIT logic senses a contact between any one of the stormtrooper's beam and the good guy. This spells disaster for the good guy because a signal from GHIT automatically stops the game, resetting the position of any remaining stormtroopers to the top of the screen.

If the good guy is successful in his attempt to kill off all eight of the stormtroopers, the ALL S DEAD block senses the condition and ends the game.

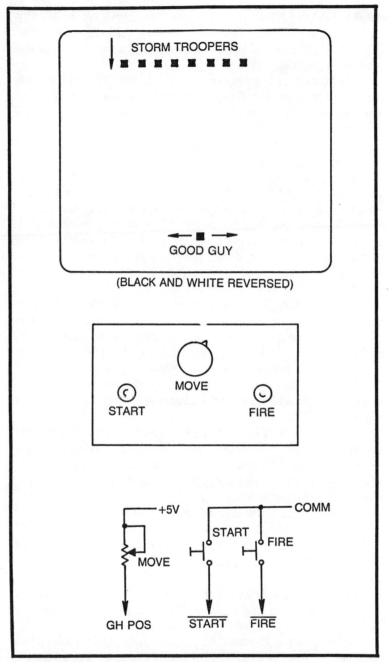

Fig. 8-28. Control panel diagram and schematic, and screen diagram for Stormtrooper Attack.

The GAME END block also responds to a condition signalled by the GV=SV block. The GV=SV block is responsible for sensing the fact that one or more of the live stormtroopers have reached the good guy's position.

The figure board shown in Fig. 8-30 contains all the circuitry for the game's master $\overline{R}$-$\overline{S}$ flip-flop control, stormtrooper motion, figure-position information for the good guy, and the good guy's firing circuit.

Depressing the START pushbutton sets the $\overline{R}$-$\overline{S}$ flip-flop, IC2-A and IC2-B, to a condition that allows counters IC7 and IC8 to increment (count upward) at a rate determined by VRST, 60 Hz. These counters provide position-programming information to comparators IC5 and IC6. According to the equations in Fig. 8-13, the counter/comparator system ought to move the stormtrooper figures through one complete screen cycle in 71 seconds. The stormtroopers, however, do not have to make one complete cycle before they reach the good guy's position. So the actual playing time is no longer than about 60 seconds.

The signal from pin 6 of IC6 is thus a 1V-wide horizontal line that moves slowly down the screen. IC4-F inverts this signal and applies it to a monostable multivibrator, IC9-A, where the position pulse is transformed into a wider bar that is about 8V wide. This timer actually sets the height of the stormtrooper figures.

Inverter IC4-A merely inverts the signal so that it has a phase that is appropriate for some of the control operations on the Control board in Fig. 8-32.

IC9-B in Fig. 8-30 is part of a motion-control circuit described in Chapter 5. Its GHPOS input comes from the MOTION potentiometer and lets the player set the horizontal position of the good-guy figure. Capacitor C2 is part of a pulse-generator circuit that fixes the width of the good-guy figure.

The horizontal position of the good guy is fixed by the V-count inputs to IC1-A, and then transformed into a pulse by IC1-B and IC4-E. Capacitor C3 fixes the height of the good-guy figure, while IC1-C is used merely for generating a GV signal for control purposes.

IC3 is the FIRE timer for the good guy. Whenever the player depresses the FIRE pushbutton, this timer generates a positive GFP pulse that lasts about 0.5 second.

A $\overline{RST}$ pulse at the input of IC2-B signals the end of a game sequence, generating a logic-0 $\overline{CLR}$ level that stops the counters and initializes the position of the stormtroopers.

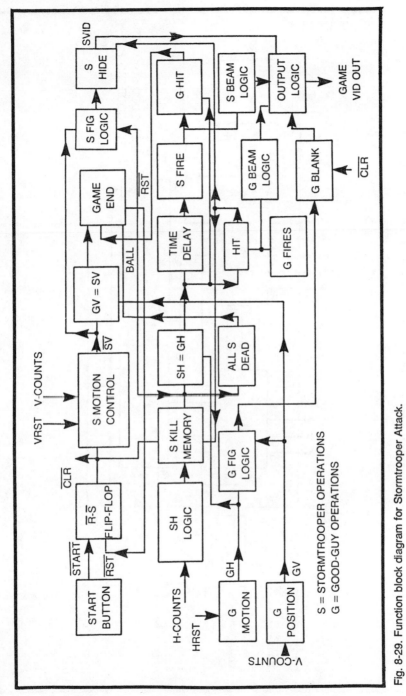

Fig. 8-29. Function block diagram for Stormtrooper Attack.

367

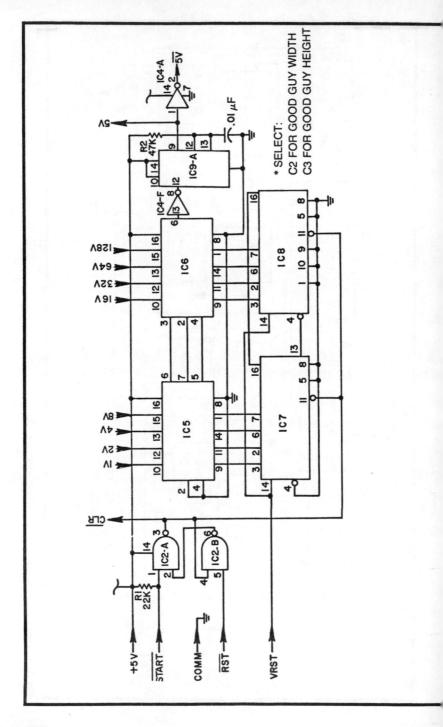

* SELECT:
C2 FOR GOOD GUY WIDTH
C3 FOR GOOD GUY HEIGHT

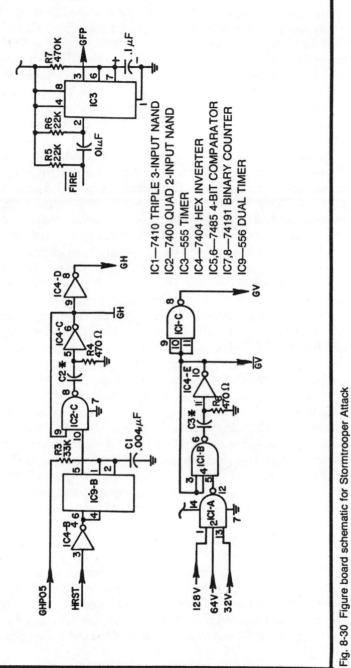

Fig. 8-30 Figure board schematic for Stormtrooper Attack

369

The Stormtrooper board in Fig. 8-31 keeps track of the live stormtroopers, generates the horizontal component of the stormtrooper figures, and senses when they are all killed. IC3 in Fig. 8-31 determines which one of the eight stormtroopers is hit and changes the state of the appropriate J-K flip-flop, IC6-A through IC9-B. Information from the "live" flip-flops is then recombined in IC5 to generate the horizontal component of the remaining stormtroopers. IC4 senses the condition where all eight stormtroopers are killed before any of them reach the good guy's position at the bottom of the screen.

IC3 and IC5 in Fig. 8-31 make up an addressable de-multiplexer/multiplexer combination having a set of eight J-K flip-flops standing between them. The demultiplexer and multiplexer circuits are addressed from the same source of counting signals: 32H, 64H, and 128H. (The board's 128H input is inverted by IC2-B before it is applied as the $\overline{128H}$ address bit.) Since the demultiplexer and multiplexer ICs are operated from the same three address lines, it follows that they scan their data in precisely the same sequence.

These are 8-line devices. That is to say, the demultiplexer (IC3) takes a single input line and splits the data into eight scanned output lines. The multiplexer (IC5) works just the other way around, accepting eight scanned inputs and reassembling them into a single output line, SH or $\overline{SH}$. The eight outputs from the demultiplexer go to eight different J-K flip-flops, each representing the dead-or-alive status of each stormtrooper. The active-high Q output of each flip-flop then makes up an input line to the multiplexer.

Each address count represents the horizontal position of a stormtrooper. When the address inputs to the demultiplexer/multiplexer combination are $32H=64H=\overline{128H}=0$, for example, the beam on the screen is generating the horizontal component of the first stormtrooper on the left. When the count changes to $32H=1$, $64H=128H=0$, the beam is scanning the second stormtrooper from the left. This demultiplexer/multiplexer scanning process continues through the eighth address combination, $32H=64H=128H=1$, the point on the screen representing the horizontal position of the last stormtrooper on the right.

This addressing scheme thus scans the stormtroopers one at a time, beginning at the left-hand end of the line. In Fig. 8-31, IC6-A determines the dead-or-alive status of the first stormtrooper, IC6-B takes care of the second stormtrooper from the left, and so on through IC9-B that determines the status of the last stormtrooper on the right.

Putting this information all together, the three address lines to the scanning system causes IC3 to generate a sequence of outputs representing the horizontal position of each stormtrooper, the flip-flops determine whether the stormtrooper being scanned is supposed to be dead or alive, and the multiplexer reassembles the information into a single string of sequential dead-or-alive information.

IC2-A uses 128H and 256H inputs to window the line of stormtrooper figures. This EXCLUSIVE-OR gate makes certain there are never more than eight stormtroopers on the screen at any given time, and causes them to appear fairly well centered where the 128H and 256H signals have opposite colors. This windowing information from IC2-A is combined with a HIT signal (HIT inverted by IC2-C) at IC1-B. The interaction between the HIT signal and window information will be described in a moment.

The stormtrooper information at IC5 is also windowed by the output of IC2-A, but the windowing information in this case is further refined by the 8H and 16H inputs to IC1-A. These two additional windowing parameters reduce the horizontal size of each stormtrooper to 8H and inserts a 24H blank space between each of them. The 24H blank is inserted so that the good guy has a chance to slip between two adjacent stormtroopers without getting shot by one of them.

Now suppose the game is reset for any one of three reasons: (1) all eight stormtroopers are successfully killed, (2) any one of them reaches the bottom of the screen, or (3) the good guy is shot by one of the stormtroopers. This reset condition sets CLR in Fig. 8-31 to logic 0, where it remains until the player depresses the START button to begin another attack sequence. While CLR remains at logic 0, the preset inputs to all eight J-K flip-flops are pulled down to logic 0. And taking for granted that all eight outputs from IC3 are at logic 1 at the time, the flip-flops are all set to a state where their Q outputs to the multiplexer are at logic 1. Ultimately, this means all eight stormtrooper figures can appear on the screen. In fact any stormtrooper figure remains on the screen as long as the Q output of its corresponding flip-flop is at logic 1.

The flip-flops then remain in their "alive" logic-1 states until a successful HIT occurs. Whenever the good guy manages to shoot a given stormtrooper, a $\overline{\text{HIT}}$ pulse occurs at the windowing input (pins 2 and 14) of IC3. The addressing scheme for the demultiplexer works in such a way that its output is scanning the stormtrooper that is hit, thereby setting its flip-flop to a logic-0 state. This indicates a

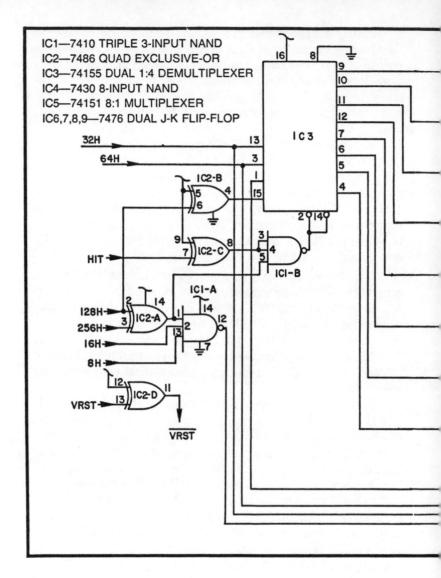

IC1—7410 TRIPLE 3-INPUT NAND
IC2—7486 QUAD EXCLUSIVE-OR
IC3—74155 DUAL 1:4 DEMULTIPLEXER
IC4—7430 8-INPUT NAND
IC5—74151 8:1 MULTIPLEXER
IC6,7,8,9—7476 DUAL J-K FLIP-FLOP

"dead" stormtrooper, and the multiplexer now sees a logic-0 input at that position on the screen. The figure for that particular stormtrooper is thus eliminated until the whole game sequence is reset again.

As far as the player is concerned, he hopes to hit all eight stormtroopers before the game is automatically reset. If he is successful, the Q outputs of all eight flip-flops are finally set to logic 0, and no stormtrooper figures appear on the screen.

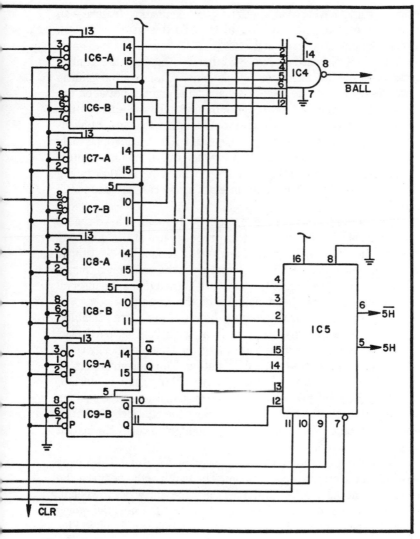

Fig. 8-31. Stormtrooper board schematic.

IC4 in Fig. 8-31 is responsible for sensing the condition where all eight stormtroopers are successfully eliminated. The inputs to this NAND gate come from the $\overline{Q}$ outputs of the flip-flops. When these active-low outputs all reach a logic-1 state, the output of IC4 drops to logic 0 to create the $\overline{BALL}$ signal, one of the three conditions required for resetting the game sequence.

The operation of the Stormtrooper board in Fig. 8-31 is far more difficult to explain than to use. Any experimenter hoping to design a game having this special figure-eliminating feature—an elementary memory system—ought to build this game and work through the circuitry first hand.

The Control board in Fig. 8-32 handles most of the control functions for the Stormtrooper Attack game. Whenever the game is in progress, for instance, IC1-A senses an alignment between the horizontal components of the good guy and any one of the stormtroopers visible on the screen. Whenever this sort of alignment occurs, a negative-going pulse from IC1-A initiates a 0.1-second monostable timer, IC8-A. And when this short timing interval elapses, the output at pin 5 of IC8-A initiates yet another timing operation from IC8-B. The timing interval in this case is close to 0.5 second.

What is the purpose of these sequential timers? These timers are responsible for making the stormtroopers fire at the good guy whenever he crosses the path of any one of them. The first timer inserts the crucial 0.1-second delay that gives the good guy a chance to fire a round and get out of the way. IC8-B then times the interval the stormtroopers' ray beam appears on the screen.

Both of these stormtrooper beam timers are disabled whenever the $\overline{CLR}$ signal to them is at logic 0. This particular condition occurs between the time the game is automatically reset and the player depresses the START button. The stormtroopers, in other words, cannot fire at the good guy until the game is started, thus giving the good guy a chance to take his initial defensive position without getting blasted off the screen before the attack really starts. Be careful, though. The stormtroopers might fire a volley the instant the game is started.

The pulse-generator circuit composed of IC1-B and IC6-A fixes the width of the stormtroopers beam. The width of the beam can be selected by the value of C4, the larger the value, the wider the beam.

This pulse generator is put into action on the negative-going (leading) edge of every $\overline{SH}$ pulse from the multiplexer circuit in Fig. 8-31. The beam, in other words, always appears to come from the left-hand edge of an advancing stormtrooper figure. Thus the stormtroopers are all right-handed, a fact that might help the good guy's strategy.

The $\overline{R}$-$\overline{S}$ flip-flop made up of IC1-C and IC1-D determines where the stormtroopers' beams begin and end. The $\overline{SV}$ signal to one of the inputs to this flip-flop ensures that the beam always starts from the line of stormtroopers, and the VRST input makes certain the beams travel all the way to the bottom of the screen.

So there are three basic elements that make up the stormtroopers' beams. IC1-A and the two timers determine when the stormtroopers fire and the duration of their volley, IC1-B and IC6-A determine the horizontal position and width of each beam, while IC1-C and IC1-D fix the position and length of the beam in the vertical plane. All three of these stormtrooper beam parameters are NANDed together at IC4-A, resulting in the complete video information for that part of the game.

A dead stormtrooper, incidentally, cannot fire a round at the good guy simply because the $\overline{SH}$ pulse at IC1-B cannot occur. That particular pulse is eliminated at the Stormtrooper board.

Whenever the good guy depresses his FIRE button, the timer circuit on the Figure board (IC3 in Fig. 8-30) generates a GFP pulse that lasts about 0.5 second. This positive-going level is fed to pin 3 of IC4-B to determine the good guy's firing-time interval.

The R-S flip-flop built around IC2-B and IC2-C fixes the vertical length of the good guy's beam. The SV input to this flip-flop always starts the good guy's beam at the line of stormtroopers, and the $\overline{GV}$ input ends the beam at the good guy's position. The good guy's beam is actually drawn from the line of stormtroopers to the good guy, but the visual impression is that the good guy is firing upward on the screen, and it is a visual impression that is more important in this case.

The pulse generator composed of IC2-D and IC6-C fix the horizontal position of the good guy's beam. The circuit operates from a $\overline{GH}$ signal, making the beam appear from the left-hand edge of the good-guy figure. The good guy, in other words, is a southpaw.

You should be able to see that the good guy's beam circuit is practically identical to that of the stormtroopers. The only real difference is that the stormtroopers fire automatically after a 0.1-second delay, whereas the good guy fires at any time the play depresses the FIRE pushbutton.

The good guy's beam parameters are all combined in IC4-B to create his beam video signal. The width of the good guy's beam is determined by the value of C5.

Thus far we have accounted only for the two beam figures generated at the Control board. We have yet to see exactly how the good-guy and stormtrooper video signals are assembled.

The horizontal and vertical components of the good-guy figure ($\overline{GH}$ and $\overline{GV}$) are effectively ANDed at IC7-B, then passed to the blanking gate, IC2-A. An active-low version of the good-guy figure emerges from IC2-A as long as the pin-1 input to that gate is resting

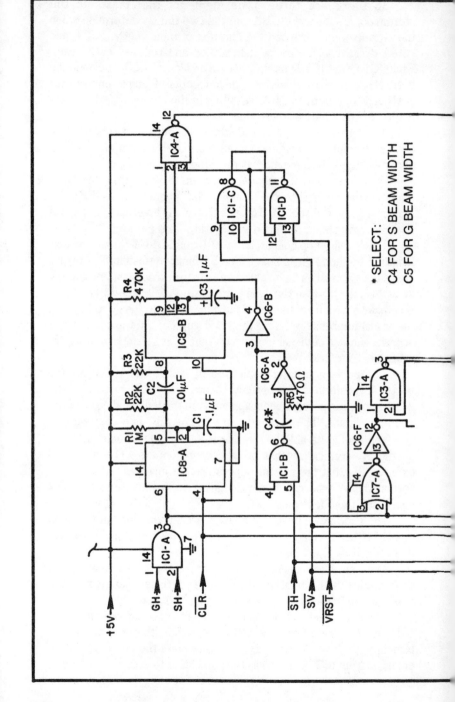

376

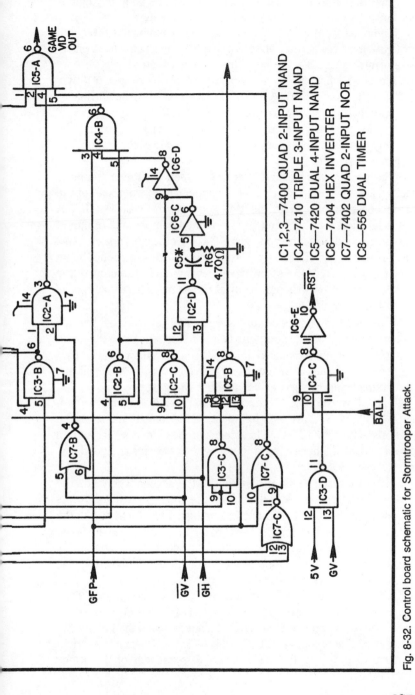

Fig. 8-32. Control board schematic for Stormtrooper Attack.

377

at logic 1. And as long as IC2-A is thus passing the good-guy figure, that figure is ORed with the other game components at IC5-A.

The pin-1 input of IC2-A drops to logic 0 and blanks the good-guy figure from the screen whenever he is hit by a beam from one of the stormtroopers. To see how this blanking feature works, note that the pin-1 input of IC2-A is controlled by the output of a $\overline{R}$-$\overline{S}$ flip-flop, IC3-A and IC3-B. A logic-0 input to IC3-B from $\overline{CLR}$ sets this flip-flop into a condition that places a logic-1 level at pin 1 of IC2-A, allowing the good guy figure to appear on the screen. The good guy, in other words, always appears on the screen whenever the game is started.

The good guy is blanked from the screen whenever the pin-1 input of IC3-A goes to logic 0. This happens only when one of the stormtroopers manages to kill the good guy. Recall that IC1-A senses an alignment between the horizontal components of one of the stormtroopers and the good guy. This logic-0 signal goes to pin 2 of IC7-A where it is effectively ANDed with the stormtrooper beam signal from IC4-A. If the stormtrooper beam and alignment of the good guy and a stormtrooper occur at the same time, the output of IC7-A goes to logic 1.

IC6-F inverts this good-guy-hit signal and sets the $\overline{R}$-$\overline{S}$ flip-flop to a condition that blanks good guy from the screen. Once the game is started, good guy remains visible on the screen until he is hit by a stormtrooper's beam. If the good guy manages to avoid being hit, his figure remains on the screen throughout the game.

The stormtroopers' horizontal- and vertical-figure components, SH and SV, are combined at IC7-C and blanked at the appropriate time by IC7-C. The stormtrooper video signal is then applied to IC5-A, where it is combined with the beams and good-guy figure.

Live stormtroopers are blanked off the screen whenever the good guy fires a round. Note that GFP, the good-guy firing signal, is applied to one input of IC7-C, creating a logic-1 level that blanks the stormtrooper figures as long as the 0.5-second good-guy beam lasts. The visual impression is that the stormtroopers take cover every time the good guy fires. Good guy can still hit one of the troopers, even while taking cover, though.

IC5-B is responsible for sensing a hit between the good guy's firing beam and a stormtrooper. This NAND gate merely senses the simultaneous occurrence of horizontal alignment and the good guy's firing pulse. The resulting HIT signal is used for blanking the stricken stormtrooper from the screen for the reaminder of the attack

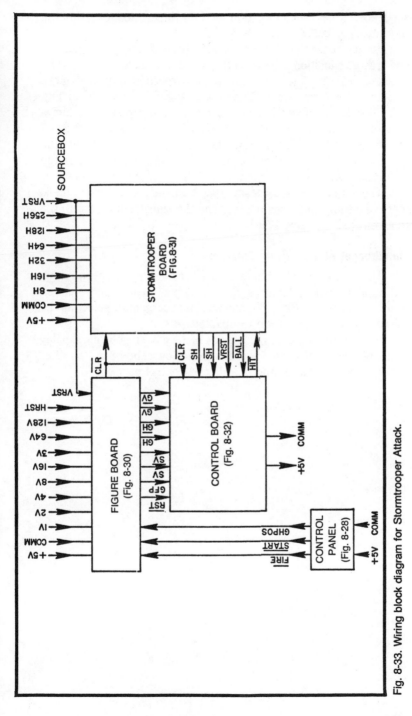

Fig. 8-33. Wiring block diagram for Stormtrooper Attack.

379

sequence. (See the application of HIT in connection with the Stormtrooper board in Fig. 8-31.)

Finally, recall that the game is automatically stopped under any one of three conditions: (1) all stormtroopers are killed, (2) good guy is hit, or (3) the line of stormtroopers reaches the good guy's position. These three conditions come together at IC4-C in Fig. 8-32. The $\overline{BALL}$ input from the Stormtrooper board senses when all troopers are killed off, the output of IC6-F senses the condition where the good guy is hit, and IC3-D senses the condition where the vertical components of the stormtroopers and good guy are on the same level—the stormtroopers reach the good guy's position.

The output of IC4-C goes to logic 1 whenever any one of these three resetting conditions occurs, and the signal is inverted to the required $\overline{RST}$ signal by IC6-E.

Stormtrooper Attack Wiring Diagram

This is a relatively simple game, considering its special slow-motion and memory features. It can be built around three circuit boards as shown in Fig. 8-33, and put into action after selecting the values of C4 and C5 on the Control board.

Since the circuit does not use any of the power-gobbling slipping counters, the +5V power sources from Sourcebox can be rather evenly divided between the boards and control panel.

Chapter 9
Scoring and Timekeeping

Virtually all fast-action video games call for automatic scoring, and of course it is nice if timed games have some provisions for displaying the elapsed time or time remaining for the play. The circuitry is practically identical in either case, a control circuit that generates binary numbers for scoring or time and a display circuit that generates the appropriate numeric figures on the screen.

The control and display circuits described in this chapter can be retrofit to most of the TV games already outlined in earlier chapters, and they can be fit into most of the game systems developed in the remainder of this book. After looking at the basic theory and suggesting some experiments, you will thus find some suggestions for expanding games you have already built to include scoring and timekeeping, or both.

Games described in the closing chapters of this book will include scoring and timekeeping boards as options. What is most important, however, is that you understand the circuitry thoroughly, making it possible to apply them effectively and efficiently to game designs of your own.

GENERATING NUMERIC CHARACTERS

The numerals used for these video games are built around the familiar 7-segment display that characterizes modern electronic calculators and digital clocks. Figure 9-1a shows this basic 7-segment format with the standard lower-case letter designations.

The a segment is always the one across the top. The alphabetical sequence then proceeds clockwise through f. Letter g is then reserved for the horizontal segment through the center of the figure.

The numeral 1 is thus generated by lighting segments b and c only. A 2 is generated by lighting segments a, b, g, e, and d, while a 3 is made up of a, b, c, d, and g. If you have never done so before, work your way through the standard 7-segment format to see how any numeral between 0 and 9 can be generated.

Seven-segment display characters (whether in a TV game, calculator, or digital clock) are normally originated by a BCD word, a binary-coded version of decimal numbers between 0 and 9. The table in Fig. 9-1b compares these 4-bit BCD words with their decimal counterparts and the segments in a 7-segment display that ought to be lighted or extinguished.

As mentioned in an earlier example, the 3 character is displayed by lighting segments a, b, c, d, and g. Note from the table that the BCD version of the number 3 is 0011. The corresponding 7-bit segment output in this particular case is 1111001, where the most-significant bit is the a segment and the least-significant is the g segment. The 1s in the segment word represent a lighted segment, and the 0s stand for a darkened segment—one that is not shown.

Study the table in Fig. 9-1b carefully, comparing the 10 BCD inputs with the segment equivalents and the 7-segment format in Fig. 9-1a.

The table in Fig. 9-1b is actually the truth table for a standard BCD-to-7-segment converter IC device. This 7448 device accepts BCD inputs A through D (a being the least-significant bit) and generates the corresponding 7-segment format at outputs a through g. Input G can be viewed as an enabling input that must be at logic 0 in order to enable the BCD-to-7-segment conversion process. Setting input G to logic 1 sets all segment outputs to logic 0, thereby blanking the figure altogether.

Assuming for the moment that you have a source of BCD numbers and a 7448 converter for translating those numbers into a 7-segment format, turn your attention to the drawing in Fig. 9-2. This figure shows how the segments are arranged for a display on the TV screen. The a segment is a bar that crosses the top of the figure, the b segment is a vertical bar that appears in the upper right-hand side, overlapping the a bar in that corner. The c segment is a vertical bar that is somewhat longer than the b-segment bar, overlapping the right-hand end of the d-segment bar.

The numeric figures appearing on the screen actually have no visible breaks between adjacent segments as the displays for most

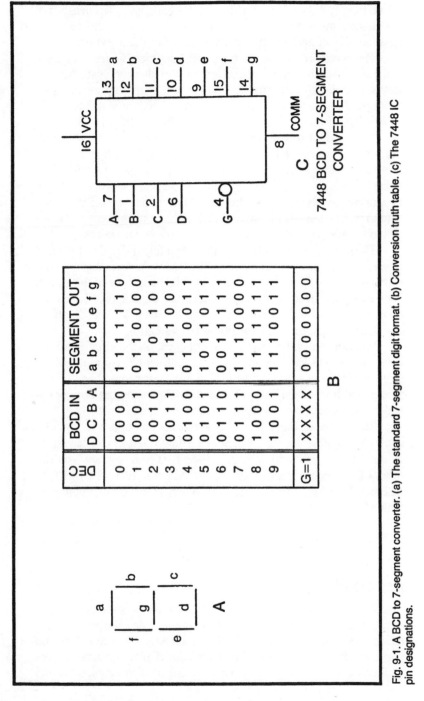

Fig. 9-1. A BCD to 7-segment converter. (a) The standard 7-segment digit format. (b) Conversion truth table. (c) The 7448 IC pin designations.

calculators and digital clocks do. This overlapping feature is not intentional, but rather a natural result of devising the simplest possible sort of numeric figure generator for video games.

The waveforms accompanying the 7-segment figure in Fig. 9-2 anticipate the theory of operation of the display system. The waveforms drawn along the bottom of the figure represent three successive H-counts from the Sourcebox. A0H, for instance, could be 8H. And if that is the case, A1H is 16H and A2H is 32H.

The V-count waveforms in Fig. 9-2 are drawn vertically, from the top downward, along the side of the 7-segment figure. These waveforms represent three successive V-count sources, with A0V being the least significant. To get a figure having the proper relative dimensions as shown here, the A0V input should be on the same count level as the A0H input. If A0H is taken from source 8H, for instance, A0V should be taken from the 8V count source.

The 7-segment pattern is thus completely defined in terms of three successive H-count and three successive V-count signals. The actual size of the figure is determined by the magnitude of the H- and V-count signals used. You can build a rather large figure, for example, by using 32H and V, 64H and V, and 128H and V. Actually those specifications generate the largest possible figure.

You can generate a much smaller figure, on the other hand, by using the H- and V-count sequence of 2, 4, and 8. No matter how large or small you want to make the figure, just remember that the proper width-to-height ratio comes about by taking the horizontal- and vertical-count signals from corresponding sources.

Regardless of the size, the waveforms and figure in Fig. 9-2 shows that segment a can be generated only when all vertical-count inputs are at logic 0 and A2H is at logic 0. The b segment, on the other hand, can be displayed only when $A2V=0$, $A0H=A1H=1$, and $A2H=0$. Then note that it is possible to generate the g segment only when $A0V=A1V=1$ and $A2V=A2H=0$.

You can check your understanding of this display scheme by making up a truth table that shows which segments are enabled at the various combinations of H- and V-count inputs.

DIGIT-GENERATOR CIRCUITS

After working your way through the circuits and experiments suggested in this chapter, you should be able to devise digit displays having any display format and control scheme you want. For the purposes of our discussion, however, the display formats are organized as follows: single digit display, 2-digit numeric display, and

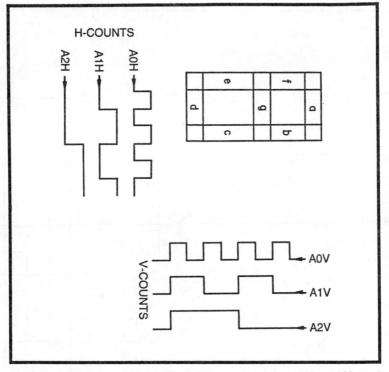

Fig. 9-2. The basic 7-segment video digit, showing relevant H- and V-count waveforms.

double 2-digit display. These formats cover most video game situations. Naturally we will describe a numeric character generator board that is capable of being programmed for any one of the standard formats. The idea here is to provide a single circuit board that can be used for a large number of different games.

A Single-Digit Display Circuit

The circuit in Fig. 9-3 is capable of displaying a single-digit numeric figure having any desired size and position on the screen. This is a relatively simple circuit that can be assembled on a breadboard in a short time. So why not build it, connect its output (SCO) to the video input of the Sourcebox, and play with the circuit while working your way through the theory of operation.

The numeral to be displayed is presented in BCD form at inputs A through D to IC6. IC6 is the BCD-to-7-segment code converter described in Fig. 9-1, and its seven outputs go to various inputs points on a pair of 8:1 multiplexer ICs, IC7 and IC8.

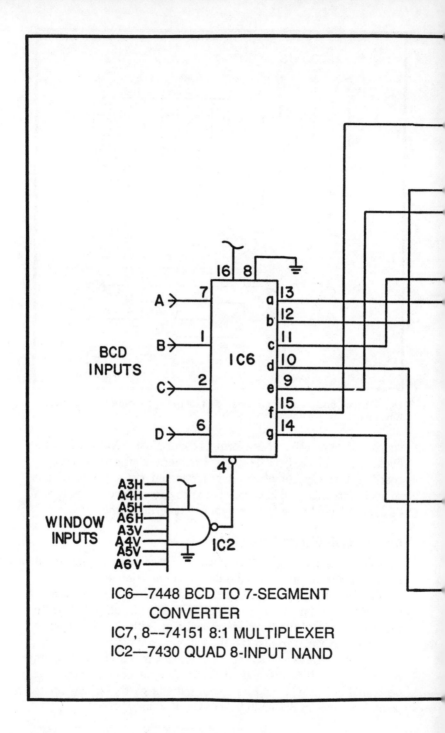

A → 7

B → 1

C → 2

D → 6

BCD
INPUTS

16 8

IC6

a 13
b 12
c 11
d 10
e 9
f 15
g 14

4

WINDOW
INPUTS

A3H
A4H
A5H
A6H
A3V
A4V
A5V
A6V

IC2

IC6—7448 BCD TO 7-SEGMENT
    CONVERTER
IC7, 8—74151 8:1 MULTIPLEXER
IC2—7430 QUAD 8-INPUT NAND

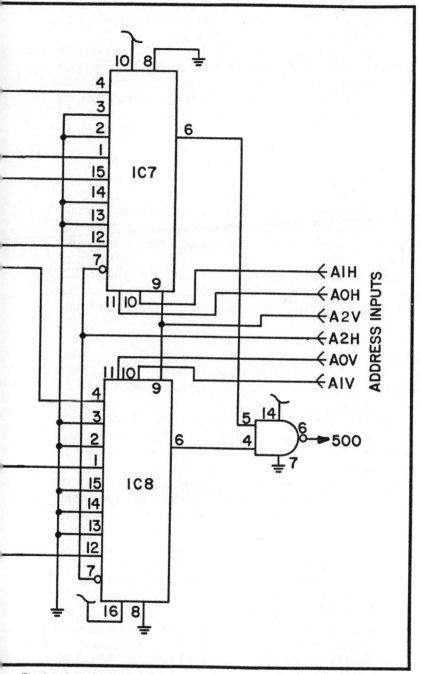

Fig. 9-3. A single-digit numeric character generator

IC6 takes care of the task of converting BCD to 7-segment information, while IC7 and IC8 perform the figure-forming logic described in connection with the drawings in Fig. 9-2.

Recall from the material in Chapter 4 that such multiplexers can be programmed to generate complex figures of all sorts. The figure in this particular case is a 7-segment numeric figure. The eight data inputs to each of the multiplexers is either an output from the BCD-to-7-segment converter or logic 0 (ground potential). The addressing inputs for IC7 and A0H, A1H, and A2V, while the addressing inputs for IC8 and A0V, A1V, and A2V.

These addressing inputs are the same ones described for the discussion of Fig. 9-2—three successive H- and V-count signals from Sourcebox.

Suppose the system is to display numeral 3. The BCD input to IC6 in this instance is 0011. And according to the truth table in Fig. 9-1b, the outputs at logic 1 are a, b, c, d, and g. Outputs f and e are at logic 0 in this case.

The a-segment output of IC6 goes to pin 4 of multiplexer IC8; so whenever that multiplexer is being addressed in such a way that the pin-4 input logic level appears at the pin-6 output, an a-segment logic level appears at SCO. If you have done your homework suggested earlier in this chapter—making up a truth table relating the H- and V-count inputs to the generation of 7-segment information—you will find that the SCO output generates the designated segment output information at the proper place in the H- and V-count signals.

And whether you have done this homework or not, you can breadboard this circuit, apply valid BCD codes to the BCD inputs to IC6 and find the corresponding 7-segment numeric character appearing on the screen.

As in the case of any complex-figure generating process, the figure must be windowed to restrict its image to a single figure on the screen. Without proper windowing, the figure would appear any number of times all over the screen.

The windowing process is rather simple, once you have determined the H- and V-count signals to be used for generating the character itself. Select three successive H- and V-count signals for the six address inputs to IC7 and IC8, using the general rules outlined in connection with Fig. 9-2. After that, apply all higher-order H- and V-count signals to the window inputs, inverting some of them as needed for fixing the figure's position on the screen.

Suppose, for example, you choose to let A0H=8H, A1H=16H, and A2H=32H. This decision makes it necessary to set A0V=8V,

A1V=16V, and A2V=32V. That takes care of the addressing inputs for the multiplexers. Now the remaining higher order Sourcebox signals—64H, 128H, 256H, 64V, 128V, and 265V—must go to the window inputs of IC2. You will want to invert some of these signals before applying them to IC2 thereby placing the figure at some convenient position on the screen. Review the material concerning figure windowing in Chapter 4 if you find you are getting lost at this point.

After fixing the address and windowing inputs, you can generate some figures by applying logic 1 and 0 levels to the BCD inputs. Connect all four BCD inputs to COMM, for instance, and you should find a 0 on the screen. The size of the figure is determined by your selection of address inputs, and its position is fixed by your selection of inverted or noninverted inputs at the windowing NAND gate, IC2.

Disconnect the grounding wire from input A, leaving the other three grounded, and you should see a figure 1 on the screen. If you connect nothing at all to the four BCD inputs, they automatically assume logic-1 states, resulting in no figure on the screen. You have most likely discovered this little fact for yourself while setting up the circuit initially. Just remember that this system responds only to valid BCD inputs, binary versions of numbers 0 through 9. Any input number larger than 9 results in either a meaningless figure or none at all.

If you want to have some more fun with the circuit in Fig. 9-3, remove all your programming jumper wires from inputs A through D and replace them with a BCD counter as shown in Fig. 9-4a.

This counter circuit can be clocked, using either the circuit in Fig. 9-4a or 9-4b. The circuit in Fig. 9-4b is a 555 timer wired as a monostable multivibrator. Each time the experimenter depresses the COUNT pushbutton, the timer generates a 10-ms pulse that increments the counter, ultimately advancing the count appearing on the screen. The count can be cleared to 0 at any time by simply depressing the CLEAR pushbutton. A numeric display system used in this fashion is typical of game-scoring operations. Every time a score pulse (COUNT operation) takes place, the numeral on the screen advances one unit.

The 555 timer in Fig. 9-4c is connected as a free-running multivibrator that has a frequency between one pulse every 6 or 8 seconds and 10 Hz, depending on the value of R2. The larger the value of R2, the slower the oscillator runs.

The circuit in Fig. 9-4c can be used as a CLK source for the counter, making the display increment automatically at the CLK frequency. The clock can be stopped and started by means of the

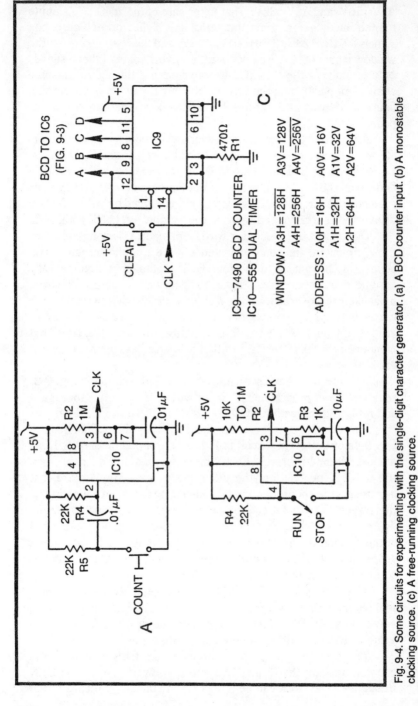

Fig. 9-4. Some circuits for experimenting with the single-digit character generator. (a) A BCD counter input. (b) A monostable clocking source. (c) A free-running clocking source.

STOP/RUN switch, or the display can be cleared to zero by depressing the CLR pushbutton on the counter.

Free-running display counters of this sort are used for displaying game times.

A Two-Digit Display Circuit

The single-digit display works fine as long as the score or game time never exceeds a figure 9. It is capable of registering single digits between 0 and 9, but many games call for scoring and timing larger numbers.

Figure 9-5 shows the general display scheme for a 2-digit video display. The two digits have identical segment designations, but are separated by a space that is one digit wide. For most counting and timing applications, the digit on the left is a 10s digit, while the other is a units digit.

The scheme for generating the figures is identical to that used for a single-digit dispaly, except for an A3H signal that is used for

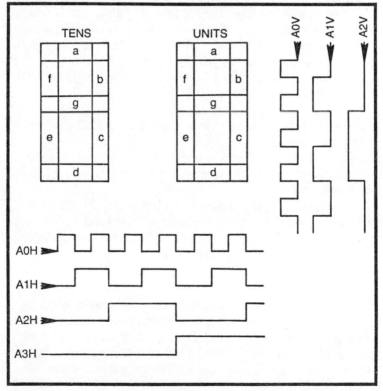

Fig. 9-5. A two-digit numeric display, showing relevant H- and V-count waveforms.

distinguishing one digit from the other. Whenever A3H is at logic 0, the system generates the 10s digit, but when this H-count input rises to logic 1, the system uses the same circuitry to generate the units digit.

The circuitry for decoding BCD numbers and generating the 7-segment figures on the screen is identical to the single-digit output circuit in Fig. 9-3. The windowing circuit is also the same.

Figure 9-6, however, shows how the basic output circuit can be modified to generate the 2-digit format. IC12 in Fig. 9-6 is a quad 2:1 multiplexer circuit that must be used for selecting the BCD words for the two digits. Whenever the SEL (SELECT) input is at logic 0, this multiplexer feeds IC6 in Fig. 9-3 the BCD word from counter IC9, the units counter. As the A3H signal to SEL rises to logic 1, however, IC12 provides the BCD word from the 10s digit counter, IC11.

The output circuit in Fig. 9-3 is thus sampling one of two different BCD words at any given time. It samples and displays data from IC9 when A3H is low and from IC11 when A3H is high. IC9 and IC11 in Fig. 9-6 are connected as a 2-decade BCD counter system, and this display scheme merely decodes the BCD numbers and translates them into the 2-digit screen format in Fig. 9-5.

The counters in Fig. 9-6 can be incremented from either one of the two circuits in Fig. 9-4a and 9-4b.

Figure 9-6 also shows a set of recommended window, select, and address specifications for experimental purposes. The address specifications are three successive H- and V-counts, the select specification is always the next higher-order H-count, and the windowing is a combination of inverted and noninverted, higher-order H- and V-counts.

As in the case of the single-digit display, the address inputs determine the size of the figures and the window specifications fix the figures' position on the screen. In this case, the SEL input distinguishes the 10s from the units digit.

A Dual Two-Digit Display

Many video games call for keeping score for two players. This means there should be two distinctly different sets of figures on the screen, generally on in the upper left-hand corner and another in the upper right-hand corner. The circuit in Fig. 9-7 is capable of doing this sort of job, presenting two pairs of numbers on the screen. An added advantage of this particular circuit is that it can also be used for generating simpler numeric displays. This one circuit board, in other

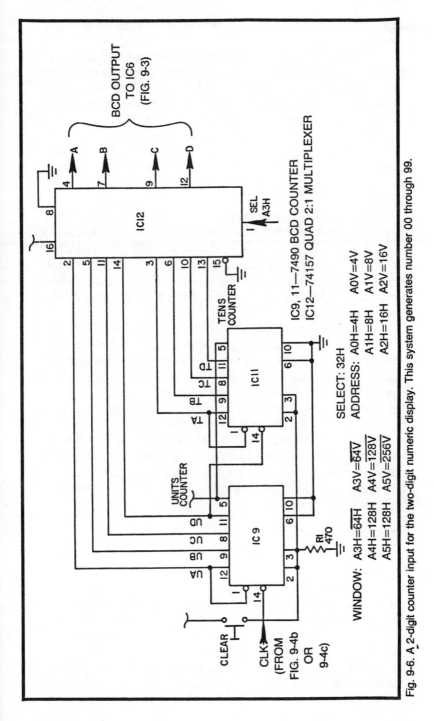

Fig. 9-6. A 2-digit counter input for the two-digit numeric display. This system generates number 00 through 99.

393

words, can be used for a wide variety of scoring and timekeeping situations.

The theory of operation is basically the same as that for the single and two-digit displays already described. The only difference is that the BCD to 7-segment decoder, IC6, is fed one of four different BCD codes at any given moment. These signals come from four 4:1 digital multiplexers built into IC4 and IC5.

Multiplexers IC4 and IC5 select one of four sources of BCD numbers according to their select inputs at pins 14 and 2. The A3H input to the multiplexers sets the blank between the two digits in each display. The 256H select input separates one 2-digit display from the other.

Whenever the select inputs to IC4 and IC5 and 00, for example, the system receives BCD information relative to the 10s digit in the left-hand display (digit LT). As A3H switches to logic 1 and 256H remains at 0, the system selects data for the units digit in the left-hand display (LU). The 10s and units digits in the right-hand display (RT and RU) are selected when 256H is at logic 1 and A3H is 0 or 1 respectively.

IC2 windows the display with inverted and noninverted versions of all higher-order H- and V-counts not used elsewhere. Whether these windowing inputs are to be inverted or non-inverted depends on where the display figures are to appear on the screen. Experimenting with the window inputs for a while can lead to some useful programming information for future design work.

The circuit in Fig. 9-7 can be tested by operating it from two sets of 2-decade counters such as those shown in Fig. 9-6. In instances where some of the four digits are never to appear on the screen, their respective BCD inputs can be left uncommitted, connected to nothing. The resulting logic-1 levels at these inputs blank the figures from the display.

SCOREKEEPING CIRCUITS

Keeping track of scores for video games is pretty much a matter of counting certain events—scoring events. The circuit designer merely determines which events are to increase a player's score, obtain a logic pulse that represents that scoring event, and apply it to a counter circuit. Then there should, of course, be some provisions for clearing the score to zero at the beginning of the next game. That's the basic process, anyway.

Scorekeeping can be raised to a rather sophisticated level, scoring different numbers of points for different kinds of scoring events, scoring more than one player, and making the scoring process part of the game control.

The Simplest Scoring Scheme

The simplest scoring scheme is one that merely advances a player's score one count whenever a particular scoring event occurs. Consider the Golf game in Chapter 8, for instance. A simple counter circuit can be triggered by the SWING pulse, thus keeping track of the number of swings in a game sequence.

Figure 9-8a shows a pair of binary counters cascaded to provide a BCD count from 00 through 99. The scoring event, whatever it might be, is presented as a brief positive-going pulse. The count increments on the negative-going edge of that particular pulse. The circuit is likewise cleared to zero by a positive pulse on the CLEAR bus. These counters, incidentally, can be cleared and held at zero, in spite of scoring events, by holding the CLEAR bus at logic 1.

The U outputs in Fig. 9-8a are the units BCD code that is to operate either the left or right units input to the score pattern generator in Fig. 9-7. The T outputs from IC2 in Fig. 9-8a are the 10s units.

A pair of counters can be used for scoring two players at the same time. The block diagram in Fig. 9-8b shows how they can be interfaced with the complete score figure generator. Player A's score increments whenever his particular scoring event occurs, and B's increments as his scoring events occur. The two counters in this instance have a common CLEAR bus. They are both cleared at the same time and under the same set of circumstances.

The ORing circuit in Fig. 9-8b merely indicates that the output of the scoring generator is to be ORed with the game's primary video information before it is applied to Sourcebox's video input.

Scoring and Game Control

Many kinds of TV games call for ending a game sequence or changing the game pattern whenever the score reaches a certain point. The scoring is an integral part of the game control.

Figure 9-9a shows a typical control circuit for a TV game. It is mainly an $\overline{R}$-$\overline{S}$ flip-flop that is manually set by depressing a START pushbutton, and it is reset by an active-low $\overline{STOP}$ pulse. Depressing the START button begins the game, and the occurrence of the $\overline{STOP}$ pulse ends it. Scoring becomes an integral part of the game control when STOP is generated by a scoring circuit.

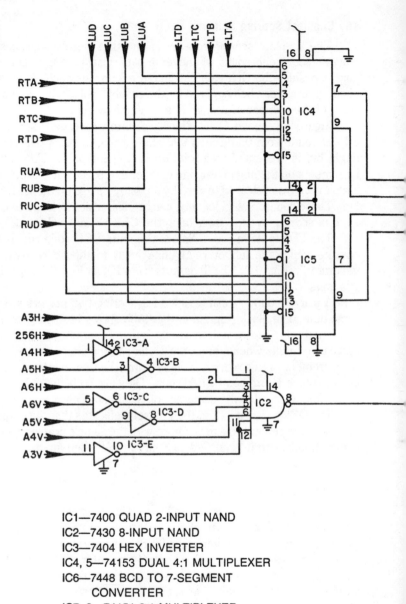

IC1—7400 QUAD 2-INPUT NAND
IC2—7430 8-INPUT NAND
IC3—7404 HEX INVERTER
IC4, 5—74153 DUAL 4:1 MULTIPLEXER
IC6—7448 BCD TO 7-SEGMENT
    CONVERTER
IC7, 8—74151 8:1 MULTIPLEXER

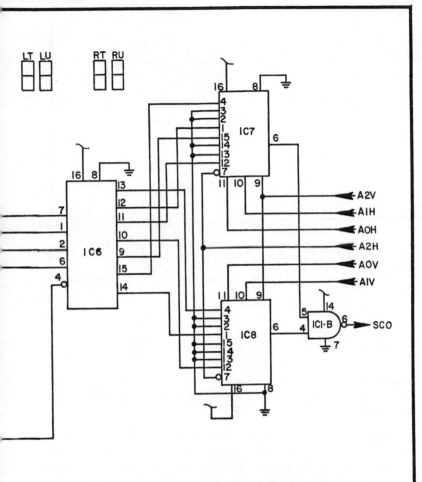

RECOMMENED SPECIFICATIONS

WINDOW: A4H=$\overline{32H}$ A3V=$\overline{16V}$
A5H=$\overline{64H}$ A4V=32V
A6H=128H A5V=$\overline{64V}$
A6V=$\overline{128V}$

SELECT: A3H=16H AND 256H
ADDRESS: A0H=2H A0V=2V
A1H=4H A1V=4V
A2H=8H A2V=8V

Fig. 9-7 A complete dual 2-digit display generator

397

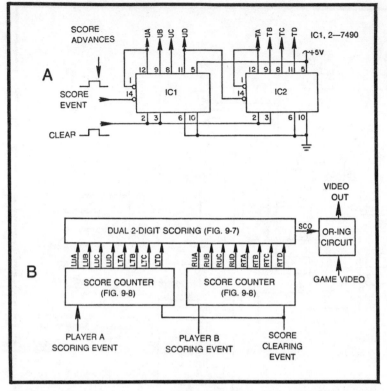

Fig. 9-8. A simple scoring scheme. (a) A 2-digit score counter. (b) Interfacing two score counters to the dual 2-digit generator circuit.

Suppose the 2-digit, single player scoring circuit in Fig. 9-8a is to control this game. Depressing the START button causes the output of IC3-B in Fig. 9-9a to drop from logic 1 to 0, and the pulse generator produces a brief pulse that is inverted to a positive-going pulse from IC4-B. This pulse is applied to the counter's CLEAR bus to clear the two digits to zero.

As the game progresses, the score presumably increments, advancing the count from IC1 and IC2 in Fig. 9-8a toward some game-ending score. Now suppose that game-ending score is 25. So when the 10s counter reaches the binary version of 2 (0010) and the units counter reaches 5 (0101), the game should stop. In other words, this game should stop the first time TB=1, UA and UC=1.

The 3-input NAND gate in Fig. 9-9c is wired to sense this particular count. The output of that gate is normally at logic 1, but drops to 0 when the counters show the BCD version of 25. At that moment, the little pulse generator in Fig. 9-9c produces a negative-

398

going pulse that is fed to the $\overline{STOP}$ input of the game control circuit in Fig. 9-9a, thus stopping the game action and holding the 25 scoring figure on the screen.

The score is cleared and the game is restarted by depressing the START button once again.

The basic idea behind the score-stopping control is to sense the score at which the game is to stop, connecting the counter outputs that are at logic 1 to the input of a NAND gate. The chart in Fig. 9-9b

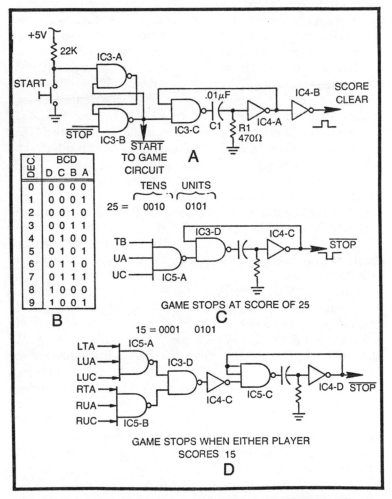

Fig. 9-9. Circuits for controlling the game from the scoring. (a) Automatic score clearing at the start of a game. (b) Score counter truth table. (c) Stopping the game when a single-player score reaches 25. (d) Stopping the game when either of two players' score reaches 15.

summarizes the output status of a counter at its 10 different counts. The NAND gate that senses the stop count must be large enough to handle all the 1s from both the units and 10s counter. A 3-input NAND gate is normally adequate, but a 4-input gate would be required in the rather odd case where one might want to stop the game at score of 47 (0100 from the tens counter and 0111 from the units counter).

The circuit in Fig. 9-9d shows how to stop a game whenever one of two player's score reaches 15. This score-sensing circuit is used in conjunction with a two-player scoring format such as the one illustrated in Fig. 9-8b, and the idea is to stop the game and fix the final scores when either player reaches the winning score.

IC5-A senses the terminal score at the left-hand display and IC5-B senses the score at the right-hand display. IC3-D effectively ORs the outputs, generating a logic-1 level when either player reaches the winning score. That logic level is inverted by IC4-C before it is applied to a pulse generator and ultimately to the STOP input of the game-control flip-flop. Of course IC5-A and IC5-B can be wired to sense any desired terminal score.

The circuit in Fig. 9-10 is a complete two-player, 2-digit score-oriented game control board. It combines all the circuit features described in Fig. 9-9 into a single board. The terminal score for both players is fixed at 45 in this case. But if the input connections to IC2-A and IC2-B are jumper wires, this one board can be used for stopping a game at any desired score having no more than three 1s in its BCD format.

This board must be interfaced with the score generator in Fig. 9-7 by connecting the counters' outputs to the corresponding BCD inputs on the score generator. The PLAY and PLAY terminals from IC1-A and IC1-B should go to the game's initialization circuitry. A later section in this chapter shows this interfacing procedure in greater detail.

Before leaving the general topic of game control from scoring circuits, it must be pointed out that the same scheme can be used for controlling sequences within a single game. Target speeds, for instance, can be increased when the score reaches a certain point, and then the game can be ended when a player's score reaches yet some higher level.

Weighted Scoring

Many games in the real world call for weighted scoring, making some game scores count more than others. A touchdown in football, for instance, is worth 6 points, a field goal is worth 3, and a point after touchdown is good for 1 point. We can do the same thing with video games.

The circuit in Fig. 9-11 shows a rather simple weighted scoring circuit. It has nine scoring inputs labeled S1 through S9, and a CLK output. The CLK output clocks a scorekeeping counter such as any of those described in the previous two sections of this chapter. The S inputs accept active-low scoring-event pulses from the game system.

Suppose a certain game event calls for scoring 2 points for one of the players. The game system generates a negative-going pulse that is applied to the S2 input, and the ultimate result is that two clock pulses emerge from the CLK output. An event in the same game might then call for a 4-point score, and in this case the event-scoring pulse is applied to S4, causing the CLK to generate four output pulses.

Since the CLK output triggers a counter, it follows that the player's score will increment either two or four units, depending on which scoring event takes place. This circuit actually handles weighted scores anywhere between 1 and 9. The experimenter has the option of using any one or all the available weighted-scoring inputs.

To see how this circuit works, use the waveforms in Fig. 9-11 while tracing the action of the ICs. And for the sake of this discussion, suppose a particular scoring event is to increment the player's score by 5 points.

When the 5-point scoring event occurs, a negative-going pulse from the game circuit appears at the S5 input of IC5. This pulse should last at least 100 μs, a requirement that is easily satisfied by the scoring procedures described in this book.

IC5 is listed as a priority encoder in most digital manuals, but it also works as a decimal-to-BCD converter. Its inputs and outputs are both active low, so pulling its pin-2 input down to logic 0 causes its four outputs to take on an inverted, or active-low, BCD version of decimal 5. The active-high version of BCD 5 is 01001, and the active-low version from IC5 is 1010. Pulling pin 2 down to logic 0 thus causes the four outputs to show 1010, where pin 9 is the least-significant-bit position and pin 14 is the ICs most-significant-bit output.

A 4-input NAND gate, IC2-B, senses the fact that a scoring pulse has been applied to IC5 and generates an active-high version of it. See the IC2-B output waveform. This waveform is applied to a resettable monostable multivibrator, IC3-A, which generates a positive pulse having a duration of about 25 μs.

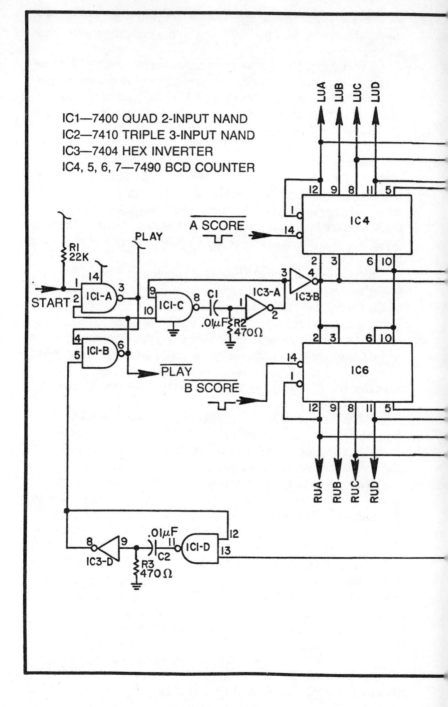

IC1—7400 QUAD 2-INPUT NAND
IC2—7410 TRIPLE 3-INPUT NAND
IC3—7404 HEX INVERTER
IC4, 5, 6, 7—7490 BCD COUNTER

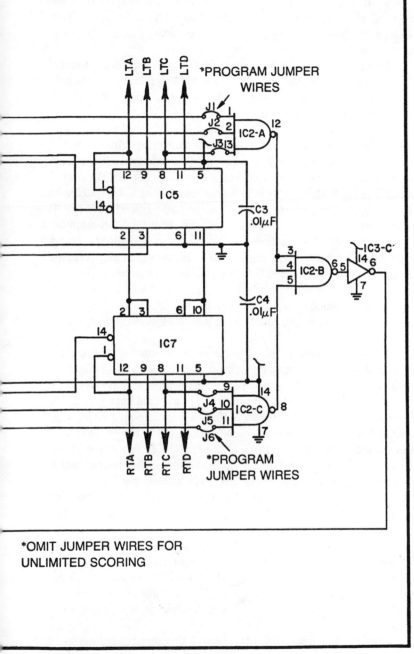

Fig. 9-10. A complete two-player game control circuit

403

The pulse from IC3-A always begins at the start of the scoring waveform. And after being inverted by IC1-D, it is applied to the pin-11 loading input of IC4, a presettable binary counter. This counter, in other words, is loaded with the binary output of IC5 the moment any scoring pulse occurs.

The negative-going pulse from IC1-D also triggers a second monostable multivibrator, IC3-B, causing it to generate a second 25 μs pulse. Note from the waveforms that the pulse from IC3-B occurs as the first pulse ends.

This second pulse sets an R-S flip-flop composed of IC1-A and IC1-B. Setting the flip-flop in this fashion snaps the output of IC1-A to logic 0 and the output of IC1-B to logic 1. These two outputs from the R-S flip-flop cause two important events to happen simultaneously: The logic-0 level from IC1-A enables counter IC4 by pulling its pin-4 enabling terminal to logic 0, and the logic-1 level from IC1-B opens gate IC2-A so that 1V pulses can appear at the CLK output.

Summarizing the action to this point in the discussion, a negative-going pulse at any one of the scoring-event inputs creates an inverted BCD number at the output of IC5, a number representing how much the scoring should advance. The same input pulse initiates a sequence of two 25 μs pulses, the first loads the counter and the second starts the counter and lets clock pulses emerge from the CLK output.

Now the question is this. How does the circuit know when it is supposed to stop chalking up points? By the time the counter is enabled at pin 4, a number has already been loaded into the counter's preset inputs. Suppose that number is an inverted binary 5, 1010. The counter, however, interprets this as an active-high input, seeing it as binary 10. So when the counter is enabled, it begins counting upward from 10 at the 1V rate. (Note that 1V is connected to the pin-14 clock input of IC4.) And when the count reaches the maximum of binary 15 (1111) the pin-12 max/min output rises to logic 1, resetting the flip-flop made up of IC1-A and IC1-B. This resetting action both disables the counter and turns off the gate that has been allowing CLK pulses to appear.

In short, the number of 1V clock pulses required to make counter IC4 reach its maximum count is equal to the score value entered at the $\overline{S}$ inputs. Pulling $\overline{S1}$ to logic 0 makes this circuit generate one CLK pulse, pulling $\overline{S2}$ to logic 0 makes it generate two CLK pulses, and so on through $\overline{S9}$, which causes nine CLK pulses to occur.

Figure 9-12 shows a pair of weighted-scoring circuits interfaced with the two-player score counters and figure generators described

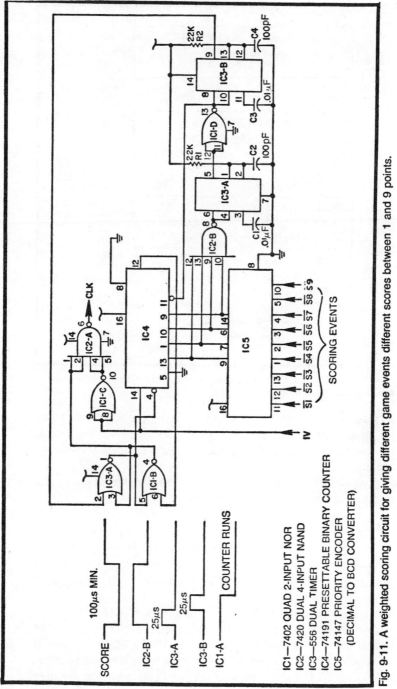

Fig. 9-11. A weighted scoring circuit for giving different game events different scores between 1 and 9 points.

405

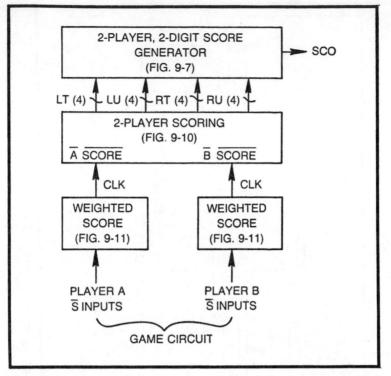

Fig. 9-12. Interfacing the weighted scoring circuits with 2-player scoring and full score character generator.

previously in this chapter. Whether used in this particular configuration or any other scoring scheme, the weighted-scoring circuit merely replaces the CLK or score-event pulse inputs to the scoring counters.

The Pinball game in Chapter 11 uses the weighted-scoring scheme in its most sophisticated form.

TIMEKEEPING CIRCUITS

Timekeeping operations are relatively straightforward: Pick up a 1-Hz source of pulses, apply them to a counter that counts seconds and minutes, then attack any sort of desired automatic start, stop, and clearing controls.

Figure 9-13 shows how to generate a precise 1-Hz timing pulse from the 60-Hz VRST source. The scheme uses two counter circuits composed of a 7492 cascaded with a 7490. The 7492 is a special clock-operation binary counter that automatically counts the sequence 0 through 5, then resets to 0 again. This particular counter serves the dual function of a divide-by-6 frequency counter and a binary counter for 10s of seconds. In Fig. 9-12, the 7493 is used as a divide-by-6 circuit.

VRST pulses applied to the pin-1 input of the 7492 thus emerge from pin 8 at the rate of 10-Hz (60 Hz divided by 6). The 10-Hz pulses are then applied to the pin-14 input of a 7490 BCD counter which is connected as a symmetrical divide-by-10 counter. The 7490 thus divides the 10-Hz signal from the first counter to a precise 1-Hz waveform having a duty cycle of exactly 50%. This 1-Hz signal serves as the main clocking source for all timekeeping operations.

The circuit generates its 1-Hz output only as long as the START input is at logic 0. Whenever START input goes to logic 1 for any reason, the 1-Hz pulses no longer appear at the output because the counters are effectively cleared and stopped. Pulling the START input back down to zero makes the 1-Hz pulses appear once again.

This 60-Hz-to-1-Hz converter, or frequency divider, is incorporated in the most useful kind of timekeeping circuit, shown in Fig. 9-14. VRST is applied to pin 1 of IC3, and as long as the game is in its PLAY mode, the precise 1-Hz pulse appears at pin 11 of IC5.

IC6 in Fig. 9-14 serves the dual purpose of a BCD counter and a divide-by-10 frequency divider. The 1-Hz pulses appearing at its pin-14 clocking input increment this counter at the 1-Hz rate, making its four outputs generate the appropriate BCD code for units of seconds.

The most-significant-bit output of IC6 changes at a rate of once every 10 seconds, the input clock rate of 1 Hz divided by ten. This output pulse clocks IC4, another 7492 divide-by-6 counter. The three outputs of IC4 increment once every 10 seconds, generating the 10s-of-seconds cycle of 0 through 5.

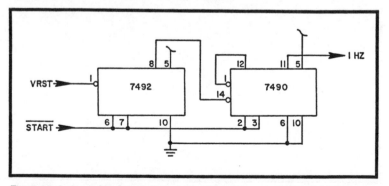

Fig. 9-13. A simple frequency divider circuit that converts the 60 Hz VRST pulse from Sourcebox into 1 Hz timing pulses.

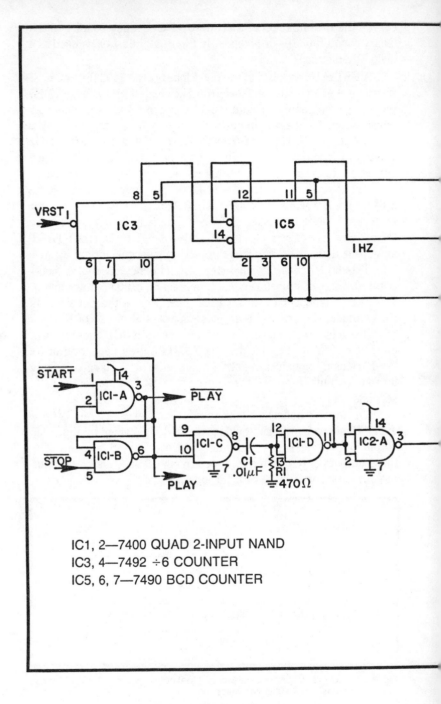

IC1, 2—7400 QUAD 2-INPUT NAND
IC3, 4—7492 ÷6 COUNTER
IC5, 6, 7—7490 BCD COUNTER

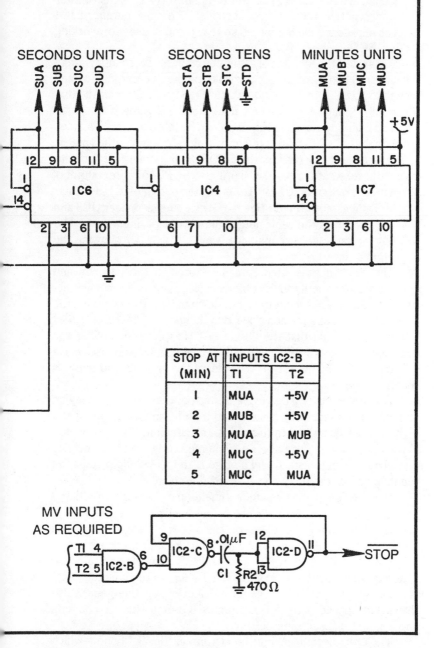

STOP AT	INPUTS IC2-B	
(MIN)	TI	T2
1	MUA	+5V
2	MUB	+5V
3	MUA	MUB
4	MUC	+5V
5	MUC	MUA

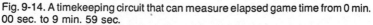

Fig. 9-14. A timekeeping circuit that can measure elapsed game time from 0 min. 00 sec. to 9 min. 59 sec.

Considered together, IC6 and IC4 make up a seconds counter that cycles between 00 and 59 seconds. The pin-8 output of IC4 changes state once each minute, so that pulse is used for clocking another BCD counter, IC7.

IC7 serves the function of a minutes counter. Its counting range is between 0 and 9, making it possible for the overall timekeeping system to count from 0 min. 00 sec. through 9 min. 59 sec. And that is certainly enough time for executing good TV games.

The counting circuit in Fig. 9-14 can be interfaced with a video game via the $\overline{\text{START}}$ and $\overline{\text{STOP}}$ control logic. Whenever the game is to be stopped for any reason, the STOP input momentarily goes to logic 0, thereby setting the $\overline{\text{R}}$-$\overline{\text{S}}$ flip-flop to its PLAY state: output of IC1-A=0 and output of IC1-B=1. Setting the output of IC1-B to logic 1 in this fashion stops the 60-Hz-to-1-Hz frequency divider (IC3 and IC5), and deprives the remaining counters of clocking pulses. The counting operation thus stops with IC6, IC4, and IC7 showing the elapsed time interval.

The elapsed time then remains stored in the seconds and minutes counters until the next game cycle is started by momentarily pulling the START input to IC1-A down to logic 0. Triggering the $\overline{\text{START}}$ input in this fashion does two things: It sets the output of IC1-B to logic 1 so that the 60-Hz-to-1-Hz frequency divider can begin generating its 1-Hz timing pulses again, and it triggers a pulse generator (IC1-C and IC1-D) that clears the seconds and minutes counters to zero.

Whenever a new game cycle is started, then, the timekeeping outputs are automatically cleared and then begin incrementing at a 1-Hz rate. As described to this point, the circuit in Fig. 9-14 works like a stopwatch, a pulse at $\overline{\text{START}}$ immediately clears the display then allows timing to start, and a pulse at the $\overline{\text{STOP}}$ input stops the counting action and holds the elapsed time display.

Most video games using a timekeeping feature are timed games. That is, the games are to be automatically stopped after a certain amount of time has elapsed. The three NAND gates shown in the insert in Fig. 9-14 can be added to make a time-stop game.

This circuit is simply a NAND gate connected to a pulse generator. The input NAND gate, IC2-B, senses the time the game is to be stopped, and IC2-D generates a brief negative-going pulse that can be applied to the STOP input of IC1-B to stop the counting and hold the elapsed-time display.

The chart accompanying the circuits in Fig. 9-14 show which timing outputs should be connected to the inputs of IC2-B. If the game is to be stopped after 3 minutes, for instance, the inputs to

IC2-B should be MUA and MUB from IC7. Once the game is started by a negative-going pulse at the $\overline{\text{START}}$ input of IC1-A, it runs until MUA and MUB both go to logic 1 at the end of 3 minutes. The resulting negative-going pulse from IC2-D then stops the clocking operation.

If the game, itself, is controlled by the PLAY and $\overline{\text{PLAY}}$ outputs of IC1-A and IC-1B, the game operation is tied to the clocking operations, as the timer goes, so goes the game.

Figure 9-15 shows how the timekeeping circuit can be interfaced with the figure generator from Fig. 9-7 and the game logic system.

RETROFITTING SCORING AND TIMEKEEPING TO EXISTING GAMES

Many of the video games described in earlier chapters can be retrofitted with certain versions of the scoring and timekeeping circuits presented in this chapter. Retrofitting the circuits is generally a matter of adding two more circuit boards, calling for little, if any, surgery on existing systems.

Golf Score and Hole Designation

Perhaps the simplest game to retrofit is the Golf game featured in Chapter 8. Adding the circuit in Fig. 9-16 to the Golf game

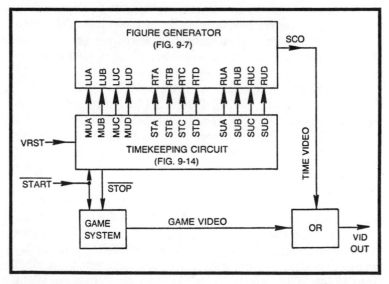

Fig. 9-15. Interfacing the timekeeping circuit with the character generator and some sort of video game that must be ended after a certain amount of time has elapsed.

provides a nine-hole score between 00 and 99, as well as a numeric designation of the hole being played.

IC1 and IC2 make up the scoring portion of the game. These two BCD counters are cascaded to count binary numbers 00 through 99, and they increment each time the pin-14 clock input of IC1 sees a positive-going pulse from BT, the ball timer in Fig. 8-18. Recall that this timer outputs a positive pulse each time the player depresses the SWING pushbutton. So the counter increments one unit each time the player takes a swing at the ball.

The tally can be reset to zero at the beginning of each game by depressing the SCORE RESET pushbutton. This pushbutton, of course, should be added to the Golf control panel.

The BCD outputs of IC1 and IC2 go to the numeric-figure generator circuit board shown in Fig. 9-7. Using the connections shown here, the Golf score appears on the screen in the left-hand set of digits.

The right-hand units numeral on the screen will show which hole is being played. IC9 in Fig. 8-18 is the hole counter for the Golf game. Its output is a BCD number between 0 and 8; so if its "C" outputs were applied directly to the RU inputs on the score figure generator, the player would see the holes being numbered between 0 and 8, instead of the proper 1 through 9.

The count from the Golf hole counter must be corrected by adding 1 to it. When the hole counter is reset to 0, then, the screen will show hole number 1. Then when the hole counter generates the BCD equivalent of 1, the screen will indicate hole number 2, and so on.

Correcting the hole count is a simple matter of adding binary 1 via an adder circuit. IC3 in Fig. 9-16 is a 4-bit binary adder that is wired to add 1 to whatever BCD number appears at its C inputs. The C inputs in this case are taken form the corresponding C connections running between the logic and figure boards for Golf. The number is summed with 1 to yield the corrected hole-number at the RU outputs of IC3 in Fig. 9-16.

The right-hand 10s (RTA through RTD) are connected to ground, thus disabling that digit and blanking it from the screen.

IC1 and IC2 thus keep track of the Golf score, while IC3 puts the hole-count designation into the conventional golf format. All that remains to be done is combine the main game video with the number video. IC4-A, IC4-B, and IC4-C in Fig. 9-16 take care of this job by effectively ORing together the game and number video.

412

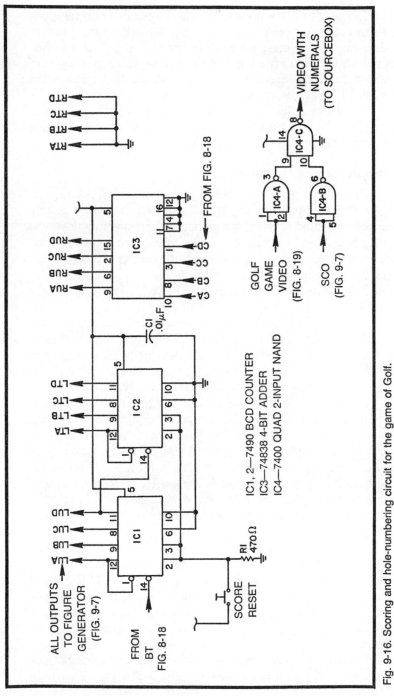

Fig. 9-16. Scoring and hole-numbering circuit for the game of Golf.

The input to IC4-A is the Golf video output that normally goes directly to the Sourcebox. The input to IC4-B is the SCO, or score video, from the figure-generating circuit in Fig. 9-7. IC4-C then effectively ORs these two active-low signals to yield a combination of game and scoring video. The output of IC4-C thus goes to the GAME VID IN on Sourcebox.

The circuit in Fig. 9-16 can be built into a plug-in board, and it, along with the board from Fig. 9-7, can be added to the existing boards for Golf.

Automatic Scoring for Ambush

The Ambush game described in Chapter 8 is a fast-action game that makes automatic scoring a practical necessity. The scoring scheme presented here scores as though there are two sides, the good guy and the bad guys. A 2-digit display in the upper left-hand corner of the screen keeps track of the total number of bad guys that appear on the screen, and another 2-digit display in the upper right-hand corner scores the number of bad guys the player actually shoots.

Adding the automatic scoring is thus a matter of applying the two-player scoring circuit from Fig. 9-10. Of course this board must be interfaced with the standard double-scoring figure generator in Fig. 9-7. So it turns out that the rather simple Ambush game can be expanded to include full scoring by adding two more circuit boards.

Figure 9-17b shows the wiring block diagram for interfacing the two scoring circuits. Connecting the scoring circuitry to the existing Ambush system is even simpler. Note that there are only three inputs to the two-player scoring board from the Ambush circuitry: a $\overline{\text{START}}$ input from the control panel in Fig. 8-22, a LOAD connection from Fig. 8-25 to the board's $\overline{\text{A SCORE}}$ input, and a special connection from pin 5 of IC7-A in Fig. 8-25 to the $\overline{\text{B SCORE}}$ input.

Allow unlimited scoring by removing all six jumper wires shown in Fig. 9-10.

Depressing the START button on the Ambush control panel thus starts the game and clears both score displays to zero. Each time a new bad guy appears on the screen, the PLAYER A score increments one unit; and each time one of the bad guys is shot, the PLAYER B score increments. The Ambush game automatically ends after 3 minutes, leaving the final scores displayed on the screen.

The Ambush video output is combined with the scoring output by means of the simple circuit shown in Fig. 9-17a. This circuit uses three 2-input NAND gates that happen to be uncommitted on the

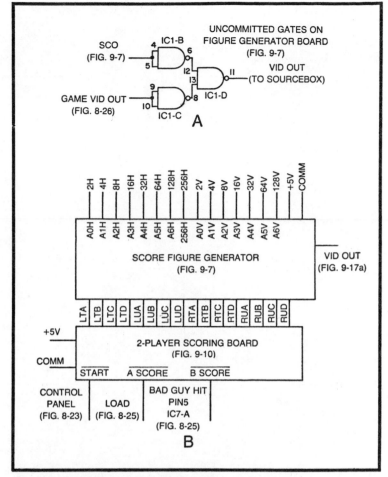

Fig. 9-17. Scorekeeping circuit for Ambush.

score-figure generator. Wire IC1 on the score-figure generator as shown here, applying the SCO terminal from Fig. 9-7 to the inputs of IC1-B and the GAME VID OUT from Fig. 8-26 to the input of IC1-C (instead of to the Sourcebox).

Connecting the pin-11 output of IC1-D to the GAME VID IN of the Sourcebox completes the operation. Ambush with full scoring is then ready to go to work for you.

Chapter 10
Figure Rebound Effects

The classic table-tennis and squash video games rely on a bouncing, or rebounding, effect. Whenever the ball strikes a paddle or one of the fixed barriers, it instantly changes its direction of motion.

Such effects are appropriate for a lot of other kinds of video games as well, and the purpose of this chapter is to provide the background necessary for working the rebound effect into any desired custom game.

Most of the examples cited here assume the rebounding figure works from a slipping counter. As pointed out near the end of the chapter, however, it is just as easy to achieve the same effects with a figure generated by one of the position programming circuits in Chapter 8.

The basic idea behind the rebound effect is to sense the moment a moving object makes contact with a second object, generally a stationary one, then reverse the horizontal or vertical direction of the moving object.

Suppose, for example, a ball figure is moving horizontally to the right. It then strikes a fixed figure on the right-hand side of the screen and immediately switches direction so that it is moving horizontally to the left. That is one particular rebound effect. The same idea can be applied to vertical figure motion, with the object's direction of motion switching from up to down as it hits a figure near the top of the screen.

Figure 10-1 shows an up/down rebound scheme. It includes figures for generating fixed top and bottom figures as well as a ball

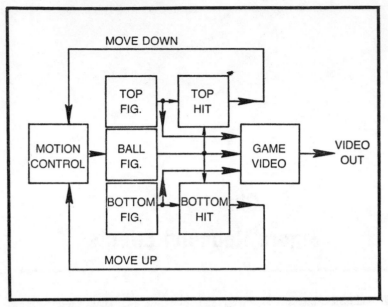

Fig. 10-1. Basic block diagram for rebound effects.

figure that is made movable from a motion-control circuit. The outputs of the three figure generators are combined in the game video circuit to produce a video output for displaying them on the TV screen.

Whenever the ball figure and top figure meet, however, the TOP HIT block generates a logic level that sets the ball's motion-control circuit for downward motion. Presumably the ball then moves in a downward direction until it contacts the bottom figure. At that moment, the BOTTOM HIT block generates a logic level that makes the motion control circuit move the ball figure upward.

The ball can thus bounce up and down between the top and bottom figures at a rate determined by the ball's velocity and the spacing between the fixed lines.

Of course the same general idea applies to horizontal ball motion, substituting left and right fixed figures for the top and bottom ones, and using a horizontal-motion-control circuit. Figure 10-2, however, shows the circuitry for the vertical ball-bouncing circuit.

The ball figure in this instance is a simple 4H × 4V square, and the fixed figures are white lines near the top and bottom of the screen. The horizontal position of the ball figure is fixed near the center of the screen by the $\overline{128H}$ signal being fed to a negative-edge

418

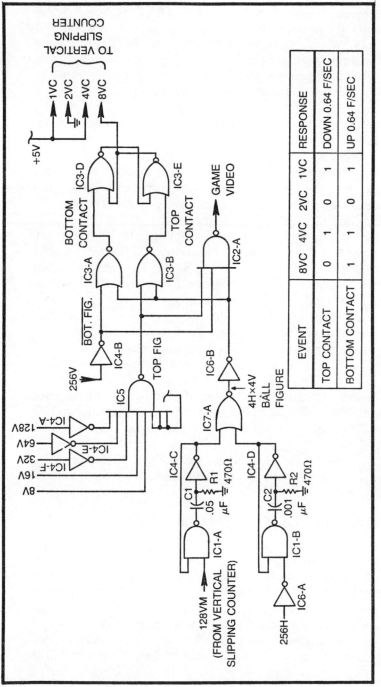

Fig. 10-2. A vertical rebound demonstration circuit.

419

pulse generator made up of IC1-B and IC4-D. The vertical, movable portion of the ball figure comes from another pulse generator (IC1-A and IC4-C) which gets its input information from the 128V output of a vertical-slipping counter circuit.

The ball figure is assembled at IC7-A and then inverted by IC6-B. One portion of this inverted ball signal goes to IC2-A where it is essentially ORed with the top and bottom figures, and another portion goes to the bottom and top contact sensing circuits, IC3-A and IC3-B.

The bottom figure in this case is simply the narrow 256V line, while the top figure is an 8V white line located about 8V from the top of the screen. The outputs from both of these fixed-figure generators are combined with the ball figure in IC2-A to produce the game's composite figure video signal.

IC3-D and IC3-C make up an R-S flip-flop. This flip-flop is SET (output of IC3-D goes to logic 1) whenever IC3-B senses contact between the ball figure and the top figure. The flip-flop is then RESET (output of IC3-D goes to logic 0) whenever IC3-A senses contact between the ball figure and the bottom one.

The table accompanying the circuit in Fig. 10-2 shows how the top and bottom contacts affect the vertical control word delivered to the vertical-slipping counter. Whenever top contact occurs, the VC control code is set to 0101. According to the speed and direction control table in Fig. 7-22, this means the movable figure (the ball in this case) is set for downward motion at the rate of 0.64 frames per second. Whenever bottom contact occurs, the VC control code is set to 1101, making the ball figure move upward at 0.64 frames per second.

Constructing the circuit as specified in Fig. 10-2 thus produces a bouncing-ball effect whereby the ball bounces vertically at a rate of about 1 Hz.

A FLEXIBLE REBOUND CONTROL SYSTEM

Figure 10-3 shows a circuit that is adaptable for both horizontal and vertical rebounding of a single figure. There can be as many as four fixed-figure inputs: bottom, top, right, and left figures. Whenever the movable figure (FIG) makes contact with any one of the fixed figures, an R-S flip-flop (IC1-B and IC1-D or IC2-B and IC2-D) is set to a state that reverses the direction of figure motion. If the figure is moving to the right and makes contact with the $\overline{RT}$ figure, for instance, the flip-flop composed of IC2-B and IC2-D changes state and ultimately reverses the direction of horizontal motion.

420

The horizontal- and vertical-motion codes are generated by a pair of quad 2:1 data multiplexers, IC3 and IC4. The experimenter can program the directions and rates as desired, and the R-S flip-flops automatically select the codes whenever a contact takes place.

The UP PROGRAM inputs to IC3 must be connected to a combination of 1s and 0s that will set the figure motion in an upward direction and at a rate determined by the experimenter. Likewise, the DOWN PROGRAM inputs fix the rate of motion in the downward direction. The same general idea applies to the RIGHT and LEFT PROGRAM inputs to the horizontal-motion selector, IC4.

The table in Fig. 10-4 shows the recommended pairs of UP and DOWN or RIGHT and LEFT program inputs. If the experimenter programs downward motion using 0101 for example, the UP PROGRAM should be 1101 after contact is made. Compare the data in this table with the master-control table in Fig. 7-22.

Figure 10-5 is a block diagram of a complete horizontal- and vertical-motion rebounding circuit. Inverted versions of the top, bottom, right, left, and movable figure are generated at the FIGURE BOARD. The diagram assumes the fixed and movable figures are ORed to yield the composite-figure video.

The REBOUND CONTROL BOARD (Fig. 10-3) senses any contact between the movable figure and a rebound object and then adjusts the horizontal- and vertical-control codes fed to a standard slipping-counter board (Fig. 5-15). The velocity of the ball is fixed by the program inputs to the REBOUND CONTROL BOARD.

The circuit in Fig. 10-6 is a sample figure-generator for the rebound control scheme described here. The figure in this case is a black field of play surrounded by a white border. A small rectangle, 4H × 4V moves about in the black field, rebounding from the top, bottom, and sides of the field. The circuit can be built on a breadboard arrangement in a rather short time. And if the suggested ball speed programming parameters listed in Fig. 10-6 are fixed at the designated inputs of the rebound control board, Fig. 10-3, the ball bounces around at a fairly high speed.

A PINBALL GAME

A video pinball game relies heavily on rebound effects. The game illustrated here represents only one of many possible pinball games, and it ties together some of the main features of game controls, figure generators, and scoring. The main emphasis is on the rebounding effects, however, with weighted scoring being a close second.

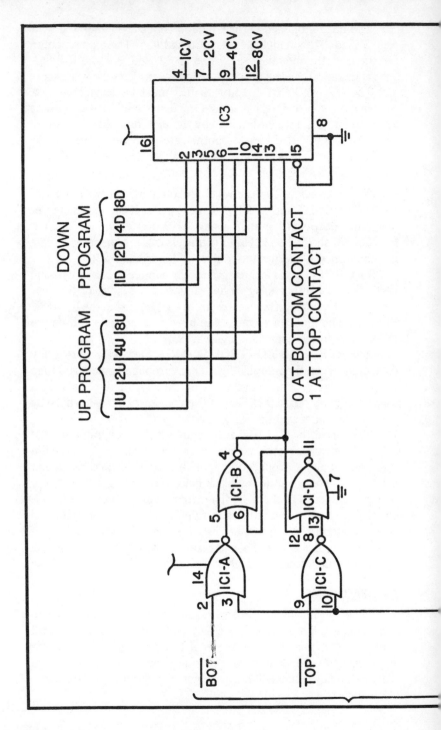

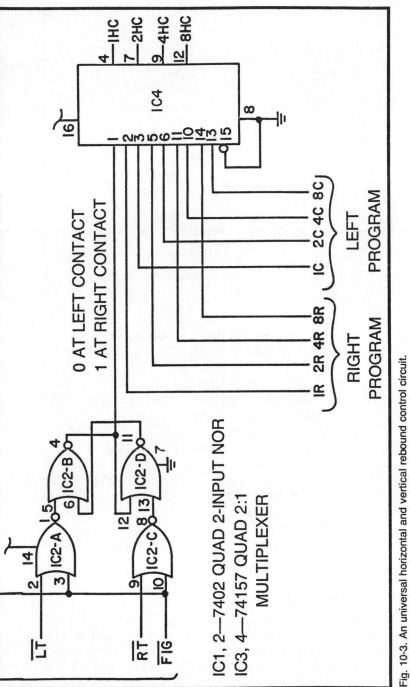

Fig. 10-3. An universal horizontal and vertical rebound control circuit.

IC1, 2—7402 QUAD 2-INPUT NOR
IC3, 4—74157 QUAD 2:1
MULTIPLEXER

0 AT LEFT CONTACT
1 AT RIGHT CONTACT

LEFT PROGRAM

RIGHT PROGRAM

IC 2C 4C 8C

IR 2R 4R 8R

1HC 2HC 4HC 8HC

LT
RT
FIG

IC2-A
IC2-B
IC2-C
IC2-D

IC4

423

CONTROL CODE									
	BEFORE				AFTER				
	8	4	2	1	8	4	2	1	
DOWN OR RIGHT (FAST)	O	O	I	I	I	I	I	I	UP OR LEFT (FAST)
	O	I	O	O	I	I	I	I	
	O	I	O	I	I	I	O	I	
	O	I	I	O	I	I	O	O	
	O	I	I	I	I	O	I	O	
	I	O	O	O	I	O	I	O	
STOP	I	O	O	I	I	O	O	I	STOP
UP OR LEFT (FAST)	I	O	I	O	I	O	O	O	DOWN OR RIGHT (FAST)
	I	O	I	I	O	I	I	O	
	I	I	O	O	O	I	I	O	
	I	I	O	I	O	I	O	I	
	I	I	I	O	O	I	O	O	
	I	I	I	I	O	O	I	I	

Fig. 10-4. Motion code table for rebound effects based on slipping-counter motion.

Figure 10-7a shows this pinball game as it appears on the screen. The main playing area is the black rectangle situated near the center of the screen. The ball is a 4H × 4V square that remains in the playing area by virtue of the rebounding effects. It rebounds to the left or right from the white sides of the playing area, and it rebounds up or down from the five fixed barriers and either of the two movable paddles near the bottom of the screen.

The player's control panel is shown in Fig. 10-7b. It consists of three normally-open pushbuttons labeled PLAY, BALL and PADDLE. Depressing the PLAY button starts the playing action, setting the ball counter and score to zero. Depressing the BALL button launches a ball, and depressing the paddle button makes the two paddle figures move from their normal resting positions at the edges of the playing field to the center as shown in Fig. 10-7a.

Figure 10-7c shows the wiring diagram for this simple control panel.

Figure Generator Board for Pinball

The playing field is shown in much greater detail in Fig. 10-8a. A white line across the top of the screen, labeled TE, is the top of the playing area, while the line across the bottom, BE, is the bottom of the playing area. The left and right edges, LE and RE, aren't lines at all, but rather borders marking the sides of the black playing field.

424

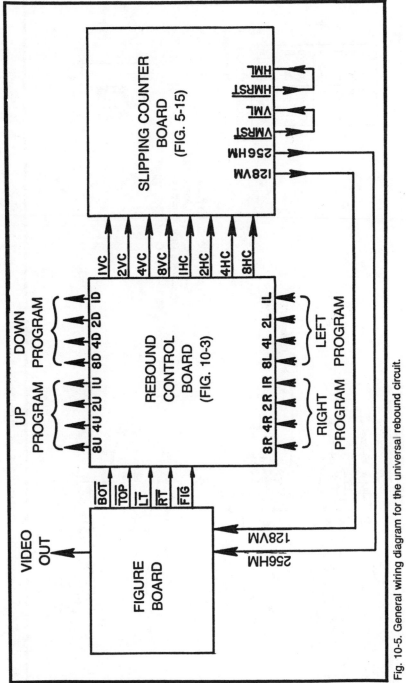

Fig. 10-5. General wiring diagram for the universal rebound circuit.

425

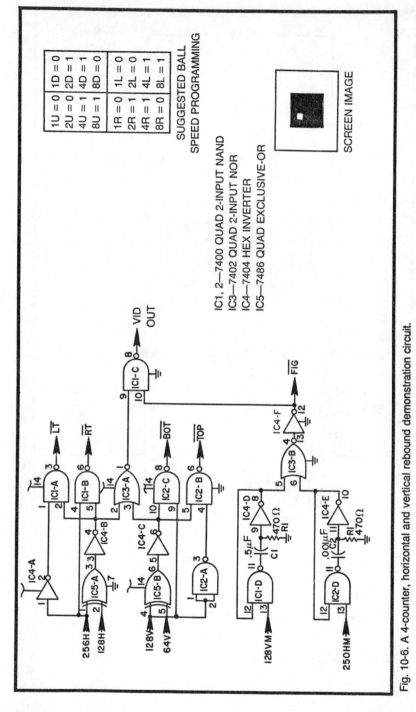

Fig. 10-6. A 4-counter, horizontal and vertical rebound demonstration circuit.

426

The fixed rebound barriers are labeled A through F, and are arranged in a symmetrical pattern about the vertical axis of the playing area.

PL and PR are the player's left and right paddles as they appear in their normal resting positions. The dashed figures labeled PL' and PR' indicate the same paddles as they appear when the player depresses the PADDLE pushbutton on the control panel.

This entire figure—the four edges, fixed barriers, and paddles—is generated by an 8 × 8 extended foldover-matrix generator of the type described in Chapter 4. The extension in this case is from top to bottom, while the foldover is around the vertical axis. Note, for instance, that the right-hand half of the figure is a mirror image of the left-hand half. The data programming for the matrix generator refers to the upper left-hand quadrant, and the remainder of the figure comes about by extension and foldover.

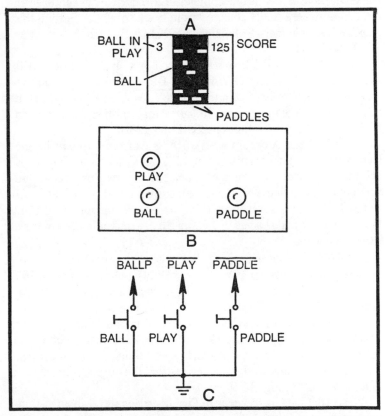

Fig. 10-7. A pinball game. (a) Figures appearing on the screen. (b) Player's control panel layout. (c) Control panel schematic diagram.

The waveforms shown in Fig. 10-8a and the matrix-programming parameters in Fig. 10-8c are vital to this figure-generating scheme. The truly unique feature, however, is the technique used for making the top and bottom edges, fixed barriers, and paddle figures appear as lines instead of the usual matrix squares and rectangles. This will be explained in connection with the actual figure-generating circuit in Fig. 10-9.

Note from the image and waveforms in Fig. 10-8a that a white line appears only where 16V makes a transition from 1 to 0. A line does not appear each time this sort of transition occurs, but it occurs only when 16V shows a 1-to-0 change.

The horizontal TE line, for instance, begins as 16V goes from 1 to 0. This line, like all the others, is 4V wide; so its position and vertical size are fixed by the vertical-count specifications, $\overline{128V}$, $\overline{64V}$, 32V, 16V, $\overline{8V}$, and $\overline{4V}$. The horizontal length of the TE line, and indeed the field of play, is one complete 128H cycle long, centered on the screen where 256H changes from black to white. Setting this length is a simple matter of doing an EXCLUSIVE OR operation on 256H and 128H.

The horizontal BE line is generated in a similar fashion. It is situated vertically where 16V makes a 1-to-0 transition. But in this case, the higher-order V-counts are $\overline{128V}$, $\overline{64V}$, and $\overline{32V}$, putting it near the bottom of the screen. Its horizontal width is also set by an EXCLUSIVE OR operation on 256H and 128H.

Fixed barrier A occurs where 16V goes from 1 to 0 while the higher-order vertical counts are at $\overline{128V}$, 64V, and $\overline{32V}$. Barrier B has the same vertical specifications, but the two are separated horizontally by having A occur at 128H and $\overline{64H}$, and B occur at $\overline{128H}$ and 64H. Barrier B is actually nothing more than a mirror image of A. In fact the right-hand halves of TE and BE are mirror images of their left-hand halves.

A similar kind of analysis can be applied to any of the lines on the screen. They all occur at $\overline{16V}$, $\overline{8V}$, and $\overline{4V}$ (4V pulses high when 16V shows a transition) and are separated vertically by various combinations of higher order V-counts 128V, 64V, and 32V.

All of this information is summarized in the D-programming specifications in Fig. 10-8c. This data sets the positions of all the figures in the playing area, using an 8 × 8 extended foldover format. The figures are narrowed vertically to 4V at the output of the matrix generator, IC7 in Fig. 10-9.

The 16:1 data multiplexer in Fig. 10-9 uses the D-input specifications derived from the figure and waveforms in Fig. 10-8a. As indicated by the presence of 128V and $\overline{128V}$ in the data program-

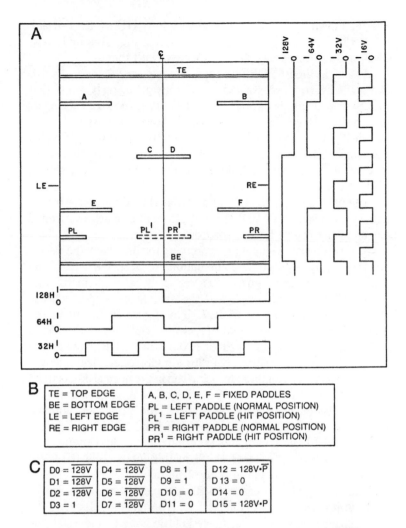

B

TE = TOP EDGE	A, B, C, D, E, F = FIXED PADDLES
BE = BOTTOM EDGE	PL = LEFT PADDLE (NORMAL POSITION)
LE = LEFT EDGE	PL¹ = LEFT PADDLE (HIT POSITION)
RE = RIGHT EDGE	PR = RIGHT PADDLE (NORMAL POSITION)
	PR¹ = RIGHT PADDLE (HIT POSITION)

C

D0 = $\overline{128V}$	D4 = $\overline{128V}$	D8 = 1	D12 = 128V·$\overline{P}$
D1 = $\overline{128V}$	D5 = $\overline{128V}$	D9 = 1	D 13 = 0
D2 = $\overline{128V}$	D6 = $\overline{128V}$	D10 = 0	D14 = 0
D3 = 1	D7 = $\overline{128V}$	D11 = 0	D15 = 128V·P

Fig. 10-8. Pinball playing area figure. (a) Basic figure and relevant H- and V-count waveforms. (b) Nomenclature for the Pinball figure. (c) D-input programming for the playing-area matrix generator.

ming, the figure is extended vertically by 128V: the upper half of the figure is generated while 128V is low, and the lower half is generated while 128V is high. This feature is implemented in Fig. 10-9 by the $\overline{128V}$ connection to a number of D inputs to IC7.

The paddle figures are to be in their resting position as long as the PADDLE button is not depressed, but then they should move to their center-screen positions when that button is depressed. This effect is shown by the D-input specifications $D12 = 128V \cdot \overline{P}$ and $D15 = 128V \cdot P$. This effect is implemented in Fig. 10-9 by IC1-A, IC1-B, and the three inverters associated with them.

As long as the PADDLE button is *not* depressed, the $\overline{\text{PADDLE}}$ input to the figure board is at logic 1, thereby gating on IC1-A so that the 128V signal passes through to pin 19 of IC7, the D12 data input. The same logic level that gates on IC1-A, however, passes through inverter IC6-C to gate off IC1-B so that pin 16 of IC7 (the D15 input) sees a logic 0. Depressing the PADDLE button, on the other hand, sets the $\overline{\text{PADDLE}}$ input to logic 0 to reverse the situation, setting pin 19 at 0 and pin 16 at 128V.

The programming for D12 and D15 is thus determined by the status of the player's PADDLE pushbutton, altering the horizontal position of the paddle figures accordingly.

So much for the D-input programming for IC7. Now the device is addressed by appropriate combinations of 32H, 64H, 32V, and 64V. Since the circuit is generating a vertically extended matrix, the V-count addresses go directly to the two higher-order address locations, pins 13 and 11 of IC7. The figure is folded in the horizontal-count direction, however, so the 32H and 64H address inputs must pass through a pair of EXCLUSIVE OR gates before applying them to the matrix-generating multiplexer. The foldover effect makes the horizontal addressing run in the normal up-counting fashion as long as 128H is low. But when this input goes to logic 1 halfway across the playing area, it reverses the direction of horizontal addressing to create the mirrored left-hand half of the figure.

The EXCLUSIVE OR gates for creating the foldover effect are IC5-B and IC5-C. The "gear shift" in this instance is the 256H connection that is common to both of them.

You might find it necessary to study the extension and foldover effects in greater detail in Chapter 4. Without understanding the basic principles involved here, there is little hope of understanding this particular circuit or, more importantly, you will find it virtually impossible to modify the game or design any of your own.

The pinball figure is not windowed at all in the vertical direction. It occupies the entire height of the screen. It must be windowed horizontally, however. And in this case it is windowed by means of another EXCLUSIVE OR operation on 256H and 128H. These specifications put the playing area near the center of the screen, spanning one complete 128H cycle.

The windowing is implemented in Fig. 10-9 by the EXCLUSIVE OR gate, IC5-A . After the output of this gate is inverted by IC6-D, it is applied to the enabling input of IC7 at pin 9.

Even after going through all these D-input, addressing, and windowing steps, the figure information coming from the pin-10 output of IC7 only vaguely resembles that shown in Fig. 10-8a. Aside from being inverted (blacks and whites reversed) this output shows groups of 32H × 32V squares instead of 4V lines. What remains to be done to complete the figure-generating process is to invert the logic and narrow all the figures to 4V.

IC2-B in Fig. 10-9 uprights the contrast between blacks and whites, while the inputs to IC3-A narrow the figures to 4V. The figure information from IC2-B is thus NANDed with $\overline{16V}$, $\overline{8V}$, and $\overline{4V}$ to trim down the height of each element in the playing area to a 4V level whenever 16V shows a change from 1 to 0.

The white sides of the figure are added at IC3-B to create the basic pinball game figure. Narrowing the white top and bottom edges, fixed barriers, and paddles to 4V is the unique part of the operation. The rest of it comes from material already outlined in Chapter 4.

The little ball figure is generated by the pulse circuits composed of IC1-C, IC1-D, IC4-A, and IC4-C. It is assembled into a square by IC4-B. The original information for creating this movable ball figure comes from a slipping-counter board generating the necessary 256HM and 128VM signals.

The BALL signal from IC4-B is used for control as well as figure-generating purposes. IC2-A, for instance, NANDs the ball image with data from the main figure generator to produce a HIT pulse, a pulse that signals a contact between the ball and any of the main figures in the playing area.

The ball figure is to be blanked from the screen whenever it is not in play, so there is a need for a ball-blanking circuit built around NAND gate IC2-C. The unblanked ball figure is then combined with the main playing figure in IC2-D, and this composite game figure is finally combined with the scoring data in IC5-D.

IC5-D, another EXCLUSIVE OR gate, makes the ball count and scoring figures appear black on the white areas to the left and right of the main playing area.

The purpose of the ball's control signals and the origin of the SCO (scoring data) and BBLANK (ball blanking) signals will be described later.

Before leaving this discussion of the figure board, however, we must point out the origin of the $\overline{LT}$ and $\overline{RT}$ signals from IC8-B and IC8-C respectively. These two signals represent the two sides of the main playing area, and are ultimately used for setting the horizontal-rebounding directions for the ball figure.

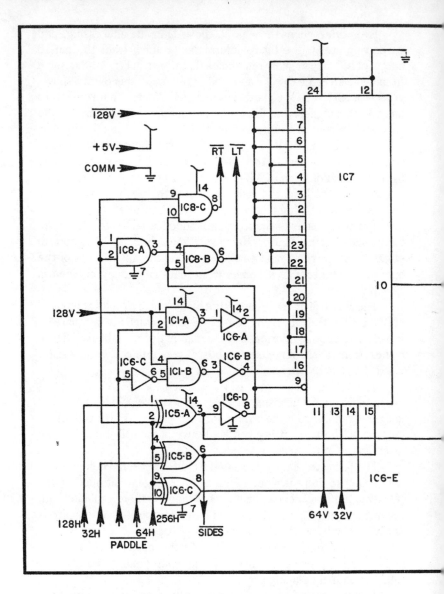

The left and right edges of the playing area are generated as a single unit at IC5-A and IC6-D. They must be separated for rebounding purposes, however. This is accomplished by gating IC8-C with 256H and IC8-B with a version of 256H that is first inverted by IC8-A. It makes some sense that the system is generating the left-hand side of the playing area when 256H is at logic 0 and it is generating the right-hand half when 256H = 1.

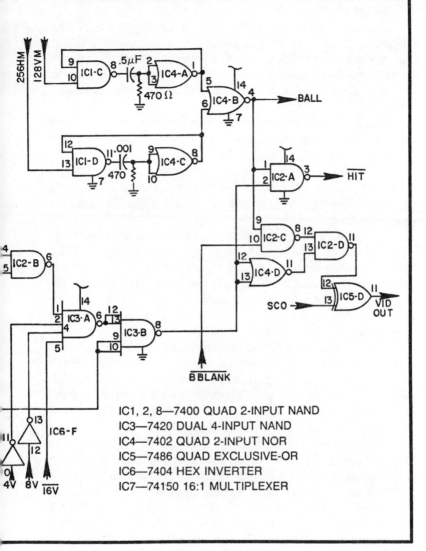

Fig. 10-9. Pinball figure board schematic diagram.

So when 256H is at logic 0, IC8-C is gated off, and the inversion of IC8-A inverts 256H to gate on IC8-B. The $\overline{LT}$ output is thus enabled in its active-low format. When 256H goes to logic 1, signifying the right-hand half of the screen is being serviced, IC8-C is enabled and IC8-B is effectively switched off.

That completes the theory of operation of the figure-generator portion of this pinball game.

Scoring the Pinball Game

The scoring portion of the pinball game consists of four 7-segment digits. One digit is located near the upper left-hand corner of the screen to designate which one of five balls is in play at the moment. A complete game consists of playing five balls which is, of course, the number used for conventional electromechanical pinball games.

Three other figures, located near the upper right-hand side of the screen, indicate the score. Scoring in this case can run anywhere between 000 and 999.

The figure-generating scheme for the ball counter and scoring is a variation of the 2-player scoring system described in Chapter 9 (the dual 2-digit display). The only difference is that the digits are grouped differently.

Figure 10-10 shows the numeral format, required waveforms, and programming. The circuit based on this rationale is in Fig. 10-11. Since this whole scheme is practically identical to the one already detailed in Fig. 9-7, it is left to the reader to sort out the finer details.

While the score-figure board in Fig. 10-11 requires little additional explanation, the score-control board (Fig. 10-12) calls for some special discussion.

This counting-control board is responsible for keeping track of which ball is in play and the total score at any given moment. Of special interest is the section of the circuit labeled WEIGHTED SCORE CIRCUIT. This pinball game, like its electromechanical counterparts, scores different amounts according to the type of contact the ball makes with various figures in the playing area.

The scores in this case can be 1, 2, or 4 points per contact. The origins of the weighted-scoring inputs is described in detail when we get to the theory of the main control board. For the time being, it is sufficient to say that the three scoring digits—those generated by IC6, IC7, and IC8—increment 1, 2, or 4 units whenever certain ball contacts occur. The theory behind the weighted scoring is described in connection with the circuit in Fig. 9-11.

IC5 in Fig. 10-12 is the ball counter. This counter is incremented by a BCOUNT pulse, which occurs each time the player depresses the BALL pushbutton. When the count reaches binary 5, IC9-A generates a logic-0 level the signals the end of the game (the $\overline{END}$ output).

The ball and score counters are all reset to zero by a pulse from IC9-D, a pulse that occurs whenever the player depresses the PLAY pushbutton.

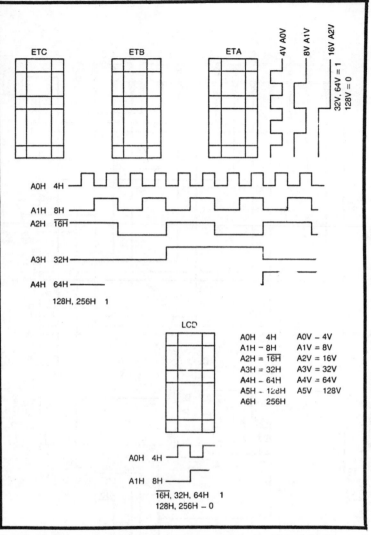

Fig. 10-10. Figures, waveforms, and programming for the Pinball "ball in play" and scoring figures.

In summary, the counter board in Fig. 10-12 keeps track of the weighted score and increments the ball count. Both counters are initially cleared to zero by depressing the PLAY pushbutton, the score counter increments 1, 2, or 4 points whenever the ball in play makes contact with certain objects in the playing area, and the ball counter increments each time a new ball is launched. The ball counter automatically stops the game when the fifth ball is played.

435

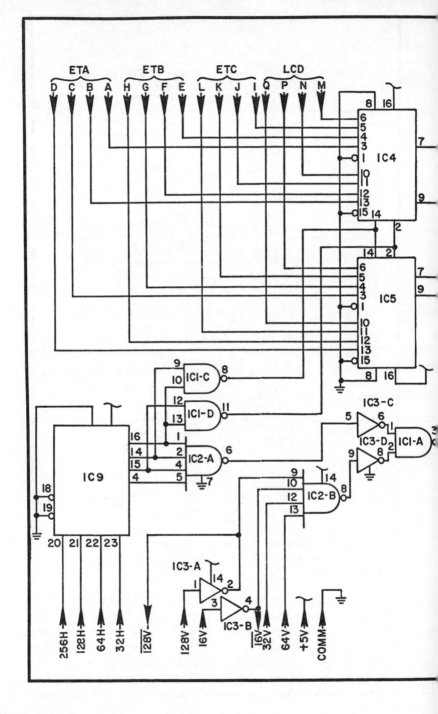

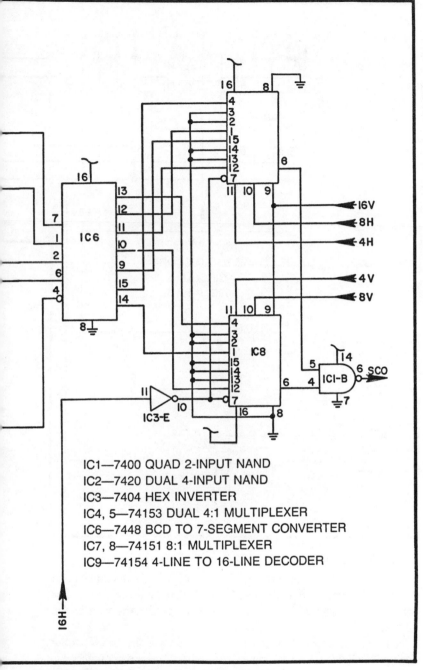

IC1—7400 QUAD 2-INPUT NAND
IC2—7420 DUAL 4-INPUT NAND
IC3—7404 HEX INVERTER
IC4, 5—74153 DUAL 4:1 MULTIPLEXER
IC6—7448 BCD TO 7-SEGMENT CONVERTER
IC7, 8—74151 8:1 MULTIPLEXER
IC9—74154 4-LINE TO 16-LINE DECODER

Fig. 10-11. Pinball score board schematic diagram.

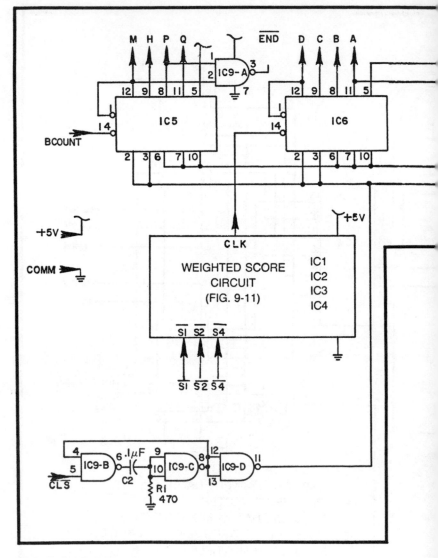

Pinball Control Board

The pinball control board in Fig. 10-14 is mainly responsible for controlling the motion of the ball figure and setting the score. The ball-rebound and scoring features are summarized in the table in Fig. 10-13a.

The table shows that the vertical motion of the ball does not change at all if it is moving downward when it makes contact with TE, the top edge of the playing area. When the ball touches TE while

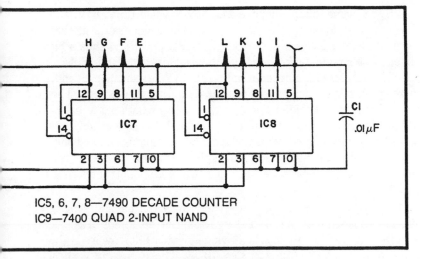

IC5, 6, 7, 8—7490 DECADE COUNTER
IC9—7400 QUAD 2-INPUT NAND

Fig. 10-12. Pinball counter board schematic diagram

moving upward, however, its direction is reversed. Neither kind of contact with TE causes a score.

The second line in the table in Fig. 10-13a shows a more interesting set of effects whenever the ball makes contact with fixed barriers A or B (designed A + B). If the ball is moving downward at the time, making contact with either A or B causes it to change to an upward direction and score 2 points. Further down the truth table, it can be seen that the ball traveling upward can contact either of the same two barriers, change its direction to down and score 4 points.

A brief study of the table in Fig. 10-13a can show the entire ball-motion and scoring rationale. The technical problem in this case is to know which barriers, edges, or paddles the ball touches. This can be done rather easily by means of the 3-line-to-8-line decoder shown in Fig. 10-13b.

Whenever a hit occurs, but not one of the two sides, this IC is enabled. (Horizontal rebounding from the left and right sides of the playing area is handled separately.)

The decoder circuit is addressed from the same three V-counts used for addressing the vertical portion of the figure matrix generator in Fig. 10-9. If a hit thus occurs when 128V, 64V, and 32V are all at logic 0, for example, the ball must be hitting the bottom edge of the playing area (BE), simply because that is the only figure being generated when 128V, 64V, and 32V are all at logic 0 at the same time.

439

By the same token, suppose a hit occurs while 128V, 64V, and 32V are all at logic 1. The only figures being generated at that moment are the paddles, PL and PR, or PL' and PR'. Thus a hit under those circumstances must be the paddles, and nothing else.

The outputs of the decoder in Fig. 10-13 thus indicate a hit and, more specifically, a hit against a particular object on the screen. The only relevant information missing is that telling whether the ball is moving upward or downward at the time. And that little problem is solved by using a pair of identical decoders, one that is enabled only when the ball is moving upward and another that is enabled when the ball is moving downward. See IC7 and IC8 on the control board in Fig. 10-14.

Before it is possible to see exactly how the hit and scoring decoders do their jobs, it is necessary to explain the origins of signals determining whether the ball is moving upward or downward at the time. Note the VC outputs in Fig. 10-14. These are the vertical speed and direction codes for the ball's slipping-counter circuit.

1VC and 4VC are fixed at a logic-1 level, while 2VC is fixed at logic 1. According to the vertical-speed control table in Fig. 7-22, this means the vertical section of the slipping counter will see either 0101 or 1101, where the most-significant bit (8VC) is the only one allowed to change. It turns out that the ball moves downward at a rate of about 0.64 frames per second when 8VC=0, and upward at the same rate when 8VC=1.

The 8VC output of the control board—or more specifically, the output of IC5-B—determines the ball's direction of vertical motion: 0 yields down, and 1 yields up.

Now suppose the ball happens to be moving upward. The output of IC5-B is at logic 1, and the logic-1 level is fed back to the pin-5 input of NAND gate IC4-A. This particular NAND gate responds with a logic-0 output only when three conditions are satisfied at the same time: the ball is moving downward, a hit pulse is taking place, and the hit is NOT against one of the sides of the playing area. IC8 is thus the down-motion hit detector and score decoder.

IC7, on the other hand, is the up-motion detector/decoder which is enabled only when: the ball is moving upward (a logic 1 from IC5-A), a hit occurs, and the hit is NOT against one of the two sides of the playing area. The output of IC5-A, incidentally, is always the complement of that from IC5-B; therefore, it is virtually impossible to enable IC7 and IC8 at the same time.

The next step in explaining the operation of this system is to work through the logic standing between the detector/decoders

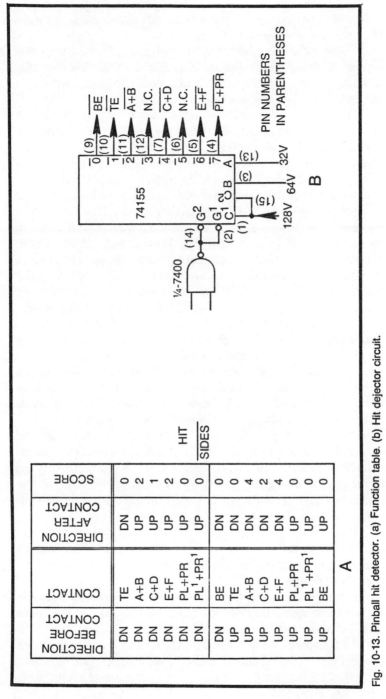

Fig. 10-13. Pinball hit detector. (a) Function table. (b) Hit dejector circuit.

(IC7 and IC8) and the output circuit that determines the ball's direction of vertical travel (IC5-B).

Suppose the ball is moving upward when it strikes the bottom of barrier A. According to the table in Fig. 10-13a, this particular situation should switch the ball's vertical motion to downward and, at the same time, score 4 points.

When the ball is moving downward, the pin-5 input of IC4-A is at logic 1 as explained earlier. And when the ball hits the A barrier (or any other one for that matter), the HIT input goes to logic 0, and inverter IC9-A inverts the signal to a positive-going pulse. Since the hit is not against one of the sides of the playing area, $\overline{SIDES}$ is at logic 1, and it turns out that all inputs to IC4-A are at logic 1 as long as the $\overline{HIT}$ pulse lasts. This NAND-gate action enables IC8.

From Fig. 10-8, it can be seen that the A barrier is being drawn on the screen as long as 128V=0, 64V=1, and 32V=0. These V-count lines to the select inputs of IC8 cause its pin-11 output to drop to logic 0, the active-low signal state for the decoders. The pin-5 output of that same IC is fixed at that same time, so NAND gate IC2-D passes the pin-11 output of IC8 as a positive-going pulse.

This pulse is inverted again by inverter IC9-F, and then goes to the $\overline{S4}$ connection on the weighted-scoring circuit. This accounts for an additional 4 points on the score readout.

That same negative-going pulse from IC9-F also passes through NAND gate IC3-D, emerging as a positive-going pulse to the pin-6 input of IC5-B. IC5-B is one-half of an R-S flip-flop circuit that also includes IC5-A. The positive pulse at IC5-B in this case resets the flip-flop so that two things happen simultaneously: the output of IC5-B is switched to logic 0, thereby reversing the direction of motion of the ball, and the output of IC5-B is switched to logic 0, thereby reversing the direction of motion of the ball, and the output of IC5-A, is switched to logic 1 to enable the downward-motion decoder, IC7.

Recall that this entire sequence of activity began when an upward-moving ball hit barrier A. The final results of this action is 4 additional points in the score and changing the direction of ball motion from up to down.

A similar kind of analysis shows that the decoders and logic circuits perform all the direction-changing and scoring operations specified in the table on Fig. 10-13a.

All the operations described for the control board to this point have concerned the VC outputs and changes in the vertical direction. It can be seen that changes in the horizontal direction of ball motion is a bit more straightforward.

The outputs controlling the ball's horizontal motion are 1HC through 8HC in Fig. 10-14. 1HC and 4HC are fixed at logic 1, while 2HC is fixed at logic 0. Only the 8HC bit is concerned with the ball's changes in horizontal motion.

The horizontal motion codes to the horizontal portion of the slipping-counter board are thus 0101 or 1101, depending on whether the ball is to be moving to the right or left respectively. In either case, the horizontal velocity is 0.98 screens per second, and whether the ball is moving to the right or left is determined by the status of an R-S flip-flop composed of IC5-C and IC5-D.

The inputs to this little horizontal-direction control circuit are BALL (the ball figure), $\overline{LT}$, and $\overline{RT}$ (signals indicating the two sides of the playing area.

To see how this circuit works, suppose the ball figure is moving toward the right. This means the 8HC bit and the output of IC5-D are at logic 0; and since this is one output of a flip-flop, it follows that the output of IC5-C is at logic 1. Now there is a contact between the ball and the right-hand side of the playing area. IC6-D senses this particular hit, and generates a positive-going pulse that resets the flip-flop. This action resets the flip-flop, changing the direction of the ball's horizontal motion to the left.

The complementary action takes place as the ball strikes the left-hand side of the playing area. IC6-C senses the contact and changes the status of the flip-flop so that the ball moves to the right again.

If the experimenter finds the ball speed seems too fast, the vertical- and horizontal-motion codes at 1VC, 2VC, 4VC, 1HC, 2HC, and 4HC can be changed, using the information in the speed-control table (Fig. 7-22) as a guide. The 8VC and 8HC bits should remain as shown in Fig. 10-14.

The control circuit board also includes some housekeeping logic that is mainly concerned with starting and ending the game. Note, for instance, that the $\overline{PLAY}$ and $\overline{BALLP}$ signals from the control panel each go to a separate $\overline{R\text{-}S}$ lip-flop—IC1-A and IC1-B, and IC1-C and IC1-D.

Depressing the PLAY pushbutton on the control panel forces the $\overline{PLAY}$ input to the control board to logic 0, thus setting the output of IC1-A to logic 1 and the output of IC1-B to 0. The logic-0 level from IC1-B leaves the board via the $\overline{CLS}$ connection and ultimately clears the ball counter and score counter on the score-counting board (Fig. 10-12). The ball count and score are thus cleared whenever the player depresses the PLAY pushbutton at the beginning of a new game sequence.

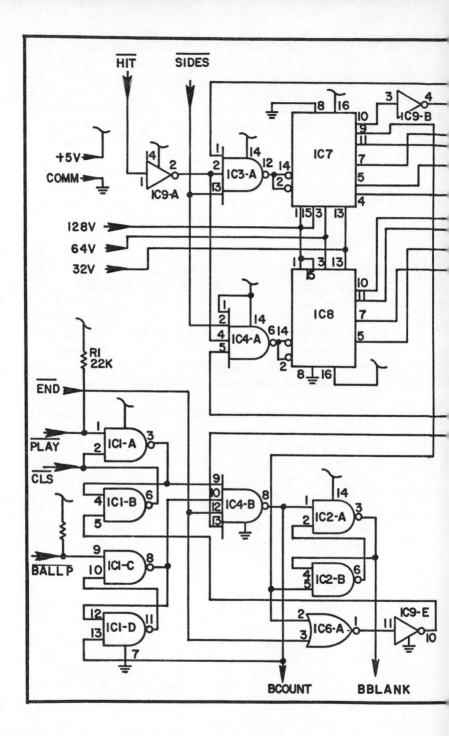

444

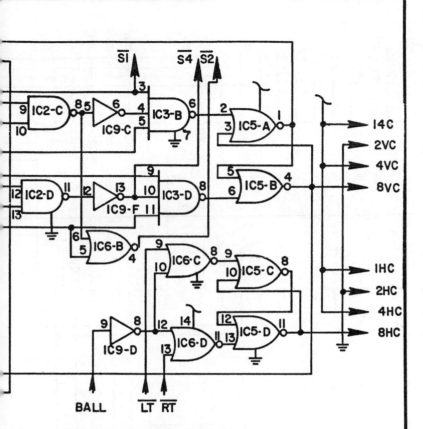

BALL $\overline{LT}$ $\overline{RT}$

IC1, 2—7400 QUAD 2-INPUT NAND
IC3—7410 TRIPLE 3-INPUT NAND
IC4—7420 DUAL 4-INPUT NAND
IC5, 6—7402 QUAD 2-INPUT NOR
IC7, 8—74155 DUAL 2-LINE-TO-4-LINE
         DECODER
IC9—7404 HEX INVERTER

Fig. 10-14. Pinball control board schematic diagram.

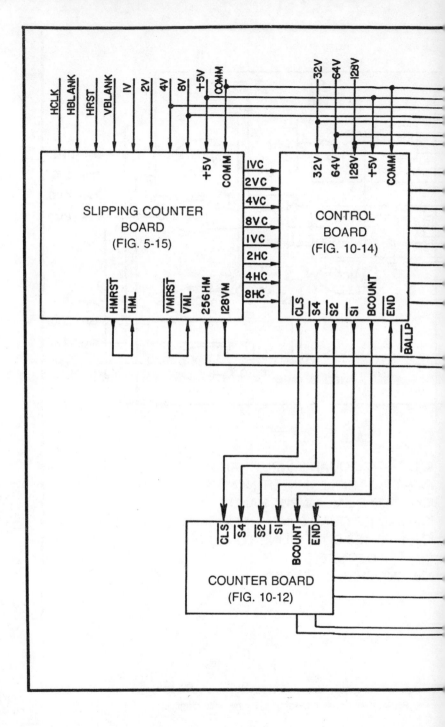

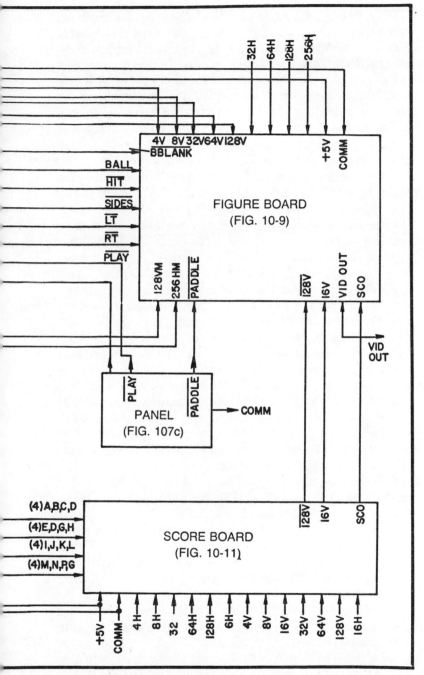

F 10-15. Pinball wiring block diagram.

Once the PLAY flip-flop is set in this fashion, the only way it can be reset is by means of a negative-going pulse at the pin-5 input of IC1-B. Two conditions must be met before this can happen, however. First, the ball counter must be showing numeral 5 as indicated by a logic 0 level at the END input and the pin-3 input of NOR gate IC6-A. Second, the ball must contact BE, the bottom edge of the screen, as signaled by a negative-going pulse at the pin-9 output of IC7. This pulse is effectively ANDed with the $\overline{\text{END}}$ pulse at IC6-A to produce a positive-going pulse that indicates the end of a game sequence: end of play for the fifth ball in the series.

That same end-of-game pulse is inverted to a negative-going pulse by inverter IC9-E and finally resets the PLAY flip-flop so that the next game can be started by depressing the PLAY pushbutton.

Once a game sequence is started, a new ball is launched by depressing the BALL button. This action sets the $\overline{\text{R-S}}$ flip-flop composed of IC1-C and IC1-D. The pin-8 output of IC1-C is thus set to logic 1, and that logic level is fed to a 4-input NAND gate, IC4-B.

IC4-B considers four different game parameters simultaneously, and the only way its output can be set to logic 0 (its active state) is by having the following parameters at logic 1: the PLAY output of IC1-A, the BALL-LAUNCH output of IC1-C, the END signal from the ball-counting circuit, and the TE contact signal from pin 10 of IC7. The output of this 4-input NAND gate is normally at logic 1, dropping to 0 only when all four of these conditions are met.

Whenever the output of IC4-B does drop to logic 0, it sets the condition of yet another $\overline{\text{R-S}}$ flip-flop composed of IC2-A and IC2-B. Setting this particular flip-flop causes the output of IC2-A to go to logic 1, thereby blanking the ball figure from the screen via the $\overline{\text{BBLANK}}$ terminal of the control board.

Also note that a logic-0 level from IC4-B, the 4-input NAND gate, both generates a BCOUNT pulse and resets the BALL-LAUNCH flip-flop composed of IC1-C and IC1-D.

What does all this mean? One thing it means is that a newly launched ball does not appear on the screen until it crosses TE while moving downward. The flip-flop responsible for blanking the ball figure is not set until IC7 senses the ball figure crossing TE while moving downward.

The same signal that unblanks the ball figure serves as a BCOUNT pulse that increments the ball counter, thus advancing the ball-count display on the screen. The BCOUNT pulse also resets the BALL-LAUNCH flip-flop (specifically at pin 13 of IC1-D), preparing it for the next ball-launching operation.

The ball-blanking flip-flop is reset only when the ball crosses BE (the bottom edge of the playing area) while traveling downward. This effect is detected by the pin-9 output of IC7, the same one responsible for resetting the entire game at the end of play for the fifth ball.

Overall Pinball Block Diagram

A final wiring diagram for the pinball game appears in Fig. 10-15. You will note that the game requires five circuit boards and a special control panel. Of course you should already have the slipping-counter board available from previous experiments and games.

The slipping counter and control boards can be powered from one of the +5V sources, while the remaining boards ought to be connected to a second source to avoid overloading any one of the power supplies.

Chapter 11
Animation and
Rotation of Complex Figures

Figure animation and rotation belong to a class of special effects that is seldom critical to the operation of a video game system. These effects can, however, lend a special touch of interest that heightens the players' sense of reality.

The circuits suggested in this chapter can actually be applied without reference to any particular game. Most experimenters will agree that building the complex figures in Chapter 4 offered a unique opportunity to create some fascinating images on the screen. Now there is the chance to add the dimension of motion, animation and rotation, to them.

Figure rotation is a special class of motion calling for rotating the figure on the screen about an imaginary axis extending at right angles to the plane of the screen—in and out of the screen. One of the more common figure rotation effects can be found in connection with a popular commercial combat game where two tanks chase each other around the screen. The tank figure moves only in a forward direction; the player has the ability to rotate the figure, making it possible to move it in virtually any direction.

This figure-rotation feature is actually a form of animation, but as demonstrated later in this chapter, it is a form of figure animation and motion that calls for an unusually high degree of system planning.

An experimenter cannot hope to master the fundamentals of figure animation and rotation without first getting a complete understanding of how complex figures are built in a matrix format. Readers who feel they are not prepared to design animated figures would do well to study the principles outlined in Chapter 4 once again.

FIGURE ANIMATION

The basic idea behind figure animation (and rotation as well) is to present a series of figures on the screen in a fashion that creates the illusion of motion. The scheme might consist of four different complex figures, each differing from the others in some peculiar way. And when they are flashed onto the screen in a relatively rapid sequence, the observer gets the impression of motion or animation.

The idea is identical to filmed animation. In this video situation, however, the length and complexity of the animated sequence is necessarily limited by the cost and complexity of the circuitry involved.

So the following discussion presents the basic formula for generating a simple animated sequence. While the examples are kept on a rather simple level, the basic scheme can be extended indefinitely, or at least as far as time, money, and patience can carry it.

One of the principle IC devices required for generating an animated sequence is a dual 1-line-to-4-line decoder, 74155. This particular device has been specified in earlier game systems, but it is not important to understand its modes of operation in greater detail.

Figure 11-1 shows the 74155 device, first in a functional block diagram form (Fig. 11-1a), then the pinout (Fig. 11-2b), and finally in a truth-table form (Fig. 11-1c).

The device is divided into two separate sections as shown in Fig. 11-1a. As illustrated in the truth tables, any logic level present at a C input is delivered to one of the four outputs of each section, depending on the status of select inputs A and B.

Suppose, for example, A=0 and B=1. This select status selects output Y2 for both sections, delivering an inverted version of C1 to output 1Y2 and a noninverted version to output 2Y2. A given C input can appear at one, and only one, of its respective Y outputs.

Setting one of the G inputs to logic 1 effectively turns off the device, causing all Y outputs for that section to take on a logic-1 condition, regardless of the status of the C input.

As clearly shown in the sections that follow, this decoder device plays a vital role in altering the data directed to the matrix-generating schemes already presented in Chapter 4.

Figure 11-2 shows a simple 4-frame animation sequence. The figure in this case is that of a man walking into or out of the plane of

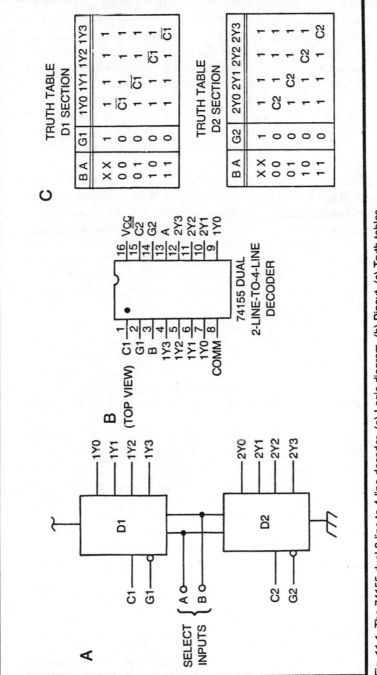

Fig. 11-1. The 74155 dual 2-line-to-4-line decoder. (a) Logic diagram. (b) Pinout. (c) Truth tables.

the screen. In frame 1, his feet are both on the "ground" and his arms are straight down at his sides. He then takes a step with the left foot in frame 2, extending his right arm and bending up the left one slightly. He returns to the basic position once again in frame 3, and then takes the next step with his right foot in frame 4. Presenting these four frames in sequence and at a rate of about 2 Hz creates the illustration of a walking figure.

Any one of these four figures can be generated by the 8 × 8 extended matrix circuit shown in Fig. 4-17. The trick is to generate all four figures without having to build four separate matrix-generator circuits.

Notice, for instance, that frames 1 and 3 are identical in every respect. It is thus possible to generate both of these frames from the same matrix-generator programming. Frame 2 is obviously different from frames 1 and 3, but it is quite similar to frame 4. Frames 2 and 4, in fact, are simply mirror images of one another, with the mirror axis running vertically through the middle of the matrix. The significance of this mirror effect is that frame 4 can be generated from the same matrix generator for frame 2, but making the horizontal counting take place in the opposite direction.

To express the differences between frames 2 and 4 in another fashion, consider the matrix fold-over scheme described in Chapter 4. In that instance, the size of a symmetrical figure could be doubled in complexity by simply reversing the direction of the matrix addressing half way through the operation. In this case, the direction of addressing for horizontal counts is reversed through the entire frame, frame 4.

The four-frame sequence in Fig. 11-2 can thus be digested down to two basic figures, frames 1 and 2. The programming for the data fed to the matrix generator takes on one particular form when generating frame 1, then the data is changed to generate the image in frame 2. The animation sequence returns to the first set of data programming to generate frame 3. And finally, two things happen at once to generate frame 4: The data programming is returned to that of frame 2 and the direction of horizontal counting is reversed.

So the first step in building an animated video sequence is to plan the frames, keeping them as simple and as much alike as possible. The second step is to analyze the frames, attempting to take advantage of their similarities and reducing the amount of data programming required.

Ultimately the four frames in Fig. 11-2 will be called up in sequence, and since there are four frames, the calling operation

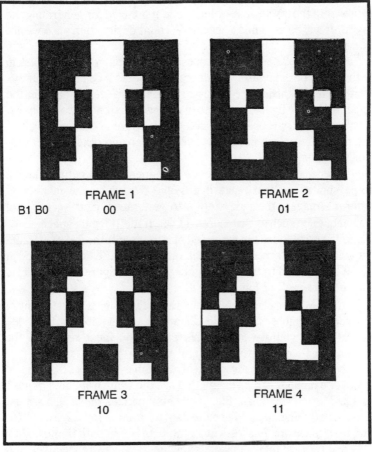

B1 B0

FRAME 1
00

FRAME 2
01

FRAME 3
10

FRAME 4
11

Fig. 11-2. A simple 4-frame animation sequence.

requires two address lines. The frame addresses, designated B1 and B0, determine which one of the four frames will appear on the screen at any given moment. When B1=B0=0, for example, the first frame should appear on the screen. Then when B1=0 and B0=0, the second frame should appear, and so on through the sequence. If this 2-bit counting sequence is taken from a binary counter circuit, the sequencing will take place automatically, thereby generating the desired animation effect.

The table in Fig. 11-3a shows a complete breakdown of frames 1 and 2 in terms of the data inputs required for an 8 × 8 extended matrix generator circuit. The procedure for determining the data requirements is identical to that described in connection with the basic 8 × 8 extended matrix in Fig. 4-18. The "X" in this case

455

represents the 3rd lowest-order V-count bit used for generating the figure. It will be assigned a specific V-count designation once we are in a position to specify the size of the figure.

In Fig. 11-3a, a 0 entry represents a matrix cell that is black in both halves of the figure. A 1 entry represents a cell that is always white. The X entries are necessary where the cell is black in the upper half of the figure, but white in its lower, extended counterpart. Finally, a $\overline{X}$ entry represents a cell that is white in the upper half of the frame, but black in the lower. There are no other logical possibilities than these.

After making up the sequence of frames and, hopefully, finding some similarities that make it possible to reduce the number of different images, the next step is to generate a figure-generating data sequence such as that in Fig. 11-3a. If the D inputs specified for frame 1 are applied to the extended matrix circuit, the image in frame 1 appears on the screen. If, on the other hand, the data specified in frame 2 is applied to the matrix generator, the figure will appear as shown in frame 2 of Fig. 11-2.

It ought to be clear at this point that a thorough understanding of the complex figure schemes in Chapter 4 are all important to video animation. If you are lost at this point, you must return to the material in Chapter 4 to get caught up.

Now a careful study of the truth table in Fig. 11-3a should uncover a number of data inputs that are the same from both frame 1 and 2. The information in Fig. 11-3b summarizes these similarities. There are 11 instances where the data for frames 1 and 2 are both 0, and then there are 7 cases where the data is 1 in both frames. Only D17 and D25 are totally unique, showing 01 and $\overline{1X}$ respectively. So of the two pairs of 32 data inputs required for this particular animation sequence, there are only 8 different combinations of 0s, 1s, Xs and $\overline{X}$s. Simplification. That is the key to the successful design of video animation circuitry.

The eight different combinations are summarized in Fig. 11-3c. The eight sequences, for the sake of simplicity, are designated according to the first term in the equality expressions in Fig. 11-3b. Bear in mind, for instance, that the programming for D1 in Fig. 11-3c will also apply to data inputs D6 and D26, as specified in Fig. 11-3b.

The next step is to derive some logic circuitry that will alter the data inputs to a single 8 × 8 extended matrix circuit, distinguishing frame 1 data from that required for frame 2 by the status of a control bit, B0. When B0=0, for example, D2 should be equal to logic 0, but

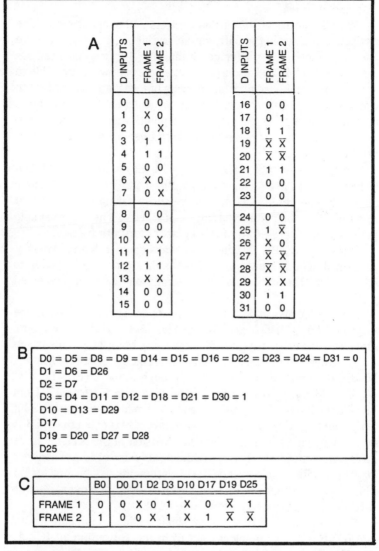

Fig. 11-3. Truth-table analysis of the 4-frame animation sequence in Fig. 11-2.
(a) D-input programming for frames 1 and 2. (b) Equations showing data inputs
having identical programming for both primary frames. (c) simplified truth table
for matrix D-input programming.

when B0 is changed to logic 1, input D2 to the matrix generator
should be changed to X.

Making this step calls for a rather experienced outlook on digital
logic design. The procedures are rather straight-forward for experi-

enced technicians, but a beginner will find the task a rather troublesome one at times.

What is the result of all this analysis and simplification? The answer is contained in the fairly simple circuit in Fig. 11-4. Here we have the complete circuit for generating the 4-frame animated sequence in Fig. 11-2, and also a prime example of how it is possible to devise some simple circuitry for carrying out what appears at first to be an exceedingly difficult task. In this particular example, a 4-frame animated sequence is simplified to a point where it can be implemented with an 8 × 8 extended matrix generator and only four outboard IC devices.

Comparing the tables in Fig. 11-3 with the circuit in Fig. 11-4, it can be seen that the data inputs requiring a logic 0 in all cases can be connected together to COMM, while those calling for a constant logic-1 level can be connected together at +5V. These two simple operations take care of 18 of the D inputs for both frames.

Furthermore, the D10 input is always equal to X and D19 is at the $\overline{X}$ level. The X input in Fig. 11-4 is thus connected directly to D10, while D19 sees a version of the same input that is first inverted by IC3-B.

All that remains as far as the D inputs are concerned are those designated D1, D2, D7, and D25 in Fig. 11-3c. This set of inputs differs from the others inasmuch as they vary according to the frame being displayed. Input D1, for instance, is equal to X during frame 1 (B0=0), but must be set at logic 0 through frame 2 (B0=1).

The B0 signal—the one distinguishing data for frame 1 from that of frame 2—is generated by the least-significant output of a 2-bit binary counter, IC2-A and IC2-B. Whenever B0 is equal to 0, IC3-A is effectively gate on, and an inverted version of the $\overline{X}$ signal from IC3-B is presented to D1. D1, in other words, is set to X whenever B0=0 (a condition that satisfies the requirements established for D1 in Fig. 11-3c). Whenever B0 switches to logic 1, however, it gates off IC3-A and guarantees a logic-0 level at D1.

The data for D2 is derived in a similar fashion, taking its $\overline{X}$ data from IC3-B and frame-select data from the $\overline{B0}$ output of IC2-A. When B0=0, then $\overline{B0}$ is equal to logic 1, and IC3 is effectively gated off to feed a guaranteed logic-0 level to D2. Whenever B0 switches to logic 1, however, $\overline{B0}$ is set to logic 0, and D2 sees an X signal. These conditions meet the requirements spelled out for D2 in Fig. 11-3c.

According to Fig. 11-3c, D25 is simply an inverted version of the D2 input. That is, D25=1 when D2=0, and D25=$\overline{X}$ when D2=X. All that is necessary for generating the D25 input, then, is an

458

inverting operation between D2 and D25, and that is performed by IC3-D.

Finally, it can be seen from Fig. 11-3c that D17 is equal to B0. So the final D connection is one where the B0 output of IC2-A is connected directly to the D17 input of the matrix generator.

The circuit as described to this point is capable of distinguishing frames 1 and 2. What remains is the procedure for inverting the direction of horizontal counting in order to produce the mirror images for frames 3 and 4. This is accomplished by inverting the H-count inputs to select lines S0, S1, and S2 while B1=1. And it is a simple matter of running these H-count levels through EXCLUSIVE OR gates, IC4-A through IC4-C. Whether these select lines count forward or in reverse depend on the logic level from IC2-B, counting forward while B1=0 (frames 1 and 2) and counting in reverse while B1=1 (frames 2 and 3).

The 2-bit binary counter composed of IC2-A and IC2-B thus generates a sequence of four binary numbers, each representing one of the four frames in the animation sequence. The rate of counting is fixed by the 555-type astable multivibrator, IC-1. Adjusting the RATE control sets the animation rate.

The H-count specifications shown in Fig. 11-4 generate a figure that is 32H × 32V in size. The recommended window inputs set the position of the figure near the lower right-hand corner of the screen. Of course all these H- and V-count signals can come from a slipping-counter circuit, thereby making it possible to move the animated figure around the screen while it is going through its walking motions.

The RUN/STOP input to IC-1 gives the experimenter the option of fixing the figure in its frame-1 position, while the BLANK/UNBLANK input to the matrix generator allows the entire figure to be blanked from the screen.

This particular animation sequence does not call for an application of the 2-line-to-4-line decoder described in Fig. 11-1. Before leaving this discussion of figure animation, we should look at a somewhat more complicated case where this circuit becomes a valuable asset.

Figure 11-5 shows an 8-frame animation sequence. The object in this case is a teeter-totter on a pedestal. Ultimately the eight frames will be flashed onto the screen in rapid sequence, giving the visual impression of a teeter-totter action (an action, incidentally, that is part of a very popular coin-operated TV game).

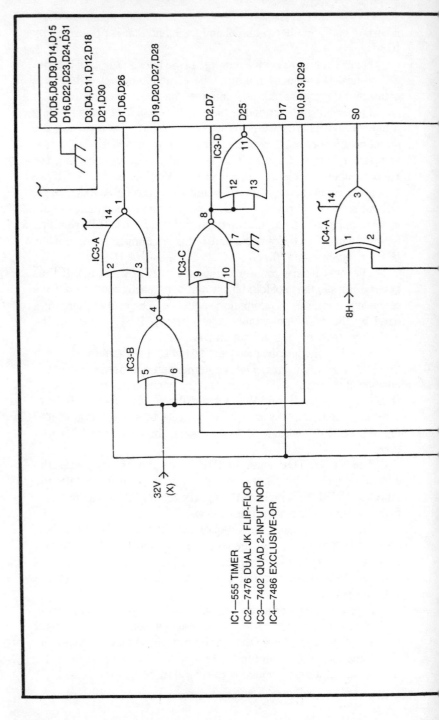

IC1—555 TIMER
IC2—7476 DUAL JK FLIP-FLOP
IC3—7402 QUAD 2-INPUT NOR
IC4—7486 EXCLUSIVE-OR

460

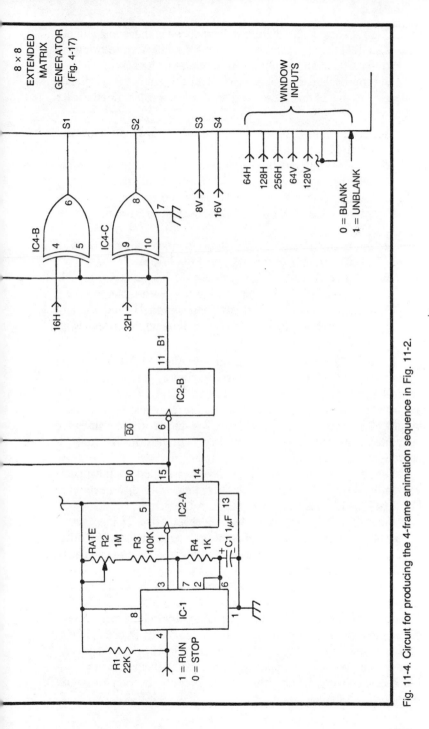

Fig. 11-4. Circuit for producing the 4-frame animation sequence in Fig. 11-2.

There is some figure distortion introduced in these images, but it turns out that the distortion is far more apparent when viewing the static frames than when they are in motion on the screen.

The approach to designing a circuit for this animation sequence is identical to that of the 4-frame walking sequence described earlier in this chapter:

1. Draw the basic figure sequence in standard matrix formats (Fig. 11-5).
2. Reduce the number of images, if possible, by noting whether any are simple mirror images of others.
3. Assign logic levels to the nonextended portion of the matrices, using an X or $\overline{X}$ to indicate the third-order H-count (Fig. 11-6a).
4. Note any D inputs that show identical combinations of inputs through all the frames (Fig. 11-6b).
5. Prepare a truth table for each class of D inputs (Fig. 11-6c).
6. Devise logic circuits for solving the truth table.
7. Complete the circuit design and assign H- and V-count parameters for figure size and position on the screen (Fig. 11-7).

It can be seen from the drawings in Fig. 11-5 that half the figures are mirror images of others. Frame 8, for instance, is a vertical mirror image of frame 1, and so are frames 7 and 2, 6 and 3, and 5 and 4. There are thus only four unique frames to be generated by an 8×8 extended matrix generator. The mirror-image frames are generated from the same data circuitry, but with the H-count addresses running backward instead of forward.

Figure 11-6a shows the logic levels assigned to the matrix generator's D inputs for the four basic frames, while the equations in Fig. 11-6b show those D inputs that are the same.

Figure 11-6c summarizes the representative D inputs that require something other than constant 0, 1, or X. It shows, in other words, those D inputs calling for some sort of logic manipulation between the four basic frames.

Now it is time to appreciate the operation of the dual 2-line-to-4-line decoder described in Fig. 11-1. Note the sequence in Fig. 11-6c for D0, D8, D16, and D24. Grouping them together yields a pattern of logic levels that closely resembles the truth tables in Fig. 11-1. These D inputs to the matrix generator can be derived directly from a 4-line decoder by applying B0 and B1 to the select inputs, A and B respectively, feeding the four 2Y outputs through inverters, and applying X to the C2 input. See this done with IC3-A in Fig. 11-7.

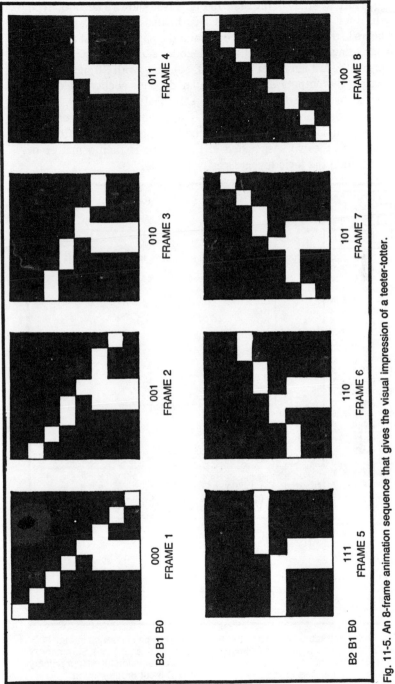

Fig. 11-5. An 8-frame animation sequence that gives the visual impression of a teeter-totter.

463

A further study of the table in Fig. 11-6c shows a decoder-type pattern for D22, D23, D15, and D6. In this instance, a single X appears in the company of three 0s, and the pattern is that achieved by inverting the outputs of the 1Y decoder section in Fig. 11-1. So applying the X input to pin 1 of IC3-B, selecting with B0 and B1, and inverting the outputs of that particular decoder section yields the information required for D22, D23, D15, and D6.

A single dual-decoder package, IC3, is thus capable of generating programmable data inputs for 12 cells in the animation matrices. Completing the work specified in Fig. 11-6c is then a matter of manipulating the logic levels already available.

A

D	FRAME 1	FRAME 2	FRAME 3	FRAME 4
0	$\overline{X}$	0	0	0
1	0	0	0	0
2	0	0	0	0
3	0	0	0	0
4	X	X	X	X
5	0	0	X	X
6	0	0	0	X
7	0	0	0	X
8	0	$\overline{X}$	0	0
9	$\overline{X}$	0	0	0
10	0	0	0	0
11	X	X	X	X
12	X	X	X	X
13	X	X	0	0
14	0	X	X	0
15	0	0	X	0
16	0	0	$\overline{X}$	0
17	0	$\overline{X}$	$\overline{X}$	0
18	X	0	0	0
19	$\overline{X}$	X	X	X
20	X	X	X	X
21	0	0	0	0
22	X	0	0	0
23	0	X	0	0
24	0	0	0	$\overline{X}$
25	0	0	0	$\overline{X}$
26	0	$\overline{X}$	$\overline{X}$	$\overline{X}$
27	1	1	1	1
28	X	X	X	X
29	0	0	0	0
30	0	0	0	0
31	X	0	0	0

B

D0 = D9 = D18
D1 = D2 = D3 = D10 = D21 = D29 = D30 = 0
D4 = D11 = D12 = D19 = D20 = D28 = X
D5
D6 = D7
D8
D13
D14
D15
D16
D17
D22 = D31
D23
D24 = D25
D26
D27 = 1

C

	B1	B0	D0	D5	D6	D8	D13	D14	D15	D16	D17	D22	D23	D24	D26
FRAME 1	0	0	$\overline{X}$	0	0	0	X	0	0	0	0	X	0	0	0
FRAME 2	0	1	0	0	0	$\overline{X}$	X	X	0	0	$\overline{X}$	0	X	0	$\overline{X}$
FRAME 3	1	0	0	X	0	0	0	X	X	$\overline{X}$	$\overline{X}$	0	0	0	$\overline{X}$
FRAME 4	1	1	0	X	X	0	0	0	0	0	0	0	0	$\overline{X}$	$\overline{X}$

Fig. 11-6. Truth-table analysis of the 8-frame animation sequence in Fig. 11-5. (a) D-input programming for primary frames 1, 2, 3 and 4. (b) Summary of equations showing data inputs having identical programming for all four primary frames. (c) Simplified truth table for the matrix D-input programming.

Input D17, for example, uses two $\overline{X}$ terms that can be derived by ORing together D8 and D16. IC6-A accomplishes this task, taking advantage of the fact that inverted data at the input of a NAND gate yields an OR function. D14 is obtained in a similar fashion, effectively ORing together D15 and D23. IC7-A and IC4-E work together to OR D17 and D24 to produce the D26 input.

D5 and D13 could be derived from ORed combinations of other D inputs, but more for the sake of illustration than anything else, the circuit in Fig. 11-7 shows them being generated in a different manner. D5 seems to have a close relationship with the B1 frame-select bit (D5=0 when B1=0, and D5=X when B1=1). So it is possible to generate the D5 signal by gating it off while B1=0 and allowing X to emerge when B1=1. This is a simple AND operation performed by the NOR gate, IC7-7, operating from inverted versions of B1 and X.

D13, on the other hand, shows Xs as long as B1=0, and it outputs 0s as long as B1 = 1. This is, again, a basic AND operation that can be carried out by IC7-B.

The data inputs to the 8 × 8 extended matrix generator are thus completely satisfied for all eight frames of the animation sequence. All that remains to be done is force the H-count select inputs to run in reverse for frames 5 through 8. This is easily accomplished by the three EXCLUSIVE OR gates, IC8-A through IC8-C. Select inputs S0, S1, and S2 run forward as long as B2 is at logic 0—through the first four frames. As B2 rises to logic 1 through the last four frames, the H-count data is inverted by the EXCLUSIVE OR gates, effectively forcing the count at the select inputs to run in reverse and creating the mirror images of frames 1 through 4.

The rate of the teeter-totter effect is adjusted by the RATE ADJUST resistor which, in turn, sets the counting frequency of IC2, the frame counter.

Using the H- and V-count specifications in Fig. 11-7, the teeter-totter figure measures 32H × 32V and is located near the lower right-hand corner of the screen. Of course these specifications can be altered to select any desired size and position.

It is not easy to design and build a video animation sequence. But the possibilities are unlimited. In fact some experimenters have chosen to make a hobby of figure animation alone. Animation effects can add a great deal of interest to TV games, but the designer must have the experience and patience to do the job in his own way. Beginners are encouraged to avoid complex animation sequences until they feel they have the necessary experience and know-how to take on the job.

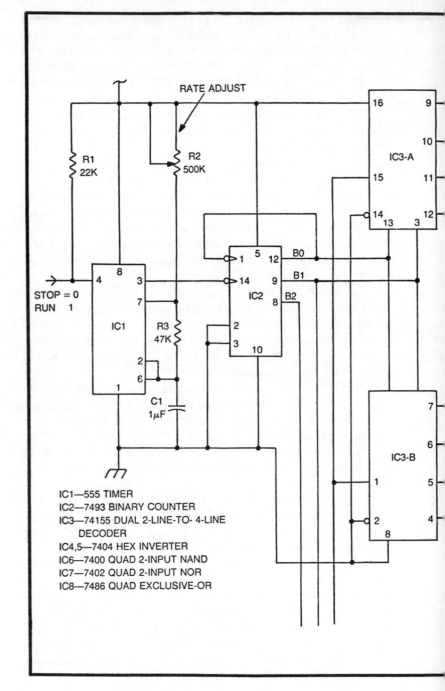

RATE ADJUST

R1
22K

R2
500K

IC3-A

16   9

10

15   11

14   12
13   3

STOP = 0
RUN   1

IC1

8

4   3

7

2
6

1

R3
47K

C1
1μF

IC2

1   5   12   B0

14   9   B1

8   B2

2

3   10

IC3-B

7

6

5

4

1

2

8

IC1—555 TIMER
IC2—7493 BINARY COUNTER
IC3—74155 DUAL 2-LINE-TO- 4-LINE
    DECODER
IC4,5—7404 HEX INVERTER
IC6—7400 QUAD 2-INPUT NAND
IC7—7402 QUAD 2-INPUT NOR
IC8—7486 QUAD EXCLUSIVE-OR

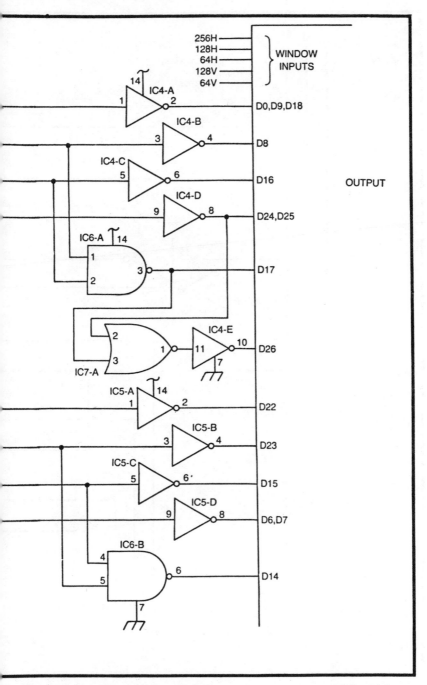

Fig. 11-7. Circuit for producing the 8-frame animation sequence in Fig. 11-5

467

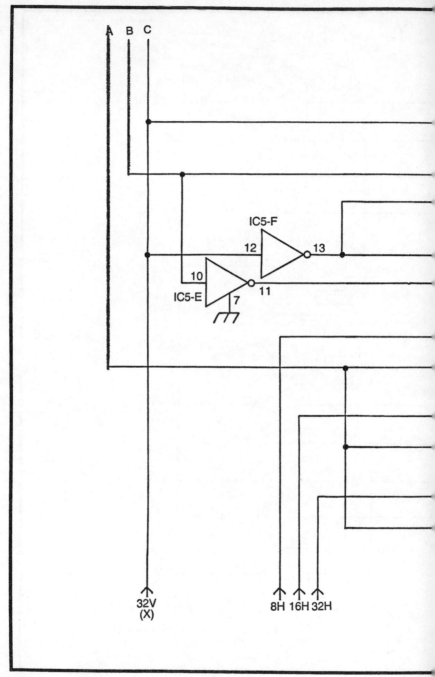

Fig. 11-7. Continued.

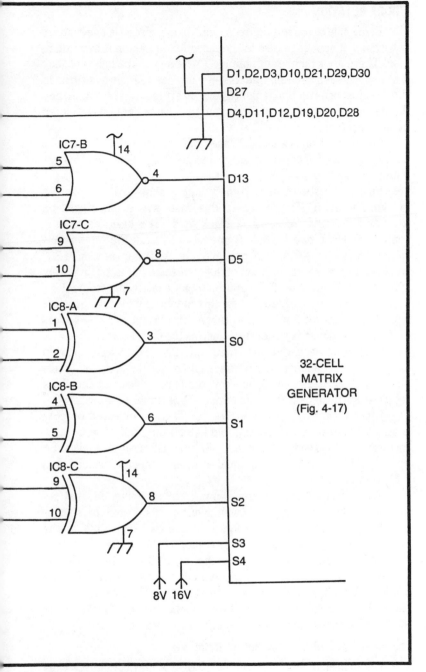

Fig. 11-7 Continued.

469

FIGURE ROTATION

Being able to move a figure around on the screen is one matter, but making it appear to turn in the direction of motion is something else. There are a number of popular TV games on the market today that feature such rotation effects—an airplane that always turns in the direction of its motion; a tank figure that rotates and moves in any direction, but always forward; or a gun that can be rotated and aimed in any direction.

Figure rotation is a special case of figure animation, but it calls for even closer preliminary analysis and greater patience and insight with the circuit design.

Figure 11-8 shows an extremely simple, almost trivial, example of figure rotation. The image in this case is one that might be described as an X figure on a black field. The basic position is represented by frame 1, while frames 2 and 3 show the same figure rotated clockwise 30° and 60° respectively. A further rotation of 30° would carry it to a total rotation of 90°; but since this is a completely symmetrical figure, the 90° rotation looks exactly like frame 1.

The appearance of rotation for this simple figure is thus possible with three different frames, and those three frames can be generated by a 4 × 4 matrix generator, such as the one shown in Fig. 4-5. The D inputs for each frame are specified below the drawings. And in keeping with the animation processes outlined in the first part of this chapter, Figs. 11-8b and 11-8c show the truth tables and equalities required for designing the appropriate D-programming circuitry.

D0, D1, and D2 appear in Fig. 11-8b to be inverted outputs from a 2-line-to-4-line decoder. And indeed they can be generated that way. See IC3 and IC4 in Fig. 11-9. Input D5 is simply logic 1. So it, along with the four others equal to it, is connected directly to a +5V source.

These steps complete the D-input programming. All that remains is to apply the select and windowing inputs. Using the specifications in Fig. 11-9, the little figure measures 32H × 32V and is located just below and right of the center of the screen.

As the experimenter adjusts the frequency of the 555-type astable multivibrator, IC1, the 3-count counter (IC2) generates the sequence 00, 01, 10, 00, 01...at a variable rate. The overall impression is that the figure rotates clockwise on the screen. The faster the multivibrator runs, the faster the figure appears to rotate.

The Importance of 90°-Increment Rotation

The matter of rotating complex, nonsymmetrical figures calls for some techniques that aren't required for the simpler forms of

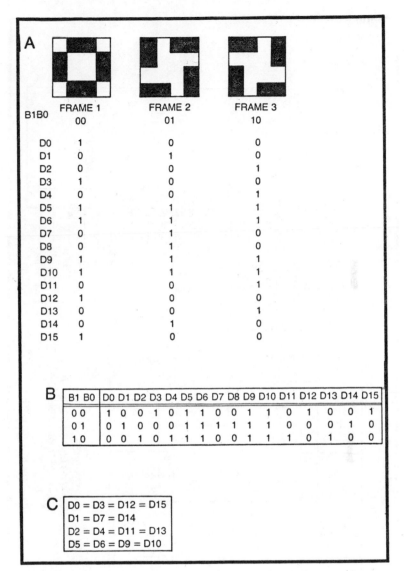

	FRAME 1	FRAME 2	FRAME 3
B1B0	00	01	10
D0	1	0	0
D1	0	1	0
D2	0	0	1
D3	1	0	0
D4	0	0	1
D5	1	1	1
D6	1	1	1
D7	0	1	0
D8	0	1	0
D9	1	1	1
D10	1	1	1
D11	0	0	1
D12	1	0	0
D13	0	0	1
D14	0	1	0
D15	1	0	0

B

B1 B0	D0	D1	D2	D3	D4	D5	D6	D7	D8	D9	D10	D11	D12	D13	D14	D15
0 0	1	0	0	1	0	1	1	0	0	1	1	0	1	0	0	1
0 1	0	1	0	0	0	1	1	1	1	1	1	0	0	0	1	0
1 0	0	0	1	0	1	1	1	0	0	1	1	1	0	1	0	0

C

```
D0 = D3 = D12 = D15
D1 = D7 = D14
D2 = D4 = D11 = D13
D5 = D6 = D9 = D10
```

Fig. 11-8. A very simple animation/rotation sequence. (a) Figures and corresponding D-input matrix programming. (b) Simplified truth table. (c) List of D inputs having identical programming through all three frames.

figure animation. To get an appreciation for the situation, suppose you want to rotate a figure through a full 360° turn at increments of 45°. Now that is a very coarse rotation sequence. The figure will appear to jump from one 45° angle to the next in a very unrealistic fashion. But this is simply an example.

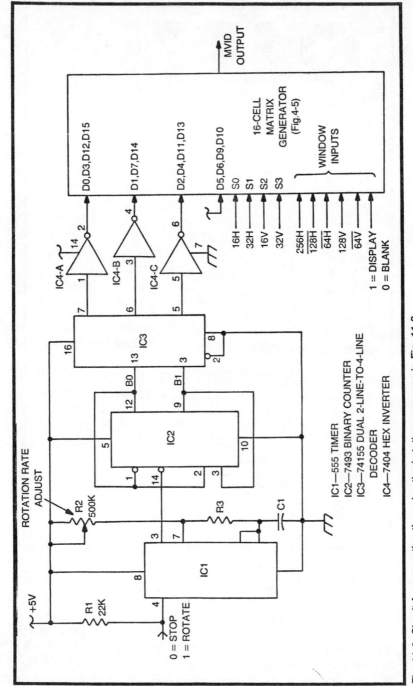

Fig. 11-9. Circuit for generating the animation/rotation sequence in Fig. 11-8.

Now if the figure is going to rotate in 45° steps, it follows that the sequence will use eight animation frames: 0°, 45°, 90°, 135°, 180°, 225°, and 315°. An additional 45° rotation carries the figure back to its original 0° position. See the sequence in Fig. 11-10.

From the foregoing discussion of animation sequences, it might be assumed that one doesn't need eight different sets of D-input matrix programs to accomplish this rotation effect. The 180° figure, for instance, is a vertical reflection of the 0° figure, the 270° figure is a horizontal reflection of the 90° one, the 135° figure is a vertical reflection of the 45° version, and finally the 315° image can be derived by a vertical reflection of the 225° figure. The eight figures can thus be obtained by performing either a horizontal- or vertical-reflection operation on just four of them. It would be possible to generate this sequence by establishing a D-input matrix program for four of them, then reversing the direction of horizontal or vertical counting to get the other four.

That's not too bad. But notice how coarse the rotation effect would be. The player would not see anything resembling a smooth rotation. The figure would appear to snap around in 45° intervals. And overcoming that problem is a matter of rotating the figure in finer angular increments.

So let's suppose you try rotating a complex figure in 22½° increments, cutting the minimum angular increment in half. Does this double the number of images in the animation/rotation sequence? No, it quadruples the number of figures, apparently making

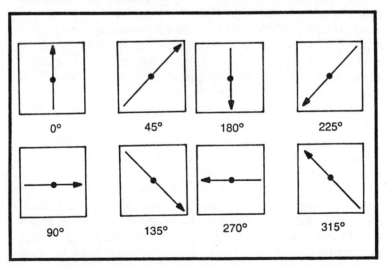

Fig. 11-10. Definitions of rotation through 360 degrees at 45-degree increments.

the whole affair four times as complicated! If anything useful is to be done with this matter of rotating complex figures in a realistic fashion, there has to be a special trick for simplifying the whole thing. That trick is 90° rotations.

The previous analysis of the rotation sequence in Fig. 11-10 showed that it could be done with four programmed figures (0°, 90°, 45°, and 225°) by reversing the horizontal or vertical counting to obtain the other four figures. Using a 90°-shift operation, however, it is possible to generate all eight figures from just two matrix programs, the 0° and 45° images.

While the sequence in Fig. 11-10 is built around 45° increments, it can be seen that the 0° image can be shifted by 90° to get the images for 90, 180, and 270 degrees, while the 45° image can be shifted in 90° increments to get the images for 135, 225 and 315 degrees. Using this 90°-shift technique, it is possible to get all eight frames from the D-input matrix programs for 0° and 45°. And in fact a 16-frame rotation sequence (22½° intervals) can be derived from just four D-input matrix programs.

Figure 11-11 shows the rationale behind rotating a single 4 × 4 matrix image in 90° increments by varying the select format, rather than the D-input programming. In this case, the basic 0° matrix is generated in the usual fashion, applying the least-significant H-count bit (H0) to S0 of the matrix generator, the most-signifcant H-count (H1) to S1, and so on. The numerals in the matrix cells indicate their relative positions, with the first digit being the decimal value of select inputs S0 and S1, and the second being the decimal value of the bits applied to select inputs S2 and S3.

Achieving a 90° clockwise rotation from the basic matrix is a matter of shifting the counts around the matrix. In the 90° figure, 00 replaces, 03, 03 replaces 33, and so on. Any complex figure constructed within the 0° matrix will appear shifted 90° clockwise if it is again constructed in the 90° matrix.

Making this 90° shift calls for applying the two V-count inputs to what is normally considered the H-count inputs, S0 and S1. Furthermore, the H-count bits are inverted before applying them to S2 and S3 of the matrix generator, effectively reversing their direction of count.

Another 90° shift in the clockwise direction takes us to the 180° matrix, where the H- and V-count bits are applied to their usual select inputs, but inverted to force both to count in reverse. A final 90° shift yields the matrix for 270°. The connections to the select inputs are similar to those required for the 90° image, but in this case it is the V-count inputs that run in reverse.

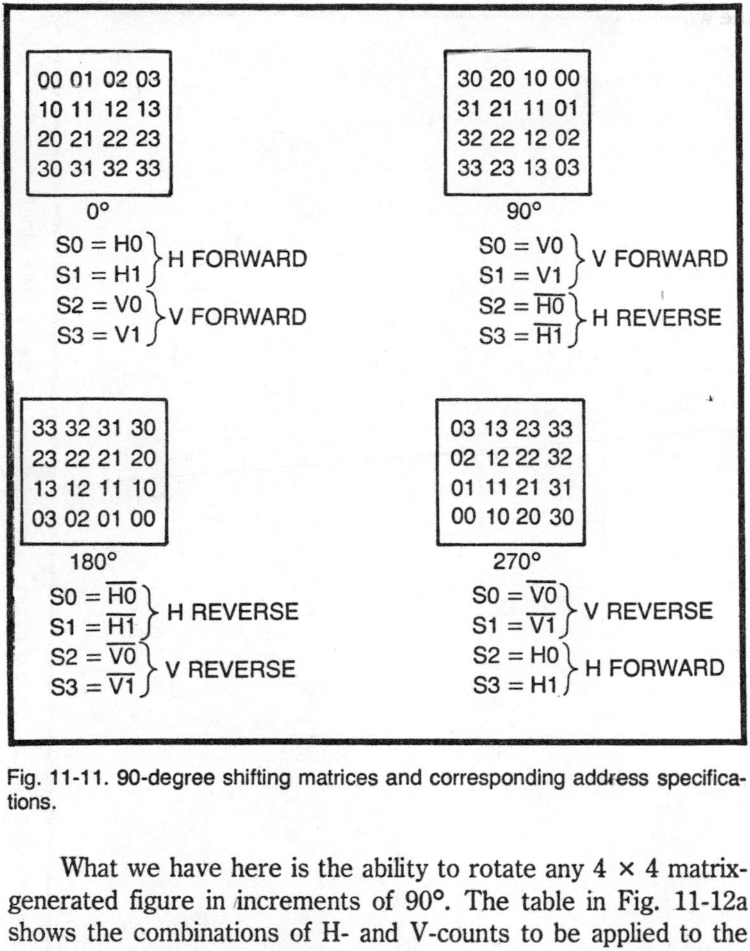

```
00 01 02 03              30 20 10 00
10 11 12 13              31 21 11 01
20 21 22 23              32 22 12 02
30 31 32 33              33 23 13 03
```

0°   90°

S0 = H0 ⎫   S0 = V0 ⎫
S1 = H1 ⎬ H FORWARD   S1 = V1 ⎬ V FORWARD
S2 = V0 ⎫   S2 = $\overline{H0}$ ⎫
S3 = V1 ⎬ V FORWARD   S3 = $\overline{H1}$ ⎬ H REVERSE

```
33 32 31 30              03 13 23 33
23 22 21 20              02 12 22 32
13 12 11 10              01 11 21 31
03 02 01 00              00 10 20 30
```

180°   270°

S0 = $\overline{H0}$ ⎫   S0 = $\overline{V0}$ ⎫
S1 = $\overline{H1}$ ⎬ H REVERSE   S1 = $\overline{V1}$ ⎬ V REVERSE
S2 = $\overline{V0}$ ⎫   S2 = H0 ⎫
S3 = $\overline{V1}$ ⎬ V REVERSE   S3 = H1 ⎬ H FORWARD

Fig. 11-11. 90-degree shifting matrices and corresponding address specifications.

What we have here is the ability to rotate any 4 × 4 matrix-generated figure in increments of 90°. The table in Fig. 11-12a shows the combinations of H- and V-counts to be applied to the matrix-select inputs at the four different angles. The angles are selected by an external source of 2-bit binary numbers, B0 and B1. When B0=B1=0, for example, the figure will be in its basic 0° position. But when B0=1 and B1=0, the 90° image is selected.

The circuit in Fig. 11-12b shows how the various angle patterns can be obtained by running the two B inputs through their 2-bit binary counting sequence. It is really just a set of four 4:1 multiplexer circuits, each one providing an output for each of the four select lines to the matrix generator.

A careful study of the circuit in Fig. 11-12b shows that it satisfies the truth table in Fig. 11-12a. And since that truth table is derived from the matrix-rotation scheme in Fig. 11-11, it ultimately follows that the circuit in Fig. 11-12b will do the job. A single figure

475

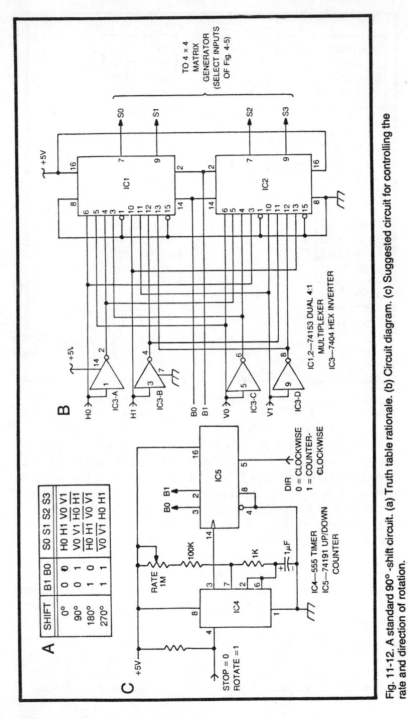

Fig. 11-12. A standard 90°-shift circuit. (a) Truth table rationale. (b) Circuit diagram. (c) Suggested circuit for controlling the rate and direction of rotation.

programmed into the D inputs of the matrix generator can be rotated to any one of four different positions.

The circuit in Fig. 11-12c shows a circuit for controlling the rotation. Adjusting the RATE potentiometer sets the rate of rotation. The logic level presented to the DIR (direction) input determines whether the figure rotates in a clockwise or counter clockwise direction.

So how can this 90°-shift procedure be used for simplifying the rotation of figures through much smaller increments? Rotating a figure through 45° increments is first a matter of working out two D-input programs, one for the basic 0° position and another for the 45° position. One additional rotation bit is required for selecting one of the two basic figures, while the two shown in Fig. 11-12 are necessary for determining how much either figure is shifted.

The table in Fig. 11-13 shows the rotation sequence for turning any 4 × 4 matrix figure through a full 360 degrees in a clockwise direction and at intervals of 45°.

Rotation of an 8 × 8 Figure at 22½° Intervals

The 45° rotation sequence just described is presented as an example of how such a scheme should work. For an acceptable visual impression of relatively smooth rotation, the figure should advance at angles no greater than 22½°. This section uses a specific example, a tank figure, to show how the principles of figure animation and 90° shifting can be combined to transform a very complicated rotation situation into a reasonably simple format.

ROTATION CONTROL			OPERATION	ROTATION EFFECT
B1	B0	B3		
0	0	0	0° IMAGE WITH 0° ROTATION	0°
0	0	1	45° IMAGE WITH 0° ROTATION	45°
0	1	0	0° IMAGE WITH 90° ROTATION	90°
0	1	1	45° IMAGE WITH 90° ROTATION	135°
1	0	0	0° IMAGE WITH 180° ROTATION	180°
1	0	1	45° IMAGE WITH 180° ROTATION	225°
1	1	0	0° IMAGE WITH 270° ROTATION	270°
1	1	1	45° IMAGE WITH 270° ROTATION	315°

Fig. 11-13. Table of rotation/frame selection for rotation a complex figure through 360 degrees at 45-degree increments.

A

```
00 01 02 03 04 05 06 07
10 11 12 13 14 15 16 17
20 21 22 23 24 25 26 27
30 31 32 33 34 35 36 37
40 41 42 43 44 45 46 47
50 51 52 53 54 55 56 57
60 61 62 63 64 65 66 67
70 71 72 73 74 75 76 77
```
0°

```
70 60 50 40 30 20 10 00
71 61 51 41 31 21 11 01
72 62 52 42 32 22 12 02
73 63 53 43 33 23 13 03
74 64 54 44 34 24 14 04
75 65 55 45 35 25 15 05
76 66 56 46 36 26 16 06
77 67 57 47 37 27 17 07
```
90°

```
77 76 75 74 73 72 71 70
67 66 65 64 63 62 61 60
57 56 55 54 53 52 51 50
47 46 45 44 43 42 41 40
37 36 35 34 33 32 31 30
27 26 25 24 23 22 21 20
17 16 15 14 13 12 11 10
07 06 05 04 03 02 01 00
```
180°

```
07 17 27 37 47 57 67 77
06 16 26 36 46 56 66 76
05 15 25 35 45 55 65 75
04 14 24 34 44 54 64 74
03 13 23 33 43 53 63 73
02 12 22 32 42 52 62 72
01 11 21 31 41 51 61 71
00 10 20 30 40 50 60 70
```
270°

B

	0°	90°	180°	270°
	S0 = H0	S0 = V0	S0 = $\overline{H0}$	S0 = $\overline{V0}$
	S1 = H1	S1 = V1	S1 = $\overline{H1}$	S1 = $\overline{V1}$
	S2 = H2	S2 = V2	S2 = $\overline{H2}$	S2 = $\overline{V2}$
	S3 = V0	S3 = $\overline{H0}$	S3 = $\overline{V0}$	S3 = H0
	S4 = V1	S4 = $\overline{H1}$	S4 = $\overline{V1}$	S4 = H1
	S5 = V2	S5 = $\overline{H2}$	S5 = $\overline{V2}$	S5 = H2

Fig. 11-14. Matrix rationale for shifting 8×8 complex figures at 90-degrees. (a) 8×8 matrices with each cell showing the octal equivalent of the applied counting sequence. (b) Truth-table summary of addressing required for each 90-degree shift.

Figure 11-14 shows the 90° shifting rationale for an 8 × 8 matrix. The procedure for generating these matrices is identical to that of the simpler scheme in Fig. 11-11. The number of cells, however, has been increased substantially.

Using an 8 × 8 matrix generator calls for six select lines, designated S0 through S5. (Compare Fig. 11-14b and the matrix generator in Fig. 4-17.) Three of the select lines have inverted or noninverted H-counts applied to them, while the other three have inverted or noninverted V-counts connected to them. The 90° shifting is accomplished by varying this pattern of H- and V-count inputs as shown in Fig. 11-14b.

478

The circuit in Fig. 11-15, derived from the rationale in Fig. 11-14, can be considered a universal 90° rotator for 8 × 8 matrix figures. The circuit calls for six 4:1 multiplexers, each feeding the appropriate data to a select input on the matrix generator. The circuit satisfies the truth table in Fig. 11-15, and that table is based on the data derived from the basic 8 × 8, 90° shifting requirements in Fig. 11-14.

So much for the basic 8 × 8 90° shifter. Now consider how it can be combined with an animation sequence to rotate the figure of a tank on the screen.

Figure 11-16 shows a tank figure built within an 8 × 8 extended matrix. This is a 4-frame animation sequence that can be programmed at the D inputs of the matrix generator in Fig. 4-17.

Frame 1 shows the tank in its basic 0° position. This is probably the best tank figure that can be constructed within an 8 × 8 matrix. Frame 2 then shows the tank figure rotated clockwise by 22.5°. The image is terribly distorted, but it is the best we can do with a 64-cell matrix. And besides, the distortion really doesn't seem so bad to players lost in the action of a video game.

Frame 3 then shows the tank figure rotated to 45°, an additional 22.5° from that in frame 2. The distortion is somewhat less objectionable in this case.

And finally, frame 4 shows the same figure rotated to 67.5°.

The scheme involves a total of four unique animation frames. There is no way any one of these frames can be derived from another by performing any sort of shifting operation. It is possible, however, to generate 12 additional frames by rotating each of them through a complete sequence of 90° intervals. If frame 1 is rotated 90°, for instance, the impression is that of a tank figure pointing to the right. Another 90° shift on that same frame yields a total of 180°, thereby making the tank figure point toward the bottom of the screen. Yet another 90° shift transforms frame 1 into a tank figure pointing to the left (a total of 270° angular shift).

This 90°-shifting sequence can be applied to any one of the four basic frames, producing a total of 16 tank images, images giving the impression of a full 360° rotation at 22.5° increments.

Before carrying the discussion of 90° shifting any further, it is necessary to work out the circuit for generating the four frames in Fig. 11-16. This is done using the same procedures outlined in the first part of this chapter. The data resulting from this procedure is summarized in the tables in Fig. 11-17. Figure 11-18 then shows the appropriate circuitry.

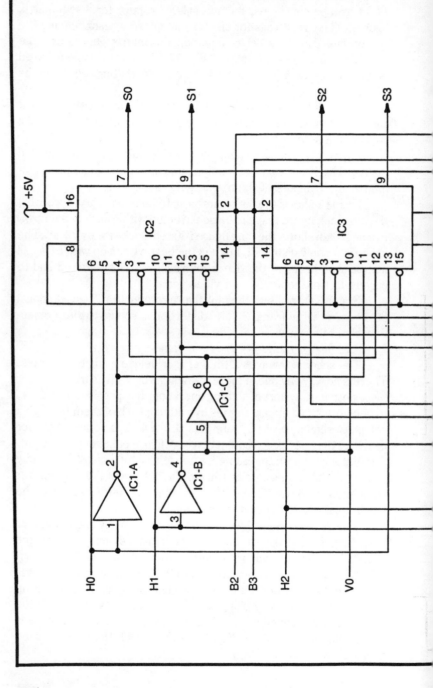

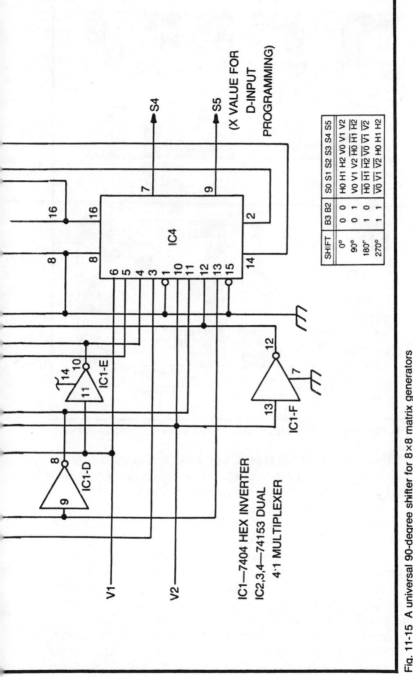

Fig. 11-15 A universal 90-degree shifter for 8×8 matrix generators

SHIFT	B3 B2	S0 S1 S2 S3 S4 S5
0°	0 0	H0 H1 H2 V0 V1 V2
90°	0 1	V0 V1 V2 H̄0 H̄1 H̄2
180°	1 0	H̄0 H̄1 H̄2 V̄0 V̄1 V̄2
270°	1 1	V̄0 V̄1 V̄2 H0 H1 H2

S4

S5 (X VALUE FOR D-INPUT PROGRAMMING)

IC4

IC1—7404 HEX INVERTER
IC2,3,4—74153 DUAL
4·1 MULTIPLEXER

IC1-E
IC1-D
IC1-F

V1
V2

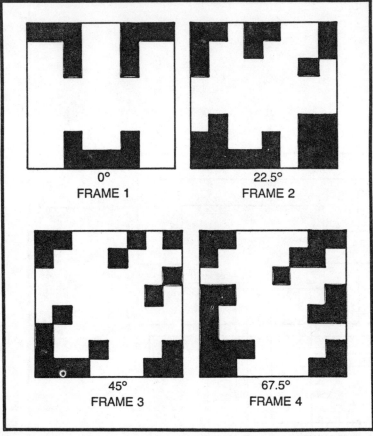

Fig. 11-16. Four critical frames for rotating a tank figure at 22.5-degree intervals.

There should be no reason to explain the derivation of the circuit in Fig. 11-18 in great detail because it follows the principles already outlined for a 4-frame animation sequence.

What is most important here is to combine the 8 × 8 90°, shifting circuit (Fig. 11-15) with the 4-frame animation generator (Fig. 11-18) with the 8 × 8 extended matrix generator in Fig. 4-17. Figure 11-19 shows how these circuits are combined. If the scheme is combined with the control circuit in Fig. 11-20, the result is a tiny 8H × 8V tank figure that can be rotated into any one of 16 positions, in a direction set by the logic level at the DIR input, and at a rate determined by the setting of the RATE control.

Any custom-designed figure can be worked into this circuit. The 90° rotator circuit never changes. Only the D-input programming changes. Of course the whole system can be systematically expanded to accommodate more complex and less distorted figures. If it appears to an advanced experimenter that the complexity of the whole scheme is getting out of hand, he can resort to using a programmable read-only memory (PROM). This device is most often used by engineers who design high-quality commercial video games calling for fine rotation of complex figures.

COMBINING ROTATION AND FIGURE MOTION ACROSS THE SCREEN

All of the animation and rotation effects described thus far assume the figure will not move across the screen as the rotation takes place. It is often desirable to combine rotation and slipping-counter motion effects to heighten the impression of reality.

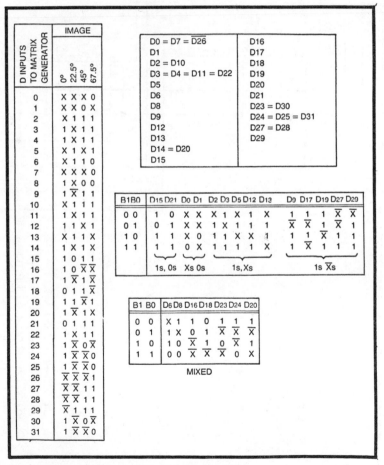

Fig. 11-17. Truth-table analysis of the tank rotation.

483

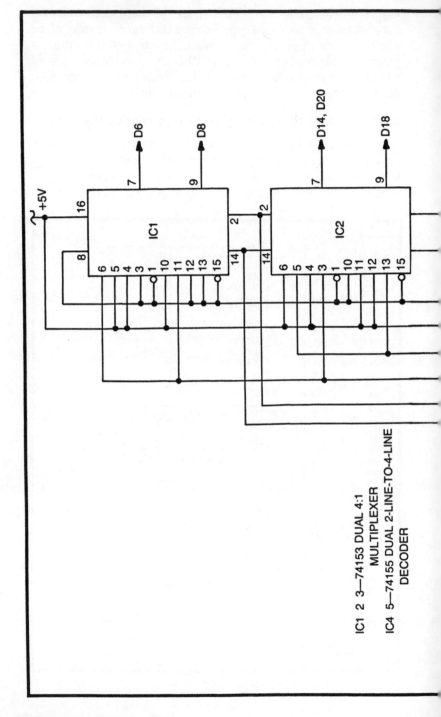

IC1 2 3—74153 DUAL 4:1
MULTIPLEXER
IC4 5—74155 DUAL 2-LINE-TO-4-LINE
DECODER

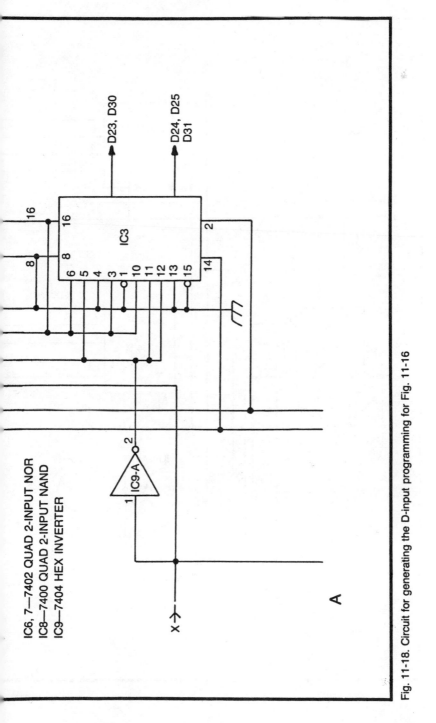

Fig. 11-18. Circuit for generating the D-input programming for Fig. 11-16

485

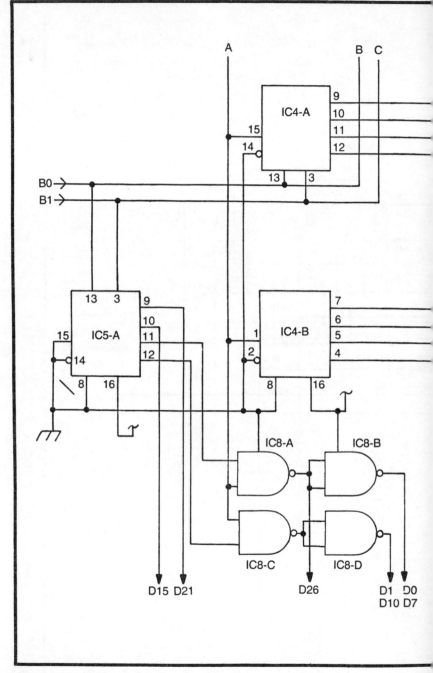

Fig. 11-8. Continued.

486

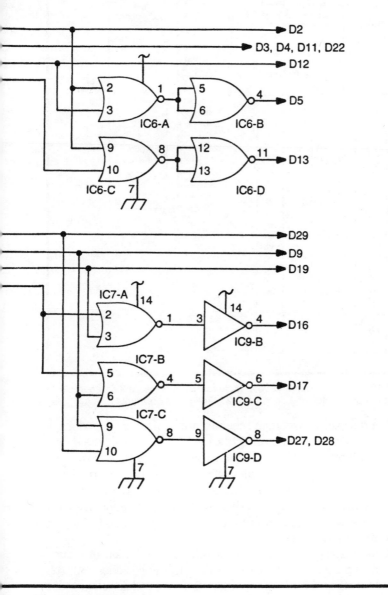

Fig. 11-8. Continued.

487

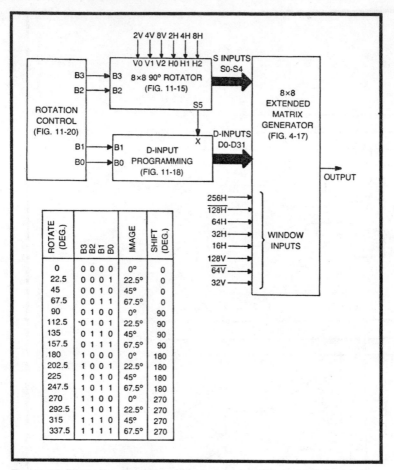

Fig. 11-19. Block diagram and code table for rotating the tank figure in either direction through a full 360 degrees at 22.5-degree increments.

In principle, the rotation schemes are devised as described in this chapter, and the motion effects are achieved by using the H- and V-count outputs of a slipping-counter board, rather than those from the Sourcebox. The only difficult part is coordinating the direction of motion across the screen with angle of rotation of the figure.

If the tank figure in Fig. 11-16 is set for a 45° rotation, it should move up the screen and toward the right. If it is rotated to 180°, it should move straight down.

Coordinating the rotation angle with the direction of motion across the screen is a matter of translating the angle codes (B3, B2, B1, and B0 in Fig. 11-18) into appropriate speed and direction codes for a set of horizontal and vertical slipping counters.

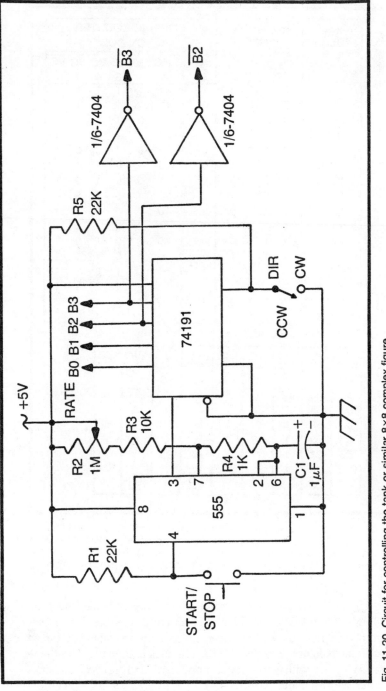

Fig. 11-20. Circuit for controlling the tank or similar 8×8 complex figure.

A	ANGLE* (DEG.)	ROTATION CODE				SLIPPING-COUNTER MOTION CODES							
		B3	B2	B1	B0	HC 8	HC 4	HC 2	HC 1	VC 8	VC 4	VC 2	VC 1
	0	0	0	0	0	1	0	0	1	1	1	1	1
	22.5	0	0	0	1	0	1	1	1	1	1	1	0
	45	0	0	1	0	0	1	1	0	1	1	0	1
	67.5	0	0	1	1	0	1	0	1	1	0	1	1
	90	0	1	0	0	0	1	0	0	1	0	0	1
	112.5	0	1	0	1	0	1	0	1	0	1	1	1
	135	0	1	1	0	0	1	1	0	0	1	0	1
	157.5	0	1	1	1	0	1	1	1	0	1	0	0
	180	1	0	0	0	1	0	0	1	0	0	1	1
	202.5	1	0	0	1	1	0	1	1	0	1	0	0
	225	1	0	1	0	1	1	0	0	0	1	0	1
	247.5	1	0	1	1	1	1	0	1	0	1	1	1
	270	1	1	0	0	1	1	1	0	1	0	0	1
	292.5	1	1	0	1	1	1	0	1	1	0	1	1
	315	1	1	1	0	1	1	0	0	1	1	0	1
	337.5	1	1	1	1	1	0	1	1	1	1	1	0

B *0° = STRAIGHT UP

	8HC	4HC	2HC	1HC	8VC	4VC	2VC	1VC
D0	1	0	0	$\overline{B2}$	$\overline{B3}$	$\overline{B3}$	1	1
D1	B3	$\overline{B3}$	1	1	$\overline{B3}$	1	$\overline{B3}$	B2
D2	B3	1	$\overline{B3}$	0	$\overline{B3}$	1	0	1
D3	B3	1	0	1	$\overline{B3}$	B3	1	$\overline{B2}$
D4	B3	1	B3		1	0	0	-
D5	B3	1	$\underline{0}$		B3	$\overline{B3}$	1	-
D6	B3	1	$\overline{B3}$		B3	1	0	-
D7	B3	$\overline{B3}$	1	-	B3	1	B3	-

Fig. 11-21. Truth-table analysis of the relationships between angle of rotation and direction of motion across the screen. (a) Table of code translations between rotation codes and slipping-counter motion codes. (b) Summary of slipping-counter speed control codes as a function of D-input programming for translating them from rotation-code inputs.

Figure 11-21 shows the truth-table analysis behind such an angle-to-motion translator. Figure 11-21a specifies the desired set of rotation angles as well as the rotation codes established for an 8 × 8 matrix figure. See Fig. 11-13. The task is then to relate these rotation codes with appropriate horizontal and vertical slipping-counter-control codes.

490

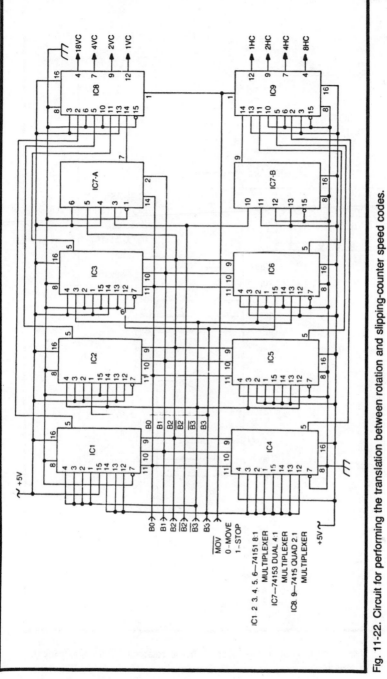

Fig. 11-22. Circuit for performing the translation between rotation and slipping-counter speed codes.

491

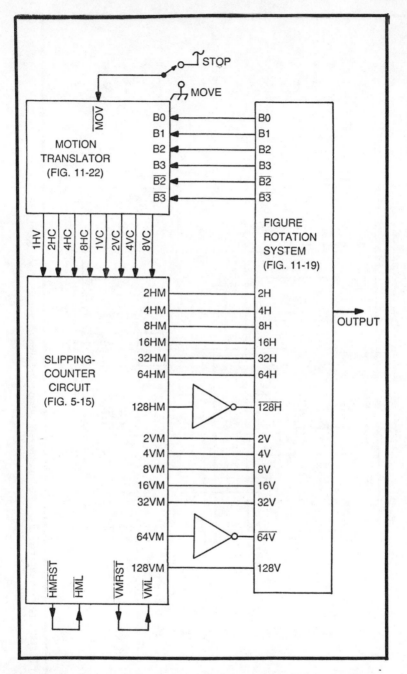

Fig. 11-23. The translator interfaces with the rotatable figure and slipping-counter board.

The general procedure is to determine the sine and cosine of the angles, then use the table in Fig. 7-22 to find the closest possible velocities for each. The sine of the angle determines the vertical velocity, while the cosine determines the horizontal velocity.

Table 11-21b shows the results of this translation process, assuming it will be carried out by means of a set of multiplexer circuits.

The resulting circuit diagram for the angle-to-motion translator is shown in Fig. 11-22. Figure 11-23 shows how the translator interfaces with the 8 × 8 rotatable figure and a slipping-counter board.

A similar approach using universal position programmers (Chapter 8) would provide a much wider range of figure speeds, but only at the cost of greater circuit complexity.

Chapter 12
Sound Effects

Most commercial video games feature some interesting sound effects. Such effects are rarely a vital part of the games, themselves, but they add to the fun of the whole thing.

Rather than presenting a wide variety of sound-generating circuits that have specific applications, this chapter shows how certain classes of sounds can be generated, leaving it to the know-how and imagination of the experimenter to apply them as desired.

TONES FROM THE V-COUNT SIGNALS

Figure 12-1 lists some of the frequencies in the audio range that are available directly from the V-count outputs of the Sourcebox unit. These tones are available continuously as long as the Sourcebox unit is turned on. To get a good idea how these signals sound, connect any one of them directly to the AUDIO IN pin on the Sourcebox, adjusting the volume control for a comfortable listening level.

Steady tones are rarely useful for video games, however, so there must be some provisions for switching them on and off at the appropriate times. Figure 12-2 shows an experimental breadboard circuit for controlling the tone from a negative-going control pulse.

The circuit in Fig. 12-2 is basically a monostable multivibrator built around a 555-type timer. Whenever switch S is depressed, a short negative-going pulse is coupled through C1 to the trigger input of the monostable circuit. Its output from pin 3 then goes to a logic-1

V-COUNT OUTPUT	FREQUENCY (Hz)
1V	7893
2V	3945
4V	1973
8V	987
16V	493
32V	247
64V	123
128V	62
256V	62

Fig. 12-1. Approximate frequencies from V-count sources.

level for a period of time determined by the product of 1.1 times the values of R3 and C2.

Setting the pin-3 output of the 555 to logic 1 in this fashion opens the 2-input NAND gate, allowing the 4V signal to pass through to the audio amplifier in the Sourcebox unit. The player thus hears a 1973-Hz tone which, in this particular case, lasts about 110 ms. The sound is very much like that of a table-tennis ball hitting a paddle.

Of course the tone duration can be modified by altering the values of R3 and C2, and the tone frequency can be changed by selecting a different V-count input.

The circuit is perfectly compatible with any of the video games that include a figure-contact operation. Most of these operations generate a negative-going pulse that can be connected to the timer through C1. R1 and S can be normally omitted in such cases.

This circuit can also be connected to the SWING pushbutton on the Golf game (Chapter 8). The effect is a "plink" sound every time the player hits the ball.

Connect this circuit to the HIT terminal in the Pinball game (Chapter 10), and you will hear the "plink" sound every time the ball rebounds from one of the barriers or paddles.

It is sometimes desirable to generate more than one "plink" frequency in a game. Suppose, for example, you want two different sounds of this sort, each switched on by a different event on the screen. Figure 12-3 shows how this can be done.

Basically, the circuit ORs together the tones from the two "plink" circuits. The occurrence of event A switches on IC1-A, and allows the 4V frequency to pass through IC2-A and IC2-B to the audio amplifier in the Sourcebox unit. By the same token, the occurrence of event B switches IC1-B to its active state, allowing the 8V frequency to pass to the audio amplifier.

In this particular example, event A causes the player to hear a 1973-Hz tone that lasts only about 0.1 second. Event B, on the other hand, causes a 987-Hz tone that lasts about 0.25 second. The overall effect is a higher-pitched and shorter "plink" sound for event A, and a lower-pitched and longer "ploonk" sound for event B.

Again, any of the timing values for the monostables and the V-inputs can be altered to suit your own needs.

Replacing IC2-B, the output that effectively ORs together the different tones, with a 4-input NAND gate allows the circuit to respond to four different kinds of events calling for an equal number of different tones and tone durations.

Deedle-Deedle Sounds

Space games and ray guns call for weird little sounds that cannot be easily generated from single V-count sources. They can be created, however, by rapidly alternating between two different tone sources. See the example in Fig. 12-4.

IC1-A in Fig. 12- 4 is connected as a free-running multivibrator having a frequency fixed by the values of R2, R3, and C2. In this particular case, the frequency is on the order of 4 Hz. This circuit determines the "deedle-deedle" rate.

The output of IC1-A alternately gates on IC2-C and IC2-B. Whenever the output of IC1-A is at logic 1, IC2-C is gated on,

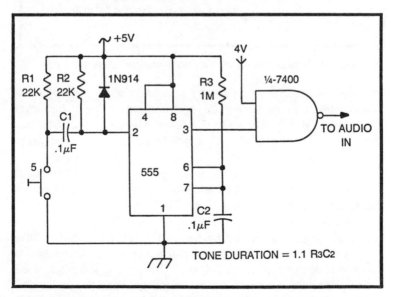

Fig. 12-2. Experimental circuit for gating V-count tones on and off.

497

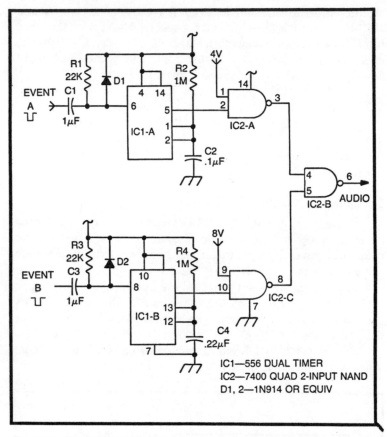

Fig. 12-3. Circuit for combining V-count tones from two different sources.

thereby allowing the 4V frequency to pass. The inverter action of
IC2-A, however, transforms the logic 1 from IC1-A to a zero level
that gates off IC2-B. Whenever IC1-A switches to its 0 output state,
the situation is reversed: IC2-B is gated on to allow the 8V signal to
pass and IC2-C is gated off.

Neither of these frequencies appears at the AUDIO output of
the circuit unless IC3-A is gated on by a logic-1 level at its pin-2
input. And that signal comes from IC1-B.

IC1-B is connected as a monostable multivibrator that is set to
its timing state only when the desired triggering event occurs.
Maybe this event occurs when the player depresses the trigger on
some sort of ray gun. In any event, a negative-going pulse at C1
starts the timing action of IC1-B and allows the "deedle-deedle"
sounds to pass through IC3-A to the audio amplifier.

The timing interval for IC1-B is fixed by the values of R4 and C3. In this example, it is set for about 1 second. The circuit is thus normally silent. But when the triggering event occurs, IC1-B allows the "deedle-deedle" sounds to be heard for 1 second.

It is possible to achieve a wide variety of audio effects from this one simple circuit. The "deedle" frequencies can be altered by applying different pairs of V-count inputs to IC2-C and IC2-B. The "deedle-deedle" rate can be changed by experimenting with the values of R2, R3, and C2. And finally, the duration of the funny sounds can be modified by changing the values of R4 and C3.

SOUNDS FROM SOURCES OTHER THAN V-COUNT SOURCES

Some of the most common sounds for video games are built around noise or static sounds. Gunshots and explosions are both good examples of this sort of audio feature.

Figure 12-5 is the schematic diagram for a noise generator. The noise (or static) is generated by the reverse-breakdown of the

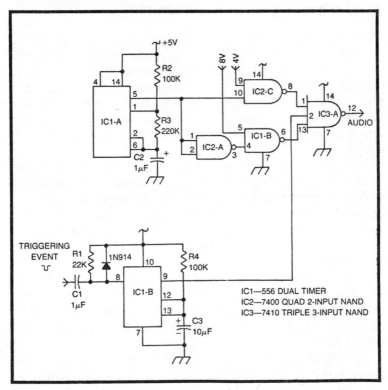

Fig. 12-4. Circuit for creating "deedle-deedle" tones from V-count sources.

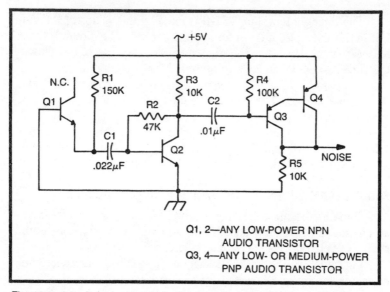

Fig. 12-5. A basic noise generator for explosion effects.

emitter-base junction of Q1. The breakdown current is controlled at a safe level by resistor R1. The collector on that same transistor is not used. But the noise it generates can be amplified by Q2, and then further amplified and adjusted to TTL logic levels by Q3 and Q4.

Since this circuit generates the noise continuously, its output must be applied to a control circuit to give the impression of explosions or gunfire. The circuits in Fig. 12-6 illustrate two kinds of noise controls.

The circuit in Fig. 12-6a uses a simple monostable multivibrator circuit to control the on-time of the noise signal fed to the audio amplifier. The monostable is set to its active timing mode whenever the SHOOT input experiences a brief negative-going pulse. The positive-going timing pulse from pin 3 of the 555 then gates on the NAND gate, allowing the noise signal to pass to the audio amplifier in the Sourcebox unit.

The monostable remains in its active condition for a period of time determined by the values of R2 and C2. In this particular instance the timing is set for about 0.1 second, giving the impression of a single gunshot each time a negative-going pulse appears at the SHOOT input.

The duration of the explosion sound can be lengthened by increasing the value of R2, thereby giving the impression of a bomb exploding.

500

The circuit in Fig. 12-6b can create the sound of machine gun fire. In this instance the noise signal is gated on and off by a free-running multivibrator. As long as the FIRE input is at the logic-1 level, this oscillator runs at about 4 Hz, gating the NAND gate on and off, ultimately producing a string of staccato-like noise bursts. The firing rate can be adjusted by changing the values of R1 or R2, or both.

Another source of game sounds takes advantage of a simple digital-to-analog (D/A) converter circuit. The idea is to translate any source of digital words into a voltage level, and then use that voltage level to create tones of various frequencies. Such a scheme is useful for generating buzzing sounds that vary in pitch with the speed of a figure moving on the screen or whistling sounds for falling bombs.

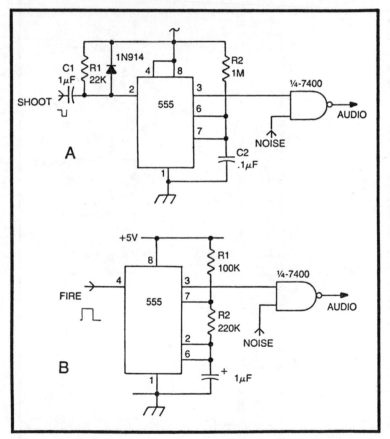

Fig. 12-6. Circuits for controlling noise sounds. (a) Single gunshots or explosions. (b) Machine gun effects.

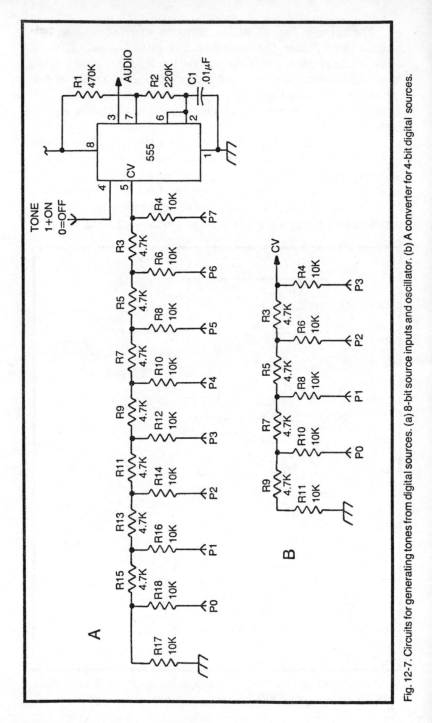

Fig. 12-7. Circuits for generating tones from digital sources. (a) 8-bit source inputs and oscillator. (b) A converter for 4-bit digital sources.

The basic D/A converter is made up of a resistor-ladder network. Two of them are shown in Fig. 12-7. The larger circuit in Fig. 12-7a can accept an 8-bit digital word at inputs P0 through P7, while the simpler one in Fig. 12-7b can be used with 4-bit digital words.

In either case, the voltage appearing at the junction of R3 and R4 is proportional to the value of the binary number applied to the P inputs. That voltage level is then used to set the frequency of a 555-type free-running multivibrator. The TONE input to the 555 oscillator is used for gating the sound on and off. When this input is at logic 1, the tones appear at the AUDIO output connection. Setting that TONE input to logic 0, however, silences the circuit.

The values of R1, R2, and C1 determine the range of frequencies available from the circuit. The larger these values, the lower the tones. The P inputs to the ladder network then determine the frequency within that selected range that will appear at the AUDIO terminal. While the analog voltage to the CV input of the 555 timer is proportional to the size of the binary number applied to the P inputs, it turns out that the selected frequency is inversely proportional to the binary number. The larger the number, the lower the audio tone.

So if the eight P inputs in Fig. 12-7a are connected to the outputs of an 8-bit binary counter, the tone sweeps downward when the counter is counting upward, and the tone sweeps upward when the counter is counting downward. Figure 12-8 shows a rather simple circuit for experimenting with the tone generator. The out-

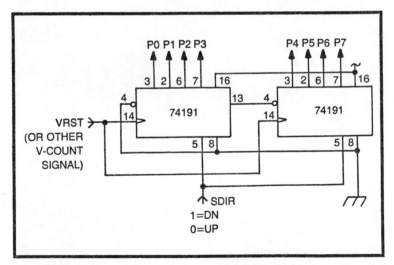

Fig. 12-8. An 8-bit counter for generating whistle effects from the circuit in Fig. 12-7a.

503

puts of the 74191 counters interface directly with the P inputs of the circuit in Fig. 12-7a.

It is possible to generate a lot of interesting sounds by combining the circuits in Fig. 12-7a and 12-8. It is left to the experimenter to play with the circuit and come up with sounds that seem fun and useful for custom TV games.

The smaller D/A converter in Fig. 12-7b is especially useful for translating the 4-bit VC or HC inputs to a slipping-counter circuit into audio tones. Simply replace the larger resistor network in Fig. 12-7a with the simpler one in Fig. 12-7b, and then connect the four P inputs to the VC or HC terminals of a slipping-counter control. Adjust the values of R1 and C1 to get the range of frequencies that seem most appropriate for the game scheme.

Appendices

Appendix I

This appendix is a complete listing of horizontal- and vertical-count binary outputs.

H- OR V-COUNT OUTPUTS

256	128	64	32	16 8 4 2 1	DECIMAL EQUIVILENT	
0	0	0	0	0 0 0 0 0	0	H AND V BLANKING BEGIN
				0 0 0 0 1	1	
				0 0 0 1 0	2	
				0 0 0 1 1	3	V SYNC BEGINS
				0 0 1 0 0	4	
				0 0 1 0 1	5	
				0 0 1 1 0	6	
				0 0 1 1 1	7	V SYNC ENDS
				0 1 0 0 0	8	
				0 1 0 0 1	9	
				0 1 0 1 0	10	
				0 1 0 1 1	11	
				0 1 1 0 0	12	
				0 1 1 0 1	13	
				0 1 1 1 0	14	
				0 1 1 1 1	15	V BLANKING ENDS
				1 0 0 0 0	16	
				1 0 0 0 1	17	
				1 0 0 1 0	18	
				1 0 0 1 1	19	
				1 0 1 0 0	20	
				1 0 1 0 1	21	
				1 0 1 1 0	22	
				1 0 1 1 1	23	
				1 1 0 0 0	24	
				1 1 0 0 1	25	
				1 1 0 1 0	26	
				1 1 0 1 1	27	
				1 1 1 0 0	28	
				1 1 1 0 1	29	
				1 1 1 1 0	30	
0	0	0	0	1 1 1 1 1	31	H SYNC BEGINS
0	0	0	1	0 0 0 0 0	32	
				0 0 0 0 1	33	
				0 0 0 1 0	34	
				0 0 0 1 1	35	
				0 0 1 0 0	36	
				0 0 1 0 1	37	
				0 0 1 1 0	38	
				0 0 1 1 1	39	
0	0	0	1	0 1 0 0 0	40	
0	0	0	1	0 1 0 0 1	41	

V SYNC

V BLANKING

H SYNC

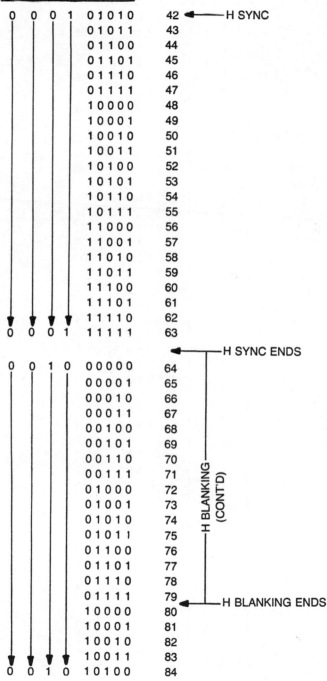

256	128	64	32	16 8 4 2 1	
0	0	1	0	1 0 1 0 1	85
				1 0 1 1 0	86
				1 0 1 1 1	87
				1 1 0 0 0	88
				1 1 0 0 1	89
				1 1 0 1 0	90
				1 1 0 1 1	91
				1 1 1 0 0	92
				1 1 1 0 1	93
				1 1 1 1 0	94
0	0	1	0	1 1 1 1 1	95
0	0	1	1	0 0 0 0 0	96
				0 0 0 0 1	97
				0 0 0 1 0	98
				0 0 0 1 1	99
				0 0 1 0 0	100
				0 0 1 0 1	101
				0 0 1 1 0	102
				0 0 1 1 1	103
				0 1 0 0 0	104
				0 1 0 0 1	105
				0 1 0 1 0	106
				0 1 0 1 1	107
				0 1 1 0 0	108
				0 1 1 0 1	109
				0 1 1 1 0	110
				0 1 1 1 1	111
				1 0 0 0 0	112
				1 0 0 0 1	113
				1 0 0 1 0	114
				1 0 0 1 1	115
				1 0 1 0 0	116
				1 0 1 0 1	117
				1 0 1 1 0	118
				1 0 1 1 1	I19
				1 1 0 0 0	120
				1 1 0 0 1	121
				1 1 0 1 0	122
				1 1 0 1 1	123
				1 1 1 0 0	124
				1 1 1 0 1	125
				1 1 1 1 0	126
0	0	1	1	1 1 1 1 1	127

256	128	64	32	16 8 4 2 1	
0	1	0	0	0 0 0 0 0	128
				0 0 0 0 1	129
				0 0 0 1 0	130
				0 0 0 1 1	131
				0 0 1 0 0	132
				0 0 1 0 1	133
				0 0 1 1 0	134
				0 0 1 1 1	135
				0 1 0 0 0	136
				0 1 0 0 1	137
				0 1 0 1 0	138 ◄——— V CENTER
				0 1 0 1 1	139
				0 1 1 0 0	140
				0 1 1 0 1	141
				0 1 1 1 0	142
				0 1 1 1 1	143
				1 0 0 0 0	144
				1 0 0 0 1	145
				1 0 0 1 0	146
				1 0 0 1 1	147
				1 0 1 0 0	148
				1 0 1 0 1	149
				1 0 1 1 0	150
				1 0 1 1 1	151
				1 1 0 0 0	152
				1 1 0 0 1	153
				1 1 0 1 0	154
				1 1 0 1 1	155
				1 1 1 0 0	156
				1 1 1 0 1	157
				1 1 1 1 0	158
0	1	0	0	0 1 1 1 1	159
0	1	0	1	0 0 0 0 0	160
				0 0 0 0 1	161
				0 0 0 1 0	162
				0 0 0 1 1	163
				0 0 1 0 0	164
				0 0 1 0 1	165
				0 0 1 1 0	166
				0 0 1 1 1	167
				0 1 0 0 0	168
				0 1 0 0 1	169
0	0	1	0	0 1 0 1 0	170

511

256	128	64	32	16 8 4 2 1	
0	0	1	0	0 1 0 1 1	171
				0 1 1 0 0	172
				0 1 1 0 1	173
				0 1 1 1 0	174
				0 1 1 1 1	175
				1 0 0 0 0	176
				1 0 0 0 1	177
				1 0 0 1 0	178
				1 0 0 1 1	179
				1 0 1 0 0	180
				1 0 1 0 1	181
				1 0 1 1 0	182
				1 0 1 1 1	183
				1 1 0 0 0	184
				1 1 0 0 1	185
				1 1 0 1 0	186
				1 1 0 1 1	187
				1 1 1 0 0	188
				1 1 1 0 1	189
				1 1 1 1 0	190
0	0	1	0	1 1 1 1 1	191
0	1	1	0	0 0 0 0 0	192
				0 0 0 0 1	193
				0 0 0 1 0	194
				0 0 0 1 1	195
				0 0 1 0 0	196
				0 0 1 0 1	197
				0 0 1 1 0	198
				0 0 1 1 1	199
				0 1 0 0 0	200
				0 1 0 0 1	201
				0 1 0 1 0	202
				0 1 0 1 1	203
				0 1 1 0 0	204
				0 1 1 0 1	205
				0 1 1 1 0	206
				0 1 1 1 1	207
				1 0 0 0 0	208
				1 0 0 0 1	209
				1 0 0 1 0	210
				1 0 0 1 1	211
				1 0 1 0 0	212
0	1	1	0	1 0 1 0 1	213

512

	256	128	64	32	16 8 4 2 1	
	0	1	1	0	1 0 1 1 0	214
					1 0 1 1 1	215
					1 1 0 0 0	216
					1 1 0 0 1	217
					1 1 0 1 0	218
					1 1 0 1 1	219
					1 1 1 0 0	220
					1 1 1 0 1	221
					1 1 1 1 0	222
	0	1	1	0	1 1 1 1 1	223
	0	1	1	1	0 0 0 0 0	224
					0 0 0 0 1	225
					0 0 0 1 0	226
					0 0 0 1 1	227
					0 0 1 0 0	228
					0 0 1 0 1	229
					0 0 1 1 0	230
					0 0 1 1 1	231
					0 1 0 0 0	232
					0 1 0 0 1	233
					0 1 0 1 0	234
					0 1 0 1 1	235
					0 1 1 0 0	236
					0 1 1 0 1	237
					0 1 1 1 0	238
					0 1 1 1 1	239
					1 0 0 0 0	240
					1 0 0 0 1	241
					1 0 0 1 0	242
					1 0 0 1 1	243
					1 0 1 0 0	244
					1 0 1 0 1	245
					1 0 1 1 0	246
					1 0 1 1 1	247
					1 1 0 0 0	248
					1 1 0 0 1	249
					1 1 0 1 0	250
					1 1 0 1 1	251
					1 1 1 0 0	252
					1 1 1 0 1	253
					1 1 1 1 0	254
	0	1	1	1	1 1 1 1 1	255

513

256	128	64	32	16 8 4 2 1		
1	0	0	0	0 0 0 0 0	256	
				0 0 0 0 1	257	
				0 0 0 1 0	258	
				0 0 0 1 1	259	
				0 0 1 0 0	260	← V BLANKING BEGINS
				0 0 1 0 1	261	
				0 0 1 1 0	262	
				0 0 1 1 1	263	
				0 1 0 0 0	264	
				0 1 0 0 1	265	
				0 1 0 1 0	266	← H CENTER
				0 1 0 1 1	267	
				0 1 1 0 0	268	
				0 1 1 0 1	269	
				0 1 1 1 0	270	
				0 1 1 1 1	271	
				1 0 0 0 0	272	
				1 0 0 0 1	273	
				1 0 0 1 0	274	
				1 0 0 1 1	275	
				1 0 1 0 0	276	
				1 0 1 0 1	277	
				1 0 1 1 0	278	
				1 0 1 1 1	279	
				1 1 0 0 0	280	
				1 1 0 0 1	281	
				1 1 0 1 0	282	
				1 1 0 1 1	283	
				1 1 1 0 0	284	
				1 1 1 0 1	285	
				1 1 1 1 0	286	
1	0	0	0	1 1 1 1 1	287	
1	0	0	1	0 0 0 0 0	288	
				0 0 0 0 1	289	
				0 0 0 1 0	290	
				0 0 0 1 1	291	
				0 0 1 0 0	292	
				0 0 1 0 1	293	
				0 0 1 1 0	294	
				0 0 1 1 1	295	
				0 1 0 0 0	296	
				0 1 0 0 1	297	
				0 1 0 1 0	298	
1	0	0	1	0 1 0 1 1	299	

256	128	64	32	16 8 4 2 1	
1	0	0	1	0 1 1 0 0	300
				0 1 1 0 1	301
				0 1 1 1 0	302
				0 1 1 1 1	303
				1 0 0 0 0	304
				1 0 0 0 1	305
				1 0 0 1 0	306
				1 0 0 1 1	307
				1 0 1 0 0	308
				1 0 1 0 1	309
				1 0 1 1 0	310
				1 0 1 1 1	311
				1 1 0 0 0	312
				1 1 0 0 1	313
				1 1 0 1 0	314
				1 1 0 1 1	315
				1 1 1 0 0	316
				1 1 1 0 1	317
↓	↓	↓	↓	1 1 1 1 0	318
1	0	0	1	1 1 1 1 1	319
1	0	1	0	0 0 0 0 0	320
				0 0 0 0 1	321
				0 0 0 1 0	322
				0 0 0 1 1	323
				0 0 1 0 0	324
				0 0 1 0 1	325
				0 0 1 1 0	326
				0 0 1 1 1	327
				0 1 0 0 0	328
				0 1 0 0 1	329
				0 1 0 1 0	330
				0 1 0 1 1	331
				0 1 1 0 0	332
				0 1 1 0 1	333
				0 1 1 1 0	334
				0 1 1 1 1	335
				1 0 0 0 0	336
				1 0 0 0 1	337
				1 0 0 1 0	338
				1 0 0 1 1	339
				1 0 1 0 0	340
↓	↓	↓	↓	1 0 1 0 1	341
1	0	1	0	1 0 1 1 0	342

515

256	128	64	32	16 8 4 2 1	
1	0	1	0	1 0 1 1 1	343
				1 1 0 0 0	344
				1 1 0 0 1	345
				1 1 0 1 0	346
				1 1 0 1 1	347
				1 1 1 0 0	348
				1 1 1 0 1	349
				1 1 1 1 0	350
1	0	1	0	1 1 1 1 1	351
1	0	1	1	0 0 0 0 0	352
				0 0 0 0 1	353
				0 0 0 1 0	354
				0 0 0 1 1	355
				0 0 1 0 0	356
				0 0 1 0 1	357
				0 0 1 1 0	358
				0 0 1 1 1	359
				0 1 0 0 0	360
				0 1 0 0 1	361
				0 1 0 1 0	362
				0 1 0 1 1	363
				0 1 1 0 0	364
				0 1 1 0 1	365
				0 1 1 1 0	366
				0 1 1 1 1	367
				1 0 0 0 0	368
				1 0 0 0 1	369
				1 0 0 1 0	370
				1 0 0 1 1	371
				1 0 1 0 0	372
				1 0 1 0 1	373
				1 0 1 1 0	374
				1 0 1 1 1	375
				1 1 0 0 0	376
				1 1 0 0 1	377
				1 1 0 1 0	378
				1 1 0 1 1	379
				1 1 1 0 0	380
				1 1 1 0 1	381
				1 1 1 1 0	382
1	0	1	1	1 1 1 1 1	383

256	128	64	32	16	8	4	2	1	
1	1	0	0	0	0	0	0	0	384
				0	0	0	0	1	385
				0	0	0	1	0	386
				0	0	0	1	1	387
				0	0	1	0	0	388
				0	0	1	0	1	389
				0	0	1	1	0	390
				0	0	1	1	1	391
				0	1	0	0	0	392
				0	1	0	0	1	393
				0	1	0	1	0	394
				0	1	0	1	1	395
				0	1	1	0	0	396
				0	1	1	0	1	397
				0	1	1	1	0	398
				0	1	1	1	1	399
				1	0	0	0	0	400
				1	0	0	0	1	401
				1	0	0	1	0	402
				1	0	0	1	1	403
				1	0	1	0	0	404
				1	0	1	0	1	405
				1	0	1	1	0	406
				1	0	1	1	1	407
				1	1	0	0	0	408
				1	1	0	0	1	409
				1	1	0	1	0	410
				1	1	0	1	1	411
				1	1	1	0	0	412
				1	1	1	0	1	413
				1	1	1	1	0	414
1	1	0	0	1	1	1	1	1	415
1	1	0	1	0	0	0	0	0	416
				0	0	0	0	1	417
				0	0	0	1	0	418
				0	0	0	1	1	419
				0	0	1	0	0	420
				0	0	1	0	1	421
				0	0	1	1	0	422
				0	0	1	1	1	423
				0	1	0	0	0	424
				0	1	0	0	1	425
1	1	0	1	0	1	0	1	0	426

256	128	64	32	16 8 4 2 1	
1	1	0	1	0 1 0 1 1	427
				0 1 1 0 0	428
				0 1 1 0 1	429
				0 1 1 1 0	430
				0 1 1 1 1	431
				1 0 0 0 0	432
				1 0 0 0 1	433
				1 0 0 1 0	434
				1 0 0 1 1	435
				1 0 1 0 0	436
				1 0 1 0 1	437
				1 0 1 1 0	438
				1 0 1 1 1	439
				1 1 0 0 0	440
				1 1 0 0 1	441
				1 1 0 1 0	442
				1 1 0 1 1	443
				1 1 1 0 0	444
				1 1 1 0 1	445
				1 1 1 1 0	446
1	1	0	1	1 1 1 1 1	447
1	1	1	0	0 0 0 0 0	448
				0 0 0 0 1	449
				0 0 0 1 0	450
				0 0 0 1 1	451
				0 0 1 0 0	452
				0 0 1 0 1	453
1	1	1	0	0 0 1 1 0	454 ← H BLANK BEGINS

Appendix II
Digital Integrated Circuits

7400	Quad 2-input NAND
7402	Quad 2-input NOR
7404	Hex inverter
7420	Dual 4-input NAND
7427	Triple 3-input NOR
7430	8-input NAND
7448*	BCD to 7-segment converter
7474*	Dual D flip-flop
7475*	Quad D latch
7476*	Dual JK flip-flop
7483*	4-bit binary full adder
7485	4-bit comparitor
7486	Quad EXCLUSIVE OR
7490*	Decade counter
7492*	÷6 counter
7493*	4-bit binary counter
74125	Quad 3-state buffer
74147	Decimal-to-BCD converter
74150	16:1 multiplexer
74151	8:1 multiplexer
74153	Dual 4:1 multiplexer
74154	4-line to 16-line decoder
74155	Dual 2-line to 4-line decoder
74157	Quad 2:1 multiplexer
74191*	Presettable binary up/down counter

*designates ICs detailed in this appendix

This appendix lists the digital ICs that are referenced within this book. Those marked with an asterisk (*) are detailed on subsequent pages.

7448* BCD to 7-Segment Converter

DESCRIPTION — The 9358/5448, 7448 and 9359/5449, 7449 are TTL, BCD to 7-Segment Decoders consisting of NAND gates, input buffers and seven AND-OR-INVERT gates. The 9358/5448, 7448 offers active HIGH, open-collector outputs for current-sourcing applications to drive logic circuits or discrete, active components. Seven NAND gates and one driver are connected in pairs to make BCD data and its complement available to the seven decoding AND-OR-INVERT gates. The remaining NAND gate and three input buffers provide lamp test, blanking input/ripple-blanking output and ripple-blanking input for the 9358/5448, 7448. Four NAND gates and four input buffers provide BCD data and its complement and a buffer provides blanking input for the 9359/5449, 7449.

The circuits accept 4-bit binary-coded-decimal (BCD) and, depending on the state of the auxiliary inputs, decodes this data to drive other components. The relative positive-logic output levels, as well as conditions required at the auxiliary inputs are shown in the truth tables.

The 9358/5448, 7448 circuit incorporates automatic leading and/or trailing edge zero-blanking control ($\overline{RBI}$ and $\overline{RBO}$). Lamp test ($\overline{LT}$) of these types may be performed at any time when the $\overline{BI}/\overline{RBO}$ node is a HIGH level. They contain an overriding blanking input ($\overline{BI}$) which can be used to control the lamp intensity or to inhibit the outputs.

PIN NAMES		**LOADING**
A, B, C, D	BCD Inputs	1 U.L.
$\overline{RBI}$	Ripple Blanking Input	1 U.L.
$\overline{LT}$	Lamp Test Input	1 U.L.
$\overline{BI}/\overline{RBO}$	Blanking Input or	2.6 U.L.
	Ripple Blanking Output	5 U.L.
$\overline{BI}$	Blanking Input	1 U.L.
a to g	Outputs	6 U.L.

DIP (TOP VIEW)

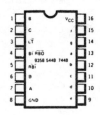

Positive logic: See truth table

LOGIC DIAGRAM

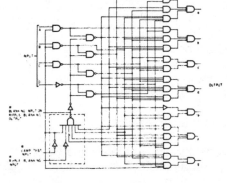

* NOT INCLUDED WITH THE 9359/5449

520

0	1	2	3	4	5	6	7	8	9	10	11	12	13	14	15

NUMERICAL DESIGNATIONS – RESULTANT DISPLAYS

TRUTH TABLE 9358/5448, 7448

DECIMAL OR FUNCTION	LT	RBI	D	C	B	A	BI/RBO	a	b	c	d	e	f	g	NOTE
0	H	H	L	L	L	L	H	H	H	H	H	H	H	L	1
1	H	X	L	L	L	H	H	L	H	H	L	L	L	L	1
2	H	X	L	L	H	L	H	H	H	L	H	H	L	H	
3	H	X	L	L	H	H	H	H	H	H	H	L	L	H	
4	H	X	L	H	L	L	H	L	H	H	L	L	H	H	
5	H	X	L	H	L	H	H	H	L	H	H	L	H	H	
6	H	X	L	H	H	L	H	L	L	H	H	H	H	H	
7	H	X	L	H	H	H	H	H	H	H	L	L	L	L	
8	H	X	H	L	L	L	H	H	H	H	H	H	H	H	
9	H	X	H	L	L	H	H	H	H	H	L	L	H	H	
10	H	X	H	L	H	L	H	L	L	L	H	H	L	H	
11	H	X	H	L	H	H	H	L	L	H	H	L	L	H	
12	H	X	H	H	L	L	H	L	H	L	L	L	H	H	
13	H	X	H	H	L	H	H	H	L	L	H	L	H	H	
14	H	X	H	H	H	L	H	L	L	L	H	H	H	H	
15	H	X	H	H	H	H	H	L	L	L	L	L	L	L	
BI	X	X	X	X	X	X	L	L	L	L	L	L	L	L	2
RBI	H	L	L	L	L	L	L	L	L	L	L	L	L	L	3
LT	L	X	X	X	X	X	H	H	H	H	H	H	H	H	4

NOTES:

(1) BI/RBO is wired-AND logic serving as blanking input (BI) and/or ripple-blanking output (RBO). The blanking out (BI) must be open or held at a HIGH level when output functions 0 through 15 are desired, and ripple-blanking input (RBI) must be open or at a HIGH level if blanking of a decimal 0 is not desired. X=input may be HIGH or LOW.

(2) When a LOW level is applied to the blanking input (forced condition) all segment outputs go to a LOW level, regardless of the state of any other input condition.

(3) When ripple-blanking input (RBI) and inputs A, B, C, and D are at LOW level, with the lamp test input at HIGH level, all segment outputs go to a HIGH level and the ripple-blanking output (RBO) goes to a LOW level (response condition).

(4) When the blanking input/ripple-blanking output (BI/RBO) is open or held at a HIGH level, and a LOW level is applied to lamp-test input, all segment outputs go to a LOW level.

ABSOLUTE MAXIMUM RATINGS (above which the useful life may be impaired)

Storage Temperature	–65°C to +150°C
Temperature (Ambient) Under Bias	–55°C to +125°C
V_{CC} Pin Potential to Ground Pin	–0.5 V to +7.0 V
*Input Voltage (dc)	–0.5 V to +5.5 V
*Input Current (dc)	–30 mA to +5.0 mA
Voltage Applied to Outputs (Output HIGH)	–0.5 V to +V_{CC} value
Output Current (dc) (Output LOW)	+30 mA

*Either Input Voltage limit or Input Current limit is sufficient to protect the inputs.

7474* Dual D Flip-Flop

DESCRIPTION – The 9N74/5474, 7474 are edge triggered dual D type flip-flops with direct clear and preset inputs and both Q and Q̄ outputs. Information at the input is transferred to the outputs on the positive edge of the clock pulse. They are designed for use in medium to high speed applications.

Clock triggering occurs at a voltage level of the clock pulse and is not directly related to the transition time of the positive going pulse. After the clock input threshold voltage has been passed, the data input (D) is locked out and information present will not be transferred to the output.

The 9N74/5474, 7474 have the same clocking characteristics as the 9N70/5470, 7470 gated (edge triggered) flip-flop circuits. They can result in a significant saving in system power dissipation and package count in applications where input gating is not required.

LOGIC AND CONNECTION DIAGRAM

DIP (TOP VIEW)

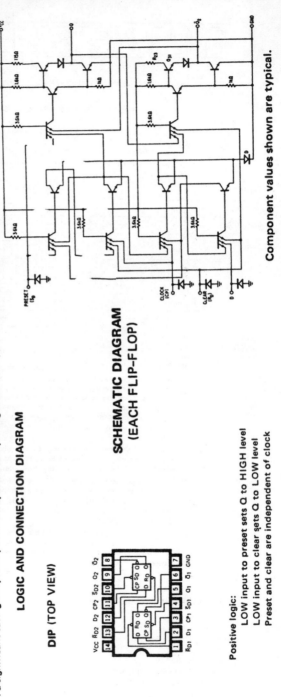

SCHEMATIC DIAGRAM
(EACH FLIP-FLOP)

Component values shown are typical.

Positive logic:

LOW input to preset sets Q to HIGH level

LOW input to clear sets Q to LOW level

Preset and clear are independent of clock

522

LOGIC DIAGRAM (EACH FLIP-FLOP)

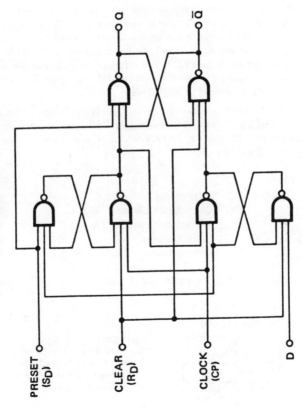

TRUTH TABLE (Each Flip-Flop)

t_n	t_{n+1}	
INPUT	OUTPUT	OUTPUT
D	Q	$\bar{Q}$
L	L	H
H	H	L

NOTES:

t_n = bit time before clock pulse
t_{n+1} = bit time after clock pulse.

523

7475*   Quad D Latch

DESCRIPTION – The TTL/MSI 9375/5475, 7475 and 9377/5477, 7477 are latches used as temporary storage for binary information between processing units and input/output or indicator units. Information present at a data (D) input is transferred to the Q output when the clock is HIGH and the Q output will follow the data input as long as the clock remains HIGH. When the clock goes LOW, the information (that was present at the data input at the time the transition occurred) is retained at the Q output until the clock is permitted to go HIGH.

The 9375/5475, 7475 features complementary Q and $\overline{Q}$ output from a 4-bit latch and is available in the 16-lead packages. For higher component density applications the 9377/5477, 7477 4-bit latch is available in the 14-lead package with $\overline{Q}$ outputs omitted.

PIN NAMES

		LOADING
D_1, D_2, D_3, D_4	Data Inputs	2 U.L.
$\overline{CP}_{1-2}$	Clock Input Latches 1 & 2	4 U.L.
$\overline{CP}_{3-4}$	Clock Input Latches 3 & 4	4 U.L.
Q_1, Q_2, Q_3, Q_4	Latch Outputs	10 U.L.
$\overline{Q}_1, \overline{Q}_2, \overline{Q}_3, \overline{Q}_4$	Complementary Latch Outputs	10 U.L.

Note: 1 Unit Load (U.L.) = 40 μA HIGH/1.6 mA LOW

TRUTH TABLE
(Each Latch)

t_n	t_{n+1}
D	Q
H	H
L	L

NOTES:
t_n = bit time before clock negative-going transition.

t_{n+1} = bit time after clock negative-going transition.

524

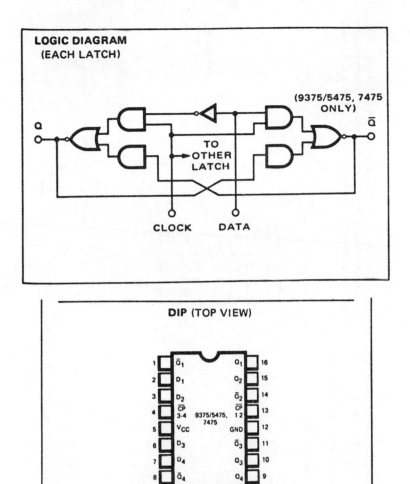

LOGIC DIAGRAM
(EACH LATCH)

(9375/5475, 7475 ONLY)

Q

Q̄

TO
OTHER
LATCH

CLOCK   DATA

DIP (TOP VIEW)

1 — Q̄₁	Q₁ — 16
2 — D₁	Q₂ — 15
3 — D₂	Q̄₂ — 14
4 — C̄P̄ 3-4	C̄P̄ 1 2 — 13
5 — V_CC	GND — 12
6 — D₃	Q̄₃ — 11
7 — D₄	Q₃ — 10
8 — Q̄₄	Q₄ — 9

9375/5475, 7475

Positive logic: See truth table.
NC — No internal connection.

7476* Dual JK Flip-Flop

DESCRIPTION – The TTL/SSI 9N76/5476, 7476 is a Dual JK Master/Slave flip-flop with separate presets, separate clears and separate clocks. Inputs to the master section are controlled by the clock pulse. The clock pulse also regulates the state of the coupling transistors which connect the master and slave sections. The sequence of operation is as follows: 1) Isolate slave from master. 2) Enter information from J and K inputs to master. 3) Disable J and K inputs. 4) Transfer information from master to slave.

LOGIC AND CONNECTION DIAGRAM

DIP (TOP VIEW)

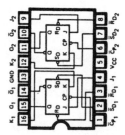

TRUTH TABLE

t_n		t_{n+1}
J	K	Q
L	L	Q_n
L	H	L
H	L	H
H	H	$\bar{Q}_n$

NOTES:
t_n = Bit time before clock pulse.
t_{n+1} = Bit time after clock pulse.

CLOCK WAVEFORM

Positive logic:
LOW input to preset sets Q to HIGH level
LOW input to clear sets Q to LOW level
Clear and preset are independent of clock

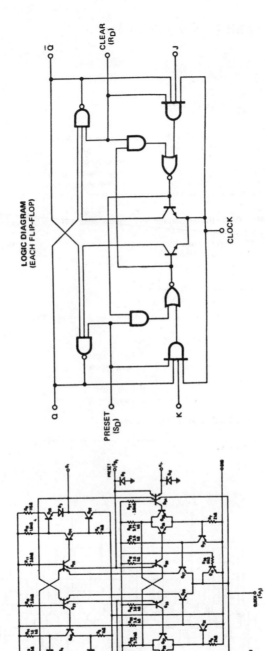

SCHEMATIC DIAGRAM
(EACH FLIP-FLOP)

LOGIC DIAGRAM
(EACH FLIP-FLOP)

Component values shown are typical.

527

7483* 4-Bit Binary Full Adder

DESCRIPTION — The TTL/MSI 9383/5483,7483 is a Full Adder which performs the addition of two 4-bit binary numbers. The sum (Σ) outputs are provided for each bit and the resultant carry (C_4) is obtained from the fourth bit. Designed for medium to high speed, multiple-bit, parallel-add/serial-carry applications, the circuit utilized high speed, high fan out TTL. The implementation of a single-inversion, high speed, Darlington-connected serial-carry circuit within each bit minimizes the necessity for extensive "lookahead" and carry-cascading circuits.

ABSOLUTE MAXIMUM RATINGS (above which the useful life may be impaired)

Storage Temperature	−65°C to +150°C
Temperature (Ambient) Under Bias	−55°C to +125°C
V_{CC} Pin Potential to Ground Pin	−0.5 V to +7.0 V
*Input Voltage (dc)	−0.5 V to +5.5 V
*Input Current (dc)	−30 mA to +5.0 mA
Voltage Applied to Outputs (Output HIGH)	−0.5 V to +V_{CC} value
Output Current (dc) (Output LOW)	+30 mA

*Either Input Voltage limit or Input Current limit is sufficient to protect the inputs.

PIN NAMES   **LOADING**

A_1,B_1,A_3,B_3	Data Inputs	4 U.L.
A_2,B_2,A_4,B_4	Data Inputs	1 U.L.
C_{IN}	Carry Input	4 U.L.
$\Sigma_1,\Sigma_2,\Sigma_3,\Sigma_4$	Sum Outputs	10 U.L.
C_4	Carry Out Bit 4	5 U.L.

1 Unit Load (U.L.) = 40 μA HIGH/1.6 mA LOW

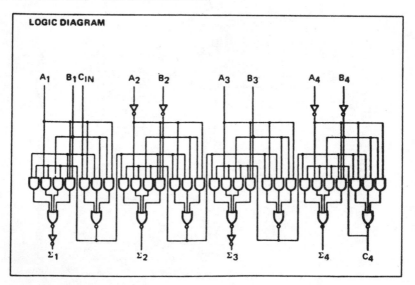

LOGIC DIAGRAM

528

LOGIC SYMBOL

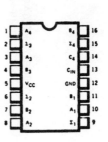

V_CC = Pin 5
GND = Pin 12

CONNECTION DIAGRAM
DIP (TOP VIEW)

TRUTH TABLE (See Note 1)

INPUT				OUTPUT					
				WHEN $C_{IN}=0$	WHEN $C_2=0$		WHEN $C_{IN}=1$	WHEN $C_2=1$	
A_1 / A_3	B_1 / B_3	A_2 / A_4	B_2 / B_4	Σ_1 / Σ_3	Σ_2 / Σ_4	C_2 / C_4	Σ_1 / Σ_3	Σ_2 / Σ_3	C_2 / C_4
L	L	L	L	L	L	L	H	L	L
H	L	L	L	H	L	L	L	H	L
L	H	L	L	H	L	L	L	H	L
H	H	L	L	L	H	L	H	H	L
L	L	H	L	L	H	L	H	H	L
H	L	H	L	H	H	L	L	L	H
L	H	H	L	H	H	L	L	L	H
H	H	H	L	L	L	H	H	L	H
L	L	L	H	L	H	L	H	H	L
H	L	L	H	H	H	L	L	:L	H
L	H	L	H	H	H	L	L	L	H
H	H	L	H	L	L	H	H	L	H
L	L	H	H	L	L	H	H	L	H
H	L	H	H	H	L	H	L	H	H
L	H	H	H	H	L	H	L	H	H
H	H	H	H	L	H	H	H	H	H

NOTE:
1. Input conditions at A_1, A_2, B_1, B_2 and C_{IN} are used to determine outputs Σ_1 and Σ_2, and the value of the internal carry C_2. The values at C_2, A_3, B_3, A_4, and B_4, are then used to determine outputs Σ_3, Σ_4 and C_4.

7490* Decade Counter

DESCRIPTION — The TTL/MSI 9390/5490, 7490 is a Decade Counter which consists of four dual rank, master slave flip-flops internally interconnected to provide a divide-by-two counter and a divide-by-five counter. Count inputs are inhibited, and all outputs are returned to logical zero or a binary coded decimal (BCD) count of 9 through gated direct reset lines. The output from flip-flop A is not internally connected to the succeeding stages, therefore the count may be separated into these independent count modes:

A. If used as a binary coded decimal decade counter, the $\overline{CP}_{BD}$ input must be externally connected to the Q_A output. The $\overline{CP}_A$ input receives the incoming count, and a count sequence is obtained in accordance with the BCD count for nine's complement decimal application.

B. If a symmetrical divide-by-ten count is desired for frequency synthesizers or other applications requiring division of a binary count by a power of ten, the Q_D output must be externally connected to the $\overline{CP}_A$ input. The input count is then applied at the $\overline{CP}_{BD}$ input and a divide-by-ten square wave is obtained at output Q_A.

C. For operation as a divide-by-two counter and a divide-by-five counter, no external interconnections are required. Flip-flop A is used as a binary element for the divide-by-two function. The $\overline{CP}_{BD}$ input is used to obtain binary divide-by-five operation at the Q_B, Q_C, and Q_D outputs. In this mode, the two counters operate independently; however, all four flip-flops are reset simultaneously.

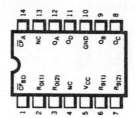

CONNECTION DIAGRAM
DIP (TOP VIEW)

PIN NAMES

		LOADING
R_0	Reset-Zero Inputs	1 U.L.
R_9	Reset-Nine Inputs	1 U.L.
$\overline{CP}_A$	Clock Input	2 U.L.
$\overline{CP}_{RD}$	Clock Input	4 U.L.
Q, Q_B, Q_C, Q_D	Outputs	10 U.L.

1 Unit Load (U.L.) = 40μA HIGH/1.6mA LOW.

530

TRUTH TABLES

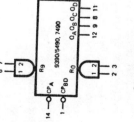

BCD COUNT SEQUENCE (Note 1)

COUNT	OUTPUT			
	Q_D	Q_C	Q_B	Q_A
0	L	L	L	L
1	L	L	L	H
2	L	L	H	L
3	L	L	H	H
4	L	H	L	L
5	L	H	L	H
6	L	H	H	L
7	L	H	H	H
8	H	L	L	L
9	H	L	L	H

RESET/COUNT (see Note 2)

RESET INPUTS				OUTPUT			
$R_{0(1)}$	$R_{0(2)}$	$R_{9(1)}$	$R_{9(2)}$	Q_D	Q_C	Q_B	Q_A
H	H	L	X	L	L	L	L
H	H	X	L	L	L	L	L
X	X	H	H	H	L	L	H
X	L	X	L	COUNT			
L	X	L	X	COUNT			
L	X	X	L	COUNT			
X	L	L	X	COUNT			

LOGIC DIAGRAM

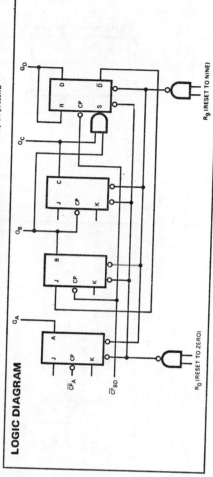

NOTES:
1. Output Q_A connected to input CP_{BD} for BCD count.
2. X indicates that either a HIGH level or a LOW level may be present.

R_9 (RESET TO NINE)

R_0 (RESET TO ZERO)

$\overline{CP}_A$

$\overline{CP}_{BD}$

LOGIC SYMBOL

9390/5490, 7490

R_9 CP_A CP_{BD} R_0

$Q_A Q_B Q_C Q_D$

V_{CC} = Pin 5
GND = Pin 10
NC = Pin 4, 13

531

7492* ÷6 Counter

DESCRIPTION — The TTL/MSI 9392/5492, 7492 is a 4-Bit Binary Counter consisting of four master slave flip-flops which are internally interconnected to provide a divide-by-two counter and a divide-by-six counter. A grated direct reset line is provided which inhibits the count inputs and simultaneously returns the four flip-flop outputs to a LOW level. As the output from flip-flop A is not internally connected to the succeeding flip-flops, the counter may be operated in two independent modes:

A. When used as a divide-by-twelve counter, output Q_A must be externally connected to input $\overline{CP}_{BC}$. The input count pulses are applied to input $\overline{CP}_A$. Simultaneous divisions of 2, 6 and 12 are performed at the Q_A, Q_C and Q_D outputs as shown in the truth table.

B. When used as a divide-by-six counter, the input count pulses are applied to input $\overline{CP}_{BC}$. Simultaneously, frequency divisions of 3 and 6 are available at the Q_C and Q_D outputs. Independent use of flip-flop A is available if the reset function coincides with reset of the divide-by-six counter.

These circuits are completely compatible with TTL and DTL logic families.

PIN NAMES

		LOADING
R_0	Reset-Zero Inputs	1 U.L.
$\overline{CP}_A$	Clock Input	2 U.L.
$\overline{CP}_{BC}$	Clock Input	4 U.L.
Q_A, Q_B, Q_C, Q_D	Count Outputs	10 U.L.

1 Unit Load (U.L.) = 40 μA HIGH/1.6 mA LOW

CONNECTION DIAGRAM
DIP (TOP VIEW)

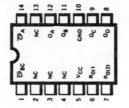

LOGIC SYMBOL

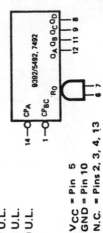

V_{CC} = Pin 5
GND = Pin 10
N.C. = Pins 2, 3, 4, 13

TRUTH TABLE
(See Notes 1, 2 and 3)

COUNT	OUTPUT			
	Q_D	Q_C	Q_B	Q_A
0	L	L	L	L
1	L	L	L	H
2	L	L	H	L
3	L	L	H	H
4	L	H	L	L
5	L	H	L	H
6	H	L	L	L
7	H	L	L	H
8	H	L	H	L
9	H	L	H	H
10	H	H	L	L
11	H	H	L	H

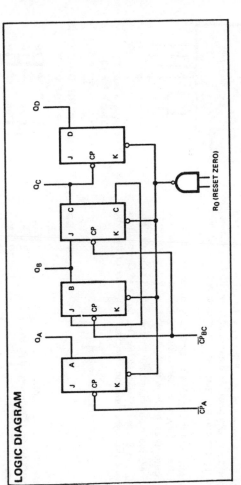

LOGIC DIAGRAM

R_0(RESET ZERO)

NOTES:
1. Output Q_A connected to input $\overline{CP}_{BC}$.
2. To reset all outputs to LOW level both $R_0(1)$ and $R_0(2)$ inputs must be at HIGH level state.
3. Either (or both) reset inputs $R_0(1)$ and $R_0(2)$ must be at a LOW level to count.

533

7493* 4-Bit Binary Counter

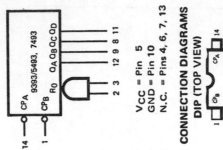

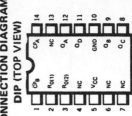

V_{CC} = Pin 5
GND = Pin 10
N.C. = Pins 4, 6, 7, 13

CONNECTION DIAGRAMS
DIP (TOP VIEW)

1	$\overline{CP}_B$		CP_A	14
2	$R_{0(1)}$		NC	13
3	$R_{0(2)}$		Q_A	12
4	NC		Q_D	11
5	V_{CC}		GND	10
6	NC		Q_B	9
7	NC		Q_C	8

DESCRIPTION — The TTL/MSI 9393/5493, 7493 is a 4-Bit Binary Counter consisting of four master/slave flip-flops which are internally interconnected to provide a divide-by-two counter and a divide-by-eight counter. A gated direct reset line is provided which inhibits the count inputs and simultaneously returns the four flip-flop outputs to a LOW level. As the output from flip-flop A is not internally connected to the succeeding flip-flops the counter may be operated in two independent modes:

1. When used as a 4-bit ripple-through counter, output Q_A must be externally connected to input $\overline{CP}_B$. The input count pulses are applied to input $\overline{CP}_A$. Simultaneously divisions of 2, 4, 8 and 16 are performed at the Q_A, Q_B, Q_C, and Q_D outputs as shown in the truth table.

2. When used as a 3-bit ripple-through counter, the input count pulses are applied to input $\overline{CP}_B$. Simultaneous frequency divisions of 2, 4, and 8 are available at the Q_B, Q_C, and Q_D outputs. Independent use of flip-flop A is available if the reset function coincides with reset of the 3-bit ripple-through counter.

These circuits are completely compatible with TTL and DTL logic families.

PIN NAMES

		LOADING
R_0	Reset-Zero Input	1 U.L.
$\overline{CP}_A$	Clock (Active LOW going edge) Input	2 U.L.
$\overline{CP}_B$	Clock (Active LOW going edge) Input	2 U.L.
Q_A, Q_B, Q_C, Q_D	Outputs	10 U.L.

LOGIC DIAGRAM

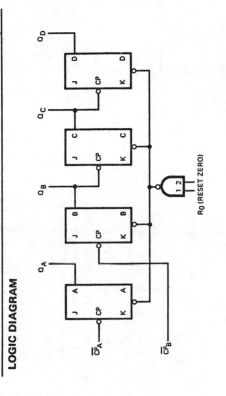

R$_O$ (RESET ZERO)

$\overline{CP}_A$

$\overline{CP}_B$

Q$_A$ Q$_B$ Q$_C$ Q$_D$

1 Unit Load (U.L.) = 40 μA HIGH/1.6 mA LOW

TRUTH TABLE (See Notes 1, 2 and 3)

COUNT	OUTPUT			
	Q$_D$	Q$_C$	Q$_B$	Q$_A$
0	L	L	L	L
1	L	L	L	H
2	L	L	H	L
3	L	L	H	H
4	L	H	L	L
5	L	H	L	H
6	L	H	H	L
7	L	H	H	H
8	H	L	L	L
9	H	L	L	H
10	H	L	H	L
11	H	L	H	H
12	H	H	L	L
13	H	H	L	H
14	H	H	H	L
15	H	H	H	H

NOTES:

1. Output Q$_A$ connected to input $\overline{CP}_B$.
2. To reset all outputs to LOW level both R$_{O(1)}$ and R$_{O(2)}$ inputs must be at HIGH level state.
3. Either (or both) reset inputs R$_{O(1)}$ and R$_{O(2)}$ must be at a LOW level to count.

535

74191* Presettable Binary Up/Down Counter

DESCRIPTION — The 93190/54190, 74190, 74191 and 93191/54191, 74191 are Synchronous Up/Down Counters with enable control presetting facility, single line up/down control, cascading for multi-decade operation and buffered inputs. The 93190/54190, 74190 is a BCD counter, while the 93191/54191, 74191 is a 4-bit binary counter. Synchronous operation is provided by having all flip-flops clocked coincident with each other so that the outputs change coincident with each other when input conditions are met. This mode of operation will eliminate the output counting spikes which are normally associated with asynchronous (ripple clock) counters.

A HIGH at the enable input inhibits counting. A LOW at the enable input and a LOW-to-HIGH clock transition triggers the four master/slave flip-flops. The enable input should be changed only when the clock is HIGH. The down/up input determines the direction of the count. When LOW, the count goes up; when HIGH, the count goes down.

These counters are fully programmable. The outputs may be preset to any state by placing a LOW on the load input and entering the desired data at the data inputs. The output will change to agree with the data inputs independently of the state of the clock input. This feature allows the counters to be used as modulo-N dividers by simply modifying the count length with the preset inputs.

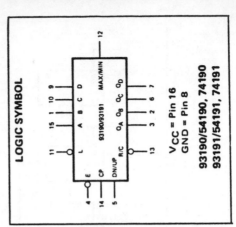

LOGIC SYMBOL

V_{CC} = Pin 16
GND = Pin 8

93190/54190, 74190
93191/54191, 74191

536

Two outputs have been made available to perform the cascading function. ripple clock and maximum/minimum count. The latter output produces a HIGH level output pulse with a duration approximately equal to one complete cycle of the clock when the counter overflows or under-flows. The ripple clock output produces a LOW level output pulse equal in width to the LOW level portion of the clock input when an overflow or underflow condition exists. The counters can be easily cascaded by feeding the ripple clock output to the enable input of the succeeding counter if parallel clocking is used, or to the clock input if parallel enabling is used. The maximum/minimum count output can be used to accomplish lookahead for high speed operation.

Power dissipation is typically 325 mW for either the decade or binary version. Maximum input clock frequency is typically 25 MHz and is guaranteed to be at least 20 MHz

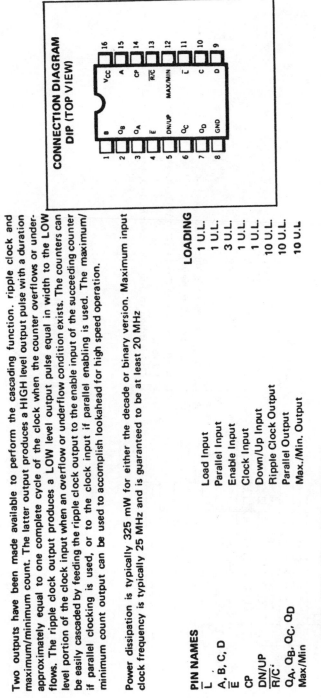

CONNECTION DIAGRAM
DIP (TOP VIEW)

Pin	Name
1	Q_B
2	Q_A
3	$\overline{E}$
4	DN/UP
5	Q_C
6	Q_D
7	GND
8	

Pin	Name
16	V_{CC}
15	A
14	CP
13	$\overline{R/C}$
12	MAX./MIN.
11	$\overline{L}$
10	C
9	D

PIN NAMES		LOADING
$\overline{L}$	Load Input	1 U.L.
A, B, C, D	Parallel Input	1 U.L.
$\overline{E}$	Enable Input	3 U.L.
CP	Clock Input	1 U.L.
DN/UP	Down/Up Input	1 U.L.
$\overline{R/C}$	Ripple Clock Output	10 U.L.
Q_A, Q_B, Q_C, Q_D	Parallel Output	10 U.L.
Max./Min.	Max./Min. Output	10 U.L.

1 Unit Load (U.L.) = 40 µA HIGH/1.6 mA LOW

537

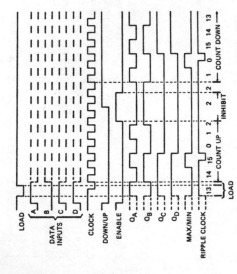

The following sequence is illustrated:

1. Load (preset) to binary thirteen.
2. Count up to fourteen, fifteen (maximum), zero, one, and two.
3. Inhibit.
4. Count down to one, zero (minimum), fifteen, fourteen, and thirteen

BINARY COUNTER
93191/54191, 74191

Index

Index